Also by Orville Schell

The China Reader: Vol. V, The Reform Years

*Virtual Tibet: Searching for Shangri-La from the
Himalayas to Hollywood*

*Mandate of Heaven: A New Generation of
Entrepreneurs, Dissidents, Bohemians,
and Technocrats Lay Claim to China's Future*

*Discos and Democracy: China in the Throes
of Reform*

To Get Rich Is Glorious: China in the Eighties

Modern Meat

Brown

*Watch Out for the Foreign Guests:
China Encounters the West*

*In the People's Republic: An American's Firsthand
View of Living and Working in China*

The Town That Fought to Save Itself

*The China Reader: Vol. I, Imperial China; Vol. II,
Republican China; Vol. III, Communist China*

Also by John Delury

"Gu Yanwu's Mixed Model and the Problem of Two
Despotisms," *Late Imperial China,* Summer 2013

"Harmonious in China: The Ancient Sources of
Modern Doctrine," *Policy Review,* Spring 2008

"North Korea: 20 Years of Solitude," *World Policy
Journal,* Winter 2008/9

WEALTH
AND
POWER

富强

WEALTH
AND
POWER

CHINA'S LONG
MARCH TO THE
TWENTY-FIRST CENTURY

Orville Schell and
John Delury

RANDOM HOUSE

NEW YORK

Published in the United States by Random House, an imprint of
The Random House Publishing Group, a division of
Random House, Inc., New York.

RANDOM HOUSE and colophon are registered trademarks
of Random House, Inc.

Owing to limitations of space, acknowledgments of permission to quote
from previously published materials will be found on p. 479, following the index.

Library of Congress Cataloging-in-Publication Data
Schell, Orville.
Wealth and power : China's long march to the twenty-first century /
Orville Schell & John Delury.
pages   cm
Includes bibliographical references and index.
ISBN 978-0-679-64347-0—ISBN 978-0-679-64538-2 (ebook)   1. China—History—
20th century—Biography.   2. China—History—21st century—Biography.
3. China—Politics and government—20th century.   4. China—Politics and
government—21st century.   I. Delury, John.   II. Title.
DS776.S34 2013
951'.050922—dc23   2013002596

Printed in the United States of America on acid-free paper

www.atrandom.com

2 4 6 8 9 7 5 3 1

First Edition

Title-page image copyright © iStockphoto.com

For my other half: Baifang
—ORVILLE

For Mom
—JOHN

Contents

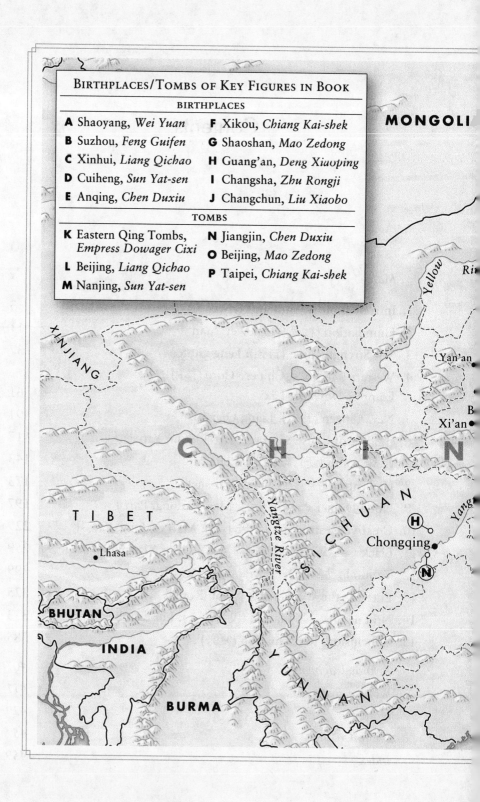

BIRTHPLACES/TOMBS OF KEY FIGURES IN BOOK

BIRTHPLACES

A Shaoyang, *Wei Yuan*
B Suzhou, *Feng Guifen*
C Xinhui, *Liang Qichao*
D Cuiheng, *Sun Yat-sen*
E Anqing, *Chen Duxiu*
F Xikou, *Chiang Kai-shek*
G Shaoshan, *Mao Zedong*
H Guang'an, *Deng Xiaoping*
I Changsha, *Zhu Rongji*
J Changchun, *Liu Xiaobo*

TOMBS

K Eastern Qing Tombs, *Empress Dowager Cixi*
L Beijing, *Liang Qichao*
M Nanjing, *Sun Yat-sen*
N Jiangjin, *Chen Duxiu*
O Beijing, *Mao Zedong*
P Taipei, *Chiang Kai-shek*

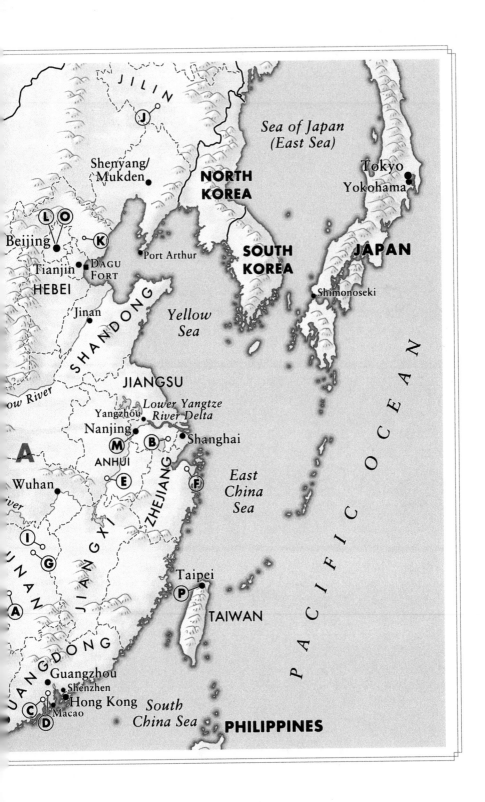

WEALTH
AND
POWER

富强

CHAPTER 1

Introduction

WEALTH AND POWER（富国强兵）

The Burden of Dreams

As the Chinese empire was unraveling at the beginning of the twentieth century under the combined pressures of internal decay and foreign assault, political essayist and reformer Liang Qichao began writing an unlikely novel, *The Future of New China*. Published serially in a popular journal, it was a strange blend of patriotic reverie and science fiction conjuring up what a rejuvenated China might look like sixty years hence—after it had reemerged as a strong, prosperous, and respected country once again. Although Liang, the most influential public intellectual of his generation, completed only a few chapters, his fictional exercise allowed his many readers, distraught by the Qing Dynasty's inability to adapt to modern times, to dream a little about what their benighted country might be like in an idealized future, circa 1962. As he imagined it then, the world's leading scholars, statesmen, and merchants would all clamor to visit and pay tribute both to China's modern present and its Confucian past at an international exposition to be held in Shanghai—strangely like the World Expo the city actually did hold in 2010. "I truly believe that this type of book can be a great help to China's future," Liang wrote.[1]

The Future of New China was not exactly great literature, and Liang admitted as much, commenting self-deprecatingly that the work-in-progress made him "laugh at myself."[2] But reading the novel's chapters today, when China is, in fact, ever more wealthy, powerful, and respected, imbues that long-ago moment with a triste sense of just how passionately Chinese then yearned to escape the bitter reality of their country's humiliating decline, even if only by projecting themselves for a moment into an imaginary future.

Such fantasies were an all too understandable antidote to China's century-long decline, and Liang was not the last to indulge in dreaming of remote triumphs. Four decades later, another well-known writer, Lin Yutang, contemplating a China largely occupied by the Japanese Imperial Army and steeped in even deeper misery, experienced a similar wishful prefiguration of the future. In his 1942 book *Between Tears and Laughter*, Lin described being visited by an "intuition," almost "mystic" in nature, which "blew like a whiff of clean air through the tortuous maze in which my will and my mind were imprisoned and paralyzed."[3] He wrote defiantly how, even with backwardness and despair everywhere around him, he nonetheless "saw China growing strong." "I know that this nation of 450,000,000 people, united and awakened and purged by the war-fire, is coming up," he insisted against all evidence. "The strength lies in her and nothing the western nations can do can stop her or keep her down."[4]

Such improbable dreams of a wealthy, strong, and proud China gave expression to widespread but frustrated yearnings for a revival of national greatness that arose in the nineteenth century, when for the first time in centuries Chinese could no longer think automatically and indisputably of their empire as *Zhongguo* (中国), the "Central Kingdom." Today, however, after three decades of dynamic economic growth on a scale and speed beyond anything the modern world has ever known, the fantasies of Liang Qichao and Lin Yutang seem prophetic.

Such a starkly unexpected ending to modern China's torturous developmental story compels us to reexamine the narrative of endless modernization failure with which we have all grown up. How did China's modern history of relentless humiliation and backwardness, of failed reform and disastrous revolution—the curse of generation after generation of would-be activists trying to create a "new China"— suddenly morph into such a story of triumph? Was it really just a sudden post-Mao miracle conjured up by Deng Xiaoping, or were the seeds of the present planted long ago, only germinating so slowly that at the time it was difficult to see, or even imagine the shape of things to come . . . except in a few fictional dreamscapes?

This is not another book heralding or bemoaning China's rise. Instead, we have chosen to engage in what is more of a historical reflection on the backstory to China's "economic miracle," an attempt to use history to find a new vantage point on its progress, emphasizing the perspectives of the Chinese themselves. In short, our goal has been to embark on a somewhat different kind of explanation for how, after over a century of decline, occupation, civil war, state repression, and socialist revolution, China finally did manage to catapult itself into an era of stunning dynamism and economic growth. To do this, we have chosen to primarily rely not on new archival material, but instead on preexisting scholarship—both the older classics in the field and some more recent research—works in which both of us have been immersed over our many collective decades of studying China's history. By standing on the shoulders of this collective body of work we hope to see a bit further toward the horizon of China's future, so bound up as it is with China's past. For it is these works that shaped, and continue to shape, our own thinking and understanding. And since both of us have also had long personal odysseys traveling, studying, living, and working in China, we have also drawn on some of these more immediate experiences that have also played an important role in helping us make sense out of how and why things have worked out as they have in this most singular of countries.

In reading through historical accounts of the lives, writings, and speeches of the diverse group of iconic political and intellectual figures presented in this book, a common chord rings through all their work— the abiding quest for *fuqiang* (富强), "wealth and power." Our account of modern China is thus the story of how these national leaders marched their people down the long road to *fuxing* (复兴), rejuvenation, and, by doing so, made Chinese society finally more ready than ever before for the possibility of a more open and democratic future.

The couplet of characters *fuqiang* has most commonly been translated as "wealth and power," and as a result the term—a shorthand version of the ancient adage *fuguo qiangbing* (富国强兵), "enrich the state and strengthen its military power"—has thus worked its way into historical literature in the English language. The expression was coined during the Warring States Period more than two millennia ago, as when the Legalist philosopher Han Feizi explained bluntly, "If a wise ruler masters wealth and power, he can have whatever he desires."[5] For Chinese reformers since the early nineteenth century, these two characters have repeatedly stood in for the profound desire among China's cognoscenti to see their country restored to the kind of greatness their ancestors had once taken for granted. Above all, these patriotic Chinese yearned for their nation to be able to defend itself against foreign incursion. Although in classical times these two characters conveyed a certain sense of aggressiveness, when the phrase was revived in the nineteenth century in a context of an empire in decline and struggling to maintain its territorial integrity, the subtext of "wealth and power" was self-defense rather than foreign conquest. A more fitting translation might actually have been: "prosperity and strength."

As China's humiliation deepened through each defeat by imperialist powers from the First Opium War (1839–42) onward, the scramble to find the keys to China's lost "wealth and power" gained an almost unbearable urgency. The ardor with which successive generations of Chinese intellectual and political leaders pursued *fuqiang*—even though most of them ended up with very little to show for their efforts—ultimately proved a unique dynamo fueling the country's constant and fervent pursuit of self-reinvention and rejuvenation.

The obverse of the elusive dream of "wealth and power" was, of course, China's chronic reality of poverty, weakness, and ignominy. As the West and Japan encroached ever more on its territorial sovereignty and as its people began to lose confidence in the superiority of their Confucian system itself, first uncertainty, and finally debilitating doubt and self-disparagement infected the entire society. When China was defeated by Japan—a presumably inferior Asian power—in the Sino-Japanese War of 1894–95, the shock was staggering. By the end of World War I, the notion of their country as a global victim had become an organic part of how Chinese looked at themselves and their place in the world, with variations on the theme of "humiliation" infecting every aspect of China's cultural, psychological, and political being. Confronting this narrative of prey versus predators, in which they were inevitably bested, Chinese reformers and leaders wrestled with the complex task of blaming the predatory great powers, while at the same time somehow absolving their own countrymen of too crippling a sense of inferiority and hopelessness. Myriad new slogans arose, and many have endured to this day, all emanating from a crushing sense of China's having fallen from a previous state of grace: "Restore the nation and erase the stain of humiliation!" "Endure humiliation to carry out our important task!"[6] By the 1940s, Chinese were speaking regularly of "a century of humiliation" and had even established a National Humiliation Day. To this day, children are still exhorted to "never forget national humiliation and strengthen our national defense."[7]

Modern Chinese intellectuals have continuously woven these grievances together into an ever more elaborate tapestry in which a weakened China is depicted as being unfairly pitted against a powerful, aggressive imperialist world. Within this frieze of history, our book examines how foreign exploitation and the ensuing humiliation that flowed from it became a deeply seductive, if painful, way of understanding their country's inescapable failures, how these failures also became organic parts of a new national identity (marked by what one scholar has described as the "sanctification of victimhood"),[8] and finally how they paradoxically provided raw material for escaping the dilemma of perpetually being both stepped on and one step behind the great powers of the world. Foreign superiority may have been humiliating and shameful, but it also served as a sharp goad urging Chinese to sacrifice for all the various reform movements and revolutions that came to be launched as a way to remove the stigma of their shame. And nationalism, which reformers and revolutionaries alike turned to as a way to galvanize the populace against their ignominy, grew directly out of China's evolving consciousness of failure and weakness, its roots well irrigated by the aquifer of historical humiliation that had long been pooling beneath it.

In the nineteenth century, the effort to efface national humiliation and restore China to wealth, strength, and respect had been largely focused on the question of how the West's military technology and economic *yong* (用), "techniques," might be harnessed to China's own national *ziqiang* (自强), "self-strengthening" effort. By the early twentieth century, however, the need for more far-reaching and radical approaches had become painfully apparent. It was in this period that Chinese thinkers first began seriously questioning the wisdom of maintaining the inner *ti* (体), or "core," of the country's traditional culture, fearing that China's backwardness and inability to adapt to the modern world was rooted in Confucian values themselves. Fin de siècle public intellectuals such as Liang Qichao and Yan Fu, for example, were ready to jettison the foundations of Chinese culture and import Western ideas in their place as part of a desperate effort to restore their country to greatness. "We have no time to ask whether this knowledge is Chinese or Western, whether it is old or new," Yan wrote imploringly. "If one course leads to ignorance and thus to poverty and weakness . . . we must cast it aside. If another course is effective in overcoming ignorance and thus leads to a cure of our poverty and weakness, we must imitate it, even if it proceeds from barbarians."[9]

Soon thereafter, even more radical skeptics had launched a cultural and intellectual uprising known as the New Culture Movement, calling for a wholesale repudiation of China's past and a new regimen of even more extensive foreign borrowing. For these activists, around whom much of twentieth-century Chinese history turned, the demolition of the country's ancient Confucian escutcheon became part of a sacred mission to "save the nation."

Unlike democratic political reform in the West, which developed out of a belief in certain universal values and human rights as derived from a "natural," if not God-given, source, and so were to be espoused regardless of their efficacy, the dominant tradition of reform in China evolved from a far more utilitarian source. Its primary focus was to return China to a position of strength, and any way that might help achieve this goal was thus worth considering. What "*liberté, egalité, fraternité*" meant to the French Revolution and to the making of modernity in the West, "wealth, strength, and honor" have meant to the forging of modern China. As a result, Chinese reformers tended to inhabit what looks to Western eyes like a pragmatic kingdom of means, rather than an idealistic world of ends. Reformers have been interested in democratic governance at various stages in China's tortuous path, not so much because it might enshrine sacred, inalienable political liberties but because it might make their nation more dynamic and thus stronger. "We cannot decide whether an idea is good or not without seeing it in practice" was the way Sun Yat-sen, "Father of the Nation," who helped bring republican government to China, once pragmatically observed. "If the idea is of practical value to us and to the world, it is good. If the idea is impractical, it is no good."[10]

By this logic, since the liberal political philosophies and governmental systems of the West had been so effective in creating such extraordinary national strength, would it not be foolish of Chinese reformers not to also experiment with them? But the same held true for communism, fascism, and authoritarianism. If one kind of "borrowing" did not do the job, the inclination was to try another, and another . . . until China could find a formula that worked. So in their relentless quest for wealth, strength, and finally greatness, successive generations of reformers bent their energies toward giving their country the equivalent of serial economic, intellectual, cultural, and political organ transplants.

Initially, conservative and sometimes xenophobic factions obstructed and inhibited this process, but over time, the scope of what might be acceptably imported from abroad kept growing. However, whatever means of borrowing were chosen, the goal was almost always the same: the "salvation" of the nation and its restoration to global preeminence. It was this pragmatic willingness to try anything that has given the drama of modern Chinese history its strangely disjointed quality, as if each succeeding act of borrowing had been imagined and written by a different playwright.

Alas, learning from foreign models turned out to have its own set of problems, for to borrow from elsewhere in such a wholesale way meant to deny the most organic aspect of being Chinese, namely, its own unique cultural tradition extending back thousands of years. Indeed, for more than a century and a half, the country found itself oscillating between attraction to and then repulsion from a culture that had for millennia served it well, yet now seemed the very cause of its weakness and failure. Finally, under Mao Zedong the project of destroying the old core of Chinese identity was carried to a grim conclusion with a violent and totalistic resolve. But, like a forest fire that clears the way for new growth, it may have ironically also helped prepare the way to usher in a spectacular new kind of economic growth under his successor, Deng Xiaoping.

As modern China's political history unfolded over the past century and a half, the country's successive efforts at self-reinvention kept crashing onto its shores like ever more powerful and destructive waves. To make sense of the unremitting upheaval that ensued, we have gathered together a dramatis personae of eleven iconic intellectuals and leaders, reformers and revolutionaries, to serve as guides. They span the years from the early nineteenth century until the present day, and all played critical roles as thinkers, iconoclasts, and leaders in this modern drama. We hope this cast of characters will not only help personalize what can otherwise appear as an opaque and bewildering sweep of alien history but also help tease out some of the leitmotifs that have kept repeating from generation to generation and thus, when understood, impart a sense of shape and coherence to the narrative of one of the world's most critical countries as it continues its difficult progress into modernity.

CHAPTER 2

Humiliation（行己有耻）

WEI YUAN（魏源）

The Temple

There is little tranquility to be found around the Temple of the Tranquil Seas, which sits on a narrow cut of land in the northwest corner of the city of Nanjing, squeezed between the banks of the Yangtze River and Lion Rock. Cars and trucks roar by on a three-lane boulevard, lancing toward downtown through a gate in the city's massive fourteenth-century fortification. A kind of metropolitan Great Wall built by the founder of the Ming Dynasty for his new capital, this rampart still rings the modern city, rising behind the steep crest of Lion Rock, where long ago Ming imperial officials planned to erect a giant tower from which visitors could be awed by majestic views of the great river to the north and the capital spread out to the south. Alas, dynastic coffers ran dry before this imperial project could be built, and it was not until six hundred years later—in September 2001—that the tower was finally completed.

At the foot of Lion Rock, nestled inside the Temple of the Tranquil Seas itself, is a small shrine to a seminal moment in modern Chinese history. It was in a back room of this temple that, in the oppressive heat of August 1842, Chinese negotiators were forced to sit with their British counterparts and hammer out the crushing terms of the Treaty of Nanjing. This bitterly humiliating document ended the three-year-old Opium War, China's first major clash with the West and the start of an interminable series of military and diplomatic defeats at the hands of imperialist powers.

Statue of Wei Yuan at Sun Yat-sen University, Guangzhou

The negotiating chamber in the temple has been restored to something resembling its original state, with another building across the small courtyard housing an exhibition on the painful history of what have come to be known as "China's Unequal Treaties." Back when this inaugural treaty was signed aboard the British warship HMS *Cornwallis*, anchored in the Yangtze not far from the temple, Chinese officials hoped it would be an "eternal document of confidence and trust."[1] Making unpleasant but unavoidable concessions, China's ruling Qing Dynasty justified the treaty as an artful ploy to placate the aggressive foreigners and, by getting rid of them, restore a state of equilibrium in which Beijing would regain its role presiding over the center of the world, as Chinese then knew it.

Today the Temple of the Tranquil Seas is a curious porthole into this past. As the exhibit's first panel explains: "Those unequal treaties were like fettering ropes of humiliation that made China lose the control of her political and military affairs . . . and seriously hindered and destroyed the social and economic development of China. It was one of the major causes that rendered China to be poor and weak in modern history." The explanatory panel adds that because the Temple of the Tranquil Seas was "the former site of negotiating the Treaty of Nanjing, the first unequal treaty of modern China, [it] has become a symbol of the commencement of China's modern history."

So here is where we open our retelling of that history, in the place that Chinese conventionally view as the starting point of their agonizing voyage into modernity, but also as the beginning of the country's long and painful road back to wealth and power. As the officially authorized birthplace of an important aspect of modern Chinese identity, the temple is a curiously vivid representation of the country's sense of its history of backwardness and impotence. It may seem strange to Westerners, accustomed to the histories of modern nations beginning with moments of triumph—the Glorious Revolution in Britain, the storming of the Bastille in France, or the signing of the American Declaration of Independence—to find Chinese beginning their modern journey by highlighting the shock of unexpected defeat and a moment symbolizing greatness lost. Yet that defeat, that moment of loss, resentment, and humiliation, would end up becoming a strangely affirmative one. Being overwhelmed by a materially stronger but culturally inferior foreign power—what Chinese leaders pejoratively referred to as *yi* (夷), "barbarians," became a counterintuitive source of motivation for China's regeneration as a great power. Humiliation was to become transmuted into a *positive* force—transformed from a depressant into a stimulant—in the construction of a new and modern national identity. The shameful sense of living in paradise lost, of having fallen so far behind other countries, would become a curious badge of distinction, one that would goad the country to strengthen and develop in order to finally catch up with the West and thus once again be able to defend itself and restore China to honor.

Since this drama has continued into the present, it is not surprising to find that the last panel in the temple's exhibit room makes modern Chinese history into a heroic morality play:

> It is hard to look back upon this humiliating history. The unequal treaties are like acts in a historical tragedy, telling sorrowfully of the misfortunes, grief and humiliation of the Chinese people. But the abolishment of the unequal treaties has shown the Chinese people's unwavering spirit of struggle for independence and self-strengthening. To feel shame is to approach courage. With history serving as a warning, our goal is to promote the great cause of our people's rejuvenation!

According to this canonical version of modern Chinese history, 1842 is year one. Every high school student preparing to take the intensely competitive and dreaded college entrance examination is now required to memorize the official national narrative that divides Chinese history neatly into pre–Opium War and post–Opium War periods. There is some truth to that historical division. After all, the Opium War did play a critical role in drawing a line between past and future, as well as in stimulating new ideas about China's place in the world and how the country would have to change in order to survive.

However, to understand the origins of the "humiliating history" that lies at the root of modern China's historical experience, as well as its self-consciousness and evolving national self-image, it is necessary to back up a bit. The recognition that something was deeply wrong had already begun to incubate within China decades *prior* to the shocking defeat by the British in the First Opium War. However, because Chinese historically had had so little experience in questioning the fundamental assumptions of their culture and its ways of governance, recognition came grudgingly slowly.

The key figure who first sensed that his country was in decline, and then initiated its search for modern *fuxing* (复兴), "rejuvenation," was a scholar-official by the name of Wei Yuan. He was among the first to confront his countrymen with a new reality: that they were falling perilously behind the seafaring powers of the modern West. Calling for a revival of an indigenous but long-ignored tradition of "statecraft reform" to fortify themselves, Wei boldly exhorted his countrymen to engage in strategic borrowing from Western powers such as England, whose ships, powered by steam and armed with the latest cannons, had wreaked havoc along China's coasts and up her riverways, into the heart of the empire.

Although an ethnic Han Chinese, Wei was intensely proud of the originally Manchu Qing Empire's eighteenth-century greatness and distraught by its early nineteenth-century decline. He left a lasting mark on modern China's intellectual and political agenda by sounding an alarm. In the process, he gave a name to the primary goal of China's elite: a restoration of the nation's *fuqiang* (富强), or "wealth and power," a phrase coined two thousand years earlier that he reprised and which has remained something of a north star for Chinese intellectual and political leaders ever since.

Apogee of Empire

The son of a middle-ranking Qing official, Wei Yuan was born in 1794 in Shaoyang, Hunan Province, near the town where Mao Zedong would be born a century later.[2] The 1790s turned out to be the political, economic, and military high-water mark for the Qing Dynasty. At least on the surface, China still seemed to be—as a literal translation of its name, *Zhongguo* (中国), indicated—the "Central Kingdom." Indeed, Qing China was enjoying what was referred to as *shengshi* (盛世), an "age of prosperity and flourishing."[3] The population had doubled since the time of the Ming Dynasty, surpassing three hundred million, making it not only the most populous empire on the globe, but also a country in which many people lived as well as, if not better than, those anywhere else. As Ken Pomeranz's work has shown, per capita standards of living in China's wealthiest region, the lower Yangtze River delta, rivaled those in Britain and the Netherlands, then the wealthiest parts of Europe, which increasingly craved Chinese tea, porcelain, and silk. And the Qing economy was an important engine driving economic globalization, such as it was, in the preindustrial world.[4]

In terms of territory, China was a behemoth. The Qing Dynasty, founded by Manchu tribes who swept down from the Manchurian forests north of the Great Wall in 1644 to capture Beijing, had more than doubled the size of the preceding Ming Empire. By the late eighteenth century, the Qing military was capable of projecting power up into the Himalayas as far as the Tibetan capital, Lhasa (where Chinese troops fought off a Nepalese Gurkha assault in 1792), and down the banks of the Red River to Hanoi (where Qing forces restored the deposed emperor of Vietnam, albeit only temporarily, in 1788). The political stability of the empire had been ensured by the longevity of the Qing emperor Qianlong, who had reigned in glory for six decades.[5]

It was at this apex of power that, just months before Wei Yuan was born, Emperor Qianlong had deigned to receive Lord George Macartney, an emissary from Britain, in what would be a defining moment in Sino-Western relations. King George III had dispatched Macartney to sail to Beijing at the head of an embassy of ninety-five men, carrying the latest in European technology and artwork as gifts. His official purpose was to seek "normal" diplomatic relations between Britain and the Celestial Kingdom based on an exchange of resident ambassadors. But Macartney's even more pressing charge was to seek an improvement in trade relations. Rather like twenty-first-century America, eighteenth-century Britain, for all its military and economic might, had been running an unsustainable trade deficit with China, because there was no British export that Chinese consumers would buy in amounts comparable to British imports of tea, for which Britons had an insatiable desire.

When Macartney's much-anticipated audience with the Chinese monarch finally took place, Emperor Qianlong dismissively informed him that the Qing Empire had no great need for England's goods or inventions, and, in any event, it was not accustomed to establishing "equal" diplomatic relations with anyone. "How can our dynasty alter its whole procedure and regulations, established for more than a century, in order to meet your individual views?" Qianlong incredulously demanded in an edict addressed to King George for Macartney to carry home with him. "As your Ambassador can see for himself, we possess all things. I set no value on objects strange or ingenious, and have no use for your country's manufactures."[6] Emperor Qianlong's rhetoric reeked of complacency, but, coming from the ruler of a vast and powerful empire, it was also a perfectly rational assessment of the balance of power between China and the West at that moment.

Macartney proved no less smug. Presciently smelling the rot that was already starting to undermine the foundations of the Chinese empire's proud political edifice, he wrote in his diary, "The Empire of China is an old, crazy, first-rate Man-of-War, which a fortunate succession of able and vigilant officers has contrived to keep afloat for these one hundred and fifty years past, and to overawe their neighbours merely by her bulk and appearance, but, whenever an insufficient man happens to have the command upon deck, adieu to the discipline and safety of the ship. She may perhaps not sink outright; she may drift some time as a wreck, and will then be dashed to pieces on the shore; but, she can never be rebuilt on the old bottom."[7]

As Macartney sensed, China's "age of prosperity and flourishing" was already drawing quickly to a close. Demographic pressures, ecological constraints, political corruption, and cultural ossification were conspiring to undo the great Qing Empire. Decades of population growth, intensified agriculture, and land reclamation were now beginning to reap a bitter ecological harvest of eroded soil, fallow fields, droughts, and floods, all of which made it ever more difficult for farmers to feed their families. An energetic government might have maintained popular support in the face of such adversity. Unfortunately for the Qing, official corruption had also become endemic, causing average Chinese to view their government as part of the problem, not the solution.[8]

A telltale sign of decline appeared in the year of Wei's birth: the eruption of a large-scale rebellion of disgruntled peasants that took the dynasty nearly a decade to suppress. This so-called White Lotus Rebellion turned out to be just the first in a series of domestic insurrections, sectarian revolts, and civil wars that would plague China until Mao's victory in 1949. Again, Lord Macartney proved prophetic: "I am indeed very much mistaken if all the authority and all the address of the Tartar [Manchu] Government will be able much longer to stifle the energies of their Chinese subjects," wrote the British emissary. "Scarcely a year now passes without an insurrection in some of the provinces. It is true they are usually suppressed, but their frequency is a strong symptom of the fever within. The paroxysm is repelled, but the disease is not cured."[9] Fear of rebellion would continue to haunt every ruler in Beijing through to modern times, even the likes of Deng Xiaoping and his successors, who have all had an abiding aversion to any kind of social or political uprising that might upset stability.

Return to Statecraft

This was the world of declining fortunes in which Wei Yuan came of age. At nineteen, he won a coveted fellowship to go to Beijing as one of Hunan Province's most promising talents. Leaving behind his new bride, he went to study with the leading lights of the intelligentsia in the capital. This was still a rather claustrophobic world in which students and teachers devoted themselves to mastering the canon of ancient Confucian texts in order to advance through the civil service examination system. The examinations, held at the county, provincial, and national levels, provided the only legitimate avenue to becoming an official in the prestigious imperial bureaucracy. Although even the lowest county degree brought a measure of prestige and privilege, it was only by passing the triennial national examination, and acquiring the degree of a *jinshi* (进士), or "presented scholar," that an ambitious student such as Wei could hope to be appointed to high office. For men of ambition in nineteenth-century China, passing the imperial exams was the be-all and end-all of one's existence.

Once in Beijing, as he crammed for the examinations, Wei gravitated toward relatively unconventional thinkers, including Liu Fenglu, a forgotten figure today, but then one of the empire's leading philosophers. Liu inducted his bright acolyte into an esoteric school of Confucianism that claimed to unlock secret teachings of the Sage through unorthodox readings of classical texts. His ideas were an exciting alternative to the rote memorization otherwise required to do well on the exams. Perhaps Liu's most radical contention was that history did not move in endless "dynastic cycles," as educated Chinese almost universally assumed to be the case, but rather progressed in a linear, teleological fashion, from an ancient era of Chaos toward a utopian future called *datong* (大同), "Grand Harmony." Confucius himself, Liu held, had lived in an imperfect in-between period of Approaching Peace, and taught a secret set of pragmatic, realpolitik methods to keep the world orderly until the era of Grand Harmony arrived. Liu believed that China was precisely in that transitional phase between Chaos and Grand Harmony, and soon Wei Yuan would apply this pragmatic and liberating form of Confucianism in bold new ways.[10]

In 1822 Wei passed the province-level civil service examination with the second-highest mark in his pool.[11] He was now a member of China's national elite, qualified to take the highest examination, which was offered in Beijing. But Wei would have to wait more than twenty years before finally attaining that coveted highest degree and ironically his failure was probably the reason for his lasting historical significance. As an unsuccessful and frustrated examination candidate, he was paradoxically freed to become an independent and original thinker.

Wei was thrust into the role of reformist in the early 1820s, when he took charge of a writing project that would prove far more influential for China's future than anything he might have done as an official. The finance commissioner of wealthy Jiangsu Province recruited him to compile a collection of writings on government administration, economic policy, and social order. Wei's *An Anthology of Statecraft Writings from the Present Dynasty*, published in 1826, exerted a profound impact on fellow scholars and officials, who were beginning to worry about what was wrong with their once "prosperous and flourishing" empire. The term for "statecraft," or *jingshi* (经世), literally meant "ordering the world," and Chinese scholars of this more pragmatic, political bent used it to distinguish themselves from fellow Confucians who were more interested in ethical self-cultivation, metaphysical philosophy, or classicist scholasticism. In the spirit of this unique form of statecraft, Wei's anthology was designed to be both a practical field guide for government officials and a compendium of theories on political and economic reform. By using the old motto of "wealth and power" and making its revival the overarching goal of his reform agenda, Wei's book laid new conceptual foundations for China's future struggle to modernize.[12]

On the face of it, all of the works chosen by Wei for inclusion in his anthology were composed by Confucian scholar-officials, who ostensibly hewed to an orthodox emphasis on family before state, moral values over material interests, and governance by means of ritual and education rather than reward and punishment. When they were read collectively, however, the message of these essays was deeply subversive to that very moralistic Confucian orthodoxy. Wei's anthology included one policy proposal after another written by hard-nosed scholar-officials who sought new, practical ways to strengthen the empire politically, economically, and militarily. Indeed, at its core, Wei's statecraft reform agenda turned out to be based less on the moral values preached by Confucians than on the precepts of the Sage's ancient rivals—a group known as the Legalists who emphasized wealth and power as primary goals.

The first Legalist statesmen emerged as critics of Confucius, who lived circa 500 BC and preached a moral code focused on filial piety to one's ancestors and loyalty to one's ruler. Known in Chinese as *rujia* (儒家), the "School of Scholars," Confucius and his disciples insisted that the virtues of benevolence, ritual propriety, and social harmony were the only legitimate and effective basis for good government. In a famous debate against Legalists, Confucians openly decried their fixation on "wealth and power," arguing that "propriety and righteousness are the foundations of the state, while power and profit are the destroyers of government."[13]

At the other extreme of the political and philosophical spectrum in traditional Chinese thinking was the rival *fajia* (法家), "School of Legalists," who rejected the Confucian ideal of a government by virtuous scholars ruling over a peaceful and harmonious agrarian society. Instead, they defined the proper goals of the ruler and his officials in one simple exhortatory phrase: *fuguo qiangbing* (富国强兵), "Enrich the state and strengthen its military power." One of the originators of this new creed was the fourth-century BC statesman Shang Yang, a brilliant consigliore who, though he had a "cruel nature," dedicated his energies to "enriching the state and strengthening the army" of the kingdom of

Qin.[14] If Shang Yang was Legalism's first great practitioner, its greatest theoretician was Han Feizi, who lived at the close of a bloody phase of Chinese antiquity known as the Warring States Period. Han Feizi's teachings inspired the unapologetically amoral first emperor of the Qin Dynasty, who ended the era of Warring States by violently unifying China in 221 BC. The core of Han Feizi's philosophy boiled down to a single dictum: "If a wise ruler masters wealth and power, he can have whatever he desires."[15] And Han Feizi dispensed Machiavellian advice in the dark arts of politics to ensure that "in times of peace the state is rich, and in times of trouble its armies are strong."[16]

Legalists offered a radical alternative to the Confucian notion of harmonious agrarian idealism. They argued instead that the key to national strength was to invest in a technologically advanced military, encourage commerce through a mixture of private enterprise and state monopoly over key industries, and maintain social order through a brutal set of laws enforced uniformly by an authoritarian state. (Their list of priorities and principles bears a sometimes uncanny resemblance to today's "China model" of authoritarian, state-led capitalism.) They were pessimistic about human nature, and viewed men as acting out of base motives such as fear and desire rather than loyalty and benevolence. This meant that the ruler's job was to impose a strict system of clear rewards and punishments, allowing no exceptions. Legalism was egalitarian in that all stood equal before the law, and, true to their name, Legalists prized *fazhi* (法治), the "rule of law," rather than the Confucians' political philosophy of *dezhi* (德治), the "rule of virtue." But according to the Legalists, rulers must use carrots and sticks to ensure that their subjects did their bidding, fashioning the common interest out of countless individual selfish impulses and deeds, thereby maintaining their own power in the process. These ancient Chinese *realpolitikers* had no patience for what they considered the moralistic blather of the Confucians. Since they put little stock in good intentions, wealth and strength alone were the ultimate arbiters of a ruler's success or failure.

The remarkable thing about Wei Yuan's anthology was that it brought these very un-Confucian ideas back into the mainstream of nineteenth-century reform thinking. By threading the language and values of Legalism throughout a guidebook for Confucian scholar-officials,

Emperor Qianlong receives Lord Macartney, 1793

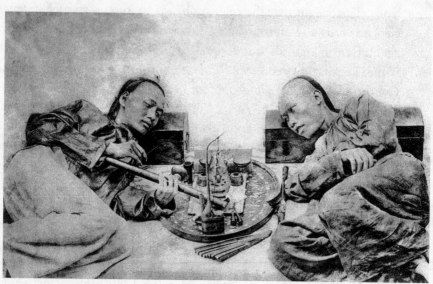

Opium smokers in nineteenth-century China

British ironclad warship HMS *Nemesis* during the First Opium War, 1841

Signing the Treaty of Nanjing aboard the HMS *Cornwallis*, 1842

Wei launched a covert revolution from within. Of course, *An Anthology of Statecraft Writings* did not attack or question Confucianism directly. Wei was far too much of a Confucian himself to be so direct. Rather, he replaced the moralist idealism of what Confucians called *wangdao* (王道), the "Kingly Way," with a pragmatic, utilitarian focus on "wealth and power"—the almost obsessive preoccupation of Legalism. After all, according to Wei, even the most virtuous "sage king" must ensure that his people are prosperous and the state is strong. "From ancient times," he wrote, "there have been wealth and power that were exercised apart from the Kingly Way, but never the Kingly Way exercised apart from wealth and power."[17] Even in the days of Confucius, he insisted, guns and butter were the keys to governance. "A sufficiency of food and a sufficiency of military power served as tools for governing the empire," he wrote. "Were not Confucius and his disciples concerned with providing for the people's material welfare and managing the state's revenue?"[18] In other words, even Confucian philosopher-kings had to ensure that their people were prosperous and the state was strong; more relevant to Wei's own day was that even flawed rulers could hope to achieve "wealth and power."

Opium War and Humiliating Peace

An Anthology of Statecraft Writings established Wei's reputation as the leading political reformer of his generation, but his promising career in government hit the bamboo ceiling as he repeatedly failed the national level of the civil service examination system, rendering him ineligible for the highest levels of government appointment. Instead he had to work as a political advisor to provincial officials, throwing himself into issues such as reforming the salt and grain transport trade, a formerly profitable state monopoly now plagued by high costs and corruption. Wei put his money where his mouth was, making a small fortune investing in the private salt transporters along the way. With his new-found wealth, he bought a villa in the Yangtze Delta city, Yangzhou, in 1834 and gave up on trying to pass the national exam.[19]

Then came the Opium War. Wei watched the stunning events unfold from the safety of his Yangzhou villa, playing only minor and intermittent roles in the conflict. He did, however, become overtly linked to some of its principal actors, and wrote a narrative of the war, *An Account of the Daoguang-Era Pacification Campaign Against the Western Ships*. The central message of his account was that China urgently needed reform, including borrowing from abroad, in order to protect and restore the empire's greatness. It was a message that would inspire and divide the political class for generations to come.[20]

Wei's telling of the war centered on the heroic role of China's first drug czar, Imperial Commissioner Lin Zexu, whom Emperor Daoguang had dispatched to Canton in early 1839 with a mandate to ban opium use and stop British traders from aggressively marketing the drug to an alarmingly growing number of addicts in China. Back in the "age of prosperity and flourishing," opium use had been limited, while England's addiction to tea had caused an annual trade deficit to run in China's favor. However, since the 1820s British traders had stumbled upon a clever, if hurtful, way to stanch the hemorrhaging of British silver bullion at Canton, the only Chinese port into which Europeans were then allowed to bring their goods. By selling high-grade opium grown in British India to Chinese middlemen, Britain's chronic trade deficit with China was turned into a growing surplus. These traders, many linked to the government-backed East India Company, were the drug cartels of their day. The opium trade became so successful that the British Parliament soon found itself under heavy pressure to expand market access beyond Canton—by force if necessary. In the meantime, Qing rulers now faced a fiscal crisis themselves, with silver bullion suddenly flowing out of rather than into the Chinese economy. In addition, Emperor Daoguang was understandably dismayed by the toll opium addiction was taking on his subjects. And so it was that China and Britain came to loggerheads in one of the modern world's first drug wars.[21]

China's one triumph in the confrontation came before war even broke out thanks to Commissioner Lin. His first act upon arrival in Canton was to cordon off the area where the British traders were confined, along with their warehouses of opium. Lin then brazenly commanded them to hand over twenty thousand chests of the narcotic. Wei Yuan vividly described the scene that followed: "At an elevated spot on the shore, a space was barricaded in; here a pit was dug, and filled with opium mixed with brine: into this, again, lime was thrown, forming a scalding furnace, which made a kind of boiling soup of the opium. In the evening the mixture was let out by sluices, and allowed to flow out to sea with the ebb tide."[22]

Commissioner Lin's men spent three weeks slowly liquidating the drugs, making a "public spectacle" of it in the process.[23] This was arguably the last triumphant moment for China in its relations with the West . . . until Mao Zedong's armies fought American troops to a standstill in the Korean War more than a century later. But the principal effect of Lin's aggressive confiscation and disposal was to give the British the casus belli they were in fact seeking. In the words of historian Peter Ward Fay, Britain's logic was, "Why not take them [the Chinese] to war, and at its victorious conclusion make them pay for the opium and for the war too?"[24]

Commissioner Lin held to a hard line, even writing Queen Victoria demanding cessation of the opium trade on moral and economic grounds. Alas, there was little hope of swaying British foreign policy, then being crafted by the hawkish Lord Palmerston. Preliminary hostilities erupted in the fall of 1839 as Commissioner Lin readied the defense of Canton. But when the full British fleet finally arrived in the summer of 1840, to Lin's surprise they did not attack the city. Instead, they simply bypassed Canton and sailed up the coast, handily capturing strategic coastal positions near Shanghai.

Wei Yuan himself became personally involved in the war in September 1840, when a British surveyor, Captain Peter Anstruther, was captured while on a reconnaissance mission in Zhejiang Province, and local officials asked Wei, already considered something of an authority on "barbarian affairs," to help interrogate him.[25] When Wei arrived at the prison, he pumped the surveyor for information about England, a place Wei Yuan had no prospect of visiting but about which he was intensely curious. With an iron ring around his neck and eighteen-pound irons weighing down his legs, Captain Anstruther answered Wei's basic questions about his far-off country as best he could. As the captive explained, because his island nation ("Ying-jie-li," as Wei transliterated it) was so small, his countrymen had been forced to rely on sea commerce, and thus had mastered new techniques in shipbuilding and firearms manufacture in the process. Anstruther also told Wei how the English government's revenue came almost entirely from maritime customs, rather than from taxes on land or labor as was the case in China. After the interrogation, Wei drafted an intelligence report, "A Briefing on England," writing pointedly, "England neither produces nor consumes opium, but rather, by enjoying the profits of opium smoking, leads the West in terms of wealth and power."[26]

While Wei was questioning his British prisoner, Lin's defenses, thanks to his installation of foreign-bought artillery, were keeping Canton safe from British attack. Wei's *Account* quoted Lin as being confident that "three million taels would buy all the ships and guns that China wanted; and, by thus imitating the enemy's best methods, we should be able to constrain him with his own weapons, and allow him to wear himself out in seeking to attack us."[27]

However, Lin's view of the need to "imitate the enemy's best methods" was decidedly in the minority. Most of Chinese officialdom instead maintained an attitude of disdain for all things foreign, a sentiment keenly felt by Westerners in China such as Duncan MacPherson, who fought in the Opium War and wrote in his memoirs, "Haughty, cruel, and hypocritical, they despise all other nations but their own; they regard themselves as faultless. Next to the son of heaven, a true Chinaman thinks himself the greatest man in the world, and China, beyond all comparison, to be the most civilized, the most learned, the most fruitful, the most ancient, in short, the only country in the world."[28] As Wei saw things, Lin Zexu was caught in a political no-man's-land between a xenophobic war party and an appeasement party, both woefully ignorant of the true nature of the new kind of threat represented by British sea power, and they scapegoated Lin for a war that was going poorly everywhere except in Canton.

In late September 1840, the court recalled Lin to Beijing for censure. His replacement in Canton foolishly reversed his fortification policies, leaving the city exposed to a British assault. It came in January 1841 and was punishing, forcing Lin's hapless replacement to promise the British seven million taels as an opium indemnity, along with rights to occupy a desolate, malaria-infested nearby island called Hong Kong. But Emperor Daoguang refused to sign off on the terms negotiated by his Canton commissioner. As Wei told it, "The Emperor was furious when he heard of the capture of the forts [at Canton] and the menacing attitude of the [British] rebels, and said he would not give a cent for the opium nor yield an inch of territory."[29]

So, in standard Chinese bureaucratic fashion, which inevitably seeks to pin blame for defeat on someone, Lin's replacement was arrested as an appeaser. In the spring of 1841, when the next, hawkish Canton commissioner ordered a foolhardy sneak attack on the British fleet, the full-scale British counterassault that followed led to the fall of the city and a final ignominious defeat. That summer Lin Zexu was banished with his two sons to Ili, a remote northwestern frontier town on the edge of the deserts of what is now Xinjiang Province. Passing through Zhenjiang on his way into exile, he spent an evening with Wei Yuan, commiserating over the sorry course of the war and the urgent need to catch up with Western military superiority, while lamenting their powerlessness to reverse China's decline. As was common practice among Confucian gentlemen, Wei composed a poem on the occasion of seeing his friend and mentor head off into exile:

> On a day fraught with countless emotions, we meet but cannot
>   say a word.
> Like worms that curl up in a storm, as time races by we must
>   laugh at our efforts to learn how to slay a dragon.
> You have studied their methods for three years, yet we are in
>   danger from both north and south.
> Even if there is a chance to go to Beijing, still we must focus our
>   strategy on the sea.
> In a single night we come together and go separate ways, like
>   joy and regret in a single body . . .
> We should not waste the moon in Zhenjiang, bosom friends can
>   escape their predicament with wine.[30]

As Lin Zexu later wrote, in plainer prose: "Now it is even more difficult to check the wildfire. After all, ships, guns, and a water force are absolutely indispensable. Even if the rebellious barbarians had fled and returned beyond the seas, these things would still have to be urgently planned for, in order to work out the permanent defense of our sea frontiers. Moreover, unless we have weapons, what other help can we get now to drive away the crocodile and to get rid of the whales?"[31]

Indeed, new military technology like the HMS *Nemesis*—the world's first ironclad, steam-powered paddle warship—gave the British an enormous advantage as they mounted another attack near Shanghai in 1842 and then brazenly proceeded up the Yangtze River. Occupying the confluence of the Yangtze River and the Grand Canal, on which southern rice was transshipped north to the capital, they had the Chinese empire by its jugular. The British had effectively cut off trade, including the emperor's food supply, at the country's commercial heart, creating a desperate situation. Wealthy salt merchants in Yangzhou (Wei presumably among them) even offered to pay a ransom of half a million silver taels so that British ships might leave their city and property unmolested. But, reported Wei, "junks docked in other Yangtze River towns . . . were put to the torch."[32] And when "over eighty foreign ships thundering in the river," as Wei described them, finally reached Nanjing, the distraught emperor gave his lead negotiator "carte blanche to act as he should see fit."[33] The once-hawkish court was now desperate for peace terms, lest the British bombard Nanjing itself. "All their anxiety, which was too powerful to be concealed," a British officer observed of the Chinese in Nanjing, "was centered upon one main object—our immediate departure."[34]

And so on August 11, 1842, a small English delegation met their Chinese counterparts at the Temple of the Tranquil Seas to negotiate the infamous Treaty of Nanjing. In their great anxiety to secure the English barbarians' swift removal, the Chinese struck a humiliating bargain. Along with being awarded Hong Kong, the British were allowed to "open up" four more coastal cities to European trade, including the town of Shanghai (which would soon become transformed into the "Pearl of the Orient"), creating the first of the so-called treaty ports, which ultimately would stretch like a chain of foreign cultivated pearls up the Chinese coast. British nationals were also granted legal immunity from standing trial in local courts based on the principle of extraterritoriality. And finally, the Qing court promised to pay an indemnity of a staggering twenty-one million silver taels in war reparations, including the cost of all the opium destroyed by Lin Zexu.[35]

Wei insisted that the British would have settled for a much smaller indemnity, and possibly even an agreement banning the sale of opium (which, ironically, was not even mentioned in the treaty ending the Opium War). But from the start, the Qing negotiators had lost their nerve and yielded to British demands. "Fighting was neglected when fighting was proper, and indulged in when out of place," Wei wrote dejectedly. "And peace was decided for exactly at the wrong time."[36]

Wei foresaw devastating historical consequences growing out of China's blindness toward the Western threat, and he again invoked his favorite Legalist motto about the need for "wealth and power" to become the basis for reform. "The millions . . . we had to spend in war indemnities to the barbarians could have been devoted to the purchase of foreign guns and ships, the training of marines and firemen to attack, etc.; thus appropriating to our own purposes the armaments and defences of the foreigners themselves, and turning their arts and devices into *our* arts and devices, and at one effort both enriching the state and strengthening our arms."[37]

Besides the need for a radically new approach to defense, the other great lesson Wei took from the Opium War was that, in order to exploit divisions between the imperialist powers to its own advantage, China urgently needed to study international relations. He could see that China's skills in diplomacy were woefully inadequate. For example, both the Americans and the French had made overtures to China during the war, but in their ignorance of Anglo-American and Anglo-French tensions, Qing officials had not attempted to use these advances to play one power off against the other. In fact, in a supplemental treaty signed in 1843 the Qing supinely gave away most-favored-nation rights, automatically extending to the British any privileges accorded to any other countries. American negotiators then arranged to have such rights extended to them as well, setting the stage for an unprecedented scramble by each foreign power to automatically claim whatever privileges were won by any one of the others. This most-favored-nation clause made it almost impossible for Beijing to employ the age-old Chinese strategy of *yiyi zhiyi* (以夷制夷), "using barbarians to control other barbarians." Instead, each foreign power could count on automatically enjoying all the imperialist spoils claimed by the others.[38]

The Opium War spun Wei into a whirlwind of research and writing.

The same month that the Treaty of Nanjing was signed, he finished a new book, *Records of the Conquest*, a paean to the rise of the Manchus and their mighty Qing Empire. Based on historical research he had been carrying out for over a decade, his report rang familiar notes, memorializing the Qing's earlier success in using statecraft based on the quest for wealth and power not only to fend off foreign threats but also to continually expand the empire. "When the state is rich and powerful, it will be effective—it deals with the traitors and they will not persist in their ways; it administers revenue and [the revenue] will not be wasted; it acquires weapons and they will not be flawed; it organizes armed forces and the troops will not be understrength. What then is there to fear about barbarians anywhere—what is there to worry about as to defense against aggression?"[39]

As his compatriots contemplated the implications of their military and diplomatic defeat in 1842, Wei's *Conquest* presented them with a timely reminder that the halcyon days of China's "age of prosperity and flourishing" had been based on a dynamic and expansive foreign policy, at least around its periphery—including a willingness to borrow from foreigners, whether such borrowings involved Dutch cannons or Jesuit cartography.

Wei also introduced another concept in *Conquest* that would prove significant for decades to come. He counter-intuitively argued that Chinese needed to feel a more acute sense of humiliation over their current fallen status. His monumental history of Qing China's rise was intended to induce in its readers not a sense of pride but a profound sense of shame over their decline. In an ancient Confucian classical text, Wei found the perfect motto for the Qing's nineteenth-century predicament—indeed, for modern China's struggle as a whole—which he used prominently in the preface to *Records of Conquest*: "Humiliation stimulates effort; when the country is humiliated, its spirit will be aroused."[40] This idea would be expressed again and again by others for the next century and a half. In fact, it remains the inspiration for the phrase inscribed today in the museum at the Temple of the Tranquil Seas: "To feel shame is to approach courage."

Wei's *Conquest* described how Qing China had once marched boldly west, extending the empire's borders across the Eurasian continent. As his readers knew all too well, since the time of Wei's own birth in the 1790s, the Qing had been able to claim no more such grand conquests. And few could probably then imagine that the Treaty of Nanjing represented only the first of an endless string of defeats and sacrifice of Chinese lives and territory.

Knowing the Enemy

Wei's next pioneering book, *Illustrated Treatise on Sea Powers*, published in 1843, turned its attentions to the new maritime powers that were already reaping the benefits of China's decline. Wei had been inspired by what he learned from his interrogation of Captain Anstruther, as well as by the efforts of his hero Lin Zexu, who had hired assistants in Canton to start collecting materials about Western nations. Lin shared the modest results, *Treatise on the Four Continents*, with Wei and, as he headed into exile, urged him to carry on the work in a more systematic fashion. So Wei began compiling as much credible new information as he could find on the rising maritime powers now encroaching on the Central Kingdom.

In carrying out this unprecedented research, Wei was groping in the dark. He was hindered not only by the paucity of original source material but also by the fact that he had never left China or studied a foreign language. He had to rely on the meager and miscellaneous assortment of translations and Chinese-language writings by Westerners such as the Prussian missionary Karl Gutzlaff and the Macau-born missionary's son John Robert Morrison—both of whom interpreted for the British military during the Opium War.[41]

Wei's task was further complicated by the fact that most educated Chinese still rejected the very idea of learning from "barbarians"— even after the shock of a war in which he estimated that three thousand British troops had managed to vanquish two hundred thousand Chinese fighting on their own soil.[42] In fact, Wei himself risked being seen as fatally contaminated by foreign influences simply for his efforts to alert his fellow countrymen to China's peril. As he pointed out, merely studying the West was potentially criminal behavior. "Nowadays, if Chinese are involved in translating foreign books, imitating barbarian skills, and briefing themselves on the foreign situation in the same way as the foreigners spy on all aspects of our situation," he wrote, "these people will be punished for committing crimes, causing trouble, and communicating with foreigners."[43] As a result, while the West was learning more and more about China, Chinese continued to know next to nothing about the West.

But Wei would not be deterred by the xenophobic tendencies of Confucian orthodoxy. He was convinced of the need to subject these new maritime challengers to strategic analysis. He was also acting in accordance with the classic teaching of the ancient military strategist Sunzi, a kindred spirit to the Legalists, who wrote in the *Art of War*, "Know yourself and know your enemy, and fighting a hundred battles you will win every one." True to that dictum, Wei's book *Sea Powers* was, in the words of scholar Jane Kate Leonard, "the first Chinese work to make a realistic geopolitical assessment of the worldwide dimensions of Western expansion and of its implications for Asian trade and politics."[44]

Britain of course stood out as the model most urgently demanding careful study. Although Wei had only the faintest notion of where England actually was on a world map, he displayed a pretty good grasp of the essential nature of commercial imperialism and the threats it posed. "[The British] promote trade by sending out soldiers," he explained in *Sea Powers*. "Soldiers and trade are mutually dependent. By overpowering [their rivals], they have become the most powerful of the island barbarians."[45]

Wei did not suggest that the Qing replicate Britain's maritime imperialism; he simply hoped his country could learn enough "barbarian techniques" to defend itself, hold on to its existing territory, and perhaps reestablish its central position at sea in maritime Asia. As Leonard explains, "Although he urged the adoption of Western naval and arms technology, he rejected thoroughly the Western use of naval power and the rampant and aggressive expansionism it included."[46]

Wei's foreign policy strategy boiled down to a core principle: "Before the peace settlement, it behooves us to use barbarians against barbarians. After the peace, it is proper for us to learn their superior techniques in order to control them."[47] Wei concluded, "The superior techniques of the barbarians are three: (1) warships, (2) firearms, and (3) methods of maintaining and training soldiers."[48] He did not idealize Europe or the West as alternative sources of values or civilization.

In fact, he described parts of Europe, for example, as populated by "many barbarian tribes, who cherish only profit and power, and indeed are as treacherous as the owls."[49] But he insisted that China could not afford to ignore their "superior techniques," if it wished to regain its own wealth, strength, and standing in the world.

Notably, Wei thought quite positively about democracy, especially in the section of *Sea Powers* describing the United States, where at that time suffrage was expanding (at least to all white men) in the name of Jacksonian democracy. "More than any other political regime past or present," Wei wrote, "because it so closely adheres to the will of the people, this system may truly be called public!"[50] Homing in on the fundamental difference between democratic America and authoritarian China, he observed, "Decisions on governmental policy, and the selection of high officials, all derive from [the people] below"[51]—not, as in China, from the emperor and his mandarins above.

Although he praised the United States, Wei was by no means suggesting that China adopt even selective elements of the American democratic model, nor copy the ways in which the United States Constitution sought to constrain the power of a strong central state. As historian Philip Kuhn observed, "The tripling of China's population under Qing rule and the resulting danger to social stability left the elite particularly vulnerable. It was a time not for weakening authoritarian rule, but for strengthening it. This last point was to emerge insistently as Western aggression made nationalism the central theme of elite politics during the dynasty's last years."[52] Indeed, the need to strengthen the state was a theme that would be echoed until the present day by almost every Chinese leader and thinker of note.

The year after the publication of *Sea Powers*, Wei finally passed the national-level civil service examination in Beijing, and, at long last, became eligible for a senior government appointment. Over the next decade he held a series of postings in Jiangsu Province, where he had advised provincial officials since he was a young man. But, perhaps because he had become too accustomed to his independence, these positions proved only a succession of frustrations, interrupted by a three-year hiatus to return home to Hunan to mourn his mother's death as required by the Confucian principle of "filial piety."

When Wei finally retired from public service, he was a thoroughly

Painting of Lin Zexu, circa 1840

disillusioned mandarin. By 1854, with the Taiping Rebellion raging, a new generation of thinkers and actors was emerging to "order the world," as Wei's pragmatic reformist brand of Legalist-Confucian amalgam described it. Wei himself soon disappeared into oblivion. In 1856 he left his family to join a Buddhist monastic community in Hangzhou, and early the next year he died. While his practical achievements as an official were insignificant, the body of writings he left behind, all motivated by his overriding patriotic concern to see China better understand the encroaching Western world as a way to both defend itself and restore itself to "wealth and power," were to profoundly influence generations of Chinese reformers thereafter.

CHAPTER 3

Self-Strengthening（自强）

FENG GUIFEN（冯桂芬）

The Ruins

The Qing Dynasty's old Summer Palace, known as Yuanmingyuan (圆明园), the "Garden of Perfect Brightness," is situated to the northwest of Beijing at the foot of the Western Hills. Emperor Kangxi began work on the first palace complex in the early eighteenth century as a gift for his son. In the 1750s, his grandson, Emperor Qianlong, with the help of resident European Jesuits missionaries, turned it into a resplendent complex of parks, gardens, lakes, hills, pagodas, and palaces—a Chinese Versailles.[1] At a time when European designers were toying with a new aesthetic of chinoiserie, Qianlong decided to mix Chinese and Western architectural styles to create a marvel of East-West hybrid landscape architecture. Indeed, Lord Macartney described with awe how the Yuanmingyuan was made up of "hundreds of pavilions scattered through the grounds and all connected together by close arbors, by passages apparently cut through stupendous rocks, or by fairyland galleries." The mesmerized Macartney wrote in his diary, "The various beauties of the spot, its lakes and rivers, together with its superb edifices . . . so strongly impressed my mind at this moment that I feel incapable of describing them."[2]

The eighteenth century had been a time when the West had accepted a distant, if constrained, working relationship with China—whether it was the Catholics in the court in Beijing, who as a condition of residence adopted Chinese customs, or the European traders sequestered

Rendering of Feng Guifen

in the port of Canton, who made what profits they could in the restrictive system created by the Qing to manage and limit commerce with Westerners. But with the First Opium War (1839–42), this period of controlled accommodation came to an abrupt end. And with the Second Opium War (1856–60), a whole new relationship was thrust on the Chinese, one in which they found themselves on the losing side of an increasingly unequal relationship with the West.

This Opium War redux began in 1856, when Qing authorities in Canton interdicted a commercial ship (the *Arrow*), formerly of Hong Kong registry, on suspicion of piracy and opium smuggling. The British peremptorily claimed the boat to be under the protection of the crown, thereby making its seizure an act of war. The incident soon became another casus belli, just like Commissioner Lin's confiscation of British opium in 1839—exactly the justification the British now needed to re-instigate hostilities and extend their commercial power up and down the Chinese seaboard. On the pretext of what they called the "Arrow War," the British navy quickly took control of Canton, then steamed north to seize Dagu Fort at the strategic port of Tianjin, the gateway to Beijing. By June 1858, they had strong-armed the Qing into signing another unequal treaty, the Treaty of Tianjin, which forced China to accept a British ambassador in Beijing, open up ten more treaty ports, allow Christian missionaries to proselytize in the Chinese interior, standardize the duty on opium, and lower transit fees on foreign goods (a major source of Qing revenue).[3]

But this initial armistice did not hold. The court in Beijing demurred on the Treaty of Tianjin, hoping to amend the terms of defeat by means of delaying tactics. The British, joined by the French, soon lost patience and reopened hostilities in the summer of 1859. To their chagrin, however, their joint forces were unable to retake the Dagu Fort, a Pyrrhic victory for the Chinese that foolishly led the Qing Dynasty to overestimate its own strength and then take hostage a small Anglo-French negotiating party. The infuriated British and French promptly formed a thirty-five-hundred-man expeditionary force and marched on Beijing virtually unopposed. When the British and French hostages were finally returned—nineteen of them dead, with others in the group tortured— the Europeans decided to take their revenge on the Chinese emperor's most prized possession—his Garden of Perfect Brightness.

The destruction of Yuanmingyuan was to be a "solemn act of retri-bution," said the British commander Lord Elgin, in which no blood would be spilled, but an emperor's "pride as well as his feelings" would be crushed.[4] Indeed, before the foreign expeditionary force arrived in Beijing, the young emperor Xianfeng had already fled along with his concubine (soon to become known as the Empress Dowager Cixi) to safe haven in Manchuria. With the Son of Heaven in hiding far to the north in his hunting lodge, British and French soldiers set about teach-ing the Qing a lesson they would never forget: that the British crown would not tolerate having the rights of Englishmen violated, even in faraway China. "As a deliberate act of humiliation," historian James Hevia explains, "it was an object lesson for others who might contem-plate defying British power."[5]

The work of pillaging the garden complex was systematic chaos. The French arrived first and began sacking and looting the imperial palaces. Lieutenant Colonel G. J. Wolseley, attached to the British ex-peditionary force, who arrived soon thereafter, saw in the French ram-page "the love of destruction that is certainly inherent in man," and described the event vividly: "The far-famed palaces of a line of mon-archs claiming a celestial relationship . . . were littered with the *débris* of all that was highly prized in China. Topsy-turvy is the only expres-sion in our language which at all describes this state. The ground around the French camp was covered with silks and clothing of all kinds, whilst the men ran hither and thither in search of further plun-der, most of them, according to the practice usual with soldiers upon such occasions, being decked out in the most ridiculous-looking cos-tumes they could find, of which there was no lack as the well-stocked wardrobes of his Imperial Majesty abounded in curious raiment."[6]

British troops soon also arrived to complete the sorry task. On Oc-tober 18, 1860, they "set fire to all the royal palaces which lay scat-tered about in that neighborhood," recorded Wolseley. "Throughout the whole of that day and the day following a dense cloud of black and heavy smoke hung over those scenes of former magnificence."[7] "By the evening of the 19th October, the summer palaces had ceased to exist, and in their immediate vicinity, the very face of nature seemed changed: some blackened gables and piles of burnt timbers alone indicating where the royal palaces had stood," he recounted.[8]

A twenty-seven-year-old captain in the Royal Engineers, Charles George Gordon, observed somberly, "You can scarcely imagine the beauty and magnificence of the places we burnt. It made one's heart sore to burn them; in fact, these places were so large, and we were so pressed for time, that we could not plunder them carefully. Quantities of gold ornaments were burnt, considered as brass. It was wretchedly demoralizing work for an army."[9]

Hinting at some measure of remorse, Lieutenant Wolseley mused: "When we first entered the gardens they reminded one of those magic grounds described in fairy tales; we marched from them upon the 19th October, leaving them a dreary waste of ruined nothings."[10]

But, in the end, Wolseley accepted the logic behind humbling the Qing Dynasty, instinctively understanding how to hit the Chinese where it hurt most. "The great vulnerable point in a Mandarin's character lies in his pride," he observed. "The destruction of the Yuanmingyuan was the most crushing of all blows which could be levelled at his Majesty's inflated notions of universal supremacy."[11] Reducing the gardens to ruins was "the strongest proof of our superior strength" and "served to undeceive all Chinamen in their absurd conviction of their monarch's universal sovereignty."[12]

Captain Gordon, on the other hand, surmising that this act of foreign plunder might instead inspire Chinese ire rather than humble self-reflection, wrote in a letter home: "I think the grandees hate us, as they must after what we did to the Palace."[13] He was, indeed, proved right. A few years later one of the most powerful ministers in the Qing court invoked the trauma of 1860 to chastise those in favor of engaging with—even studying—the West. "The barbarians are our enemies," this official, an ethnic Mongolian by the name of Woren, reminded the emperor. "In 1860 they took up arms and rebelled against us. Our capital and its suburb were invaded, our ancestral altar was shaken, our Imperial palace was burned, and our officials and people were killed or wounded. There had never been such insults during the last 200 years of our dynasty. All our scholars and officials have been stirred with heart-burning rage, and have retained their hatred until the present. Our court could not help making peace with the barbarians. [But] how can we forget this enmity and this humiliation even for one single day?"[14]

Today the Yuanmingyuan's fabled palaces still lie in ruins, looking like so many oversized but half-assembled Lego blocks. Preserved by the Chinese Communist government, the despoiled palaces remain a glaring showcase of China's painful treatment by the Western powers, an outdoor museum of victimization. On weekends and during national holidays, the grounds of the old Summer Palace make for a popular outing for Beijingers and a pilgrimage destination for out-of-towners (foreigners are few). Locals come for the lakes, leafy gardens, and quiet refuge from the city's concrete jungle and relentless traffic. However, people from across the country are also drawn here for a history lesson. Families, couples, and student groups traipse amid the smashed pillars and fallen structures of what was once the Garden of Perfect Brightness, stare at the rubble, and try to imagine the lost grandeur of a long-gone China. Official guides remind them to focus on the paradise lost, or, as an exhortation on a signpost admonishes: "Do not forget our humiliation."

One father on holiday in Beijing from the provinces with his family expressed a typical sentiment. Not quite clear on the historical details—he confused the British-French expeditionary force of 1860 with a later one after the Boxer Rebellion in 1900—still he grasped the essential point: "China was weak back then," he said firmly. "But now we are getting stronger." And the lesson taken from the sacking of Yuanmingyuan by the leading reformers in the generation immediately following Wei Yuan was hardly different: A weakened China desperately needed to strengthen itself. Among them, none was bolder in his ideas than Feng Guifen, the heir to Wei's reformist agenda and a leading political thinker of the latter part of the nineteenth century. Building on Wei's insights, Feng devised a new plan for restoring wealth and power to China, through something he called *ziqiang* (自强), "self-strengthening." He believed that these marauding foreign powers would have to be studied more deeply, and, as a result, the scope of "techniques and methods" copied from them would have to become much broader than even Wei had allowed himself to imagine. Out of the double trauma of foreign aggression and civil war, Feng Guifen devised a program for change that he promised would be the ideal solution to his country's sense of deepening crisis.

Anxiety Within, Calamity Without

Feng was born in 1809, when China's hegemonic place at the center of East Asia still appeared unchallenged. He hailed from a distinguished lineage in the wealthy metropolis of Suzhou, in Jiangsu Province, but came of age in modest circumstances. The only surviving portrait, depicting him late in life, shows a severe mandarin with a long goatee and thick mustache compensating for the bald crown of his head. His high cheekbones and eyes lined with wrinkles leave only a hint of the youth who had been consumed with memorizing Confucian classical texts and commentaries in preparation for the endless rounds of examinations needed to make it into China's famed civil service.[15] Feng excelled in the early stages of the system, passing the county level in one of the most competitive regions in the empire. That brought him to Nanjing, where Wei Yuan was then applying his talents to reforming the region's grain and salt transportation systems. Here Feng passed the provincial exam on his first try in 1832, writing an essay that won him praise as the kind of talent that comes "once in a hundred years."[16] But he failed the imperial qualifying exam. And then, to the immense disappointment of his family, he failed the provincial requalifying exam in 1835. Like so many others, Wei Yuan included, Feng had become trapped in what the scholar Ichisada Miyazaki termed "China's examination hell."[17]

Fortunately, Feng, like Wei, drew the attention of Lin Zexu, then governor of Jiangsu Province, who recruited him for his staff. It was a way for the young man to gain administrative experience, make political connections, and support himself as he continued studying for the exams, which he finally passed in 1840 with high honors. A national-level civil service examination degree was his payoff for more than twenty years of unremitting dedication to classical studies, and Feng quickly wrote a letter of gratitude to his patron, Lin, who was just being sent into exile for his role in the Opium War.

In the unsettled years after the First Opium War, distraught scholar-officials and examination students met to agonize and strategize over the failed war effort and to ponder China's newly revealed impotence. At one such meeting, Feng heard a speech by an Opium War hero who had aggressively fought off the British (on the island of Taiwan) yet was punished by the Qing court. According to Feng, this veteran finished his speech by saying, "It is up to you gentlemen! Keep up your pride! Keep up your pride!" Whereupon, Feng added, "all of us who had been listening suddenly cast down our gaze with shame."[18] It was a textbook example of the deeply held Confucian idea that humiliation can be a spur to action.

At another Beijing gathering of like-minded literati, Feng actually met Wei Yuan. Yet despite the overlap in their reformist patronage networks, they never became close. Although Feng did credit Wei with being the first to advocate studying the strengths of "barbarians," he also criticized him for naiveté about how easy it might be to turn one against the other and for some factual errors in *Sea Powers* due to his reliance on outdated materials.[19] Still, despite his criticisms, Feng was deeply influenced by Wei's writings on wealth and power, statecraft reform, and Western studies. In fact, Feng's defining concept of "self-strengthening," for which he later became renowned, had actually first been used by Wei in his account of the Opium War, in which he had written of China's need for *zixiu ziqiang* (自修自强), "self-improvement and self-strengthening."[20]

Feng rose steadily through the imperial bureaucracy in the years after the Opium War, but in 1845 his mother died, obligating him to retire for three years of mourning. However, by 1850 his star was again rising, and his political patrons even managed to secure him a coveted personal audience with the newly enthroned twenty-year-old emperor Xianfeng. Alas, before Feng could avail himself of this chance to whisper into the young sovereign's ear, his father died, and once again he was obliged to return home and desist from all official activities—even a meeting with the emperor himself—to mourn his father in a properly filial manner.[21]

By the time this second retirement-in-mourning ended, the empire was yet again in crisis mode. By 1853 Feng and his fellow scholar-officials found themselves thrust into a daunting universe of civil war sparked by the rebellion of a Christian cult that had taken the name Taiping (太平), or "Supreme Peace." And when the Qing Dynasty became embroiled in the Second Opium War, China found itself mired in a double jeopardy, what the ancient Legalists described as *neiyou wai-huan* (内忧外患), "anxiety within, calamity without."[22] In the 1850s and 1860s, the Qing was put to the ultimate test of having to quell domestic rebellion and repel foreign invasion at the same time, the anvil on which Feng Guifen forged his ideas for reform.

The Taiping Rebellion began in 1850 as a standoff between a small crypto-Christian sect and local officials in a remote southwestern region of the country. However, the movement quickly metastasized into a full-blown dynasty-threatening civil war in which twenty million Chinese would eventually perish. The sect's leader, Hong Xiuquan, was a failed examination student who, in the course of an ensuing psychological breakdown, had visions of himself as a messiah figure. Interpreting his fevered dreams through biblical tracts he had acquired from Protestant missionaries in south China, Hong became convinced that he was the younger brother of Jesus Christ, or, as historian Jonathan Spence put it, "God's Chinese son." He went on to proclaim a theocratic state, *Taiping Tianguo* (太平天国), the "Heavenly Kingdom of Supreme Peace," a bizarre bastardization of Christian theology and Confucian classics backed by millions of armed peasant followers.[23]

The rebellion spread like lava across south China, winning over dispossessed peasants with the promise of overthrowing both hated local landlords and despised alien Manchu rulers. The Taiping repeatedly defeated demoralized and underfunded Qing armies, and in 1855 even captured the city of Nanjing, which they turned into their new "imperial" capital. The Qing Dynasty appeared to be not only in irreversible decline but also on the brink of total collapse.

Under such dire circumstances, Feng, like many of his fellow scholar-officials, felt that he could no longer play the part of disinterested Confucian gentleman cum public servant patiently awaiting a posting to some far corner of the empire. Instead, he raced back to his native city, Suzhou, to lead the armed resistance against the Taipings, who coveted Suzhou as a jewel on the path to the bigger prize, the treaty port, Shanghai. Thanks to European trade allowed by the Treaty of Nanjing, Shanghai was already booming. And although it was well armed with foreign-led forces and ready to defend itself, only local resistance stood in the way of the Taipings around Suzhou. So even though Feng had been summoned to Beijing in 1856 for an enticing court position, feeling the urgent need to help with local resistance, he opted to stay in his home town.

In addition to the ongoing Taiping Rebellion, after the eruption of hostilities with the British over the *Arrow* incident in Canton in 1856, the Qing faced a foreign menace, and both efforts went poorly. When in the spring of 1860 the Taiping rebels decimated an imperial army in the Yangtze region and then poured into Suzhou, Feng barely escaped, fleeing to the last sanctuary left in southern China, Shanghai.

Dissenting Views

Feng arrived in the famed port city late in 1860, settling initially in the Chinese part of town. Soon enough, however, he began visiting the British and French concession areas, even watching the horse races at the Shanghai track. A translator at the London Missionary Society Press named Wang Tao—later China's first modern journalist—at one point arranged for Feng and his son to visit the home of a friendly Briton for whom he worked as interpreter. This was Feng's first intimate contact with the Western world, akin to Wei Yuan's chance to interrogate Captain Anstruther. Here Feng was able to observe the texture of European material life—leather upholstered furniture, foreign musical instruments, a realist painting hanging on the wall next to a well-stocked bookcase, and other manifestations of Western treaty port life.[24] If these were but fragments of this parallel world, at least they were tangible and within reach. In early 1861 he moved his family into a neighborhood where the British and French concessions met—about as close as an educated Chinese could hope to get to the West and still be in China.[25] Here, in this strangely foreign world transplanted onto Chinese soil, Feng began to think in new ways, and write down his thoughts.

Just as the defeat of 1842 had spurred Wei Yuan to reconsider recent Chinese history and reevaluate the nature of Western power, so the disasters of 1860 and his otherworldly refuge in Shanghai now inspired Feng to propose a new direction for China drawn in part from foreign models. Though suffering from a liver ailment, the fifty-year-old Confucian scholar-official nonetheless managed to author a slim volume of *kangyi* (抗议), "dissenting views," that outlined his new ideas on "self-strengthening," thinking that would leave a deep imprint on the evolution of his country's modern intellectual history.

In typical Confucian fashion, the title of Feng's work, *Dissenting Views from a Hut near Bin*, tipped off his classically educated readers that this was a book about resisting foreign aggression. They would immediately have recognized the place-name Bin, near modern Xi'an, as the birthplace of the ancient Zhou Dynasty's King Wu, who symbolized fierce resistance to barbarian threats. Xi'an had in antiquity been near the border of China's "barbarian" neighbors—today, Bin was Shanghai in the middle of a barbarian settlement. And by placing himself in a humble dwelling—the "hut" of his title—Feng meant to suggest his temerity. After all, despite his middling rank as a local official, Feng had dared to write a book proffering sweeping strategic counsel to the Imperial court on matters ranging from national policy to foreign affairs, articulating core principles for what was China's first indigenous plan for modernization, one that remains surprisingly relevant even today.

The central question that Feng posed was radical in its simplicity: "Our territory is eight times that of Russia, ten times the size of America, one hundred times bigger than France, and two hundred times England," he wrote. "Why is it that they are small and strong, yet we are big and weak?"[26] His answer was no less bold: China would have to master the secrets of its new adversaries by admitting their superiority and adopting some of their ways, or else perish.

The West's superiority, according to Feng, was more than simply steamships, firearms, and military training. Deeper, systemic factors were at work. The West, he declared, surpassed China in four critical ways: education ("employing people's talents"), economic development ("profiting from the land"), political legitimacy ("keeping the rulers and people close"), and intellectual inquiry ("calling things by their true names").[27] Feng concluded that in order to close the gap with Britain, Chinese would have to swallow their pride and become more like their adversary in these fundamental areas.

His plan called on Chinese to *self*-strengthen: learn from the West, yes; borrow from the West, yes; but not rely on the West. He warned of the dangers of accepting military aid from foreign governments, and

The Jiangnan Arsenal in Nanjing, 1872

Li Hongzhang and Ulysses S. Grant in Beijing, 1879

Fall of Dagu Fort during the Second Opium War, 1860

Tourists at the Yuanmingyuan, destroyed by Anglo-French troops in 1860

insisted not simply on acquiring foreign weaponry but also teaching
Chinese how to manufacture, maintain, and employ new technology
themselves.[28] In the short term, China would have to hire foreign military experts for instruction in the skills of modern warfare, but over the
long term native Chinese should be trained to take their place. This
balancing act of borrowing from foreign powers without falling irre-
trievably into their debt would, in fact, trip up China's leaders for the
next century and more. Culturally conservative isolationists were always ready to pounce on advocates of adaptation as traitors. Considering that the general attitude toward Western "barbarians" had changed
little since Emperor Qianlong's days, Feng's *Dissenting Views*, written
while the embers of the Summer Palace were still smoldering, took no
small amount of courage. Indeed, a British interpreter, Thomas Taylor
Meadows, described in 1852 what it was then like working with Chinese involved in "barbarian management," as relations with the West
were still called. "Those Chinese who have had direct opportunities of
learning something of our customs and culture," Meadows observed,
"may amount, taking all Five Ports [into account], to some five or six
thousand out of three hundred and sixty millions." And, he added,
they "mostly consider us beneath their nation in moral and intellectual
cultivation . . . I do not recollect conversing with one, and I have con-
versed with many, whose previous notions of us were not analogous to
those we entertain of savages. They are always surprised, not to say
astonished, to learn that we have surnames, and understand the family
distinctions of father, brother, wife, sister, etc.; in short, that we live
otherwise than as a herd of cattle."[29]

If such disdain typified the attitude of his countrymen, Feng's *Dissenting Views* had a radically different starting point: an invigorating
sense of shame. In his eyes, the Confucian virtue of humiliating *chi* (恥),
"shame," was not merely an embarrassment but—as was suggested on
placards in the Temple of the Tranquil Seas—also a useful catalyst for
strengthening the nation. Feng believed that if a human being could
feel shame over his inferiority, it was the beginning of doing something
about it to make oneself stronger. "Once one feels a sense of shame,
nothing is better than self-strengthening," he proclaimed.[30]

At the core of Feng's self-strengthening program was the military,
because national self-defense was the top policy priority, and also the

form of foreign borrowing that was most acceptable to China's still conservative establishment. As Feng became intimately involved in the exiled Suzhou gentry's efforts to raise and fund a Western-run mercenary force to recapture their city from the Taipings, the experience gave him tangible experience in borrowing from the West.[31] He even wrote short biographies of the three most famous foreign generals active in Shanghai: Frederick Townsend Ward, Henry Burgevine, and Charles George "Chinese" Gordon, the last of whom had described the destruction of the Yuanmingyuan and then later fought against the Taipings. Feng watched as English and American officers helped Qing forces triumph over the rebels by using advanced technology and Western tactics, and he was impressed. So, in *Dissenting Views*, he called on his government to fund the creation of Western-style shipyards and arsenals in strategic ports up and down the coast. "Only then," he wrote, "can we restore our original strength, only then can we erase our recent humiliations, only then can we fully count as the number one great power on this vast earth."[32]

As he wrestled with the question of technological modernization, Feng was way ahead of his contemporaries in recognizing the relevance of Japan, a nearby alternate model of adaptation that would later come to haunt China. Feng praised Japan's incipient efforts at opening and reform, which were already under way in the late 1850s. He lamented that while China had made no progress at all in the twenty years since the first Opium War, the Japanese—within a couple of years of being forced to open their markets to Western powers—were already manufacturing modern ships. If China could not bring itself to act similarly, he warned grimly, "We Chinese will be meat and fish for the hundred other nations of the world."[33]

Feng's interests were not limited to defense. He was also out ahead of his peers in exploring the political foundations of the West's superiority on the battlefield. He argued that a critical part of the West's dynamism and strength was the accountability of their governments to their people—or, as Chinese statecraft thinkers such as Feng described it, "the closeness of the ruler and the ruled."[34] Such intimacy, he believed, grew naturally from political models such as Britain's parliamentary democracy and America's presidential one. In his view, Chinese officials, by contrast, had become totally alienated from their subjects.

"During my life I have been simple and straightforward," he wrote. "Therefore I asked high officials, as well as those in the prefectures and counties, about the suffering and bitterness among the people. Most were alarmed and said they had never heard about such things. This deficiency results from a lack of communication."[35] Feng believed that such alienation of the rulers from the ruled helped explain the spread of the Taiping Rebellion. "The rebels in the Empire are not born as rebels," he wrote, "but they become insurgents as a result of being neither fed nor educated."[36]

A rare manuscript version of *Dissenting Views* includes Feng's fascinating assessment of American democracy written just after the 1860 election of Abraham Lincoln. Notably, Feng drew an explicit connection between the democratic electoral process and American "wealth and power," an instrumentalist view of liberty that would have a long shelf life in Chinese political discourse. "Various barbarian books show that, in America, the president rules the nation, and that political power is transmitted not to [the president's] son but to the wise," he wrote. "People reportedly write down the name of their favorite leaders on ballots and throw them into the ballot box, and the one who wins the most ballots rises to the presidency. The state governors are elected through the same procedure. Thereby, the nation became wealthy and powerful, gradually surpassing in national strength even Russia, England and France. Who dares say that there is no man [of greatness] among the barbarians?"[37]

Feng did not stop at admiring America from afar; he suggested that China introduce a small-scale version of "village democracy." "In each village people will write on slips of paper the name of those whom they nominate for these positions. The votes will then be submitted to a public office, where they will be tallied. The persons with the most votes will be elected to the offices."[38] He also proposed to open up the ranks of candidates for government office to men who were widely recommended by "all scholar-gentry, all groups of students, village headmen, and their assistants in local communities"—rather than to just those who did well on the examinations and had the right political connections in Beijing.[39] This was one of the first, albeit tentative, arguments made by a Chinese for popular consent of the governed. "As to whether we should stress the private opinions of one or two persons or public opinion derived from a large body of people, our focus ought to be on the latter," Feng insisted.[40]

Among his most original proposals, Feng dared the Qing government to open its budgetary process to public scrutiny—a revolutionary suggestion at the time (as it would still be today).[41] And he praised northern European social welfare and popular educational systems he had heard about, such as reform schools in Holland and mandatory education for literacy in Sweden.[42] From his reading of translated material about the West and discussions with other "barbarian experts"— perhaps even a few living, breathing barbarians in Shanghai—he cobbled together a picture of how foreign political systems worked, and what might be useful to China. Defying orthodox Confucianism's emphasis on traditional models from China's ancient past, Feng argued: "If a system is no good, even though it is from antiquity, we should reject it; if a system is good, then we should follow it, even if it originates from uncivilized peoples. I have picked up one or two such things from barbarian books, and they should not be dismissed simply because of that."[43]

Feng's political philosophy, however, can hardly be called democratic. It was closer to what we might today call "participatory authoritarianism." After all, he still conceived of political authority as flowing from the emperor, the Son of Heaven, downward. In the end, like generations of reformers who followed him, Feng concluded that Western democracy was not suitable for China. In addition, he remained confident in the superiority of Chinese values and Confucian principles. Yes, China would have to learn "techniques for wealth and power" from the West, but its social fabric, moral code, and cultural forms would, and should, remain intact. They were, after all, nonpareil.

"Today we must once again study foreign countries," Feng advised. "They exist in the same time and space, yet they have attained wealth and power on their own. Is it not clear that we have similarities, and that we can easily adopt their strong points? If we use Chinese ethics and teachings as the foundation, but supplement them with foreign countries' techniques for wealth and power [*fuqiang zhi shu*, 富强之术], would it not be ideal?"[44] As a Chinese reformist dream, this vision of using Western means for Eastern ends would echo down the decades to Deng Xiaoping, and still resonates today in China's halls of power.

Arsenals and Institutes

As soon as Feng finished writing *Dissenting Views from a Hut near Bin*, he sent a copy to the most powerful person in China—not, as one might presume, the newly enthroned Tongzhi emperor, who was only a five-year-old Manchu boy, but a Confucian gentleman-general whose army was the Qing rulers' last hope to stop the Taiping rebels: General Zeng Guofan, the Chinese equivalent of Ulysses S. Grant.

Zeng's life paralleled Feng's in that he, too, passed the civil service exams at a young age, but in 1853 returned to his native province, Hunan, to lead the fight against the Taiping rebels. But, unlike Feng, Zeng Guofan had been remarkably successful in quelling the "anxiety within" of Taiping insurrection by mobilizing local gentry and commoners to fight together in defense of their homes, spawning a whole new species of military organization, the Hunan Army. By 1860, hopes for defeating the Taiping rested almost entirely on his shoulders. Imperial troops had proven so ineffective that the court in Beijing was forced to cede power to Zeng's regional Hunanese force. As any reader of Wei Yuan's *Conquest* would have appreciated, such desperate decentralization of imperial power was unprecedented in the Qing era. It also marked the first time that Beijing had suspended the time-honored "rule of avoidance," which barred imperial officials from holding positions in their native provinces. Scholar-officials were now fighting in and for their hometowns.[45]

It was not just the Manchu rulers and Qing officials in Beijing who pinned their hopes for survival on Zeng and his regional Hunan Army; Feng Guifen himself, while in Shanghai, personally sought out Zeng's help. In November 1861—the same month he finished *Dissenting Views*—he wrote Zeng, beseeching him to send a division of his army to Shanghai to link up with Anglo-American mercenary units fighting under a Qing flag in order to retake Suzhou from the Taipings. Initially reluctant to overextend his troops or overstep his mandate, Zeng was finally persuaded to dispatch his star lieutenant, Li Hongzhang, to Shanghai.[46]

Li was only in his late thirties at the time, but he commanded immediate attention. Over six feet tall, with eagle eyes and an implacable gaze, Li was an imposing figure. "He is colossal, with very prominent cheek-bones, and small, very small, quick and searching eyes," wrote the French novelist Pierre Loti after meeting him.[47] At General Zeng's orders, Li now created his own regional fighting force, drawn from his native Anhui Province.[48] In order to ensure the swift and safe passage of Li's Anhui Army, Feng and fellow displaced gentry in Shanghai hired seven British steamships to transport the new troops. Li arrived in Shanghai with his Anhui Army in April 1862 and had retaken Suzhou by the end of 1863.

With his close ties to Li and Zeng, Feng Guifen had reason to hope that his ideas about "self-strengthening" might now receive an official hearing. After all, General Zeng had written in his diary that *Dissenting Views* was the work of a "great scholar," and had had copies distributed to his staff.[49] And, he began echoing Feng's language and ideas: "If we wish to find a method of self-strengthening," he told his officers, "we should begin by considering the reform of government service and the securing of men of ability as urgent tasks, and then regard learning to make explosive shells and steamships and other instruments as the work of first importance."[50] He even offered to publish Feng's pamphlet, but Feng turned down the offer. No doubt Feng was fearful of conservative enemies pouncing on his "dissenting views," and so chose instead to circulate his essays unofficially in manuscript form produced by the countless underemployed, highly literate men who worked for leading figures such as Zeng.[51]

As soon as Li Hongzhang arrived in Shanghai, he made Feng a top advisor and hired him to help ghostwrite his reformist policy proposals.[52] In fact, Li first used the phrase "self-strengthening" just after he arrived in Shanghai and Feng had entered his orbit.[53] He also soon embraced Feng's idea that humiliation could serve as a catalyst for self-strengthening. As Li wrote to Zeng Guofan: "I feel deeply ashamed that the Chinese weapons are far inferior to those of foreign countries. Every day I warn and instruct my officers to be humble-minded, to bear the humiliation, to learn one or two secret methods from the Westerners in the hope that we may increase our knowledge."[54]

Feng's vision of manufacturing Western-style armaments to save

China became a reality when Li finally established China's first modern arsenals in Shanghai and Suzhou. Feng drafted the memorial that Li sent to Beijing in 1863 explaining the need to borrow not just military hardware but also training methods from the West. "If China desires to make herself strong, there is nothing better than to learn about and use the superior weapons of foreign countries," Li and Feng stated in their memorial. "If we wish to seek machines which will make machinery, and the men who can make the machinery, we might specially set up a course for students."[55]

Li's memorial went to Beijing's newly established *Zongli Geguo Shiwu Yamen* (总理各国事务衙门), or "General Bureau for Foreign Affairs," a Western-style foreign ministry created at the insistence of the victorious British after the Second Opium War. The General Bureau forwarded Li's request to the throne, also couching its endorsement in Feng's new language of reform through self-strengthening: "The way to govern the state lies in self-strengthening, and in the present time and circumstances, the most important matter regarding self-strengthening is to train troops, but the training of troops must be preceded by the manufacture of weapons," the General Bureau argued.[56] In 1865, Li Hongzhang combined his small arsenals into an ultramodern munitions plant in Nanjing to serve as the main site of a regional network of factories known as the Jiangnan Arsenal, making Feng's recommendations in *Dissenting Views* a reality.

Today, a visitor to the former Jiangnan Arsenal, located just outside the south gate of Nanjing's old city wall, can step back in time, walking amid the solid, European-style gray brick buildings, imagining the time when they represented an almost dangerous modernity, the cutting edge of a new and heretical notion of how China could reverse course and arrest its gathering decline. The structures have miraculously survived the ravages of the twentieth century—Japan's Rape of Nanjing, civil war between the Communists and Nationalists, and Mao's Cultural Revolution—virtually unscathed. Now the complex has become a new neon-lit development, called "1865" (in a nod to Li Hongzhang), and is a potpourri of hip restaurants, artists' studios, five-star hotels, and software companies. In its own way, it represents Feng Guifen's vision of a new and strong China, at long last updated and fleshed out in full contemporary "wealth and power" regalia.

As supplements to the arsenals and the military reforms that were to go with them, Feng also had a scheme to create several other novel institutes of learning. For here was yet another cause for Chinese shame—an enterprising corps of Western missionaries, diplomats, and scholars had been learning Mandarin, studying the Confucian classics, and then repeatedly besting China in the grand competition to master the other's culture. In Feng's view, the mind-set and education of China's elites had to be revolutionized: "Since the opening up of trade twenty years ago, there are now many foreigners who understand our written and spoken language, and even some who read our classics and histories. Thus they can speak about our dynastic laws, administrative regulations, geography, and people's characteristics. Is it not shameful that, from our senior officers down, we remain completely ignorant about them?"[57]

To redeem China from this ignorance, he proposed sweeping reforms of the civil service examination system, heretically suggesting that students who could excel at foreign languages should be granted local and provincial degrees just like those who had mastered the Confucian classics.[58] He further argued that instead of just memorizing ancient texts, half of all civil service examination students should instead follow a curriculum in weaponry and industrial crafts.

After China's first Interpreters College was set up under the General Bureau in Beijing in 1862, Feng began to lobby for the creation of a similar institute for the study of foreign languages and science in Shanghai—just as he had proposed in *Dissenting Views*. When Li Hongzhang requested that the imperial court authorize such a school, the language for his proposal was lifted directly from Feng's book: "Are Chinese wisdom and intelligence inferior to those of Westerners?" the memorial asked. "If we have really mastered the Western languages and, in turn, teach one another, then all their clever techniques of steamships and firearms can be gradually and thoroughly learned."[59]

Feng's recommendation was accepted by the throne, and China opened pioneering foreign studies schools in Shanghai (1863), Guangzhou (1864), and Fuzhou (1866), with Feng himself appointed founding director of China's first "modern" educational establishment in Shanghai.[60] But the move provoked fierce and protracted resistance

Li Hongzhang in the 1860s

from conservatives. After all, studying the classics had been the sole route to power and privilege in imperial China for centuries, and to now alter both the educational philosophy and the curriculum by opening it up to an alternative learning pathway was to disturb the whole political and social order. So when in 1867 advocates of Western learning pushed to expand the math and science curricula, and even add courses in political economy and international law, conservatives decried the move as a craven betrayal of Confucian "rites and morality" in the name of Legalist "power and plotting."[61] Western studies proponents at the General Bureau countered this conservative opposition with arguments based on Feng's new theory of "self-strengthening": "Proposals to learn the written and spoken languages of foreign countries, the various methods of making machines, the training of troops with foreign guns, the dispatching of officials to travel in all countries, the investigation of their local customs and social conditions, and the establishment of six armies in the area of the capital in order to protect it—all these painstaking and special decisions represent nothing other than a struggle for self-strengthening."[62] They won the argument, but narrowly. And in such a tradition-bound political culture, the space for "barbarian studies" remained constricted.

Feng spent the final decade of his life in Suzhou, teaching and writing. Li Hongzhang recommended him for promotions in rank in 1867 and again in 1870. Despite all the honors bestowed on him, Feng dressed simply and abjured the colorful—if not decadent—social life of Suzhou elites.[63] He died in 1874. Although a core group of committed reformers found inspiration in *Dissenting Views from a Hut near Bin*, the manuscript did not appear in published form until a decade after his death. And, it was not until 1898 that the Son of Heaven himself at last read Feng's essays and then had a thousand copies of the treatise printed and distributed to his entire senior bureaucracy, who were ordered to suggest which parts of his proposals should be implemented.[64] By that time China not only had failed to strengthen itself relative to faraway Britain but also had fallen perilously behind an even more threatening power, neighboring Japan. Despite Feng's pioneering ideas and Li Hongzhang's valiant efforts to turn those ideas into action to restore the Qing Dynasty's strength, China had continued to decline, to ignominiously become the "sick man of Asia."

Rendering of Cixi circa 1855

CHAPTER 4

Western Methods, Chinese Core (体用)

EMPRESS DOWAGER CIXI (慈禧太后)

Dragon Lady

It took a Dragon Lady to destroy the Dragon Throne . . . or so the conventional telling of the story would have it. Empress Dowager Cixi, the last paramount leader of China's last empire, whose de facto reign spanned five decades, has gone down in the history books as a national femme fatale on par with the notorious Empress Wu Zetian of the Tang Dynasty and, more recently, the much-reviled wife of Chairman Mao, Jiang Qing. By the time Cixi passed from the scene in 1908, just three years before the Qing Dynasty itself collapsed and the country fell into terminal disarray, her name was so freighted with Confucian chauvinism and Orientalist aspersion that it had become virtually impossible to separate fact from fiction, or the fall of imperial China from her own failures.

It did not help that Cixi was the first Qing ruler to open up the Forbidden City—the vast imperial compound at the center of Beijing—to Westerners. Despite her xenophobia, in a desperate effort to lessen Western pressure and hostility the elderly Empress Dowager finally did meet over cups of tea with a host of diplomatic wives and other foreign visitors within the previously sacrosanct imperial grounds to curry their favor. "Above all things else," wrote an American missionary who was one of the barbarians allowed within the gates, the invited guests "were anxious to see her whom they called the 'She Dragon.' "[1]

Sequestered in the still-magnificent Forbidden City, Cixi was fawned

over by phalanxes of eunuchs, arrayed in exotic Manchu robes, en-
meshed in endless court rituals, and understandably appeared to straitlaced sojourners from the West as the very embodiment of the exotic
Other. In the heated imaginations of more-excitable foreigners, she conjured up an elaborate phantasmagoria of intrigue and fantasy. No one
contributed more to such mythmaking than the brilliant but decadent
British sinologist and fantasist Sir Edmund Backhouse, an Oscar Wilde
wannabe who arrived in Beijing from Oxford in 1899 and stayed in
China until World War II, leaving in his wake a sea of forged documents, diaries, and remembrances purporting to chronicle palace life
behind the veil of the failing Qing Dynasty. In Backhouse's depictions
of the Empress Dowager, the all-powerful "Old Buddha," as she liked
to be called, was not only a usurping and tyrannical concubine but a
woman obsessed by power and possessed by other exotic and voracious
appetites. Such depictions were lapped up by Westerners denied access
to the workings of the Chinese court and continued to color Western
views of the imperial court long after its fall. In fact, in one contemporary review, Backhouse's writings came to be extravagantly extolled as
coming "as near as any book could to explaining the enigmatic character of the Empress Dowager."[2] It was only later that his bestseller, *China
Under the Empress Dowager* (1910), which he coauthored with J. O. P.
Bland from the *Times* of London, was discovered to be based on forged
diaries by Manchu officials. But perhaps his most outrageous fabrica-
tion came only posthumously, in the form of his own "memoir," which
was so pornographic in describing the world of sexual deviance in old
Peking and the palace that it was not published until 2011. Littered as it
is with obscure annotations in Chinese, Latin, French, Japanese, Italian,
Manchu, and even classical Greek, which Backhouse used to embel-
lish epic sexual perversions behind a screen of erudition, *Décadence
Mandchoue: The China Memoirs of Sir Edmund Trelawny Backhouse*
is surely one of the strangest and most bawdy "scholarly" works ever
penned about China by a Westerner.

The explicitness of Sir Edmund's descriptions of his supposed intimate relations with the Empress Dowager herself is still startling in its
prurience. In one of countless lurid passages, he wrote about being
prepared by a eunuch for his assignation with Cixi: "Li talked sex dur-

ing the meal: 'The Old Buddha,' said he, 'loves to rub her person (*credo experto*) against her *vis-à-vis*: You will probably find that she will Ts'eng 蹭 (frictionner) your anus (*Yen'rh* 眼儿) with her clitoris (*Yin T'i* 阴蒂, in Japanese *Inkaku*, or *Yin Ho* 阴核) which is abnormally large."[3] Even though she was approaching her seventh decade and he was not yet thirty, Backhouse somehow managed to overcome his confirmed homosexuality for the sake of numerous *nuits d'amour* with the emphatically heterosexual Empress Dowager, each allegedly replete with endless bouts of highly diversified lovemaking.[4] According to Backhouse, their first orgy took place in Cixi's newly completed Summer Palace, built to replace the Yuanmingyuan, which had been destroyed in the Second Opium War. "Her whole body, small and shapely, was redolent with *la joie de vivre*; her shapely buttocks, pearly and large were presented to my admiring contemplation," he reports in one of the few descriptions that might pass censorship. "I felt for her a real libidinous passion such as no woman has ever inspired in my pervert homosexual mind before nor since."[5]

Western views of the Empress Dowager's court were strongly influenced by this prolific, learned, linguistically accomplished, and quite convincing con man, who was among other things the main conduit of information about the Qing court for the West's two leading foreign correspondents, J. O. P. Bland and George Ernest Morrison. They filed stories from Shanghai and Beijing for the *Times* of London and had a significant ability to influence—and distort—world opinion of the Empress Dowager, about whom they passed on much from Backhouse. The mold cast by these three British men still shapes views of Cixi and her time today.

To get a more balanced view of this seminal figure and her role in the failure of the self-strengthening movement requires scraping off layers of Orientalist fantasy and Confucian misogyny. The "Old Buddha" was a complex personage, but her real significance lay not in the exoticism of Backhouse's reveries but in her ability—or lack thereof—to guide China through the treacherous straits of decline in an increasingly globalized and predatory world. Surprisingly, it turns out that even she was driven by a desire to restore China to wealth, power, and prestige—yet her lasting historical legacy was to reign over the critical

period when her empire missed the boat to modernity and fell perilously behind the emerging powers of the twentieth century.

Joint Rule

The future Empress Dowager's political career commenced in 1861,
when, as British troops marched on Beijing at the height of the Second
Opium War, the young and beautiful imperial consort fled along with
Emperor Xianfeng, hastening far north to a summer retreat in Rehe,
nestled safely in the ancestral lands of the Manchus beyond the Great
Wall.[6] The twenty-six-year-old concubine, known by the demur moniker "Little Orchid," had urged the emperor to stay and defend Beijing,
but she was overruled.[7] Leaving her brother-in-law, Prince Gong, behind with the unenviable task of negotiating the Westerners away, she
and the emperor fled to anxiously await the European withdrawal
from the capital. Shortly after the court-in-exile learned that their beloved Yuanmingyuan had been ravaged by British and French troops,
which Backhouse reported Cixi to have called "an act of senseless vengeance" that "broke the emperor's heart,"[8] Emperor Xianfeng, not yet
thirty years of age, died. His only male heir was Little Orchid's four-
year-old son, who was duly proclaimed Emperor Tongzhi.

At this perilous moment of dynastic succession, during a time of
foreign occupation of the capital and Taiping rebel control of south
China, the new emperor's mother, Cixi, demanded to be anointed co-
regent along with the deceased emperor's principal wife, the Empress
Dowager Ci'an. And so, as powerful factions of the Manchu court
nobility and Han Chinese bureaucracy vied for influence, the boy monarch and the two dowagers, widows in their mid-twenties, suddenly
found themselves valuable pieces on a chessboard. In the brutal power
struggle that ensued for control of the succession process, Cixi quickly
displayed her political skills by forming an alliance with her brother-in-
law Prince Gong, soon appointed to the Qing state's highest body, the
Grand Council. By Chinese tradition, the emperor's brothers were to
be kept out of the bureaucracy, but Cixi broke sharply with precedent,
elevating her husband's brothers to powerful government posts as a
way to buttress her own position.[9]

The meaning of the name given to the boy emperor upon ascension said it all: Tongzhi means "joint rule." Cixi and Prince Gong's first joint action was to eliminate a rival group of Manchu officials, who were summarily executed on the return trip to Beijing. Now in possession of the Qing imperial seal—without which no document had the authority of the Dragon Throne—the two dowagers and the prince were nominally in control of the vast Chinese bureaucracy and military, at least until the young emperor came of age.

The "joint rule" of the so-called Tongzhi Restoration (1861–75) would come to represent not just a new court alliance among Manchu royalty—that is, the wives and brothers of the deceased emperor—but also an alliance with leading Han Chinese reformist officials working out in the provinces, men such as Zeng Guofan and Li Hongzhang, who were just then initiating the self-strengthening movement. Contrary to the stereotypical image of the Empress Dowager as an archconservative, during the 1860s she supported many of Li's reform-minded self-strengthening projects at the provincial level—including the modernized munitions arsenals and institutes of foreign study proposed by Feng Guifen. But what her court fatally failed to do was to broaden and intensify these scattered and localized reform efforts into a comprehensive, empire-wide initiative.

And so, a decade after Feng Guifen wrote *Dissenting Views*, leading reformers found themselves more discouraged than ever about the dynasty's inability to reform the country. Zeng Guofan departed from an audience with Cixi in 1869 deeply worried about a leadership vacuum. "The ability of both Empresses-Dowager is anything but exceptional," he wrote. "They had not a single important word to say. The Emperor was young and quiet, thus making any guess [about his ability] impossible. . . . The rest are more mediocre—truly a cause for great concern."[10] "When the peace negotiations were complete [with the British in 1860] everybody spoke of the necessity for self-strengthening," another high official complained a few years later. "Yet during the last ten years or more there has been little achievement."[11]

Younger and less easily thwarted by the signs of weak leadership in Beijing, Li Hongzhang pressed on with the self-strengthening cause after Zeng Guofan's death in 1872 and Feng Guifen's in 1874. Because he had helped put down the Taiping Rebellion and had displayed diplomatic finesse in dealing with the Western "barbarians," Li had won the trust of the Empress Dowager, who allowed him to emerge as the key figure in late Qing reform and foreign relations.

Having established a base of loyal troops, talented advisors, and revenue streams in the lower Yangtze River region during the 1860s, Li was transferred north in 1870 to the port city of Tianjin and made viceroy of this strategic region near Beijing, where he equipped and trained a new northern fighting force, the Beiyang Army. Although he struck the figure of a classic mandarin, with a shaven pate, long queue, mustache, and goatee, Li understood that behind the West's ability to build superior gunboats and win wars lay an infrastructural matrix that depended on research institutes, transportation networks, communications systems, and new kinds of finance. So he and his circle girded themselves for a more systematic push for technological and infrastructural modernization. Transportation, for example, became a new priority. "Now all the European countries are competing with one another for wealth and strength and their rise to prosperity is rapid," one of Li's protégés wrote. "What they rely upon are steamships and railroads. . . . [I]f the system of railway trains is not used, China can never be rich and strong."[12]

With the Empress Dowager's indulgence, Li pioneered early efforts to introduce railroads and steamboats, telegraphs and textile mills, and modern coal and iron mining to China.[13] As Feng Guifen had warned, if Chinese didn't industrialize the country themselves on their own terms, foreigners would do it on theirs. The gap with the West was not yet unbridgeable, Li argued, so long as China hurried up. Toward that end, in 1872 he created a novel kind of joint public-private enterprise called the China Merchants Steam Navigation Company, a farsighted model of *guandu shangban* (官督商办), or "government supervised, merchant managed" enterprise that anticipated the state-led developmental capitalism and state-owned enterprises of twenty-first-century China. "If we can really and thoroughly understand their methods," he wrote about Western industrial management in 1872, "the more we learn, the more we improve—[then] can we not expect that after a century or so we can reject the barbarians and stand on our own feet?"[14]

In 1873, Cixi officially stepped down from the regency, allowing her teenage son, Tongzhi, to reign in his own name. Renouncing for the time any interest in the affairs of state, she turned her energies to a vanity project—building an extravagant new Summer Palace to replace the ruined Yuanmingyuan. The project was rich in symbolic value in terms of wiping clean the slate of China's humiliations at the hands of foreigners, but its cost would weigh on the nation's increasingly strapped finances.[15] She was still battling to get her pet project fully funded when, in 1875, her son followed in his father's footsteps and died of smallpox at a tender age. Once again Cixi found herself embroiled in a succession struggle, this time made more volatile by the absence of a direct heir to the throne. Qing imperial precedent dictated selecting a royal nephew to maintain continuity from one generation to the next. But Cixi again overturned precedent and placed her son's cousin—the offspring of her younger sister and her political ally Prince Chun—on the throne as the Guangxu Emperor. Since Guangxu, whose name meant "Glorious Succession," was all of two years old, this power play ensured that she would again be thrust back in the imperial driver's seat.[16]

Cixi's Wars

During her second tour of duty as imperial regent, Cixi openly espoused the "statecraft" reformers' discourse of humiliation and self-strengthening, as demonstrated in her 1878 meeting with Zeng Guofan's son. "How can we forget our grievances for a single day?" she asked. "We must gradually make ourselves strong."[17] So she continued to support the reformist efforts of progressive provincial officials at the regional level, including those of Li Hongzhang, who was now convinced that it was "necessary to be wealthy first before a country can be strong," as he put it in 1882. But it sometimes became difficult to distinguish his wealth-first approach from charges of corruption that increasingly hovered over him.[18]

When it came to China's foreign relations, Cixi also increasingly entrusted them to Li and other "self-strengtheners," who continued to believe that, if played right, China's humiliation over falling behind the West could be put to good purposes. The pioneering journalist Wang Tao, for example, wrote in 1880, "The fact that nowadays powerful neighbors and ruthless enemies continually eye us from all sides is actually a blessing for China and not a misfortune. This is just the thing we need to stimulate our determination to forge ahead. . . . For if we can become ashamed at not being as good as the Western nations, it may yet be possible for us to do something about it."[19]

In 1880, illness forced the Empress Dowager to withdraw from court duties for more than a year. During her convalescence, the court dispatched Zeng Guofan's son to Russia to negotiate the Treaty of St. Petersburg, which reestablished control over a large swath of far north-western territories that Russian troops had formerly occupied. Emboldened by this rare diplomatic victory, hawkish Chinese officials rallied to the so-called Purist Party, counterattacking against moderate "self-strengtheners" and demanding a more aggressive foreign policy against the West. Unfortunately, they did so without first making the kinds of reforms that might have equipped China's military to win against these formidable adversaries in modern warfare.[20] For at this very time, the French were pushing to wrest Vietnam from China's sphere of influence, and the Purists foolishly lobbied for war. Cixi's streak of hawkishness now inclined her to back their militancy. "The Xianfeng Emperor regarded the war of 1860 with great remorse," she told her top ministers on the Grand Council in 1884, "but he died with an ambition unfulfilled. Now we ought to wipe out the humiliation for the former Emperor."[21]

So China went to war with the French over Vietnam and once again was ignominiously defeated by a European power. This newest loss was alarming in part because China's evident weakness was no longer entirely technological. Self-strengthening reforms had, in fact, built up a decent naval force at the southern port of Fuzhou. It just could not hold its own against the strategy and tactics of the French. More worrisome was that the decentralized, piecemeal nature of China's self-strengthening effort now revealed itself in a devastating way. The northern Beiyang Navy built up by Li Hongzhang—who disapproved of the war—sat at anchor in Tianjin, while the French routed the Southern Navy and then demanded another "unequal treaty," which Li Hongzhang ended up having to sign on behalf of Cixi in 1885.[22]

Everywhere the old configuration of Qing power now seemed to be disintegrating. The ring of once loyal Asian kingdoms—Burma, Nepal, Thailand, Vietnam, the Ryukyu Islands, and Korea—that had all traditionally paid annual "tribute" to Beijing in exchange for trade rights and diplomatic protection, thus buffering the great Qing Empire, was flaking off like old paint. Feeling increasingly at bay and fearful of another defeat, Cixi supported Li's ambitious plan to expand his Northern Navy, which over the next decade did grow to be a flotilla of some twenty-five warships and considered the strongest fleet in Asia. But soon Li was bedeviled by a new set of fears. By the latter part of the nineteenth century, China was not only still trailing the West but also slipping behind Japan, a neighbor that Chinese had long considered "uncivilized" and inferior. "In about ten years, Japan's wealth and power will be considerable," Li prophesied in 1885. "She is China's future disaster."[23]

The contrasts between Li and his Japanese counterpart, Itō Hirobumi, revealed a widening gulf between the two powers—one rising steadily and rapidly, the other struggling to stop its decline. Whereas Li had never left his native China, Itō had made numerous trips abroad, including a two-year mission to study Western political models in preparation for devising a new constitution for Japan. As Itō would explain to an audience in Sacramento, California: "We came to study your strength, that, by adopting widely your better ways, we may hereafter be stronger ourselves."[24] And when he returned to Japan from his constitutional window-shopping trip around the world, Itō was given full authority to design and implement national policies for the Meiji emperor.[25] Li Hongzhang, by contrast, had never been abroad, had to rely only on translations and secondhand reports of the West from Chinese living abroad, and had been able to experiment with foreign self-strengthening methods only at the provincial level.

Li was not the only scholar-official looking to the Japanese model with a mixture of admiration and trepidation. One twenty-seven-year-old, self-made Cantonese reformer, impudently wrote Li around this time, asking to be dispatched on an Itō-like mission to France to acquire more advanced weaponry. "Now that the nation is sparing no effort to make itself wealthy and strong," he wrote hopefully, "it will not be long before we can march side by side with Europe in terms of achievement.... [Just] look at Japan."[26] This young patriot was named Sun Yat-sen, but Li turned down his request without even offering an interview.[27]

As self-strengtheners, conservatives, and Purists jockeyed for power, the Empress Dowager had by the late 1880s returned to her escapist fantasy of building a new Summer Palace, which she called *Yiheyuan* (颐和园), the "Gardens of Nurtured Harmony." Although the Qing Dynasty's fiscal situation was now worse than ever, sycophantic officials caved in to her whims, helping divert the nation's desperately needed revenues from self-defense and economic modernization to this personal extravagance. Even Li Hongzhang was inveigled into contributing significantly from his own reservoir of personal wealth. And Prince Chun, father of Cixi's adopted son, the Guangxu Emperor, also now diverted money from a special fund needed to build a more modern navy to Cixi's new project, which included an eighteenth-century marble replica of a leisure boat that had been partially destroyed in 1860 and was now to be reassembled as a modern double-decker paddle steamer.[28] It was an expensive and ironically useless illustration of the vaunted reformist principle of grafting *xiyong* (西用), "Western function," onto *zhongti* (中体), a "Chinese core." This ironic symbol of the failure of self-strengthening still sits "docked" on the north shore of the Summer Palace's Kunming Lake for the rueful sightseeing pleasure of tourists. Towering over this totally useless stone ship on its equally useless man-made lake is a labyrinth of intricately designed yellow-tiled Buddhist, Lamaist, and Taoist temples where, after a cruise on Kunming Lake with Her Majesty, Sir Edmund Backhouse collected notes for one of *Décadence Mandchoue*'s most lurid chapters, chronicling his heroic efforts to satisfy the Empress Dowager's supposedly insatiable "carnality."[29] This vast complex was, rather narcissistically, to be completed by November 1894, in time for the Empress Dowager's sixtieth birthday. Unfortunately, the celebration had to be canceled due to the eruption of the third and most devastating war to shake the Cixi era.

Nemesis

The Empress Dowager was heir to centuries of Chinese supremacy over much of East Asia, including one neighboring kingdom in particular—Korea. Indeed, as the most thoroughly Confucianized and politically loyal of China's bordering states, Korea, ruled by the Yi family's Choson Dynasty since 1392, had been the linchpin in the Ming and Qing

Empires' elaborate "tributary system" of client states. Cixi's advisors therefore began to panic as Beijing's grip over Korea was pried loose bit by bit by the rising might of Meiji Japan. When peasant revolt broke out in 1894, both China and Japan raced troops to the Korean Peninsula to fight over the question of who would "restore order." Asia's ancient Central Kingdom and upstart Empire of the Rising Sun were, for the first time in three hundred years, suddenly at war.[30]

The decisive naval engagement of the Sino-Japanese War took place on September 17, 1894, at the point where the Yalu River flows into the Yellow Sea. Cixi had good reason to hope that Li Hongzhang's Northern Navy, stronger on paper than the Japanese fleet, would prevail. Alas, Meiji superiority in training, strategy, and coordination quickly spelled catastrophe for China. Half of Li's fleet ended up being sunk in a single day of fighting. And in an amphibious assault, Japanese forces took a key Chinese base at Port Arthur on the northern side of the Shandong Peninsula, marched overland to capture the Chinese fort at Weihaiwei on its southern side, and promptly turned Chinese guns on the rest of the Northern Navy moored at port there. This time it was the Qing's Southern Fleet's turn to stand idly by.[31]

Defeat at the hands of the Japanese, whom Chinese still condescendingly referred to as "the dwarf people," was devastating. To add insult to injury, the Japanese victors insisted that the venerable Li Hongzhang be dispatched to accept the terms of China's humiliating surrender on Japanese soil. For Li it was a bitter reprise of an encounter a decade earlier, when he and Itō Hirobumi had, as equals, negotiated a convention in Tianjin to stabilize Sino-Japanese relations. Now Li found himself in Shimonoseki, Japan, agonizingly pressed to explain China's weakness and defeat. "Why is it that up to now not a single thing has been changed or reformed?" Itō asked Li, twenty years his senior, in fluent English. Reflecting on his three decades at the center of China's modernization, Li plaintively answered through an English interpreter. "My country is hampered by traditions and customs: one can hardly do what one wants," he said. "China also has people who understand modern affairs; but there are too many provinces, with strong sectionalism, just like your country in the feudal period, when one was checked and hindered by others and had no full authority for anything."[32]

Gone was any hint of the invigorating effects on modernization of a little shame and humiliation, as celebrated earlier by Wei Yuan, Feng Guifen, and Li himself. Instead, the elderly statesman was now left to lament, "Affairs in my country have been so confined by tradition that I could not accomplish what I desired. In the twinkling of an eye ten years have gone by, and everything is still the same. I am even more regretful. I am ashamed of having excessive wishes and lacking the power to fulfill them."[33]

Adding to Li's sense of degradation, just before signing the treaty a Japanese radical bent on assassinating him fired on Li at close range, leaving a bullet lodged behind his nose.[34] He was thus forced to sign the Treaty of Shimonoseki on April 17, 1895, with his swollen face wrapped in bandages, a painful visual symbol of China's deeper loss of face on display for all to see. Like the British in 1860, now the Japanese also wanted to humiliate China.[35] And they succeeded beyond their wildest expectations. With the Treaty of Shimonoseki, the Japanese proved themselves as successful as the Europeans in teaching China a lesson. They not only won de facto control over the Korean Peninsula, sovereignty over Taiwan and the Pescadores, and access to four more treaty ports in China but also forced the Chinese to pay a whopping 230 million silver dollars in indemnities—which Japan pumped into its own industrial modernization, exciting intense nationalist passions and ensuring even greater economic and military domination over China in the future.[36]

The Sino-Japanese War threw the contrast between Meiji's successful modernization and Cixi's failed efforts into stark relief. The Empress Dowager enjoyed comparing herself to Queen Victoria, but the better measure would, in fact, have been the nearby Meiji emperor, who reigned from 1867 until 1912—roughly the same period as Cixi—and brought Japan into the modern world as a great power. Strikingly, reformers in Japan had shared the same vision of "self-strengthening" as in China, even reading the writings of many early Chinese reformers—including Wei Yuan.[37] But in Japan, Meiji elites had succeeded in making the vision reality.

Initially Japan had been forced open by the arrival of U.S. commodore Matthew Perry's "black ships" in 1853. Nonetheless, the Japanese held their noses and pragmatically plunged into barbarian studies. By the 1860s, their ruling class had reached a consensus on opening their country up to the outside world, reforming their political system, aggressively developing their economy in a centralized and coordinated way, and sending official delegations and students abroad to unlock the secrets behind the West's formula for development. In 1871 Tokyo even dispatched the famous Iwakura mission of fifty senior officials for almost two years of study abroad.[38] In Cixi's China, by contrast, those few scholars and officials who mastered *yangwu* (洋务), "Western affairs," were regarded as spoilers, and the one educational mission that did succeed in sending a group of Chinese boys to Connecticut for an American education not only was poorly funded and racked by political controversy but finally ended up being terminated prematurely in 1881 due to objections by cultural conservatives.[39]

Also quite unlike Cixi's world, the men around the Meiji emperor proved ready to act on Feng Guifen's insight that one of the keys to Western strength was the "closeness between the ruler and the people," a bond that was sealed through experiments with electoral democracy and parliamentary representation. Meiji reformers implemented Feng's idea of establishing participatory authoritarianism, broadening Japan's elite, and bringing about more public involvement in government—and they accomplished all of this without weakening the sacred authority of the emperor or Japan's traditional culture. To be sure, there were plenty of political struggles along the way, but by 1889 the Meiji regime was proudly able to unveil a modern, written constitution—Asia's first.[40]

As with politics, so too in economics: Meiji Japan acted decisively to embrace a new formula for development based on domestic industrialization and imperialist expansion. Having borrowed the Legalist motto "rich country, strong army" (pronounced *fukoku kyōhei* in Japanese) from Wei Yuan,[41] Meiji leaders linked it to a term of their own, one conspicuously absent in late nineteenth-century China: *hatten* (发展), "expansion and development."[42]

In all of this, the most significant contrast with Cixi's China was the way Meiji Japan coordinated these disparate educational, political, economic, and military initiatives in a centralized manner, choreographed by Itō Hirobumi and other architects of reform in the name of the Meiji emperor. At the same time, China was moving in precisely the *opposite* direction—from a highly centralized empire toward fragmentation, re-

Empress Dowager Cixi hosts U.S. ambassador's wife, Sarah Conger, 1903

Rendering of Emperor
Guangxu with Liang Qichao
and Kang Youwei, 1898

Japanese soldiers standing over beheaded Chinese Boxers, 1900

American troops marching through a Qing imperial temple in Beijing, 1900

gional autarky, and warlordism. Under Cixi, self-strengthening ended up becoming a patchwork of isolated and controversial provincial efforts, rather than a cohesive, centrally coordinated national plan to catch up with the West by learning from it.

Perils of Reform

As demoralizing as China's defeat in the Sino-Japanese War was, it did spur another bout of self-strengthening, overseen this time by the elderly Empress Dowager herself. Finally, Li Hongzhang got to make a journey to the West. President Grover Cleveland received him with pomp and circumstance in New York harbor, Queen Victoria knighted him in England, and Otto von Bismarck shared advice on military strategy in Prussia.[43] But this world tour came too late in Li's career, after his status and influence at home had already been severely compromised.

Back in China, the next generation of reformist provincial officials, led by Zhang Zhidong and Yuan Shikai, was already replacing Li at the head of the self-strengthening movement. Zhang had once been a Confucian hawk in the Purist faction, but after the debacle of the Sino-French War in Vietnam, he refashioned himself as a member of the "Western affairs" clique. And in 1896 Cixi's court approved his proposal to create a new Self-Strengthening Army, along with an Academy for Self-Strengthening in Nanjing. Zhang would soon coin the most famous motto of the self-strengthening movement: *Zhongxue weiti, xixue weiyong* (中学为体, 西学为用), which translates as "Chinese learning should remain the core, but Western learning should be used for practical use."[44]

Zhang's catchy phrase was, of course, a repackaging of Feng Guifen's idea of supplementing "Chinese ethics and Confucian teachings" with foreign "techniques for wealth and power." By the end of the century, however, Feng and Zhang were beginning to look rather outmoded in comparison with the even more radical visions of how to achieve wealth and power that were starting to be articulated among other Chinese intellectuals like the unorthodox Cantonese philosopher Kang Youwei. In the immediate wake of the Treaty of Shimonoseki, Kang led a daring, public demonstration against government inaction by submitting a ten-thousand-word memorial to the throne calling for far-reaching reform on behalf of the students assembled in Beijing to take that year's top civil service examination. China's public sphere was being forced open by voices such as Kang's, and when another of his reform petitions was ignored by the court in 1897, a newly founded Shanghai newspaper published it for him.[45]

Another of this new species of public intellectuals was Yan Fu. He burst onto the national stage in 1895 with a series of stirring essays, including "On Strength," that challenged the Chinese government to embrace new reforms, such as parliamentary assemblies, that would transform passive imperial "subjects" into spirited modern "citizens." The writing of intellectuals such as Yan and Kang ignited the minds of still-younger scholars including Liang Qichao, who would emerge as his country's leading public thinker in the early twentieth century.[46]

By 1898, a new coalition of political thinkers and actors who saw China's sun as setting just as Japan's was rising was ready to stage a bold, even desperate attempt at radical reform. Curiously the principal figure in this drama was Cixi's sickly, sensitive nephew, the twenty-seven-year-old Guangxu Emperor, who, having been tutored in foreign studies as a boy, was now sailing in the same winds of change as other younger thinking elites. In June 1898 the audacious young emperor threw the Qing establishment into an uproar when he suddenly began commanding officials and subjects to enact sweeping changes in government and education, including the creation of a modern Imperial University of Peking (the forerunner of today's Peking University), modeled on the Imperial University in Japan.[47]

A key inspiration for these reforms was none other than Feng Guifen. That summer the emperor had ordered the printing and distribution of Feng's *Dissenting Views from a Hut near Bin*, and then asked for comment from his top one thousand officials. Guangxu did the same thing with the timely essay by Zhang Zhidong, "On the Encouragement of Learning," which proposed the westernization of parts of China's educational system, the better to preserve the "core" of Confucian values and texts.[48]

But the young emperor was also listening to bolder ideas about reform coming from a small coterie of upstarts including Kang Youwei and Liang Qichao, and he was eager to push change beyond the comfort zone of his aunt Cixi and the ruling establishment. Without any real strategy to win political support, the young emperor began calling on the imperial bureaucracy to implement a whole series of dramatic and unexpected changes. The advice he received from his advisors was no less naive. During his first imperial audience on June 16, 1898, Kang Youwei offered the emperor this wildly optimistic thought: "With your majesty's intelligence, the self-strengthening of China should be as simple as turning the palm of your hand."[49] Not surprisingly, the political effect of the neophyte emperor's demands for reform struck powerful conservative officials more like a slap in the face.

Cixi had been briefed by the young emperor in the early summer of his Hundred Days' Reform and had raised no objection. However, by September, as opposition began to coalesce in the imperial bureaucracy, she was ineluctably drawn into its ranks. The final straw may have been the visit to Beijing of Itō Hirobumi for a private audience with the emperor.[50] The image of the leader of a nation of inferiors who had just sunk much of the Chinese fleet during the Sino-Japanese War and forced China into signing a humiliating treaty now being welcomed into the Forbidden City by the young ruler may have been more than Chinese conservatives could tolerate.

Itō's presence in Beijing would have been particularly disconcerting for the Empress Dowager, given recent events on the nearby Korean Peninsula. In Seoul, as in Beijing, a woman had managed to reach the pinnacle of political influence in the 1890s. But Queen Min, wife of the reigning Korean monarch, had opposed Japan's rising influence among Korean reformers, so in 1895 Japanese agents broke into the royal palace, stabbed her to death, and then burned her corpse on the palace grounds. Now, a mere three years later, Cixi would have had reason to fear a similar plot, spearheaded by Kang Youwei himself, who had taken to calling her the "False Empress."[51] With Itō in Beijing to cabal with the young reformist clique around her nephew, it was not illogical for her to fear that she might be next on Japan's hit list.[52]

So it was that, three days after Itō's visit ended, Cixi forced the emperor to issue a pathetic memorial announcing the abrupt resumption of her regency. His brief spurt of imperial activism had lasted only 102 days, thus inspiring the name "Hundred Days' Reform."

The conservative backlash was severe. Cixi had seven leading reformers executed, including Kang Youwei's brother. Kang and his star protégé, Liang Qichao, barely escaped with their lives, fleeing to Japan, where they opened a new chapter in modern Chinese history by forming an exile dissident movement. The hapless Guangxu Emperor was locked in a tower adjacent to the Forbidden City, where his health collapsed along with his political clout and he was left to lament: "I have plenty of ideas regarding the development of this country, but, you know I am not able to carry them out as I am not my own master."[53]

Crushing the Hundred Days' Reform almost immediately became one of the main charges leveled against Cixi on the historical balance sheet—and it started with an account of those events published in exile by Liang Qichao.[54] But the image of the aged Empress Dowager as an archconservative, power-hungry Dragon Lady who masterminded a coup against her enlightened and progressive nephew is an oversimplification. She was not so much against reform as she was unsure how to go about it. Indeed, soon after returning to power, she reaffirmed her personal commitment to the goal of self-strengthening. In a November 1898 edict she insisted, "A moment does not pass that I do not think about planning for self-strengthening. . . . Although the customs and governmental systems of Western countries differ in more than one way from those of China, their methods and techniques . . . are, as a rule, capable of [helping the country] to attain prosperity and strength. . . . If we can select what are good among these and apply them, putting them into use one by one, we shall be able to achieve the desired results promptly and consistently."[55]

Cixi cited an old aphorism to express her determination to persist in this new iteration of statecraft reform and self-strengthening: "When we have been choked, it does not follow that we are to cease eating, merely for fear it may happen again."[56] Curiously, a *People's Daily* editorial would quote the very same expression a century later in urging the continuance of "reform and opening-up" in the wake of the 1989 democracy movement![57]

Autumn of the Matriarch

Confucius famously posited that, reaching sixty years of age, the cultivated *junzi* (君子), "gentleman," should be able to satisfy all his heart's desires without ever overstepping the line of moderation. As she entered her sixties, the Empress Dowager seems to have become adept at satisfying her desires, at least. Moderation was another question. And for spiritual sustenance, Cixi looked not to moralistic Confucianism but to ritualistic Buddhism, and her religiosity only fed into her vanity. She enjoyed being photographed, and grainy images capture her garbed as Guanyin, the Buddha of Mercy, surrounded by her eunuchs, also in divine costume. "Whenever I have been angry, or worried over anything, by dressing up as the Goddess of Mercy it helps me to calm myself, and so play the part I represent," she once explained to her lady-in-waiting and interpreter Der Ling. "I can assure you that it does help me a great deal, as it makes me remember that I am looked upon as being all-merciful. By having a photograph taken of myself dressed in this costume, I shall be able to see myself as I ought to be at all times."[58]

It is unlikely that many people in late Qing China would, however, have associated the Empress Dowager with the trait "all-merciful." Even the admiring Der Ling hinted at a sadistic streak: "It was a characteristic of Her Majesty to experience a keen sense of enjoyment at the troubles of other people."[59] She also evidently experienced bouts of depressiveness, describing herself to Der Ling as "disappointed with everything."[60] And she frequently exploded in fits of rage. When her notorious temper blew, according to one Qing official who witnessed her wrath, her eyes "poured out straight rays; her cheekbones were sharp and the veins on her forehead projected. She showed her teeth as if she was suffering from lockjaw."[61]

Overshadowing everything about Cixi was the highly un-Confucian impropriety of her being a woman. Always presiding over policy discussions with her brothers-in-law or with members of the Grand Council from "behind a screen" in accordance with Confucian biases against women, she must have wondered what court life would have been like if she had been a man. Biographer Marina Warner surmised that Cixi favored "scholar-soldiers" such as Zeng Guofan and Li Hongzhang because "the men in her life—her incompetent father, her dissolute husband, her weakling son and the thousands of eunuchs who now surrounded her—made her yearn for the virile, valorous and strong."[62] In the end, however, the only reliable alpha male for Cixi was *herself*.

"Her Majesty always wanted to be a man," wrote Der Ling in her memoirs of being in Cixi's service, "and compelled everyone to address her as if she were actually one."[63]

Within the court, Cixi's self-confidence—which could sometimes lead to self-deception—was only reinforced by the servility of those around her. But during the last decade of her life, she fought a losing battle to stay ahead of popular sentiment in the empire at large, and the so-called Boxer disturbances of 1898–1901 became the point of no return.

Around the time of the emperor's ill-fated Hundred Days' Reform, discontented peasants in poor areas of north China began banding together in martial arts groups (thus the name "Boxers") and targeting Chinese Christian converts, who were widely resented for the legal and economic privileges they enjoyed through the protection of foreign missionaries who had been given extraterritorial rights under the unequal treaties. As the Boxer movement grew in scale, armed bands soon threatened not only Chinese Christians but also foreign missionaries scattered around the countryside, and eventually even the Western government emissaries residing in the Foreign Legation Quarter in the heart of Beijing. The Empress Dowager faced a dilemma described perfectly by Robert Hart, an Irishman who ran her Imperial Chinese Maritime Customs Service: "If the Boxers are not suppressed, the Legations [foreign embassies in Beijing] threaten to take action—if the attempt to suppress them is made, this intensely patriotic organization will be converted into an anti-dynastic movement!"[64]

Driven by her instinct for political self-preservation, but also by her abiding yearning for vengeance for China's myriad foreign humiliations, Cixi fatefully decided to back the Boxers. In a moment of delusional revanchism, she even stood by as the xenophobic Boxers laid siege to foreign embassies in Beijing, located just a short walk from the Forbidden City itself. As Robert Hart predicted, the Boxers' attack on Beijing's Foreign Legation Quarter triggered a devastating response, a joint eight-nation military expedition to lift the siege. For a second time Cixi was forced to flee the capital as barbarian armies approached.

There are perhaps few scenes as grotesque as a despot losing control, and the spectacle of the Empress Dowager's second flight from the Forbidden City, replete with scenes of eunuchs and servants suddenly abandoning her retinue, was no exception. "I had 3,000 eunuchs, but they were nearly all gone before I had the chance of counting them," she complained in a moment of tyrannical self-pity. "Some of the wicked ones were even rude to me, and threw my valuable vases on the stone floor, and smashed them. They knew that I could not punish them at that important moment, for we were leaving."[65] As she set out on this inauspicious flight, it looked as though she might finally be on her way to political oblivion. Her ragtag imperial convoy had to travel from dawn to dark, eventually reaching Xi'an, the ancient imperial capital far to the west, where two thousand years earlier the first emperor of the Qin Dynasty had unified China using brutal Legalist methods and then had himself entombed there along with thousands of perfectly cast terra-cotta soldiers. The thirty-year-old Guangxu Emperor traveled in a mule-drawn cart, while his aunt jostled and lurched along in a sedan chair in the extreme heat. As summer rains drenched the caravan and more and more servants abandoned Their Majesties to their fate, local officials did their best to receive the itinerant court properly. Under such dire circumstances, however, it was difficult to keep up much imperial pretense.

When this bedraggled imperial carnival finally arrived in Xi'an, the Empress Dowager described her lodgings as "very old, damp and unhealthy."[66] Here she finally countermanded her earlier decision to support the Boxers, now calling for their suppression. She had thus betrayed her subjects *and* been forced to countenance foreign troops yet again ransacking the sacred capital, Beijing.

Defeat, however, seemed to have at last convinced Cixi of the need for drastic reforms, and in her belatedly decisive "Reform Edict," issued on January 29, 1901, she proclaimed: "Now that peace negotiations have commenced, all affairs of government must be thoroughly overhauled, in hopes of gradually achieving real wealth and power."[67] Cixi also now openly embraced a comprehensive approach to learning from the West, acknowledging, "If China disregards the essentials of Western learning and merely confines its studies to surface elements which themselves are not even mastered, how can it possibly achieve wealth and power?"[68]

But before this last-ditch effort at reform, in order to get rid of the barbarians who had arrived to lift the Boxer siege of the Foreign Legation, she had to affix her seal to an agreement. Only then could she return safely from her exile in Xi'an. Once again she called upon the ever-loyal Li Hongzhang to clean up the mess, and the resulting Boxer Protocol, signed in September 1901, ended the conflict, though once again at the cost of crushing reparations. The Qing government was forced to pay the victorious eight nations 450 million silver taels over a thirty-nine-year period. In a callous act of humiliation, the indemnity was arbitrarily set at roughly one piece of silver per Chinese citizen.[69]

On a bitterly cold January day in 1902, Cixi slowly made her way back into Beijing. This time she traveled partway by locomotive—her first experience on a "fire vehicle," as the Chinese called trains. But her heart sank when she entered the Forbidden City. "I had another dreadful feeling when I saw my own Palace again. Oh! it was quite changed; a great many valuable ornaments broken or stolen . . . and someone had broken the fingers of my white jade Buddha, to whom I used to worship every day."[70]

The Empress Dowager learned that triumphant foreigners had even taken photos of themselves sitting mockingly on her throne—the ultimate sacrilege. One of those trespassers from the West was the prim and proper Reverend Isaac Taylor Headland, who had been teaching and proselytizing in Beijing since 1890. The curious minister took advantage of her exile to see the Forbidden City with his own eyes. "I went into her sleeping apartments. Others also entered there, sat upon her couch, and had their friends photograph them. I could not allow myself to do so. I stood silent, with head uncovered as I gazed with wonder and admiration at the bed, with its magnificently embroidered curtains hanging from the ceiling to the floor, its yellow-satin mattress ten feet in length and its great round, hard pillow, with the delicate silk spreads turned back as though it were prepared for Her Majesty's return. On the opposite side of the room there was a brick *kang* bed, such as we find in the homes of all the Chinese of the north, where her maids slept, or sat like silent ghosts while the only woman that ever ruled over one-third of the human race took her rest."[71]

Despite the invasion of her country and boudoir, Cixi swallowed her pride and, once back in the Forbidden City, endeavored to win over the hearts and minds of at least a few influential foreigners. Indeed, she undertook something of a charm offensive, going so far as to invite foreign ambassadors' wives to receptions in the Forbidden City. The American legate's observant wife, Sarah Conger, ended up being quite beguiled by her. In a scene that might have been written by Henry James, Conger described going to meet the Dragon Lady for the first time, in December 1898, only to find an elderly but "bright and happy" woman whose "face glowed with good will."[72] Meeting Cixi for a second time in 1902, Conger was again drawn sympathetically to her, describing in a letter how she "took my hands in both of hers, and her feelings overcame her. When she was able to control her voice, she said, 'I regret, and grieve over the late troubles. It was a grave mistake, and China will hereafter be a friend to foreigners. No such affair will again happen. China will protect the foreigner, and we hope to be friends in the future.'"[73]

Reverend Headland's wife, too, came under Cixi's spell. "Taking her guest by the hand, she would ask in the most solicitous way whether we were not tired with our journey to the palace; she would deplore the heat in summer or the cold in winter; she would express her anxiety lest the refreshments might not have been to our taste; she would tell us in the sincerest accents that it was a propitious fate that had made our paths meet; and she would charm each of her guests, even though they had been formerly prejudiced against her, with little separate attentions, which exhibited her complete power as a hostess."[74] This hardly seemed the same woman of Edmund Backhouse's fevered recherche du temps perdu. "When opportunity offered, she was always anxious to learn of foreign ways and institutions," reported Mrs. Headland.[75]

Sarah Conger even convinced Cixi to attempt an international public relations coup by allowing her portrait to be painted for presentation at the 1904 World's Fair in St. Louis. A friend of Conger's, portraitist Katherine Carl, spent months hanging around Beijing working on the canvas. But when Cixi saw how well Carl had captured her likeness, she ordered the bemused American artist to touch up the painting in order to take a few decades off her face—a kind of artistic plastic surgery.[76] Carl's portrait, now in the Smithsonian, is probably a good approximation of what the younger Cixi would have looked like.

In the last decade of her long life and reign, Cixi finally began allowing fundamental changes to the structure of government. "My life is not finished yet and no one knows what is going to happen in the future," she told Der Ling. "I may surprise the foreigners some day with something extraordinary and do something quite contrary to anything I have yet done."[77] Belatedly, Cixi now hoped to help fashion an Itō Hirobumi out of Zhang Zhidong, who was made the architect of a sweeping set of reforms called the *xinzheng* (新政), or "New Policies," designed, at long last, to modernize the military and police force, revise the legal code, draft a state constitution, and open up the educational system.[78]

Perhaps the most dramatic—and destabilizing—reform Cixi initiated came in 1905, when she abolished the system of civil service examinations through which, for the better part of a millennium, government officials had been tested on their knowledge of the Confucian classics and recruited to public office. She intended her move as a shortcut to opening up the political system to fresh blood and foreign ideas. However, it also pulled the rug out from under an entire generation of aspiring officials and their families. Conservative members of the local gentry recoiled at such an uncompromising abandonment of tradition. "It is all about wealth and power and they do not speak of the proper relationships or principles at all," wrote one disgruntled Confucian from his small town in Shanxi Province. "The whole aim of the system is to glorify the state and harm the people, and every aspect involves using the barbarian learning and changing China. It is terrible."[79] In one belated reformist stroke, the Empress Dowager had severely undercut the dynasty's hold on China's elite class.

At the same time that she abolished the exams, Cixi also let New Policies reformers give the imperial government a face-lift, revising the legal code and reorganizing the traditional Six Boards into ministries with modern names such as Foreign Affairs, Post and Communications, and Commerce. She even belatedly followed the Meiji emperor by sending an official delegation, the Qing Constitutional Reform Commission, abroad to study foreign constitutional models. When the commissioners returned in July 1906 to brief the Empress Dowager and release a report of their findings, their central conclusion was, "The real reason why other countries have become wealthy and powerful lies in the fact that they have a constitution and decide [important issues] through public discussion. Their monarch and people form one indivisible unity."[80] In other words, the core of the whole Confucian political system would have to be altered to realize the goal of *fuqiang*.

Still, when a committee was drawn up to implement the Constitutional Commission's suggestions, it decided that the Chinese people would need a "preparatory period" for self-government of at least ten to fifteen years.[81] This tempting notion of a transitional period of authoritarian rule on the way to constitutional government would recur repeatedly throughout the rest of the twentieth century, leaving proponents of self-government chasing an infinitely retreating horizon.

Meanwhile, anti-Manchu sentiment had begun bursting to the surface of public life in newly disruptive ways. After all, the Manchus were an alien ethnic minority presiding over a huge majority of ethnic Han Chinese, who still bridled under such practices as men being legally forced to shave their heads and wear long queues. An insurrectionary tract, *The Revolutionary Army*, published in 1903 by a Chinese teenager living in Shanghai's foreign concessions, was soon electrifying readers with its argument that the real root of China's problem lay with Cixi and her fellow Manchus. Its young author, Zou Rong, wrote: "Today's strengthening [*qiang*] is the strengthening of the Manchus; it has nothing to do with us Han. Today's enrichment [*fu*] is the enrichment of the Manchus; it has nothing to do with us Han."[82] Wealth and power, in other words, had to be enjoyed by the Han Chinese people and nation as a whole.

In 1907, Cixi's increasingly isolated and despised Manchu court was again shaken when a Han Chinese patriot assassinated the Manchu governor of Anhui Province. Cixi desperately tried to defuse all these rising ethnic tensions—for example, by repealing a ban on Manchu-Han intermarriage.[83] But enmities were now inescapably intensifying as Chinese began to entertain ever more radical solutions to their national decline and Han began to blame the ruling Manchu dynasty for all that ailed.

To almost everyone outside her immediate circle, Cixi increasingly came to symbolize everything that was wrong with the country, especially as she stubbornly insisted on yet another costly reconstruction project in her beloved new Summer Palace, which had been ravaged by the Allied expeditionary force after suppressing the Boxers in 1900. In a nod to the changing times, she had electric lights installed in 1903, which was followed by China's first telephone line, connecting the Summer Palace in the northwest suburbs with the Forbidden City. And she also became enamored of cameras, staging numerous photo sessions for private and political purposes. But these trappings of modernity were no replacement for a real program of nationwide modernization that was still incomplete, causing China to remain far behind the rest of the world.

The Empress Dowager died in the fall of 1908, one day after the death of her nephew, the Guangxu Emperor. Suspicions that she had a hand in his death resurfaced a century later, in 2008, when forensic scientists announced that, based on tests of his remains, the emperor had died of acute arsenic poisoning. But Cixi's role remains a matter of conjecture. Plans for her own funeral procession and entombment were suitably splendid. In November 1909, high officials, Lamaist monks, Manchu soldiers, Mongols on camelback, and devoted eunuchs set off from the Forbidden City, with eighty-four men carrying her remains aloft for the four-day journey to the Qing imperial tombs north of Beijing. Like China's ur-despot, the first emperor of the Qin Dynasty, Cixi had for more than a decade been making elaborate plans to be interred in a grand mausoleum. Evincing little regard for the inordinate expense, estimated at eight million taels, she spent lavishly on jade vessels, gold and silver incense burners, and other ornate ritual ornaments to keep her company in the afterlife.[84]

But even such a costly imperial grave could not protect her remains. As China later spiraled into chaos, in 1928 tomb raiders broke into her sarcophagus, stealing whatever they could carry and defiling her corpse in the process. The Manchu commission that finally secured the tomb and managed to recover her remains wrote in its report: "Very gently, we turned the Jade Body on its back. The complexion of the face was wonderfully pale, but the eyes were deeply sunken and seemed like two black caverns. There were signs of injury to the lower lip."[85] Like Li Hongzhang signing the Treaty of Shimonoseki in Japan with a bullet behind his nose, so even in death the Empress Dowager could not "save face."

Cixi had held the Qing regime together since 1861 by tacking constantly back and forth between self-strengtheners, cultural conserva-

Cixi circa 1900

tives, and Purist hawks. But in the process, she held China back from implementing the kinds of decisive centralized modernization efforts that had so successfully transformed Meiji Japan. Her ultimate failure left many critical thinkers convinced that China's problem required far deeper and broader remedies. As this recognition dawned, translator and social philosopher Yan Fu best captured the despair and bewilderment of his generation. "Most of these [self-strengthening reforms] have served as the foundations on which Europe became rich and strong," Yan plaintively wrote. "But, when we applied them in China, they were like a good orange tree on the bank of the Huai River which, after it was transplanted, produced thick-skinned [and inedible] oranges. The tree looks as if midway between life and death but we do not get the fruit we sought. What is the reason? I think the greatest difference between China and the West, which can never be made up, is that the Chinese are fond of antiquity, but neglect the present [whereas] Westerners are struggling in the present in order to supersede the past."[86] It was an evocative metaphor for the Cixi era—a tree midway between life and death—and it would be left to the next generation to decide whether to keep pruning, or chop it down and plant anew.

Liang Qichao in the 1890s

CHAPTER 5

New Citizen (新民)

LIANG QICHAO (梁启超)

The Tomb

There is something about the overgrown state of Liang Qichao's tomb that perfectly expresses the ambiguity into which his legacy has fallen. The grave of the most influential thinker of early twentieth-century China, and the godfather of Chinese nationalism and liberalism, sits largely unheralded in a corner of the Beijing Botanical Garden, just where the park rises to Fragrant Mountain. Rendered in an elegant 1920s beaux arts style, the salmon-colored granite tombstone is now gripped by vines and encircled by encroaching shrubbery. It stands erect like a memorial Chinese stele, but with the honorific names of Liang and his wife chiseled into its surface in a stylish font that imbues the ancient characters with an air of Art Deco modernity. Off to one side lurks a heptagonal gray pavilion, also of granite, but ingeniously cut to resemble a wooden pagoda, its greenish-blue ceramic roof capped by a lotus, the delicate, beautiful flower that grows from the muck of fetid ponds, a Buddhist symbol of the harmony of opposites.

Sprouting with weeds, Liang's final resting place is eerily forlorn, a forgotten memorial to a titanic reformer whose writings moved the nation at a tipping-point moment in its history. The tomb was designed by his son, the renowned architect Liang Sicheng, who studied at the University of Pennsylvania in the 1920s and would lead the doomed effort to save Old Beijing from destruction in the Mao Zedong era. As his late grandson Liang Congjie once wistfully remarked on visiting the tomb with one of the authors, "We are a family of reformers, but of failed reformers." The vines now creeping over this grave with such disregard for the man therein suggest how hard it has been for Communist Party custodians charged with managing their nation's history to know how to treat transitional figures, such as Liang, who do not comfortably conform to their rigid, but ever changing, narratives of modern China's progress.

The man entombed here was the first public figure to argue that China's revival would require the wholesale destruction of the cultural tradition that he had come to view as holding back his country's progress, and the creation of a whole new sense of national self in its place. As Liang wrote just after the turn of the century in his influential journal *New Citizen*: "If we wish to make our nation secure, wealthy, and respected, then we must discuss how to create 'new citizens' [*xinmin*, 新民]."[1]

Liang's clarion call for the creation of "new citizens" marked a radical departure from the prescriptions for reform by the likes of Wei Yuan and Feng Guifen, not to mention the Empress Dowager, who never surrendered their hope that the necessary changes could be accomplished within the framework of inherited Confucian values and the imperial political system. Although Liang shared the goal of "wealth and power," he opened up a new era by blazing a trail outside that framework. His call for a new kind of consciousness and new type of Chinese self laid the way for the monumental figures to come: Chen Duxiu's attack on Confucius in his journal, *New Youth*; Lu Xun's dark short stories during the New Culture Movement; Chiang Kai-shek's crypto-Confucian New Life campaign; and Mao Zedong's revolutionary blueprint for a New China—all owed something to Liang's inspiration.

Indeed, the Chinese obsession with starting anew can be said to begin with Liang. He was the first in a century-long line of intellectuals and politicians who, like magicians locked in a glass coffin filling with water, took on the challenge of freeing themselves and China from remaining drowned in "old thinking." Ironically, this quest for liberation from the past began with a man so steeped in this very tradition that he was never fully able to escape it. Like many reformers to follow, Liang, the youthful prophet of destruction, ended his life seeking refuge in the very traditional Chinese ways he had once attacked.

Diagnosing the Sick Man of Asia

Liang Qichao was born in a village of about five thousand farmers and seafarers in Xinhui county, outside the sprawling southern port city of Canton, in 1873, the year Feng Guifen was on his deathbed and Cixi was just allowing her son to rule in his own name. China's dire condition of "anxiety within and calamity without" was in remission after the disastrous end of the Second Opium War and final suppression of the Taiping Rebellion, but not for long. In his small village along an estuary leading out to the South China Sea, Liang received a classical education and proper Confucian upbringing, just as good sons had for centuries. He hailed from a modest gentry family—one grandfather had passed the county-level civil service examination, and his father was a teacher, but most other members in his family were peasants. Young Liang memorized a massive history of ancient China simply because it was one of the few books the family owned.[2]

Though they were not wealthy, the Liangs were ambitious for their son, and he turned out to be a prodigy: like his grandfather, he earned a county-level examination degree, and at the precocious age of eleven. The next year, in 1885, he moved to Canton to prepare for the Guangdong Province civil service exam, later enrolling at the most famous school in south China, the Sea of Learning Academy, where he was inducted even deeper into the rigors of Confucian scholarship and classical philology.[3] And in 1889, as a cherubic sixteen-year-old, he passed the test, receiving a province-level degree and qualifying to take the national exam in Beijing.

Liang was not a particularly handsome man, but his oversized skull, accentuated by the Manchu-style shaven pate required of all subjects of the Qing, seemed to embody his erudition. In fact, his performance in the provincial exams so impressed the head examiner that he arranged for Liang's engagement to his younger sister, Li Huixian, who remained Liang's lifetime companion, albeit not his only wife.[4]

As with Wei and Feng, Liang's golden touch with the brush failed him when he took the 1890 imperial examination in Beijing. Dejected by failing the test, he stopped in Shanghai on his way home, where he chanced upon a pioneering Chinese book about the West by Xu Jiyu, called *Record of the Ocean Circuit*. Observing life in the foreign conces-

sions of Shanghai for the first time, the teenage Liang began to appreciate the prescience of Xu's insight that England's wealth and power
were inseparable from its imperialist reach. "England consists merely
of three islands, simply a handful of stones in the western ocean," Xu
had written back in the 1840s. "Even if the soil is all fertile, how much
can be produced locally? The reason for her becoming suddenly rich
and strong, exerting political influence here and there beyond tens of
thousands of *li*, is that in the west she obtained America and in the east
she obtained the various parts of India."[5] Stumbling upon this early
piece of "barbarian" studies, Liang was seized by concern for his own
nation's weakness and uncertain fate. "Since my seventeenth year,"
Liang wrote, "I have known much anxiety over the signs of strength
and the signs of weakness among foreigners and Chinese."[6]

Although he had failed the exam in Beijing, he did gain something
else there: a mentor named Kang Youwei. Kang was a fellow Cantonese examination candidate and innovative Confucian philosopher.
Inspired by the same esoteric Confucian teachings that had attracted
Wei Yuan back in the 1820s, Kang was stretching the boundaries of
Chinese thought by boldly reinterpreting the figure of Confucius as a
radical political reformer, and recasting Chinese history as a linear process leading toward a utopian end, rather than an interminable series
of repetitive dynastic cycles. He also advocated constitutionalism as an
urgent necessity for China's survival. Back in Canton, Liang enrolled in
an upstart school Kang had founded, evocatively named Cottage in the
Woods Academy, and he quickly emerged as its star pupil.[7]

Of course, Kang's students still had to prepare for their imperial
exams, but they also tried to absorb some of the Western offerings now
increasingly available in Chinese thanks to prolific missionary transla-
tors such as Timothy Richard, whom Liang would soon meet in person
in Beijing.[8] They also drank from the stream of new translations coming out of the foreign studies institutes created back in the 1860s at the
suggestion of Feng Guifen. Later in life Liang would be self-critical
about these early efforts in Canton to fashion a new hybrid "school of
learning which would be 'neither Chinese nor Western but in fact both
Chinese and Western.'" Unfortunately, he said, they failed, because
"not only was the indigenous traditional thinking too inveterate and
deep-rooted, but the new foreign thought had too shallow and meager

a source, which dried up easily once tapped."[9] As Liang saw it, the students and scholars of his generation were like the proverbial frogs in the Chinese adage, sitting at the bottom of a well they were unable to see any more than the small circumference of sky directly above them.

In 1895, he again made the literati pilgrimage to Beijing to sit for the national civil service examinations. But it was no ordinary year. The old imperial order was coming apart at the seams, and even this most sacred of Confucian rituals, in which scholars were transmuted into high officials, would not be spared. "The defeat in 1895, loss of Taiwan, and two hundred million taels in reparations awoke our nation from its four-thousand-year-long dream," Liang later explained.[10] He would soon coin the phrase *dongfang bingfu* (东方病夫), "Sick Man of Asia," to describe China's debased condition, and would demand that the only cure for this parlous state of affairs was radical reform.[11]

After Li Hongzhang signed the humiliating Treaty of Shimonoseki with Japan, Liang became so exercised that he helped organize his fellow Cantonese examination students to sign a petition condemning the treaty and calling for immediate *bianfa* (变法), "institutional reform." Kang Youwei drafted the historic memorial on behalf of the outraged exam candidates, which they then attempted to present to the emperor in what Liang would later call "the beginning of the 'mass political movement' in China."[12] In the short run, however, Kang and Liang were ignored, and Liang again failed the national exam—this time, he heard, because the examiners mistook his answers for those of Kang, ringleader of the troublesome students.[13] Ironically Kang himself passed.

Liang's baptism in the waters of political activism was only the start of three more dizzying years of reformist endeavors. In Beijing, he joined Kang in commandeering the Self-Strengthening Study Society, founded by reformist Qing officials including Yuan Shikai and Zhang Zhidong. Conservative forces at court found their agenda too radical and had the society shut down after just a year. But Liang promptly founded another society, tellingly named the Sense of Shame Study Society.

From Beijing, Liang traveled to Shanghai, where he dove into the burgeoning new world of a vernacular press and political journalism, embracing the popularization of ideas in a way that had been alien to elitist Confucian scholars. When a reformist Qing official invited him to serve as editor of a new Shanghai paper to be called *Chinese Progress*, Liang accepted. But Liang proved to be a master at the new craft of journalism. (He later wrote—without exaggeration—that his "New-Style writing" possessed "a rare magical kind of power for the reader.")[14] It wasn't long before firsthand experience convinced him that a dynamic popular press was a key to national strength.[15] Although he soon left *Chinese Progress* in protest against editorial meddling by government officials, many other efforts to popularize reformist ideas would follow. In his skillful editorial hands, a series of journals and newspapers would exert the kind of powerful influence on early twentieth-century Chinese public opinion that online journalism has exerted in recent decades.[16]

Liang's next destination was Hunan Province, deep in the Chinese interior, where a reformist official invited him to teach at a new experimental school called the Academy of Current Affairs, giving Liang a free hand to try out educational reform in "one of the country's most conservative provinces," which "had now become the center of innovation."[17] He arrived in late 1897, just before Germany took control of Jiaozhou Bay on the Shandong Peninsula, and remembered it as a time when "the specter of dismemberment shook the whole nation."[18] He was able to concoct his own hybrid curriculum combining Western studies and Confucian philosophy. As he taught his forty disciples, he became even more determined to answer the elemental question once posed by Wei Yuan and Feng Guifen: Why were Western nations superior in "wealth and power" to all other countries on the globe?[19] What lay beneath the surface of the West's superiority and China's backwardness? What would China have to do to catch up? After all, China's defeat by Japan had made it abundantly clear that it would take more than weaponry to become a modern power. China, he concludes, would have to change its basic way of thinking as well.[20] In short, its cultural core would have to be altered.

The more Liang studied the West, the more he came to believe that there were systemic and philosophical foundations to the West's superiority that had laid the groundwork for material advances such as the Industrial Revolution. In his preface to a planned new edition of Wei Yuan's *Anthology of Statecraft Writings from the Present Dynasty*, he hailed Francis Bacon's *New Atlantis* as evidence that Western superiority had been born in the creation of new laws, new principles, new science, new technology, new philosophy, and new politics.[21] "Those who open themselves to the new," waxed Liang, "will prosper and grow strong. But those who confine themselves to the old will diminish and become weak."[22]

As he developed such ideas, he said, "the atmosphere within the school became more radical day by day," and when his invigorated students returned home, it caused "a great stir" throughout Hunan, where, far from the cosmopolitan treaty port cities, conservative resistance to Liang-style "new learning" was particularly strong.[23]

Yan Fu Translates the West

Liang was now one of the fastest-rising stars in China's small circle of experts working in "Western studies." Indeed, by 1897 he was exchanging letters with the movement's seniormost figure, Yan Fu, a political essayist and translator twenty years his senior who had actually studied in England. Yan was a direct product of Feng Guifen's self-strengthening educational reforms. After studying navigation and English at the Fuzhou Shipyard School in the late 1860s, Yan left China in 1879 on a rare scholarship to continue his studies at the Greenwich Naval College in England. There, he witnessed life in the epicenter of the Industrial Revolution firsthand, leading him to search for the deeper intellectual sources of Victorian Britain's global dominance. As historian Benjamin Schwartz explained, Yan took advantage of living among the barbarians to explore "the revolutionary notion that the secrets of Western wealth and power are to be found in the writings of Western thinkers."[24]

By the time he returned to China, Yan was firmly convinced that his country's only salvation lay in learning how to compete in the new global scramble for power. But even though Li Hongzhang appointed him director of his Beiyang Naval Academy in Tianjin, Yan grew increasingly despondent at China's lethargic pace of change, and suggested—prophetically—that soon even the Japanese "will pull us around by the nose like an old cow."[25] During the Sino-Japanese War, Yan, then a military academy instructor, suddenly burst onto the national stage as an outspoken public intellectual who, as he graphically put it, used writing to release "things choked up in my breast, which I had to vomit forth."[26]

China's crushing defeat in 1895 opened the floodgates for him. "The greatest difference in the principles of West and East, that which is most irreconcilable," he asserted, "is the fact that, while the Chinese love the ancient and ignore the modern, Westerners stress the new in order to overcome the old."[27] Yan and Liang were in effect searching for the solution to the grand challenge of becoming modern, while still somehow remaining Chinese. Yan spoke of the need for the Chinese people to cultivate "strength, intelligence, and virtue" as keys to regaining "wealth and power." Here he was pushing beyond the sanctity of a Chinese core. But for Yan, it no longer mattered whether knowledge was Chinese or Western, new or old, as long as it worked. "If one course leads to ignorance and thus to poverty and weakness," he wrote with a sense of urgency, "we must cast it aside. If another course is effective in overcoming ignorance and thus leads to a cure of our poverty and weakness, we must imitate it, even if it proceeds from barbarians."[28]

For Yan, the key to understanding China's backwardness lay in the doctrines of social Darwinism. While living in England, he had become entranced with Herbert Spencer, who had applied Charles Darwin's scientific theories on the "survival of the fittest" in the animal and plant kingdoms to the evolution of human societies. Spencer's corpus of ideas offered Yan a new way of understanding what was happening to China. In his essay "On Evolution," Yan described China as being engaged in a "red in tooth and claw" struggle with the developed nations for competitive advantage.[29] "At first, species struggle with species; then as [people] gradually progress, there is a struggle between one social group and another. The weak invariably become the prey of the strong, the stupid invariably become subservient to the clever."[30] Yan and Liang were thinking along parallel lines, and Yan's translations of Spencer, as well as of the liberal thinker John Stuart Mill, had a profound influence on the younger reformer.

New Citizen of the World

Even as Liang questioned the "old ways," he was still determined to climb the traditional ladder of imperial success. Once more he returned to Beijing in 1898 to sit for the civil service examination, and once more he failed. But life-changing events were now occurring for him outside the examination hall. Liang's mentor, Kang Youwei, had gained the young Guangxu Emperor's ear to explain why self-strengthening required not just the borrowing of technology but such things as constitutional political reform as well. "The secret of the strength of Japan and Western countries lies solely in their adoption of constitutional government and convening of parliament," argued Kang. "In this way the sovereign and the people are welded together into one body politic. How [then] can the nation not be strong."[31] Face-to-face with the young emperor, Kang brazenly promised him that after a mere three years of reforms China would be able to "stand on her own" and, soon after that, begin to "outstrip all the other countries in terms of wealth and power."[32] Such counsel had goaded the Guangxu Emperor into impulsively resolving to drive the Qing Dynasty in the direction of serious reform—modernizing education, administration, and defense—and trying to turn himself into a figure more like Japan's Meiji emperor.

Because Liang was by now known as an expert in Western affairs (an indicator of the relatively low standards of expertise), in early July 1898 he was granted an audience with the emperor, a rare honor. But the emperor was still dragging his feet on Kang's boldest proposal: setting up a "constitutional bureau" to plan systematic reforms of China's core political structure. The emperor did, however, do something almost as audacious when, as we have described, he invited the architect of the Meiji constitution, Itō Hirobumi, to China to advise his inner circle of reformers, a move that would mark the end of his dramatic Hundred Days' Reform. The emperor ended up under palace arrest, and Liang, because of his association with Kang, was forced into exile with a reward on his head. It was a precipitous ending to a bold but naive reform effort.[33]

Liang was in Beijing on September 21 when the Empress Dowager declared herself regent once again, dethroned the emperor, and issued a warrant for Liang's arrest. However, thanks to the protection of Japanese diplomats, he narrowly escaped Qing agents. Itō Hirobumi allegedly received specific orders from Tokyo to protect him and Kang.[34] So Liang first took refuge in the Japanese legation, just off Tiananmen Square.[35] From there he slipped out to Tianjin, where the Japanese consul personally escorted him to the gunboat *Oshima*, waiting off Dagu Fort to take him to safety in exile.

Once Liang was in Tokyo, even Prime Minister Okuma Shigenobu welcomed him with open arms and pocketbook.[36] It was here in Japan that Liang commenced his *vita nuova* as exiled dissident and cosmopolitan nationalist, a role in which he became arguably more dangerous to the Qing Dynasty than he had been at home. For in exile, he could give free voice to a potent new force in modern Chinese history: the overseas diaspora of merchants, students, and dissidents. After the Sino-Japanese War, Japan in particular became a breeding ground for reformist writers and revolutionary leaders from China. In 1895, only a sprinkling of Chinese students was there. A decade later, close to ten thousand had arrived, with more to follow.[37] National heroes such as Sun Yat-sen (already in residence when Liang arrived), Chen Duxiu, Lu Xun, and Chiang Kai-shek would all first spread their intellectual wings in rapidly industrializing imperial Japan.

As is so often the case among political exiles, internal rivalries among the Chinese in Japan were bitter. Liang briefly tried to ally Kang Youwei's reformist constitutional monarchy group with Sun Yat-sen's revolutionary republican group, for instance, but only made the antipathy between them stronger. Various cliques, clubs, and embryonic political parties emerged in a state of yeasty contention throughout the first decade of the 1900s. Just as Confucius spent fourteen years wandering the various ancient Chinese kingdoms with his disciples looking for a leader who would heed his advice, Liang now lived in this Japanese limbo for the next fourteen years. He gained fluency in the language, answered to his Japanese name, Yoshida Shin, surrounded himself with Japanese friends and patrons, and embraced and absorbed the Meiji model of modernity. His relocation, he enthused, "was like catching a beam of sunshine in a dark room, or having a cup of warm rice wine when you were starving."[38] Barely more than a year after fleeing China he wrote, "In Japan I have the feeling that here is my second home."[39] And as he headed off for a political fund-raising trip to Hawaii, Liang was struck by his own transformation. "My thinking and words," he wrote, "have become so different from before as to appear to be those of another person."[40]

Denied the chance at public service in the imperial Chinese government, Liang now poured his energies into his true gift—writing about the changes his country so urgently needed through new periodicals of his own creation such as *Remonstrance*, which was published in Yokohama (home to Japan's largest Chinatown) and featured his regular column, "Writings on Liberty." He fervently hoped that *Remonstrance* would be "a spur to the nation's sense of shame" by showing Chinese readers "our country's place in the world."[41] When a fire destroyed *Remonstrance*'s printing house in the winter of 1901, Liang kept going, this time launching his best-known periodical, *New Citizen*.

Observing his native land from a critical distance allowed Liang to generate new answers to the question of why China was so weak. The source of the country's backwardness, he now argued forcefully, was his countrymen's lack of *guojia sixiang* (国家思想), "national consciousness," and their congenital inability to imagine themselves as active participants, as *guomin* (国民), "citizens," of a modern nation-state.[42] It became his mission to imagine such a new community of citizens and the new society that could grow out of them, creating the foundation for a nation that would feel the necessity of elevating itself to an equal footing with other imperialist and industrial powers. Borrowing heavily from the language of social Darwinism (then also fashionable in Japan), Liang warned that unless China reinvented itself as a modern nation soon, it faced the real prospect of political extinction, of becoming a *wangguo* (亡国), "lost country."[43] In effect, Liang was calling for a fundamental change in China's identity, a change in the core of what it meant to be Chinese, in order to save its existence as embodying a people and a state.

In these early years of exile, Liang injected the Western political vocabulary of "liberty" and "democracy" into the existing Chinese reformist language of "wealth and power" and "self-strengthening." The result was a kind of muscular liberalism with Chinese characteristics. Strength, Liang insisted, was the necessary precondition for liberty. "In the world there is only power—there is no other force. That the strong always rule the weak is in truth the first great universal rule of nature. Hence, if we wish to attain liberty, there is no other road: we can only seek first to be strong."[44] He also promoted democracy as the surest

Liang's *New Citizen* journal

Translator and essayist Yan Fu, 1905

Liang at the Paris Peace Conference, 1919

Liang's tombstone on the outskirts of Beijing

route to strengthening the nation. "In the last hundred years, the democratic spirit has spread in the Western countries. If only China will do the same, then she will be as strong as the Western countries in a few decades."[45]

Liang's nationalistic but liberal ideas electrified readers back home in China, where the educated public voraciously consumed his essays. From the last generation of self-strengthening officials such as Zhang Zhidong and Yuan Shikai to the young future founders of Chinese communism, Chen Duxiu and Mao Zedong, anyone interested in national affairs—as many as two hundred thousand readers—kept up with the latest columns of this young political exile in Yokohama.[46] Yan Fu, then living in Tianjin, wrote to Liang: "I have read [*New Citizen*] from cover to cover repeatedly, feeling as if a strong wind were blowing and a loud tide surging toward me. They are without doubt the harbinger of a flourishing Asian civilization in the upcoming twentieth century."[47]

It was also during this period that Liang embraced what he called "destructivism" (a term he may have picked up from Itō Hirobumi).[48] The idea was that the fashioning of "new citizens" would require a complete destruction of the baggage of China's traditional value system. The old edifice had to be razed to the ground, or else nothing new would ever be able to replace it. He even coined the ism, *pohuai zhuyi* (破坏 注意), "destructivism." True revolution, Liang explained, meant "overturning things from their foundations and creating a new world."[49] "There can be no construction without destroying what's already built," Liang cried out from the pages of *New Citizen*.[50] He even made such destruction a moral imperative: "Those who say, 'Do not destroy, do not destroy,' I call people devoid of human feelings."[51]

Soon enough Liang would back away from this position, but his radical argument for creative destruction would later take on a life of its own. Liang recognized this himself before he died. Looking back and assessing his own legacy, he wrote that his "destructive force was far from negligible," while his "constructive [contributions] are not evident."[52] Indeed, long after his death, Mao Zedong would adopt with a vengeance the motto "Destruction before construction" during the Cultural Revolution. The nihilist genie that Liang had begun to conjure up would later be let out of the bottle by Mao to wreak a havoc that Liang could not have imagined.

Chinatown

From his new base in Japan, Liang also began traveling the world. He spent six months in Honolulu, raising money from overseas Chinese businessmen for a botched uprising that was to start in central China in 1900. Then in the spring of 1901 he made a grand tour of colonial outposts across the Asia-Pacific region—Hong Kong, Singapore, Ceylon, Australia, and the Philippines. But by far the most important journey he made was to the United States in 1903.

Like the famed French political voyager Alexis de Tocqueville, Liang traversed North America in search of answers to fundamental political questions that vexed his generation. When he arrived, he was the same age de Tocqueville had been during the 1831 tour of America that inspired his masterwork, *Democracy in America*. And like the Frenchman, Liang was largely charmed by American political life. He met President Theodore Roosevelt in Washington (though he was dismayed by Roosevelt's imperialistic speeches). He also sat down briefly with J. P. Morgan in Manhattan, stood in Boston harbor comparing the Tea Party of 1773 to Commissioner Lin Zexu's destruction of British opium in 1839, and even viewed the famous portrait of the Empress Dowager Cixi then on display at the St. Louis World's Fair.[53]

As Liang crisscrossed the New World, he was constantly thinking of the situation at home, and it was in San Francisco's Chinatown that he experienced a Tocquevillean epiphany. His plunge into the city's segregated Chinese quarter, embedded within Anglo-American society yet standing apart from it, came as a painful revelation. White Americans, observed Liang, lived by the rugged individualist's creed of liberty and equality, but Chinese in America tended to reproduce the traditional subservient and hierarchical habits of the motherland, even in the Wild West of California. The inability of Chinese communities in the United States to take advantage of the liberal democratic society around them disturbed Liang. But it also suggested an answer to that perennial question: why was China so weak?

The cause of China's backwardness, he now concluded, was not

outmoded military and scientific technology, not the lack of a constitution, not the antiquated imperial system of their Manchu overlords,
and not even the Empress Dowager Cixi herself. The problem lay at the
very core (*ti*, 体) of what it was to be Chinese, which reflected a total
lack of consciousness of a citizen's rights and responsibilities. What
troubled Liang was a crippling absence of any *guojia sixiang* (国家
思想), "national consciousness," by which he meant civic concern for
the Chinese nation.[54] The Chinese people, he was now convinced, remained so trapped in their attachments to clan, village, native region,
and ancient culture that they were unable to identify with the common-
weal and behave as citizens of a larger, modern nation must. The Chinese character, he concluded, was slavish, stupid, selfish, mendacious,
timid, and passive.[55]

What, then, was to be done? Liang reluctantly concluded that the
Chinese people were, at least for the present, incapable of democracy.
In his travel diary, published upon his return to Japan, he wrote despondently: "We [Chinese] can accept only despotism and cannot enjoy
freedom. . . . When I look at all the societies of the world, none is so
disorderly as the Chinese community in San Francisco. Why? The answer is freedom. With such countrymen, would it be possible to practice the election system? . . . If we were to adopt a democratic system
of government now, it would be nothing less than committing national
suicide. Freedom, constitutionalism, and republicanism would be like
hempen clothes in winter or furs in summer; it is not that they are not
beautiful, they are just not suitable for us."[56]

This was quite a volte-face for the leading constitutional reformer of
his generation. Like Feng Guifen writing about Lincoln's America back
in the 1860s, the pioneer of Chinese liberalism now suddenly found
himself starkly questioning democracy's appropriateness for his country, even as he embraced the United States in theory as the world's ideal
political system. He wrote mockingly of how when "heroic young activists hear Western nations have such-and-such a method of self-
strengthening, they all run and shout"—an ironic slight given his own
"heroic young activism" in the 1890s.[57]

Liang's pessimism about the Chinese character led him to embrace
a new and radically *anti*democratic position. "I returned from America
to dream of Russia," he wrote dejectedly. If the Chinese people were

decades away from being fit for self-government, what they needed in the interim was disciplined training in citizenship at the hands of an enlightened despot. Alluding to ancient Chinese Legalism, as well as some Western variants of authoritarianism, Liang now wrote: "I pray only that our country can have a Guanzi, a Shang Yang, a Lycurgus, a Cromwell alive today to carry out harsh rule, and with iron and fire to forge and temper our countrymen for twenty, thirty, even fifty years. After that we can give them the books of Rousseau and tell them about the deeds of Washington."[58] Only despotism could make China ready for democracy, Liang concluded. It was an idea that would have continuing allure for many of China's future political leaders.

Ironically, as Liang flirted with notions of enlightened despotism, the Empress Dowager was belatedly initiating "New Policies" to reform the country's political structure. Liang published his controversial essay "Enlightened Despotism" in early 1906, not long before Cixi promised to convene a new national assembly and dispatched a Constitutional Commission to travel the world in search of political reform models for the Qing. However, Liang's enthusiasm for the capacity of despots to act in the common interest also soon began to wane, and his political vision grew ever more blurry and inconsistent. As he himself acknowledged, his "views of one day often contradicted those of an earlier day."[59]

By 1909, the year after Cixi's death, Liang was even losing patience with the power of his own writings to bring into being any kind of new political consciousness among his countrymen. In fact he even seemed to lose the capacity to dream the kinds of dreams that had set him off writing his utopian novel in 1902, *The Future of New China*. Yet, still expecting great things of himself, he began to itch to enter the political fray . . . and not without some hubris. "The more I have studied political problems during this past year," he wrote to his brother, "the more convinced I am that there can be no hope for China's future unless I return to take the reins of government."[60]

Failed Politician

Whatever his inflated political ambitions and dreams, Liang would prove no better prepared than anyone else for the abrupt and ignominious end of the great Qing Empire in October 1911. A minor revolt by government troops in Wuhan caused the regime to unravel in a matter of months with almost no fighting. It was, as Liang said at the time, "a revolution in ink, not a revolution in blood."[61] The following month he traveled to Shenyang, the old Manchu capital, to test the political waters, only to return to Japan. Although the Republic of China was proclaimed in January 1912, and the last Qing emperor abdicated in February, it was not until that autumn that Liang, a forty-year-old exile, father of six and husband to two (his parents had sent him their domestic servant as a concubine in 1904), finally retraced his escape route of 1898.

Sailing to Tianjin, he traveled overland to the capital of the freshly minted republic to find himself courted by rival factions, all seeking the prestige of his approval.[62] Wanting to create a centrist coalition of his own, which he called the Progressive Party, and seeing his main political competition in Sun Yat-sen's Nationalist Party, he aligned himself with Yuan Shikai, last in the line of great self-strengthening provincial officials, who became provisional president of the new Republic.

In the immediate wake of the national elections of 1913—mainland China's first and last—the charismatic young leader of the Nationalist Party, Song Jiaoren, was assassinated in the Shanghai railroad station. Although the prime suspect was Yuan Shikai, Liang also came under a cloud of suspicion for possible involvement. It was a sign of how quickly a great public intellectual could become mired in the tawdry power plays of real politics. Days after the killing, Liang wrote dispiritedly to his daughter that acting on one's personal ideals in the political world was "like trying to knock down air."[63] Despite the cloud of suspicion over him, Liang accepted Yuan Shikai's offer to serve as minister of justice in his so-called Cabinet of Talent. But Liang quickly found himself politically in over his head, a pawn in Yuan's efforts to destroy the Nationalist Party, which he soon banned in order to consolidate his own increasingly dictatorial powers.

After resigning in protest against Yuan's autocratic maneuvering, Liang was soon enough lured back with the offer of a new post, director of a currency reform bureau. By then he had become an economic nationalist, believing that wealth was the key to power, and thus to national salvation. "Nothing is more important in order to save China from obliteration and plan [the nation's] strengthening," he wrote, "than putting the currency in order and ensuring the steady flow of financing."[64] But his efforts to rationalize monetary policy and stabilize the currency met with little success, and he soon quit in dismay.[65]

Outside government again, Liang once more found his voice and regained some influence, leading a public campaign in 1915 condemning Japan for its infamous Twenty-One Demands—a laundry list of imperialist designs forced on an increasingly helpless and powerless government in Beijing. His editorials pressured Yuan's government to push back against Tokyo's aggressive policies, which caused Japanese polemicists to accuse Liang of "ingratitude" for all the support their country had offered him during his many years of exile.[66]

Before long, Liang was leading the opposition to a despotic and farcical attempt by Yuan to enthrone himself as emperor. After publishing a devastating public letter castigating his malfeasance in office, Liang even helped organize a military uprising against him, none of which stopped Yuan from declaring himself emperor on January 1, 1916. Mercifully, China's latest leadership travesty ended a few months later when Yuan died.[67]

With Yuan out of the picture, in 1917 Liang accepted yet another government appointment, this time as minister of finance in the latest warlord government in Beijing, a role in which he achieved little. It would be his last fling at public office, what he would refer to as "frequent foolish political activities which sapped his energy."[68] Demoralized and bewildered, Liang compared his political career in the young republic to a movie in which no scene lasted more than a minute—an apt metaphor from the heyday era of the Keystone Kops. The failure of the republican experiment now appeared to Liang not so different from the epiphenomenal Hundred Days' Reform in 1898. Neither of these efforts, he now believed, had gotten close to the heart of the problem. "It was like when you open a bottle of cold beer," he wrote. "The foam quickly bubbles up to the surface and appears awfully busy. But when the moment is over and the foam dissipates, it is still a cold bottle of beer."[69] As in 1898, Liang again left China, this time bound for Europe, but without a price on his head.

Paris

During the first stop on his epic European tour of 1919–20, he served as an unofficial member of the Chinese delegation to the Paris Peace Conference that was to end World War I. The Treaty of Versailles would have almost as profound an impact on China and its neighbors as it did on Europe, where the punitive deals struck by the victorious Allies would fuel the rise of fascism and set the stage for World War II. And at this turning point in China's modern history, Liang was once again to play an instrumental role.

Harboring high hopes of enjoying some of the later fruits of a wished-for victory, both China and Japan had joined the Allied cause in declaring war on Germany. Liang had ardently supported a pro-war position in the belief that, should the Allies win, such support would gain his country a desperately needed footing in the new post-war international system. There was only one problem: once again, a pro-active Japan was a step ahead of China.[70]

After joining the war effort in 1917, China's primary contribution was some three hundred thousand Chinese laborers who took jobs in France and England, filling gaps in the workforce created by their mass mobilizations against Germany. Japan, on the other hand, not only had committed to the war in the summer of 1914, but also, with its robust industrial economy and effective navy, was able to make a far greater material contribution to the Allied cause than could the fledgling Chinese Republic. As a result, when Europe's winners and losers gathered for the Paris Peace Conference in January 1919, Liang was stunned to discover that China had already lost the diplomatic battle—and long before the war was even won. The Allied powers had already concluded covert deals with Tokyo, promising them Germany's colonial leases over strategic ports on China's Liaodong and Shandong peninsulas in exchange for support during the war. More devastating for Liang and his Chinese colleagues in Versailles was the discovery that these "secret" pacts were, in fact, known at the time to the president of the Republic of China, who, deeply indebted to Japan for loans, had raised no objections.[71]

Apprised of these shocking revelations in Paris, Liang fired off a telegram to civic leaders in Beijing exposing their government's complicity in the imperialist machinations of their "robber neighbor."[72] His report helped to spark the famous student demonstrations that culminated in the May Fourth Incident.[73] Once again Liang had played a historic role as a catalyst of public opinion and incipient Chinese nationalism. But, curiously, his telegram was the full extent of Liang's involvement in the May Fourth Movement. For Paris was just the first stop on a European voyage that, like his earlier trip to the United States, would cause him to question his most deeply held beliefs and lead to yet another major course correction in his erratically evolving vision for remaking China.

After Paris, Liang set off across Europe with a small band of disciples. But rather than enjoying the glories of Western culture as he had imagined, he found himself horrified by the postapocalyptic scenes of the Great War's destructive power and the ruin left in its wake. He was similarly stunned by the chasm between rich and poor that he found in 1920s Europe. Sounding suddenly almost like a Marxist, he began prophesying that Europeans would soon be engulfed by "social revolution," a war between labor and capital.[74] Even more than the diplomatic hypocrisy at Versailles, the ruin and misery of the war had revealed to him an unexpected dark side of the West, the West to which he and fellow Chinese reformers had looked so hopefully as young men in their quest for models of wealth, power, and respect. Now, the man who had done so much to open his countrymen's eyes to Western thought and civilization found himself staring into the self-destructive heart of what Oswald Spengler was calling, in his zeitgeist-catching new book *Decline of the West*, its "Faustian" bargain with the devil.

"New authority after all has difficulty establishing itself, and yet old authority is abolished beyond restoration," wrote Liang plaintively as he toured war-ravaged Europe. "Consequently the entire society is thrown into skepticism, despair, and fear, just as a ship without a compass caught in a storm and enshrouded with a heavy fog at the same time. No one has any idea of what the future will be like."[75]

Reoriented

Back in China, May Fourth and New Culture Movement intellectuals were celebrating the Western ideals of "Mr. Democracy and Mr. Science." But thousands of miles away from home, Liang was taking new measure of the West and finding it a dubious model. Indeed, he now saw Europe trapped in a disastrous cul-de-sac, thanks precisely to its worship of science. Europeans "are like travellers in the desert and have lost their direction," he wrote home. "At a distance they saw a big black shadow and tried hard to catch up with it, thinking it might be depended upon as a guide. How were they to know that, after they caught up a little, the shadow would disappear? . . . The European people have had a big dream about the omnipotence of science. Now they are talking about its bankruptcy."[76]

Yan Fu was now also writing with similar newfound dismay about this civilization he had once idealized. "As I have grown older and observed the seven years of republican government in China and the four years of bloody war in Europe—a war such as the world has never known," he wrote despondently, "I have come to feel that their [the West's] progress during the last three hundred years has only led to selfishness, slaughter, corruption, and shamelessness."[77]

As his ship departed Marseilles for Shanghai, Liang continued to ponder the significance of the "skepticism and despair" he had unexpectedly found at the core of Western civilization.[78] He was seeking a way to turn his disorientation into a reorientation. Not inclined to wallow in self-doubt and despondency, he wrote to his son Liang Sicheng, then struggling to make his own way as an architecture student, "Even if you cannot find a good job don't be disappointed or demoralized. That would be the most dreadful enemy in our lives; we should not allow it to overtake us."[79]

Sure enough, Liang did find a way forward. The challenge was no longer merely how to learn from, copy, or catch up to the West, but also how to avoid its mistakes. Perhaps, as a late entrant in the race for modernization, and thanks to the negative example of the war-torn West, China could now industrialize more wisely. "Our advantage is that ours is still a country lagging behind. We have witnessed all the wrong roads they took; we also have access to all the prescriptions they have used for treating the symptoms. As long as we avoid following the wrong road and take preventive measures, we will be able to develop our industry in a rational and healthy way from the outset."[80]

Most hopeful was the thought that China's great traditions might have something positive to contribute to modern civilization after all, such as the harmonious ethics of Confucianism and the spiritual discipline of Buddhism. The voice of a once young, iconoclastic, and confident Liang was now reincarnated in the writings of an older man waving a very different banner. "Our beloved youth! Attention! Forward march!" he wrote with a reinvigorated pride. "On the other shore of the great ocean there are millions of people bewailing the bankruptcy of material civilization and crying out most piteously for help, waiting for you to come to their salvation."[81] Now he was writing not about how enlightened youth in China should save their country by rejecting their own tradition and learning from the West, but rather about how the West could repair a violent modern world by rediscovering and even importing traditional Chinese values. It was no longer a one-way street. Everyone had something to learn from everyone else.

This was the culmination of Liang's long journey from nationalist self-strengthener to a far more nuanced and complex cosmopolitan self-awakener. He still thought the Chinese people would need twenty or thirty years to learn how to practice the collective "spirit of the rule of law," but he was no longer so fixated on forging a prosperous and strong Chinese state by aping the superiority of the West.[82] Instead, he began writing straightforwardly of freedom of thought and speech as ends in themselves, and he embraced the values of what he termed *shijiezhuyi de guojia* (世界注意的国家), the "cosmopolitan nation." Liang's "new citizens" would no longer be beholden to the Chinese nation-state or the West for a political identity, nor need to destroy their own Chineseness to *jiuguo* (救国), "save the nation." Instead, Liang was at last able to imagine a version of modernity that included a redeeming aspect of Chinese culture. He had been on quite an intellectual odyssey; and this new dream was the one he pursued during his last decade of life.

Returning to China of the 1920s a changed man, Liang now kept his distance from party politics, even as he allowed himself to return to his Confucian roots by steeping himself in the very traditional history, culture, language, and values that he had once called on others to reject. In a discourse increasingly polarized by Marxists and anarchists on the left and nationalists and authoritarians on the right, Liang raised the flag of centrist Confucian liberalism, calling on Chinese to heed the ancient Sage's teaching of the "doctrine of the mean," which emphasized moderation and harmony. He invited like-minded big thinkers from around the world—John Dewey, Bertrand Russell, Rabindranath Tagore—to China to spread their enlightened humanistic and liberal teachings, and he edited a spate of new translations published by the Commercial Press in Beijing. His new journal, *Emancipation and Reconstruction*, offered up a cocktail of Keynesian economics, Deweyean democracy, and globalized Confucian humanism.[83] Shuttling between his Victorian two-story house in the Italian concession of Tianjin and his traditional courtyard-style home in Beijing, Liang taught the Chinese classics (a new field then being called *guoxue*, 国学, or "national studies") at the country's leading modern universities—Tianjin's English-language Nankai University and Beijing's Tsinghua University (founded with $10 million in Boxer indemnities forgiven by the U.S. government).

Liang's prodigious youthful literary output had been like a raft that transported his readers to the undiscovered country of "new citizens" seeking to forge a modern Chinese self. Now he was drifting back across that same body of water to the familiarity, comfort, and richness of the very classical Chinese heritage he had once rejected. In the last years of his life, he even indulged his interest in the history of Chinese Buddhism and its spiritual practice. In fact, his last request would be for a Buddhist funeral ceremony (which explains the lotus-topped pagoda next to his tomb).[84] He also devoted himself to his duties as family patriarch. His thirteenth child was born in 1924, just three weeks before the death of his principal wife, Li Huixian.

His own health took a grave turn in 1928, when he was diagnosed with cancer of the kidney. Then, in a tragic twist of fate, the surgeon operating on him at Peking Union Medical College (founded by American missionaries and funded by Rockefeller philanthropies) mistakenly removed his healthy kidney rather than the diseased one, and he died on January 19, 1929.[85] His ninth son was born, fatherless, soon afterward.

As he looked back on his intellectual life and political career, his self-assessment could sometimes be harsh. "Because Liang had too few convictions," he wrote of himself in the third person, "he would often be carried away by events and abandon positions he had held."[86] But

Liang Qichao in the 1920s

he did give himself credit for having a "crude and wide-ranging approach" to ideas that helped in "opening up new fields" and giving birth to a new intellectual world.[87]

One of his most ardent readers, the father of the May Fourth Movement, Chen Duxiu, wrote generously, "The fact that we today have some knowledge of the world is entirely the gift of Mr. Kang and Mr. Liang."[88] But perhaps the most historically significant young reader of Liang's writings was a man who would bend his energies far more fully to destroying the old and forging, "with iron and fire," a new China. This was Mao Zedong, who would tell journalist Edgar Snow in the caves of Yan'an in 1935 that he had "worshipped" Liang and Kang, and "read and reread those books until I knew them by heart."[89]

CHAPTER 6

A Sheet of Loose Sand（一盘散沙）

SUN YAT-SEN（孙中山）

Old School Hall

Old School Hall still stands under towering monkey pod trees at what is today Punahou School in Hawaii, best known as President Barack Obama's high school alma mater. Watching as hip, multicultural students spill across the beautiful campus—one is practicing his golf swing on the school's impeccably manicured lawns—it is difficult to imagine what it must have been like for the thirteen-year-old Sun Yat-sen when he, still sporting his Confucian scholar's robes and Manchu-style queue, arrived in Honolulu to live with his older brother, a merchant.[1] In 1882 he was admitted to the school, then known as Oahu College, founded by American Congregationalist missionaries to educate the Caucasian elite of the islands. The experience imbued the young Sun with a keen interest in America and an excellent grasp of English.

"Here I was brought up and educated, and it was here that I came to know what modern, civilized governments are like and what they mean," a placard in a Honolulu park now dedicated to his memory quotes Sun as saying. His familiarity with things American and the cultural androgyny he acquired while living in Hawaii left him with a rare gift for crossing the divide between East and West, a facility unequaled by anyone else of his time. In fact, no Chinese leader since has come close to matching the ease with which he was able to navigate the world outside China.

There was, however, another very different side to Sun's life, and his

Sun Yat-sen in the early 1880s

final resting place catches it perfectly. To go from Honolulu to Nanjing, the old "southern capital" of imperial China, and the Sun Yat-sen Memorial Mausoleum on Purple Mountain is to migrate from one side of Sun's divided life to the other—from the informality of Hawaii to a tradition-bound China steeped in the kind of grand imperial pretension with which the country's leaders in both life and death have sought to surround themselves since time immemorial.

Sun's mausoleum, modeled unmistakably on the tombs of Ming Dynasty emperors, signaled his supporters' aspiration to conjure up a larger-than-life imperial-style mystique around his memory. With its myriad memorial arches and inscribed stone monuments all connected by a soaring 490-meter-long stairway, or "spirit road," that ascends the mountain to his marble sepulcher at the top, Sun's tomb is far grander than that of even the Ming Dynasty's founder, Zhu Yuanzhang, just next door.[2] Having dethroned the alien Manchu Qing Dynasty, just as Zhu had overthrown the alien Mongol Yuan Dynasty, Sun liked to imagine himself as a modern-day apostle of Han Chinese liberation from foreign enslavement. But the sheer size of the monument is also an expression of his formidable ego and his abiding yearning to play a central part in the restoration of China's national greatness. What Sun and many other Chinese wanted to create were symbols of what a local newspaper of the time described as the "nation in its forthcoming glorious rejuvenation."[3] Alas, during the first two decades of the century, such rejuvenation proved elusive. In the end, although Sun's own efforts never amounted to much, yet he remains revered as *guofu* (国父), the "Father of the Nation" that he never quite succeeded in founding.

Growing Up on the Margins

Sun was born in 1866 in Cuiheng, a peasant village in southern Guangdong Province not far from Liang Qichao's hometown. Sun's family was too poor to tutor their sons to take the imperial civil service examinations and join the mandarin elite. Instead, the young Sun joined his brother in Honolulu, where he not only absorbed foreign culture and language but also became a passionate believer in Christianity, converting to Congregationalism. "I do not belong to the Christianity of the churches, but to the Christianity of Jesus who was a revolutionary," he later declared of his messianic faith.[4] But, instead of wanting to save heathen souls, Sun yearned to save his country.

After returning home in 1883, he chafed under the traditionalism of his village and quickly moved on, this time to the crown colony of Hong Kong, then a bustling outpost of the British Empire. Here he continued his Western-style education and was baptized, acquiring the name by which foreigners came to know him: Sun Yat-sen (the Cantonese pronunciation of his baptismal name, Sun Yixian). In another expression of his double identity, he also began studying the Confucian classics. But in 1892 he became one of the first Chinese students to graduate from Hong Kong College of Medicine, and he began practicing as a Western-trained surgeon in the nearby Portuguese colony of Macao.

Before long, however, Sun's interest in politics, especially his disgust at the corruption that lay at the heart of the Qing Dynasty's failure to resist China's dismemberment by the foreign powers, eclipsed his commitment to medicine. Motivated by an incipient nationalism and spirit of revolution, in 1894 he returned to Hawaii to set up one of China's first overseas patriotic organizations, the Revive China Society, dedicated to fomenting an armed uprising in Canton. Because of his anti-dynastic activities, he was soon banished not only from China but from Hong Kong as well.

The Shame of Not Being Japanese

Moving to Japan in 1895 for what would be sixteen years of exile,[5] Sun severed his last links to the dynasty he so reviled by symbolically cutting off his queue, growing a mustache, and donning Western attire. Familiarizing himself with the very different ways in which the Japanese had responded to the challenges of the West during the Meiji era, he also began to travel widely, from Tokyo to Hanoi, San Francisco to London, and Sydney to Vancouver. Being away from China for so long, however, left him teetering on the edge of cultural deracination, for, unlike other exiled reformers like Liang Qichao who had at least undergone extensive Confucian education before leaving home, Sun had spent most of his formative years abroad.

In 1911 he took another step onto the foreign side of the divide

when he married into one of China's most westernized families, that of
the wealthy entrepreneur Charlie Song, who had lived in the United
States for many years and also become a devout Christian. His daughter Song Qingling, Sun's bride, was not only the sister of the well-
known banker and later Nationalist government official T. V. Song, but
also the sister of Sun's protégé Chiang Kai-shek's wife-to-be, the Welles-
ley College–educated Song Meiling.

The fact that Sun had so many foreign associations and was so
much a product of foreign-occupied treaty ports and the overseas Chinese diaspora left many other reformers alienated from him, feeling
that he was a man too detached from China's reality, even un-Chinese.
However, Sun's long periods overseas had given him one incomparable
advantage over the others: a powerful sense of just how backward
China was when compared to Japan and the West. It was an understanding that would deeply unsettle him and leave him in sympathy
with one of the slogans adopted by some of his fellow exiles: "Know
the shame of not being Japanese."[6]

As painful as these comparisons may have been, they led Sun to
conclude that foreign domination not only menaced China territorially
but also threatened the cultural identity, pride, and psychological well-
being of the Chinese people as a race. Sun "was terribly torn between
his pride in China and his admiration for the West," wrote his biographer Martin Wilbur. "It was psychologically unbearable to him that his
country should be so poor, backward, and ignorant (by Western standards), be patronized and exploited by foreigners, and be surpassed by
'the younger brother,' Japan. His intense and lasting concern for his
country's political reformation and economic development might be
explained as psychologically compulsive."[7]

Early photos of Sun show a well-pomaded man of modest stature
and swarthy complexion whose most striking personal feature was a
Continental-style mustache that often showed a hint of waxing. He
was a stylish, even fastidious dresser. Borrowing elements from Japanese school uniforms and British hunting apparel, he even designed
what came to be know as the "Sun Yat-sen suit," which he hoped
would become a symbol of a post–Qing Dynasty modernized Chinese
citizen. This curious East-West sartorial confection—another metaphor for Sun's own hybrid nature—did not come fully into its own

until long after his death, by which time it was called the "Mao suit" and worn by leaders and ordinary Chinese alike during the Communist revolution.[8]

By most accounts, Sun was an amiable and sincere leader, if not particularly charismatic. "In youth his countenance was frank, self-confident and unsuspicious," wrote one of Sun's earliest English-language biographers, who also characterized him as showing "no tendency toward undue self-analysis" and as being a man who some-times "over-estimated the value of his thinking to the nation."[9]

Whatever his weaknesses, Sun's personal determination and force-fulness were undeniable. Over his many years of revolutionary activity inside and outside China, he became known for his persistence and unending willingness to "talk up the cause of revolution." Indeed, Sun was so garrulous that he won the sobriquet "Sun the Cannon" for his willingness to talk with almost anyone, as long as it was on the subject of China's future.[10] In his style of politics, he evinced one uniquely un-Chinese trait: a decidedly nonelitist attitude. He would talk directly to whomever crossed his path and was perhaps the first Chinese leader to style himself as a representative of the common man. "I am a coolie and the son of a coolie," he once said proudly, though it was something of an exaggeration. "I was born with the poor."[11]

This penchant for interacting with ordinary people made him a novel figure among Chinese political leaders. "If you meet a farmer, speak to him about freeing him from his miseries," Sun advised. "The farmer will then certainly warmly embrace what you have to say. Do the same when meeting workers, merchants and scholars."[12] This un-Confucian absence of elitist pretension helped attract a dedicated core of followers. "He does not produce violent emotions," wrote an early Philippino biographer. "He does not provoke passionate explosions, but he speaks without vehemence, in well considered words."[13] "His is a nature that draws men's regard toward him and makes them ready to serve him at the operating-table or on the battlefield," observed Dr. James Cantlie, his Hong Kong medical college dean, friend, and hagiographer. He possesses "an unexplainable influence, a magnetism which prevails and finds its expression in attracting men to his side."[14]

Another thing that soon came to distinguish Sun from most other turn-of-the-century reformers was his unrepentant advocacy of the overthrow of the Qing Dynasty. In 1894 he wrote a letter offering his services to the great self-strengthener Li Hongzhang. In it he pondered the nexus among wealth, power, and China's ability to defend itself. "Sources of foreign wealth and power do not altogether lie in solid ships and effective guns," he wrote. "In the West the interests of the state and those of commerce flourish together. . . . National defense cannot function without money, and money for the military will not accumulate without commerce. The reason why Westerners are ready to pounce like tigers on the rest of the world and why they bully China is also due to commerce."[15]

That Sun never received a reply from Li may have helped set him on his subsequent anti-dynastic course.[16] Early on, he lost all faith in the dynasty's ability to restore China to "a position of strength and honor among the nations of the world,"[17] and began to view the Manchus not only as unrepresentative of the country's Han majority but also as hopelessly racked by incompetence and corruption.

As Sun became increasingly outspoken, he risked increasing danger of arrest even outside China. Indeed, in 1896, while he was visiting London to do research in the reading room of the British Museum, Qing agents managed to seize him and then detain him in the Chinese legation. "I well knew the fate that would befall me—first having my ankles crushed in a vi[s]e and broken by a hammer, my eyelids cut off, and, finally, be chopped to small fragments, so that none could claim my mortal remains."[18]

Only after James Cantlie launched a vigorous press campaign on his behalf was Sun finally released. His melodramatic account, "Kidnapped in London," added greatly to his revolutionary aura and the growing image of him as a national hero determined not only to overthrow the Qing but to establish a new-style republican government. But as Cantlie put it, Sun had to start the process of overthrow and rejuvenation "from complete darkness," because within China at the time "there were not present even the very elements which go to form chaos."[19]

If the challenge of reinventing China politically was daunting, Sun was a tenacious man. "The future of China is like building a railroad," he argued in the pragmatic, technocratic language of the self-strengtheners, who had actually tried to bring railroads to China.

"Thus if we were now building a railroad would we use the first locomotive ever invented or today's improved and most efficient model?"[20]
Sun wanted to sweep China's political slate clean and start over with
the latest, and most successfully road-tested, new governmental model:
a republic.

Newspaper Headline in Denver

When the rebellion that would finally topple the Qing erupted in October 1911, Sun, who had been abroad for a decade and a half, was on
yet another fund-raising trip to the United States and Canada. "I found
him at a fourth-rate hotel, a kind of lodging-house for working men,
occupying a bare and miserable little room. His dress was modest and
his luggage scanty," recalled J. Ellis Baker, a writer, who met up with
Sun in Victoria, British Columbia. "At last I told him, 'With a reward
[put up by the Qing Dynasty] of 100,000 [British pounds] on your
head, you should not go alone through the deserted streets of a strange
town.'" Sun reacted only with "a quiet smile which was half sad and
half humorous."[21]

It was while on his way to breakfast one morning some days later in
Denver, Colorado, that Sun happened on a local newspaper bearing the
headline "Wuchang Occupied by Revolutionists."[22] Since he had already been involved in several unsuccessful military insurrections himself, this was a tantalizing shard of news. But the article was very short,
and only when he reached St. Louis was he able to learn more about
what had actually happened: a series of provincial uprisings had broken out, the Qing Dynasty was collapsing, and a republic was being
established. As it turned out, the dynasty had collapsed from within in
a curiously anticlimactic way. Rather than being overthrown by an insurrectionary force, regional support for it had just melted away. As
the American minister in Beijing, William Calhoun, wrote to the U.S.
secretary of state, Philander Knox, "The revolution was comparatively
easy; it had no opposition; but now the great strain, the great test of the
[republican] movement has come."[23]

As Sun was heading home via London—where he sought diplomatic
recognition and financial support—he received a telegram announcing
the most stunning news of all: he was being asked to become the first

provisional president of a new Chinese Republic. He arrived back in Hong Kong, where for the first time in sixteen years he did not have a price on his head, and assumed office on January 1, 1912. The U.S. consul general in Canton called him "the one honest and patriotic administrator in China" and urged Washington to treat Sun politely.[24]

Alas, Sun's presidential tenure, which ended up being painfully short, was over before the State Department had much chance even to react. The president of China's first republic found himself out of power again in a mere forty-five days after taking office. Quickly recognizing the hopeless weakness of his power base, Sun chose not to become a toothless figurehead, instead relinquishing the reins of government to the more powerful Yuan Shikai, a regional commander who controlled much of what was left of China's military and was also premier of the new National Assembly established by the dynasty before it fell.

As inexplicable as some supporters found Sun's sudden abdication at the very moment of his putative triumph, the move showed him to be a realist when it came to assessing his own strengths and weaknesses. Yuan Shikai had a strong northern power base, while Sun's southern support was weaker and far removed from the center of national power in Beijing. This left him in a position of ultimate vulnerability in and around the capital.[25] In addition, while Sun had been a tireless roving ambassador, a skilled fund-raiser, and an able popularizer of republicanism, he had not been home for more than a decade and a half, nor had he had much experience running a major political organization. Since presiding over an upstart government while trying to keep the country from falling apart was going to be an almost impossible task, stepping aside when he did spared Sun the risk of an embarrassing failure. It also gave him a chance to organize the Guomindang (国民党), or Nationalist Party, which was officially established on August 25, 1912, and would serve as the vehicle for his political career until his death.

The Anti-Imperialist

Three days after his resignation, Sun held a ceremony at Purple Mountain in Nanjing at which he genuflected before the tomb of the Ming Dynasty's founder and celebrated China's liberation from the "Tartar (Manchu) savages." Addressing the long-departed emperor as "a holy inspiration," he gave a nationalistic speech charged with racial invective against foreign interlopers, describing his people as having "wept in the bitterness of their hearts" over their country's foreign occupation. Today, he proclaimed optimistically, our "sorrow is turned to joy. Your people have come here today to inform your majesty of the final victory."[26]

Other than the fall of the dynasty, however, there was little to celebrate. As China quickly plunged ever deeper into chaos under Yuan Shikai, Sun found himself again in Japanese exile and in opposition. Briefly he allowed himself to nurture hopes that the Chinese and Japanese might unite against the West in a pan-Asian brotherhood. However, when the Japanese issued their Twenty-One Demands in 1915, paving the way for their occupation of the old German concession in Shandong Province and for new claims in Manchuria and other parts of China, Sun's dream began to look dangerously naive. And when, in 1919, Allied victors agreed at the Paris Peace Conference to give Germany's concessions to Japan, the dream became positively ludicrous. For nationalists such as Sun, it was agonizing to accept how little had actually changed since 1895, when the British vice-consul in Canton had brazenly written, "It appears indeed that the Chinese Government, though practically unarmed and helpless against a serious foreign foe, is strong enough to keep peace at home—to keep the great Chinese cow steady while foreigners extract the milk."[27]

"Formerly, the battle-cry of the revolution was the overthrow of the Manchu Dynasty," Sun would write. Now he was ready to raise a new battle cry. "Henceforth, it will be the overthrow of the intervention of foreign imperialism in China."[28] It was, as he saw it, imperialism that had imposed a backward and poverty-stricken state on China. And because the country was poor, it was weak and thus unable to defend itself against further foreign exploitation, which only made it weaker and poorer. The vicious circle in which his countrymen found themselves caught began and ended with imperialism.

Political Revolutionary, Cultural Conservative

Although Sun respected much about the West and Japan and although he hoped to see China transformed into a Western-style republic, he was not tempted to borrow other forms of Western culture and values. In his early years he had viewed traditional family and clan relationships as rivals to the kind of nationalism needed to forge a new and unified China. Later in his life, however, he became concerned that westernization might undermine social cohesion at precisely the moment when it was most needed. Ultimately, like so many other reformers had late in their lives, Sun became a proponent of protecting China as a traditional culture and the Chinese people as a race. He had hoped that with the end of the alien Manchu Dynasty, the country would achieve a new state of equipoise. But as the situation continued to unravel, he, too, found himself turning to those very reserves of traditional culture and social structure for support, even while his peers were attacking them as obstructions to the modernization process. "From my standpoint," he said, "the structural relationship between Chinese citizens and the state begins with the family, extends to the clan, and only afterward the nation."[29] The Qing Dynasty may have inflicted racial humiliation on Han Chinese by forcing them to submit to minority Manchu rule, but revolting against it did not mean that Confucianism could not continue to provide an essential field of cultural gravity for Han Chinese as they sought to rejuvenate their country.

Sun's conservatism would soon put him at odds with the New Culture Movement, which exploded onto the streets on May 4, 1919, as China's rebellious intelligentsia protested against both Japanese imperialism and the strictures of traditional culture. Not much of an intellectual himself, Sun was almost contemptuous of their lack of concern for the kind of organization and discipline he had come to view as essential in reunifying and strengthening China. In fact, after a meeting with some Tsinghua University students just before his death, he chided them for failing to appreciate the need for national discipline. "They think the goal of revolution is to seek equality and freedom," he was reported to have said. "They themselves want freedom. [But] they don't follow orders and don't accept limits set by the party."[30]

The Three People's Principles

When Sun Yat-sen died in 1925 at fifty-eight, he left behind some twenty-six hundred pages of writings, autobiographical accounts,

Punahou School, Sun Yat-sen's school in Honolulu

Sun Yat-sen with friends in Hong Kong, 1890

Yuan Shikai, president of the
Republic of China, 1915

Sun Yat-sen at the Ming Dynasty founder's tomb in Nanjing, 1912

speeches, letters, and telegrams. But his most substantial work was *san-min zhuyi* (三民主义), "the three isms of the people," which would officially come to be known as the Three People's Principles. He had been working on this compendium of ideas since 1905, when he gave a speech in Tokyo at the founding of his anti-Manchu Revolutionary Alliance (which ultimately evolved into the Nationalist Party). With these ideas, he sought to lay out his vision of China's future political development. Unfortunately, in 1922, during an armed insurrection in the city of Canton, where Sun then lived, troops bombarded his beloved library, destroying the only draft he had of the document. "My notes and manuscripts, which represented the mental labor of years and hundreds of foreign books, which I had collected for reference, were all destroyed by fire," he wrote. "It was a distressing loss."[31]

The version of these principles that was finally passed on to posterity had to be extracted from notes taken at a series of lectures he delivered extemporaneously in 1924 at Canton Higher Normal School before several thousand students and officials. He hoped that his effort to sum up the importance of nationalism, of giving rights to the people and overseeing their welfare during the ongoing revolution, would serve as a rallying cry for demoralized Chinese who had lived "under the political domination of the West for a century."[32]

Soon after Sun finished these lectures, he fell gravely ill and died, and the version finally cobbled together by acolytes is often rambling, repetitive, and lacking in elegance. Nonetheless, it came to serve as the ur-text for the Nationalist Party's "revolution," and as the foundational document for Chiang Kai-shek's subsequent rule on both the Chinese mainland and later Taiwan.

Principle #1: Nationalism

Sun described his principles as guidelines for "saving the nation" through the acquisition of a new nationalist strength, an idea that would be articulated in myriad forms by many others in the decades to come. In the first six of his sixteen lectures, he focused on the need for the birth of a genuine spirit of nationalism, "that precious possession which enables a state to aspire to progress and a nation to perpetuate its existence." Sun was blunt: "If we want to save China, we must first find a way to revive our nationalism."[33]

In discussing nationalism, Sun used a term that connoted ethnicity, *minzu zhuyi* (民族主义), "the ism of race," instead of the more political *guojia zhuyi* (国家主义), "the ism of the nation-state." His choice of terminology suggested that for him—and for many other Chinese of the era—the idea of "China" had as much to do with protecting the Chinese people as a race and culture as it did with preserving the sovereign territory of the country. Indeed, Sun did imagine the country's struggle against imperialism as a form of resistance against the threat of *miezhong* (灭种), "racial extinction," in which the "white" race would triumph over and obliterate the "yellow" race.[34]

If Sun's first lectures were a nationalist call to arms, they also represented a kind of a lament. Looking back longingly on the days when a confident Chinese emperor could tell a British envoy that his country had no need for things Western, Sun explained, "Before China was subjugated, she had a very cultured people and a powerful state. She called herself the 'majestic nation,' [and] thought that she was situated in the center of the world and so named herself the 'Central Kingdom.'"[35] However, he continued, now "our old national spirit is asleep. We must awaken it! Then, our nationalism will begin to revive. [Only] when our nationalism is revived, can we go a step further and study how to restore our national standing."[36]

Using one of his most famous metaphors, he explained, "Despite four hundred million people gathered in one China, we are, in fact, but a sheet of loose sand [*yipan sansha*, 一盘散沙]. We are the poorest and weakest state in the world, occupying the lowest position in international affairs; the rest of mankind is the carving knife and the serving dish, while we are the fish and meat. Our position is now extremely perilous. If we do not earnestly promote nationalism and weld together our four hundred millions into a strong nation, we face a tragedy—the loss of our country and the destruction of our race."[37]

Drawing on his medical training, he compared the process of understanding China's weakness to "diagnosing a sick man."[38] Unless Chinese could be goaded into actively seeking a cure for their illness, he warned, they would continue to "live in a stupor and die in a dream."[39] To those who rationalized China's plight by pointing out that while the great powers had established outright colonies throughout the rest of the world, in China they had taken only a few small concessions in coastal treaty ports, Sun argued that such semi-imperialism was actually more corrosive than outright colonization. In fact, by World War I there were forty-eight such ports, where foreigners had the right to live and work under the protection of foreign law, creating a series of foreign mini-empires within China.[40] "The people of the nation still think we are only a semi-colony and comfort themselves with this term," said Sun disdainfully. "But in reality we are being crushed by the economic strength of the Powers to a greater degree than if we were a full colony. . . . We are not slaves of one country but of all."[41]

Sun viewed the "unequal treaties," a term that he himself first popularized,[42] as the main source of China's enslavement, which he saw as growing out of two main "disasters": political oppression that left Chinese "unsure whether we can live from one morning to another,"[43] and "foreign economic domination" that was "worse than millions of soldiers ready to kill us."[44]

These treaties were, he said just a year before he died, "detrimental to China's sovereignty" and "ought to be abolished so as to leave the way open for new treaties in the spirit of bilateral equality and mutual respect for sovereignty."[45]

Principle # 2: The Rights of the People

The second of Sun's principles, laid out in March 1924, centered on the idea of *minquan* (民权), "the rights of the people." Sun fancied himself a supporter of democracy, at least in theory. In his talks, he began by saying, "All of you who have come here today to support my revolution are naturally believers in democracy."[46] He continued, "If we want China to be strong and our revolution to be effective, we must espouse the cause of democracy."[47] But for him, democracy was not so much an end, as a means to an end, the traditional end of all self-strengtheners: wealth and power. In fact, by the time his six lectures on the rights of the people were over, he had piled up so many caveats about the downside of future democracy that rights and liberties began to sound quite dangerous for China. "The aims of the Chinese Revolution are different from the aims in foreign revolutions," he warned darkly, "and the methods we must use must also be different."[48]

Perhaps fearing that some might interpret all his caveats as suggesting that the Chinese people were inherently incapable of democracy, he began rationalizing, saying that even abroad "an excess of liberty led to many evil consequences," compelling certain Western scholars to admit that sometimes "liberty must be put within boundaries."[49]

In truth, Sun had nowhere near as much ardor for his second principle as for his first, supporting the idea of civil rights, at least in theory, largely because he fancied himself a modern man, and because, like Liang Qichao, he hoped that adopting some forms of democratic rights might help release the kind of energy and drive that China needed to compete in the modernizing world. But his conception of rights was not of the kind of natural or God-given rights that Enlightenment thinkers viewed as the birthright of all human beings.[50] When Sun got down to his rather muddled discussion of rights and democracy, whatever veneration he might once have had for them in theory was easily eclipsed by worries that in a post-Qing power vacuum, they would only lead to more instability, weakness, and foreign intervention in practice.

In the end, he came to believe that Westerners prized their rights and freedom because, after centuries of royal repression, they had had to struggle to possess them. But he saw the Chinese experience in a different light. However suffocating the traditional Confucian order might have been, state intrusion into society had historically been so minimal that his countrymen had ended up with "too much liberty without any unity."[51] What they now needed was not so much more liberty, but rather more "discipline."[52] Like so many other Chinese reformers and even revolutionaries, when push came to shove, Sun came down on the side of order, not the rights of the people. China's basic challenge was not to be met by "merely copying the West," but by ensuring the overall liberty and independence of the country collectively.[53] Otherwise the Chinese people would remain nothing but his eponymous "sheet of loose sand." A strong state was to be the binding agent. "If we add cement to the sand, it forms a rock, a solid body. Once transformed into rock, this body is quite solid and the sand has no freedom."[54]

And, he was quick to add, "The individual should not have too much liberty, but the nation should have complete liberty," he proclaimed. "When the nation can act freely, then China may be called strong. To make the nation free, we must each sacrifice our personal freedom. . . .[55] If we want to restore China's liberty, we must unite ourselves into one unshakeable body and must use revolutionary methods to weld our state into firm unity. Without revolutionary principles, we shall never succeed. Our revolutionary principles are our cement."[56]

Despite the fact that Sun was China's earliest westernized leader, he was hardly a democrat.[57] In his emphasis on a new and powerful form of governance capable of making the country prosperous, strong, and respected, Sun cemented the mold for almost a century of future political orthodoxy.

Principle #3: The Livelihood of the People

In his last four lectures, given during August 1924, Sun outlined his third principle, *minsheng zhuyi* (民生主义), "the people's livelihood." He opened by acknowledging that it was "a worn phrase" that has "not held much meaning for us."[58] And, truth be told, his lectures did little to clarify the problem of "the life of the masses," not to mention solving the problem of their backwardness and penury.[59] Although he expressed interest in some sort of "equalization" of land ownership and financial resources in society, he also spent an inordinate amount of time during these lectures seeking to distance himself from both socialism and Marxism. As he bluntly said, "The facts of Western history, in the seventy-odd years since Marx, have directly contradicted his theory."[60]

Sun was, after all, an inveterate gradualist who eschewed social upheaval, much less class warfare. "Society progresses . . . through the adjustment of major economic interests rather than through the clash of interests," he declared. "Class war is not the cause of social progress, it is a disease developed in the course of social progress."[61]

What Sun seemed to be reaching for in his third principle was some expression of sympathy for the plight of ordinary Chinese. He wanted to signal that in his version of republican revolution the Nationalist Party would strive to "equalize" things through taxation and some kind of a government land buy-back program that would enable ordinary people, especially peasants, to share in the benefits of development in a more equitable fashion.[62] It was a noble idea that had very little prospect of then being implemented.

Political Tutelage

While theoretically Sun supported democracy, he believed that China's best immediate hope was to delay putting it fully into practice by adopting a three-stage program of revolutionary transformation.[63] The first was to be dedicated to the dismantling of old political structures. Echoing Liang Qichao's slogan "Without destruction there can be no construction," Sun, too, saw the necessity of "a period of destruction" during which a post–Qing Dynasty government would operate under martial law to "eradicate the corruption" of the past. The second was to be a period of "political tutelage," when a provisional constitution would be promulgated, but a strong "transitional" government would rule. (Sun described these first two stages as complementing each other "like the legs of a man or the two wings of a bird.") The final stage would be the implementation of full "constitutional government," which would happen only "after the attainment of political stability throughout the country."[64]

In Sun's view, the Chinese people were simply not ready for full emancipation into a European-style political world complete with individual freedoms and rights. As he candidly noted in a 1920 speech, "China's enslavement has already been in effect for several thousand years. Thus, in Republican China, although it is nine years old, the common people still do not know how to be their own masters. Today, we have no choice. We must use forceful methods to make them their own masters."[65]

If Sun was not a particularly deep thinker, he was at least a determined man of action, and his Three People's Principles were his effort to sketch a plan for a comprehensive new kind of leadership and government that might be able to pull China out of the backwardness, disunity, and foreign exploitation into which it had fallen. Despite Sun's deceptively westernized surface, his prescriptions centered on a strong professional leadership and a well-organized political party that could run the country with a firm hand; this did not leave much room for popular elections, idealistic student demonstrators, individualistic freethinkers, or populist organizers. "In many things," he said, "we have to trust experts and we should not set limitations upon them."[66]

In one of his lectures, Sun asked his audience to think of the state as a "great automobile" and its political leaders as "chauffeurs and mechanics" who were "essential if we use automobiles."[67] By his logic, citizens should welcome being able to look upon all the officers of the government, from president and premier down to heads of departments, as specially trained "chauffeurs" into whose hands they "should be willing to put the sovereignty of the state." What is more, said Sun, "we must not limit their movements, but give them freedom of action," for only then can a state "progress with rapid strides."[68]

Even while Sun insisted that "the people are the owners and they must be sovereign," the logic of his automotive metaphor suggested that they should not immediately be given the prerogative to actually decide how and where their chauffeurs would drive them. In the end, despite his populist-sounding rhetoric, Sun was an elitist. He wanted an effective but almost corporate-style professional leadership guided by a strong executive capable of getting things done. Chauffeurs who knew how to drive should be left alone to do their job.

Comrade Lenin Comes Courting

It was hardly surprising that with the success of the Russian Revolution, V. I. Lenin's new theories on party building soon caught the eye of Sun, who by the 1920s had come to admire the discipline with which the Communist Party in Russia was building up both its political apparatus and the Red Army.[69] At the same time, Sun had been vexed over why, since its early days as the Revolutionary Alliance in Japan, his own Nationalist Party had remained so disorganized and weak. His remedy was to formally adopt a Leninist, "democratic centralist" form of organization for the Nationalist Party, a structure built on strong leadership, party discipline, and orthodox, centralized messaging, qualities that it retained even during the most bitter decades of rivalry with the Chinese Communist Party (CCP) later on.[70] As Sun observed, the Russian Revolution had been "victorious because the entire party, assisted by the army, took part in the struggle. We must learn from Russia its methods, its organization [and] its way of training party members; only then can we hope for victory."[71]

Besides party organization, Sun had another reason to heed Lenin's new ideas.[72] In his 1916 tract "Imperialism, the Highest Stage of Capitalism," Lenin had posited that the anticolonial and anti-imperialist struggles in Asia were actually a critical part of the larger global revolution against capitalism described by Karl Marx himself.[73] Lenin had masterfully linked the interests of the proletariat in Europe with the "oppressed" peoples of Asia, allowing the latter to feel that they were now part of an irresistible new movement of world revolution in which they could serve as the vanguard of a global anti-imperialist struggle in their own benighted lands. Lenin's theories on imperialism managed to limn a grand and cathartic dream in which even the "sick man of Asia," China, was promised a critical role in changing the world.

Such an idea was deeply reassuring to Chinese nationalists because it allowed them, as citizens of a "semi-colonized" country, to feel that they were now part of a larger historical narrative of heroic worldwide struggle. Given this newly assigned role, Sun even allowed himself to imagine that the Chinese revolution might actually end up being "the preliminary announcement of the death-sentence for European imperialism."[74] What is more, after his repeated efforts to gain support from the leaders of other great powers had been ignored, in 1919 the new government in Russia began sending numerous official emissaries to China to meet with Sun. One of these was their deputy commissar for foreign affairs, Lev Karakhan, who, without demands for compensation, volunteered to relinquish all the privileges and claims that czarist Russia had earlier extracted from the Qing Dynasty. These concessions got Sun's attention. "The only country that shows any signs of helping us is the Soviet government of Russia," he effused.[75]

At the same time, Russia's attentions also helped interest Sun in exploring a Soviet-brokered "United Front" between his Nationalist

Party and the Chinese Communist Party, which had been generously supported by Comintern (Communist International) agents and funds, and founded in Shanghai in 1921. Although leaders in both the Nationalist and Communist parties were in a fierce competition, they could agree that China's two most immediate enemies were imperialist powers and the regional warlords who were carving the country up into feudatories. So, concludes Sun, why not come together in a Soviet-brokered anti-imperialist alliance?[76]

Sun was an opportunist, but his anti-Communist biases still made him a tough bargainer with both the Russians and the Chinese Communists. He would accept almost any ally in his struggle against foreign exploitation and the forces of national disunity, but he would not accept a radical social program or outright Communist leadership. If there was going to be a United Front, he was going to be boss. As Communist Party founder Chen Duxiu noted, "He would allow the Chinese Communist Party to enter the Nationalist Party only on the condition that they would submit to the *Nationalist Party* and recognize no party outside of it."[77] "Because there do not exist here the conditions for a successful establishment of either Communism or Sovietism," what Sun disparaged as "the Communistic order" was not to be introduced into China.[78]

The first United Front between the Nationalist and Communist parties was finally effected, and a joint statement was issued in Shanghai on January 26, 1923, by Sun Yat-sen and visiting Soviet diplomat Adolph Joffe. Even Mao Zedong and Chen Duxiu incongruously became active members of the Nationalist Party through this marriage of convenience.[79] "The great cause of revolution is no easy matter," wrote Mao. "The only solution is to call upon . . . [all] who suffer under a common oppression and to establish a closely knit united front. It is only then that this revolution will succeed."[80] And the United Front did bring a significant amount of Russian economic and military aid to Sun's fledgling movement, including the two million gold Russian rubles delivered in March 1923 "to work for the unification and national independence of China."[81] As part of this new alliance, Sun even sent his lieutenant, Chiang Kai-shek, to Moscow for military training prior to setting up the Whampoa Military Academy near Canton, which accepted cadets from both the Nationalist and Communist parties.[82]

Despite the fact that Sun was not tempted personally or ideologically by communism, his sensitivity to China's weakness helped him openly admire what Lenin had accomplished in Russia. Indeed, shortly after Lenin's death, and just before his own, Sun extolled the Russian leader in a speech: "You, Lenin, are exceptional!" he said. "You not only speak and teach, you convert your words to reality."[83]

Legacies of China's Savior

Sun Yat-sen managed to turn a rather weak hand into one that at least allowed him to be in the game during the chaotic years of the first quarter of the twentieth century. From his regional base in Canton, his reputation as someone engaged in insurrectionary activity against the Qing and his considerable talents at raising funds among the overseas Chinese community for a republic combined to create an aura of someone able to operate both inside and outside China. That, fired by his indignation at the disrespectful way in which the great powers had treated China, his personal tenacity, his Christian sense of righteousness, and his political messianism, helped him become a formidable self-assigned savior of China. (On his deathbed, he is reported to have said, "Just as Christ was sent by God to the world, so also did God send me.")[84] He could be grandiose about his own historical self-importance, sometimes even fatuous, but he was a relentless fighter for the restoration of Chinese greatness. In taking up this challenge, he was one of the first Chinese to appreciate the galvanic qualities of nationalism. But perhaps his most unique characteristic was his ability to penetrate the membrane that still so divided China and the West during these early years.

However, in the last analysis, Sun was neither a profound thinker, a great statesman, nor an elegant writer. His most substantial contribution before his death was the short-lived United Front between the Nationalist and Communist parties, which ended up being a dubious distinction. For much of the Communist era, scholars tended to look back on Sun as one more unsuccessful, reform-minded leader, and his

Three People's Principles as just another of modern China's many dead-end political experiments. As one biographer wrote: "If Sun Yat-sen had one consistent talent, it was for failure."[85]

Perhaps. But at the same time, Sun handed down an important legacy to future generations. When few others could imagine China without its ancient imperial system of government, Sun was already boldly calling for its overthrow. While others were still fretting about how to maintain the old order, Sun was already embracing nationalism and transforming this still nascent political force into one of the most elemental building blocks of China's future. While many colleagues fell into despair, his tireless articulation of his own yearning to see his country once again unified, wealthy, powerful, and respected played an important role in injecting almost every subsequent political discussion with these themes.

When he died in 1925, he had become so identified as the face of China's republican revolution that mass memorial services honoring him took place all over the country. And—for better or worse—his conviction that Chinese needed a protracted period of firm, authoritarian political tutelage before democracy could be risked has become the template for reform ever since. As the Deng Xiaoping era of "reform and opening up" began in the late 1970s, Sun, as the last great unifier, became a handy rallying point for both a new "united front" within China and efforts to reunify Hong Kong, Macau, and Taiwan with the mainland. It was hardly surprising, then, that during key holidays the Communist Party began prominently displaying enormous portraits of Sun in Tiananmen Square as "a pioneer of the revolution."[86] In fact, the current period of "authoritarian capitalism" borrows a leaf directly from Sun's prescriptions for a protracted period of "political tutelage" while the nation became wealthier and stronger.

Perhaps the most paradoxical contribution of Sun's Three People's Principles was their vagueness and lack of rigor. On one hand, this murkiness caused many to dismiss them. On the other hand, precisely because of their fuzziness, they invited other political leaders, factions, and parties to read into them what they wished, thereby imbuing them with a strangely unifying effect.

Finally, Sun's Three People's Principles proved to have one other important virtue: even during the most undemocratic times in China,

Sun Yat-sen in 1922

they kept an official political pathway open for the promise of democracy sometime in China's future. The period of tutelage might take a century rather than a few years to complete as Sun had originally imagined, but the fact that he had clearly set forth constitutionalism, and self-government, democracy, and republicanism as final goals made them acceptable aspirations for all Chinese thereafter.

CHAPTER 7

New Youth（新青年）

CHEN DUXIU（陈独秀）

On May 27, 1942, while China was still locked in brutal combat with Japan's occupying armies, a sixty-three-year-old scholar named Chen Duxiu passed away virtually unnoticed in mountainous Sichuan Province, in the small village of Jiangjin, about fifty miles from the Nationalist Government's wartime capital, Chongqing. A studious and excitable man, he had doggedly been doing linguistic research on the classical Chinese language, hoping to finish an etymological dictionary on the roots of ancient Chinese characters and working on a system for Romanizing the modern spoken language.[1] But living in isolation and penury while struggling with chronic heart disease had slowed his research.

When Chen Duxiu died, a few old friends and relatives paid his modest funeral expenses, with even the Nationalist Party leader, Chiang Kai-shek, making a contribution.[2] But he was buried with little ceremony in a simple grave at the foot of Ding Hill outside the west gate of the small town to which he had been exiled, his tombstone etched only with: "Mr. Chen Duxiu's grave."[3]

As a young man, Chen had been one of his country's foremost writers, editors, teachers, and revolutionaries, his most lasting contribution being the founding of the Chinese Communist Party in 1921. When he died, however, the CCP had nothing to say about his passing.[4] Although he had labored long and hard to help shape his country's destiny and had gained enormous fame as a public intellectual, his life ended in obscurity.

Chen Duxiu circa 1900

The surviving photographs of Chen are mostly of his younger self, showing a pensive young man with a moon-shaped face and receding hairline who was given to wearing the kind of round, wire-framed glasses that were popular among the intelligentsia of the time. Although he sometimes dressed in Western suits and ties, he was also fond of traditional scholar's gowns that lent him a sober Confucian air. If his sartorial habits hinted at a hybrid cultural makeup, they also bespoke the great historical divide that both Chen and China were then seeking to bridge. Though he would be celebrated as a rebel, as with Liang Qichao, the past would continue to exert a powerful gravitational pull, right up to his last days. But what most distinguished Chen's long political struggle was the tenacity with which he kept going, even as firm ground repeatedly gave way beneath his feet, leading him to change position and course again and again. Like so many reformers preceding him, Chen was driven by a relentless need to answer the same basic questions: Why had China declined so precipitously in the face of the Western challenge? Why did it remain in such a weakened state? And how might it restore itself to international standing in the future?

Rebel with a Cause

Chen was born in 1879 into a family of scholar-officials in the Anhui Province town of Anqing. His father, who had passed the lowest level of the imperial examination system, died several months after he was born,[5] leaving him in the care of a strict, traditionalist, opium-smoking grandfather, who tutored Chen from age six in the classics.[6] He was an excellent student, but his taciturn grandfather, whom the fearful children of the house called "Old White Beard,"[7] was never satisfied with the young boy's progress, and regularly insulted and beat him, instilling within him a "hot temper"[8] and a rebellious hostility toward such authoritarian treatment that lasted his whole life.[9]

In 1889, Chen's grandfather died and he was returned to the care of his mother and older brother. They continued to encourage his classical studies, and in 1896 he passed the county-level exams with the highest score in the district. A year later, an arranged marriage turned him implacably against the traditional system of betrothal. By then he had already started reading the works of Kang Youwei and Liang Qichao, and their new ideas fueled his growing iconoclasm. "These days our generation has started to learn a little something of the world," Chen would write. "The source was Kang Youwei and Liang Qichao, who gave us this gift of knowledge."[10] What Chen took from them was the liberating proposition that to study Western learning did not mean you were "a slave to the foreign devil."[11]

In 1897 Chen journeyed to Nanjing via steamboat and donkey to sit for the provincial-level examinations, spending nine days in a filthy hall where students had to write, sleep, cook, and defecate (in the hallways)—and where Chen failed the exam.[12] The experience so disgusted him that he decided to have nothing more to do with the whole system. The imperial examinations were, he said, "like a circus of monkeys and bears, repeated every so many years."[13] Chen was particularly repelled by one fellow candidate who, probably in the throes of a nervous breakdown, stalked the examination hall buck naked "except for a pair of broken shoes on his feet and a big pig-tail coiled on his head. In his hand he grasped an examination. While he walked back and forth . . . both his large head and small member were wagging to and fro," remembered Chen. "As he went, he read his favorite 'eight-legged essay' out loud in a strange long drawn-out voice. When he came to his favorite place, he would emphatically give his thigh a powerful slap, point his thumb upward and exclaim: 'Great! This time I will make it!' "[14]

For Chen, such displays were grotesque symbols of the absurdity that he had begun to associate with unquestioning veneration of Chinese traditionalism. "I could not take my eyes off him," Chen later wrote in the beginnings of a never-finished autobiography that he submitted for publication at a journal edited by Lin Yutang.[15] "As I watched, I fell to thinking about the whole strange business of the examination system, and then I began to think about how much my country and its people would suffer once these brutes achieved positions of power. Finally, I began to doubt the whole system of selecting talent through examination."[16]

The Empress Dowager would soon abolish the civil service exams, but Chen's experience in that Nanjing examination hall had pushed him beyond a tipping point: "I switched my allegiance from the examination system to the reformist party of Kang Youwei and Liang Qichao . . . and so . . . decided the course of my life for the next dozen years."[17]

There was another factor that played into Chen's life-changing decision: China's ignominious defeat by Japan in 1895. Chen came to believe that before the war he had been living in a cocoon, ignorant of all the threats facing his nation, even of the concept of China as a nation. "I was home studying, from day to day, all I knew was sleeping and eating. Thus, how could I know what sort of a thing a nation was, and what it had to do with me?" he wrote. But then he heard that "there existed some 'nation of Japan,' which had defeated our China," and from that humiliating moment onward Chen became increasingly aware of a nationalist impulse building within him.[18]

In 1902, shortly after Cixi signed the degrading treaty written by the victorious Allied eight-nation army as punishment for supporting the Boxer movement, Chen left to study in Japan. This was the decade when Chinese intellectual and political avant-garde figures were all converging on their island neighbor to study the Meiji model and first becoming familiar with the fast-changing world outside the Central Kingdom. Chen promptly set about organizing one of the most overtly revolutionary organizations among overseas Chinese students, and it wasn't long before he began offending his Japanese hosts. After forcibly cutting off the queue from the pate of a Qing Dynasty government agent and triumphantly hanging it up in the student union, he was deported.[19]

These formative years coincided with the unraveling of China's last dynasty. Like Sun Yat-sen, Chen at first blamed the hapless Manchus for the empire's enfeebled state, even going so far as to briefly join an anti-Qing assassination squad. But it soon became evident to him that China's problems went far deeper than the inept Manchu elite. The problem was the Chinese people themselves. "The spirit of our people is not filled with a single aggressive and energetic thought; hence the power of resistance cannot take root," he would later complain.[20]

The Patriot

When not in Japan, Chen spent the first decade of the twentieth century back in his native Anhui Province, teaching school, organizing youth groups, and founding *Anhui Common Speech Journal*, one of the new-style vernacular journals then proliferating among progressive reformers trying to modernize the Chinese language itself. Like so many other members of his transitional generation, he came to be deeply influenced by social Darwinist ideas made popular by Yan Fu and Liang Qichao, which helped him view China as engaged in a life-and-death struggle with other predatory nations in a highly competitive new world, whether other Chinese chose to recognize it or not. If China could not adapt, and quickly, it would perish. His analysis of China's weakness began with a harsh critique of the structure of the traditional Confucian family. Chinese, he wrote, "care about their family and do not care about their nation"; this deprived them of a critical wellspring for patriotism, which Chen viewed as the most basic building block of building a nation that could defend itself.[21]

To start remedying this lacuna, in May 1903 Chen helped found the Anhui Patriotic Society. "Because the foreign calamity is daily growing worse," read its constitution, which Chen helped write, "the society seeks to unite the masses into an organization that will develop patriotic thought and stir up a martial spirit, so people will grab their weapons to protect their country and restore our basic national sovereignty."[22] In an emotional speech at its founding, just as the Qing Dynasty was on the verge of yielding to new czarist Russian demands in Manchuria, Chen warned, "If our government allows this treaty, every nation will moisten its lips and help itself to a part of China," so in the end the country would not possess "one foot or inch of clean land."[23]

Unlike the self-strengtheners, Chen contended that what China now needed was not a technological or material fix but a "spiritual" one. "We must get rid of our usual selfish opinions and strive to uphold the goal of patriotism and union with the masses," he told the society.[24] He hoped that a new spirit would enable Chinese to "take the responsibility of struggling to the death to protect our land."[25] But whereas the "foreigners' character is such that they will struggle for glory or against insult, lightly regarding matters of life and death," Chinese "do not know how to struggle for glory or against insults, [but instead] live dishonorably in the world, willingly receiving the extermination of their country and their own enslavement."[26]

In a 1904 essay, "On Nations," Chen described how the world was dividing into two kinds of states. "Those in which all people understand *protecting the nation*, are strong," he said. And "those in which all people do not know *protecting the nation*, are weak."[27] China, he believed, was in the latter camp, and as traditional culture taught subservience before one's emperor and obedience to one's father, there was little room for radical reappraisal. The Chinese were crippled by fatalism, said Chen, and it left them "knowing how to listen to the decree of Heaven, [but] not knowing how to exert the strength of people."[28] Chen's was a damning indictment, and, because he risked appearing disloyal to his own country and culture, it came with substantial risks.

New Youth

As Chen shuttled between Anhui and Japan in the decade leading up to the 1911 revolution, it was still possible to imagine, just as Sun Yat-sen had, that once the Qing Dynasty was gone, China's situation might improve. But when the dynasty finally did fall, and things rapidly degenerated into warlordism and dictatorship, Chen's darkest fears seemed realized. "A declining nation behaves like a slave, terrified by everything," he wrote despairingly in 1914. Worrying that even with a new republican government, China might end up as a slave society, he added, "Perhaps one will say: a loathsome nation is better than no nation. I, however, say: with the disaster of oppressing the people, a loathsome nation is worse than no nation."[29]

The acerbic essayist Lu Xun, born just a couple years after Chen, was even more disparaging about China's ill-fated republican experiment. "John Stuart Mill said that tyranny makes people cynical," he wrote with characteristic acidity. "He didn't realize that there would be republics to make them silent."[30] Chen himself even contemplated giving up his "heaven-ascending ambitions" and political activism in the face of "an awareness of the hopelessness of our catching up with European and American civilizations."[31]

But by 1915 a rising tide of intellectual ferment and a new incipient youth movement had begun to reenergize cultural and intellectual circles, propelling Chen into the most active and constructive period of his life as well as into one of the most vibrant interludes of modern Chinese history. During these heady years, Chen threw himself into the project of galvanizing China for *zidong* (自动), "action." But he also continued the search for a new Chinese self-consciousness that had begun with Liang Qichao's call for a "new citizen." Both men sensed that something intangible but elemental was missing in the Chinese people's spirit, though neither knew quite how to describe it, much less awaken it. However, both came to believe that the process of "awakening" would have to reach into the very heart of the country's Confucian cultural tradition, which they saw as suffocating the process of modernization.

Where Chen found real grounds for hope was among those newly educated youths who, if they could be inspired by enlightened mentors into the right kind of nationalist pride, might yet rise to the challenge of awakening their country to all that threatened it. "What we must prove to the world," fellow revolutionary Li Dazhao wrote, "is not that old China is not dead, but that a new, youthful China is in the process of being born."[32] And in many ways it was being birthed through the journal *New Youth*. Chen played a central role in the establishment of the journal in Shanghai in 1915, and then in continuing to edit it when it relocated to Beijing in 1917. Out of this pathbreaking publication grew a whole new generation of bright, activist youth committed to creating a "new China."

While the self-strengtheners had concluded that China's "wealth and power" deficit could be remedied by fortifying a traditional cultural essence with selective practical foreign borrowing, Chen and his generation came to the opposite conclusion: China's problems lay within that very traditional cultural core itself. In his first editorial in *New Youth*, which he entitled "A Call to Youth," he railed against "the old and rotten air that fills society," lamenting that "one cannot even find a bit of fresh and vital air to comfort those of us who are suffocating in despair."[33] Yes, the foreign powers were predatory, but the first order of business was the dismantling of traditional culture in order to make possible a new patriotism. If Sun's calls for greater nationalism had focused blame for China's problems on outside causes, in his new publication Chen, like Liang, sounded a clarion call for his generation to start looking inward to China's own traditional culture as the primary obstruction.

But, how was one to excise something so ubiquitous and deepseated as one's own culture? For Chen, the main tool was to be *New Youth*, which he hoped would create a "strong, new youth" to replace the "white-faced bookworms" of the past who were "sickly and weak of disposition" and emblematic both of China's conservatism and of its decline.[34] "The strength of our country is weakening, the morals [of our people] are degenerating and the learning [of our scholars] is distressing," he proclaimed. "Our youth must take up the task [of rejuvenating China]. The purpose of publishing this magazine is to provide a forum for discussing the ways of self-cultivation and of governing the state."[35]

By attracting the most incisive and progressive minds of his time to write on culture, politics, international affairs, and philosophy, and by stressing iconoclasm, debate, and diversity of viewpoint, Chen was able to make *New Youth* an intellectual and political magnet, a force that had no equal in terms of influencing the up-and-coming generation of political activists. At the same time, it helped build a national network of thinkers that ended up impacting not only the present but also much of what would transpire in China during the rest of the century. A key contributor was Chen's former assassination squad cohort Cai Yuanpei, who had just become chancellor of National Peking University. Other important contributors included Hu Shi, the philosopher, historian, and later diplomat who studied under liberal political philosopher John Dewey at Columbia University; Communist Party cofounder Li Dazhao, another Peking University professor and early Communist activist; and even the young Mao Zedong.

The most brilliant writer Chen invited to join the *New Youth* project was Lu Xun, then emerging as a true master of modern Chinese prose and short fiction. Lu was born in the canal town of Shaoxing, Zhejiang Province, in 1881 and, like Chen, ended up in Japan, but at medical school. One day in class while watching a propaganda slideshow of Japanese troops executing Chinese "spies" during the 1904–5 Russo-Japanese War, Lu experienced an epiphany and abandoned medicine to attend to the spiritual sickness of the Chinese people, who in the slides appeared so completely passive in the face of their own dehumanization that they were unable to save either themselves or their country. At this tipping-point moment of epiphany, Lu later wrote, "I reinvented myself as a crusader for cultural reform."[36]

Lu's writing was peerless—at once sardonic and sentimental, burning with the idealism of youth in one passage, then cold, bleak, and despairing in the next. Yet his "crusade" was hindered by a deep inner anxiety over the lingering influence that China's traditional heritage, which he desperately wanted to transcend through new, modern, and accessible forms of writing, still exercised over him. "I feel very unhappy about the ancient ghosts that I carry on my back. [But] I cannot shake them off," he admitted. "So often do I feel a heavy weight that depresses me."[37]

When New Youth's editorial team first approached Lu for a contribution in 1918, he demurred. In a letter that exposed his fears—ones that Chen himself shared but had seemingly overcome (or perhaps repressed)—Lu asked if it was not futile, possibly even cruel, for a writer such as he to raise his pen to rouse ordinary Chinese from their slumber of centuries, when he could offer them no real solution. "Imagine an iron house without windows or doors, utterly indestructible, and full of sound sleepers—all about to suffocate to death. Let them die in their sleep and they will feel nothing," he wrote to the editors of New Youth. "Is it right to cry out, to rouse a few light sleepers among them, causing them inconsolable agony before they die?"[38]

Still, even Lu Xun found it hard to tolerate the bleakness of his own metaphor, and he managed to pull himself back at the very last moment. Not wanting to fall into irredeemable literary despair, he added: "But even if we succeed in waking only a few, there is still hope—hope that the iron house may one day be destroyed."[39] Eventually Lu was persuaded to join the New Youth project.

His first story, "Diary of a Madman," published by Chen in late 1918, caused an intellectual sensation and became an instant literary classic. The story is written in diary form, and the protagonist describes his dawning realization that he lives in a society that condones cannibalism. However, because he cannot just accept such a savage reality as others have, he is considered insane. "I now realize I have unknowingly spent my life in a country that has been eating human flesh for four thousand years!" Lu's "madman" exclaims.[40] The image of China as a society that ate its own proved indelible and unforgettable. Finally the diarist comes to understand that in such a society the only way for him to make "a full recovery" and find any semblance of accommodation and resolution is by consenting to become a cannibal himself.

Just as Lu felt powerless to wake the Chinese people from the retrograde grip of traditional Confucian culture, so his madman feels utter despair at being unable to awaken his fellow citizens to the obvious savageries of cannibalism. At the end of his story, all the "madman" can muster by way of hope—hope was to become a constant, and usually futile, quest of Lu's—is to cry out: "Are there children who have not yet eaten human flesh? Save the children. . . . !"[41] No one had more vividly or devastatingly captured the country's dead-end state.

Chen Duxiu instantly recognized the genius of Lu Xun's prose. Yet he refused to let himself yield to the same pessimism that in Lu verged on existential despair. After all, this was a time when public intellectuals not only had begun to hold the stage in urban China but also, as part of their so-called New Culture Movement, were beginning to allow themselves to believe that they might actually midwife the birth of a New China.

In *New Youth*, it was usually Chen who penned the opening essay, and thousands of young Chinese came to eagerly await each issue.[42] More than any other figure of his time, Chen managed to imbue these politically active young Chinese with a new confidence that, through generating a "new culture," they might somehow yet "fill the sea and move mountains" and "one day save the nation."[43]

In the first issue of the magazine, Chen dissected with unflinching honesty how being so steeped in China's past crippled his countrymen, and he challenged his generation to liberate themselves as a prelude to liberating China. Almost as if he were a general giving commands to his troops, he exhorted them to:

1. Be independent, not servile. . . .
2. Be progressive, not conservative. . . .
3. Be aggressive, not retiring. . . .

4. Be cosmopolitan, not isolationist. . . .

5. Be utilitarian, not formalistic. . . .

6. Be scientific, not imaginative.[44]

"All our traditional ethics, law, scholarship, rites, and customs are survivals of feudalism," he continued. "When compared with the achievement of the white race, there is a difference of a thousand years in thought, although we live in the same period. Revering only the history of the twenty-four dynasties and making no plans for progress and improvement, our people will be turned out of this twentieth-century world, and be lodged in the dark ditches fit only for slaves, cattle and horses."[45] By referring so relentlessly in his writing to China's enslavement, Chen was trying to provoke his fellow countrymen—just as the museum display on the Treaty of Nanjing at the Temple of the Tranquil Seas would a century later—into a state of shame sufficient to goad them to action.

For China to survive and even flourish again, his generation had to cast off what another New Culture supporter, Fu Sinian, called the "four-thousand-year-old garbage can on our backs."[46] As Chen lamented, imperial scholar-officials only knew how to "write essays and sit for the civil service exams." When it came to science, innovation, industry, and developing a dynamic economy, not only were they useless, but they put "the whole nation in a coma."[47]

With *New Youth*, Chen was in full attack mode, depicting Confucianism as unreformable. "The pulse of modern life is economic and the fundamental principle of economic production is individual independence," he wrote in a 1916 essay, "On the Way of Confucius and Modern Life." "In China, the Confucianists have based their teachings on their ethical norms. . . . [But] Confucius lived in a feudal age [and] the ethics he promoted [are] the ethics of a feudal age."[48]

For millennia, Chinese intellectuals had been reared on a Confucian deference to authority, and in Chen's view had been trapped in a *fengjian lijiao* (封建礼教), a "feudalistic code of conduct." During this activist phase of his life, when Chen was young, smart, cocky, and tired of seeing China bested by countries that were more advanced and powerful, he entertained no fears that he would ever regret the loss of the cultural world that he was seeking to extirpate. His radicalism found support in the still-popular theories of social Darwinism that had captivated Yan Fu. "Whatever cannot skillfully change itself and progress along with the world will find itself eliminated by natural selection because of failure to adapt to the environment. Then, what can be said to defend conservatism?"[49]

Chen idealized many of those aspects of Western civilization that he found lacking in China's own culture. "The Chinese compliment others by saying, 'He acts like an old man, although still young,' " Chen wrote in "Call to Youth." "Englishmen and Americans encourage one another by saying, 'Keep young, while growing old.' Such is one respect in which the different ways of thought of the East and West are manifested."[50]

Then, switching gears, he extolled the possibility that the young might play a game-changing role, even in a tradition-bound society such as China's. "Youth is like early spring, like the rising sun, like trees and grass in bud, like a newly sharpened blade," he wrote rhapsodically. "It is the most valuable period of life. And the function of youth in society is the same as that of a fresh and vital cell in a human body. In the process of metabolism, the old and the rotten are incessantly eliminated to be replaced by the fresh and living. . . . If metabolism functions properly in society, it will flourish; if old and rotten elements fill society, then it will cease to exist."[51]

Chen would return again and again, especially in his first 1915 editorial in *New Youth*, to the idea of China's culture being *chenfu xiubai* (陈腐朽败), "rotten and decayed."[52] Because he saw so much that needed to first be demolished, "destruction before construction" became one of his, and the New Culture Movement's, watchwords, just as it had been a mantra of Liang Qichao and would later become one of Mao's.[53] In his 1918 essay "On Iconoclasm," Chen volcanically wrote, "Destroy! Destroy the idols! Destroy the idols of hypocrisy!"

"My beliefs are based on true and reasonable standards. The religious, political and moral beliefs transmitted from ancient times are vain, deceptive, and unreasonable. They are all idols and must be destroyed! If we do not destroy them, universal truth and our own heartfelt belief will never be united."[54]

Chen's disciple Wang Fanxi later astutely observed that his mentor's main contribution to China's tortured progress toward modernity "lay

Qing Dynasty civil service examination cells in Guangzhou, 1900

May Fourth demonstrators in Beijing, 1919

Lu Xun with George
Bernard Shaw and
Cai Yuanpei, 1933

Chen Duxiu just before
release from prison, 1937

less in his constructive achievement than in his destructive energy: in his dauntless urge to discredit, criticise, and destroy everything traditional. . . . Like all iconoclasts and pioneers, he worked not with a scalpel but with a bulldozer. For him, the main thing was to pull down the dilapidated house of the past, and this he did to devastating effect."[55]

Sometimes Chen sounded more like a preacher warning his flock against the wages of sin than like a rationalist propounding an agenda of cultural and political reform. The rhetoric and emotion that went with his critique bespoke the sense of urgency he felt about China's uncertain future, sometimes almost to the point of desperation. An essay written in 1916 is typical: "Precious and beloved youth, if you consider yourselves twentieth-century people, you must get rid of old attitudes," he wrote. "Rid yourself of the reactionary and corrupt old thinking about officialdom and wealth and develop a new faith. . . . Forsake this narrow, selfish mentality and develop the characteristics of a *new youth*. Bury the old youth whose narrow-mindedness led to conservatism and corruption. Be different!"[56]

In 1917, Peking University chancellor Cai Yuanpei asked Chen to join his illustrious faculty as the dean of the School of Arts and Letters. Chen's influence and fame as a writer and editor was just then reaching a crescendo, and the subsequent two years he spent in Beijing, which led up to the demonstrations on May 4, 1919, would prove to be its zenith.

Not surprisingly, Chen's view of Chinese tradition as a recipe for backwardness and failure did not sit well with cultural conservatives, who remained influential in intellectual and political circles in the capital. In March 1919, the well-known translator Lin Shu wrote a long critique of Chen and sent it to Chancellor Cai, charging him and Peking University with promoting "the destruction of Confucianism and the five virtues and five ethical relations." In a nine-point defense of traditional values, Lin urged Cai to remember that "Confucius is a sage adjustable to any time."[57] Then he asked him to imagine what would happen "if all the old classical books were discarded and the vernacular used?" Why, he insisted in horror, "all the rickshaw boys and peddlers of Beijing and Tianjin could be regarded as professors!"[58] Chen would shortly learn that the bite of his more conservative colleagues could still sting.

Mr. Science and Mr. Democracy

In trying to figure out what should replace traditional Chinese culture, Chen turned to a duo that he affectionately dubbed "Mr. Science and Mr. Democracy." "There are now two roads in the world," he wrote in 1918 with Manichean clarity. "One is the road of light which leads to democracy, science and atheism; and the other, the road of darkness leading to despotism, superstition and divine authority."[59]

These conjoined twins from the West were for Chen the obvious antidotes for much of what he saw as ailing tradition-bound China. "Critics accuse this magazine of intending to destroy Confucianism," he wrote of New Youth's editorial policy. "These charges are conceded. But we plead not guilty. We have committed the alleged crimes only because we supported two gentlemen, Mr. Democracy and Mr. Science. In order to advocate Mr. Democracy, we are obliged to oppose Confucianism, the codes of ritual, chastity of women, traditional ethics and old-fashioned politics. In order to advocate Mr. Science, we have to oppose traditional arts and traditional religion."[60]

So devoted was Chen to these twins that at one point he even adopted "D. S. Chen" as an English name.[61] And the enthusiasm and energy generated around them was infectious. Years later, celebrated novelist Ba Jin remembered how "legions of young people rallied behind the banners of 'science and democracy' and marched forward resolutely towards the future . . . I eagerly bought up all publications involved with the New Culture Movement that I could lay my hands on, hungrily reading every line," he recalled. "I would not have hesitated to 'climb mountains of spikes or cross a sea of fire,' if it would have helped to overthrow the old world and create a new one. . . . We were all children of May Fourth."[62]

Chen's version of democracy was at first blush classically liberal in nature: remove the strangling influence of traditional culture, add the rule of law and protection of people's rights, and the energies of the individual would be liberated.[63] Yet Chen anticipated that instilling long-lasting democratic values in the Chinese people would not be easy. "Our task today can be said to be the intense combat between the old and the modern currents of thought," he wrote. "Those with shallow views all expect this to be our final awakening, without understanding how difficult it is to put [constitutional government] into practice."[64]

He warned that great danger lay in the old Chinese tendency of passively awaiting a "good ruler." "There is no difference between the shameful disgrace of submissiveness of men of ancient times hoping that sage rulers and wise ministers will practice benevolent government and present-day men hoping that dignitaries and influential elders will build a constitutional republic," he wrote. True democracy "cannot be conferred by the government, cannot be maintained by one party or one group, and certainly cannot be carried on the backs of a few dignitaries and influential elders. A constitutional republic which does not derive from the conscious realization and voluntary action of the majority of the people is a bogus republic and bogus constitutionalism. It is political window-dressing."[65]

Chen was also impatient with leaders, such as Sun Yat-sen, who, whenever problems occurred, were ready to delay the implementation of democracy in deference to first building up a strong state. He seconded his Cornell- and Columbia University–educated colleague Hu Shi, who in 1915 famously said, "The only way to have democracy is to have democracy. Government is an art, and as such it needs practice. I would never have been able to speak English if I had never spoken it. The Anglo-Saxon people would never have had democracy had they never practiced democracy."[66]

Although Chen evinced a deep and abiding affinity with Western democratic thought, he was also intensely patriotic and nationalistic. He thus viewed liberal democracy—like all other isms—not just as an inherent natural right or as an idealized set of principles, but as a tool for improving his nation's lot. If democracy could help release the kind of innovative energy that it had in the West, Chen was interested. If there were other pathways that could do the same thing more efficiently, fine—which is why, by the end of 1919, he became interested in Marxism-Leninism, with profound historical consequences.

The same ambiguity colored Chen's ideas about individual rights and the sanctity of the liberated individual in society. A significant part of the May Fourth zeitgeist gravitated around a highly individualistic, even bohemian lifestyle. Many supporters of New Culture ardently embraced notions of Western romantic love (even "free love") and advo-

cated all kinds of artistic license and personal self-discovery. Among
the era's many young political iconoclasts were Byronesque poets, self-
absorbed artists, sexually liberated feminists, rebellious authors, and
westernized free spirits, whom some more-traditional Chinese derogatorily took to calling *jia yangguizi* (假洋鬼子), "fake foreign devils,"
youth who excessively admired and adopted foreign ways and pretensions.

Although a ringleader of the New Culture Movement, Chen understood that such self-centered and self-indulgent behavior was not the
stuff from which national wealth and power would finally be made. In
his wariness about the kind of exaggerated, self-interested individualism that some New Culture followers apotheosized in the West, he remained closer than he probably sometimes found comfortable to the
Confucian reform tradition, which saw individual cultivation and reformation as the best way to create new energy that might better serve
society and the state.

This was not to say that Chen himself was abstemious when it came
to enjoying the hedonistic pleasures that the New Culture Movement
offered up—a version of libertine escapism involving wine, women,
and song as well as rebellious politics. Chen, who went through numerous wives and a long-term mistress and had seven children, was a
legendary womanizer.[67] In fact, in both China and Japan he was known
for being a frequent visitor to brothels, and as it happened, an embarrassing incident with a lady of the night was his undoing at Peking
University. In March 1919 the campus newspaper reported on an alter-
cation between their vaunted dean of the School of Arts and Letters
and a prostitute in a Beijing *hutong*. It included the detail, incriminat-
ing in its specificity, that Chen had scratched the woman "across her
lower body." Chancellor Cai, who in an awkward coincidence was
head of the Virtue Society (which had taken strong public stands
against opium smoking, drinking, gambling, and whoring), was pressured into removing his friend as dean by conservatives who charged
that Chen's "personal virtue was too corrupt."[68]

It was a bitter moment for Chen, made all the more so by the fact
that it happened just weeks before the May Fourth Incident, when his
life's work suddenly culminated in a dramatic way. In the spring of
1919 Chinese suddenly learned that during World War I the Western

powers had secretly agreed to transfer Germany's rights and concessions in Shandong Province to Japan. Worse yet, they were soon to
formally ratify these insults to Chinese sovereignty at the Paris Peace
Conference, representing a cynical betrayal of American president
Woodrow Wilson's much-publicized anticolonial promises enunciated
in his Fourteen Points. Wilsonian liberalism had encouraged idealistic
Chinese to believe that the war was being fought for self-determination
and a new equality among nations, and a hopeful Chen Duxiu had
even dubbed President Wilson "the number one good man in the
world."[69] So the revelation that his democratic principles were now
being so brazenly betrayed outraged young Chinese. Chen's Peking
University colleague Li Dazhao derided the great powers for organizing
endless peace conferences "while they still adhere to the old pattern of
killing people and destroying nations."[70] And none other than the
young Mao Zedong wrote a short broadside entitled "Poor Wilson," in
which he characterized the awkwardness of the American president's
explanations of American hypocrisy as like watching "an ant on a hot
skillet."[71]

Reformers throughout China, alerted by Liang Qichao's telegram
from Paris, immediately began rallying to pressure their delegation at
the peace conference to reject the treaty. For Chinese patriots, these
Japanese demands were the final indignity, a guarantee that their country would never cease to be cannibalized by foreign powers. As Li
Dazhao put it, "The shame of having lost our independent nature is a
thousand times deeper than the shame of losing territory."[72]

A mass demonstration that had originally been scheduled for Beijing on May 7 was hastily moved up (it was to mark the anniversary of
the day in 1915 when the Chinese government had conceded to Japan's
earlier predatory Twenty-One Demands; subsequently, May 7 was designated as "National Humiliation Day").[73] On May 4, 1919, several
thousand students from thirty Beijing universities flooded into a then
much smaller square in front of Tiananmen Gate to demonstrate. It
was here in 1895 that thousands of imperial scholars, including Liang
Qichao, had protested against the peace agreement that followed Japan's victory in the Sino-Japanese War.[74] Now, for a second time, the
nation's elite were coming together publically in the shadow of Tiananmen to remonstrate against their government's weakness.

"Once the integrity of her territory is destroyed, China will soon be annihilated," proclaimed the "Manifesto of All Students of Beijing," circulated at the demonstration. "Accordingly, we students today are making a demonstration march to the Allied legations, asking the Allies to support justice. . . . This is the last chance for China in her life and death struggle. Today we swear two solemn oaths:

1. China's territory may be conquered, but it cannot be given away.
2. The Chinese people may be massacred, but they will not surrender!"[75]

The mood of the demonstrators darkened as they neared the Foreign Legation Quarter, but, it being Sunday, the ambassadors from the Allied powers were not in their embassies. So, shouting, "On to the homes of Chinese traitors!" a group of frustrated demonstrators marched off to the residence of Cao Rulin, minister of communications and one of the cabinet secretaries in the warlord government.[76] Once there, marchers found their way obstructed by police and began throwing stones. Then, breaking through police lines, they looted the residence and set it on fire. One student poet summed up the day this way:

To purge clean the shame from Chinese hearts and minds
We stand today as prisoners.
Among the thirty-two arrested,
There is none who fears death.
We thrashed the traitors thoroughly and
    burned the Cao mansion to the ground.
In ferreting out traitors, we've spared no cost,
    including death.
We'd do anything to save China![77]

In a matter of days, demonstrations had spread all across urban China. In a very real way, Chen's work over the previous decade was coming to fruition—and to an end. A new phase of Chinese nationalism was about to emerge from the sea of disillusionment with the West and the debacle of the Treaty of Versailles. For many Chinese, including Chen and Liang, the West's political ideals, which had led Europeans like lambs to a pointless slaughter, now seemed far less alluring.

The shock of Versailles even caused Chen to start questioning the value of nationalism itself. "In their eyes, patriotism seems to be another word for harming others," wrote Chen of the Europeans in an essay entitled "In the End, Should We Really Be Patriotic?" "Thus, they consider patriotic killing to be fanaticism and madness. . . . In the midst of everyone's zealous, slavish, unquestioning, 'patriotic' clamor," he continued, "I would like to have a reasoned discussion: In the end, should we really be patriotic?"[78]

Even in 1915, as his nationalistic sentiments were sharpening, Chen had worried that an excessively emotional commitment to one's own country could sometimes risk overriding reason. A state's most important job was, after all, "to protect individual rights and to enrich individual happiness," not to whip its citizens into a frenzy of adoration.[79] As he became more mindful of the dangerous potency of nationalist passions, Chen also became more fearful of how a state or its leaders might exploit the willingness of individual citizens to love their country for their own destructive purposes. In the closing passage of his 1919 essay, Chen asked, "Should we in the end love our country?" His answer was, "What we [should] love is a country where the people use patriotism to resist oppression, not a country that uses patriotism to oppress. . . . What we [should] love is a country that seeks happiness for the people, not a country for which the people sacrifice themselves."[80]

Days after the May Fourth Incident, a discouraged Cai Yuanpei quit as chancellor of Peking University. "I am exhausted," he wrote in a departure note.[81] Chen was left to lament: "My head is hurting so. I would rather have the government arrest and execute me right away, so that I won't have to live in such a filthy world!"[82]

A short time later, with the situation in the capital growing ever more repressive, Chen's plea was partly answered. On June 11, he was arrested after throwing copies of a "Manifesto to the Citizens of Beijing"—listing demands aimed at the warlord government that had suppressed the May Fourth demonstrations—off a theater balcony in the New World Market.[83]

It is hard to know what exactly Chen had in mind with this act of political theater. But the image of a former dean of China's most celebrated university showering leaflets from a theater balcony like an anarchist student was an unsettling one. Nonetheless, his imprisonment precipitated a flood of protests, including from Sun Yat-sen and Mao Zedong (who had just left a library job at Peking University for home in Hunan), who sent telegrams of support.[84] "We regard Mr. Chen as a bright star in the world of thought," wrote Mao. "When Mr. Chen speaks, anyone with a reasonably clear mind assents to the opinions he expresses."[85]

After eighty-three traumatic days of confinement Chen was released from jail. His incarceration had at least given him time to think. "There are two sources of world civilization: one is the research institute and the other is the prison," he wrote with a gritty new realism just three days before his arrest. "The youth of our country must be determined: once out of the research institute, to enter the prison; once out of the prison, to enter the research institute. This is the highest and most noble life. Only the civilization that comes out of these two places is true civilization, a civilization that has life and value."[86]

When the government occupied the Peking University campus, student protesters expressed a similar sentiment. First, a sign sprouted up at the law school, just behind the Forbidden City, proclaiming it "Student Prison #1." Then another appeared at the school of science proclaiming it "Student Prison #2."[87] While the May Fourth demonstrations had run into a dead end in Beijing, the movement had spread across the country, awakening a whole new generation of students, workers, and even merchants, who showed their sympathy through strikes and work stoppages in factories. Henceforth, the May Fourth Movement stood as a milestone in modern Chinese history, a moment of popular protest from which almost all future Chinese political movements derived political inspiration.

But just as the ideas that Chen had promoted in New Youth began to be popularized around the country, he himself had begun to move irrevocably away from his once firm commitment to the form of liberalism, individualism, and democracy that had animated the so-called Chinese Enlightenment. By April 1920, he had moved back to Shanghai and lost much of his faith in the power of ideas to bring about change. He had even started calling for the abolition of private property and the equalization of wealth. Chen, in fact, was now busy organizing the first Communist cells in China.[88]

Founding the Party

In a stunning post–May Fourth Movement volte-face, Chen turned to a new remedial ism: Marxism-Leninism. Indeed, Marxism, purporting to represent the "broad masses" rather than just the narrow slice of society called the bourgeoisie, was able to present itself in China as a fairer form of "democracy." And since Marxist revolutionary theory declared itself to be fully "scientific," even Mr. Science seemed to be able to acquire a new Chinese manifestation. After the failure of the New Culture Movement, Chen was prepared to give a chance to another formula borrowed from the West, this time via Russia, a country that had experienced at least some of China's trials and tribulations.

His waning faith in his countrymen's ability to save themselves without a new savior also played a role in his decision. If China were ever to rise again, he now concluded, its people would need to be led. Describing them as "a partly scattered, partly stupid people possessed of narrow-minded individualism with no public spirit," he had become convinced that to rely on "this kind of irresponsible people with no ability, purpose or knowledge, [and] to give them responsibility[, would be] to commit national suicide."[89]

His new diagnosis was hardly roseate: "In China at this time not only is government by the whole people worthless to talk of, but it is a dream," he wrote.[90] This realization was at least part of what led him to the Leninist view that, if a new China was ever to be created, an elite of organized revolutionaries would have to take up the mantle of leadership. Strangely, on his long and torturous personal odyssey, he had finally arrived at a place that Sun Yat-sen, with whom he shared little else, would have found familiar.

Given the chaos of postimperial China, the Bolshevik Revolution's proof of the efficaciousness of what Lenin called "professional revolutionaries"—specially trained "commissars" who could serve as a leadership vanguard to organize "the people"—now seemed almost heaven-sent. At some subconscious level, it may also have helped that Lenin's vision of a new revolutionary leadership had a certain congruence with the old Confucian notion that every stable society needs an elite, enlightened scholar-official class to lead the ordinary people— "like the wind bending rice seedlings," as Confucius had put it. "A political revolution must begin with those who have knowledge," Chen argued in a melding of Confucian and Communist principles.[91]

Lenin's new theories on imperialism also offered an equally welcome unified field theory that allowed Chinese—indeed, all colonized people—not only to blame their backwardness on imperialist exploitation but also to assign their own "oppressed" and "backward areas" a crucial role in the world revolution to come.[92] Just as this new message had appealed to Sun, it now also appealed to Chen, for it presented both men with a way to look at the world that placed blame for their country's misery firmly on the shoulders of foreign powers.[93]

Then, in July 1919, as we have already noted, Lev M. Karakhan, the deputy commissar for foreign affairs of the newly founded Soviet Union, made an announcement that stunned Chinese such as Sun and Chen: Moscow agreed to relinquish all claims made by czarist Russia to territories and special colonial privileges inside China. This magnanimous offer not only put Lenin's theories of anti-imperialism into practice in a dramatic way but sharply distinguished the new Bolshevik government from the exploitative hypocrisy of the liberal West. By 1921, Chen was busy establishing Chinese Communist Party cells along with his comrade-in-arms, Li Dazhao, an effort that also involved the young Mao Zedong.[94] Their defection to communism represented an enormous sea change among Chinese intellectuals. For decades to come, the liberal democratic impulse in China would remain at best muted, at worst absent, but certainly not a prevailing motor force. It was now the turn of proponents of a well-organized, strong one-party state, led by an elite of well-trained political commissars, to try their hands at bringing greatness to the fledgling Chinese Republic. "China's governmental revolution in the next couple of years absolutely cannot effect a Western-style democracy," Chen warned just as the First Congress of the CCP in Shanghai convened in July 1921 to found the party. To move toward national greatness, he said, "it would be best to undergo Russian Communist class dictatorship."[95] By seeming to open a new and more direct pathway to rejuvenation and regeneration, Bolshevism had seduced Chen, who by 1921 had concluded that "in order to save the nation, make knowledge widespread, develop industry and not be stained with capitalist taint, Russian methods are the only road."[96]

The Old Scholar in Sichuan

Although he was now a self-proclaimed Marxist, it would not take long before Chen became uncomfortable with Stalin's rigid views on the Chinese revolution and was entertaining "revisionist" second thoughts that would cause him to end up as one of Chinese Bolshevism's most prominent victims. So, from the second peak of his career as a founder of the Chinese Communist Party, Chen once again slid to the margins of political activism. But, unlike his post–May Fourth rebirth, this time there would be no reprieve. By the mid-1920s, Russia's new rising leader, the treacherous Joseph Stalin, and his allies in the Chinese Communist Party leadership, were looking to strip Chen of his position as the CCP's first general secretary. By 1927 he had been ousted for "rightist opportunism" and blamed for the party's failures to spark proletarian revolution in China's cities, as Stalin had stubbornly commanded.[97] In 1929, Chen's final ignominy arrived: expulsion from the CCP itself.

The next decade would prove no more congenial for Chen. Married to his third wife in 1930, he was forced to live incognito for long periods of time, mourning two sons executed by Chiang Kai-shek's Nationalists. Then, in 1932, he was charged as a Trotskyite and sentenced on trumped-up treason charges to thirteen years in prison (but given an early release in 1937 because of poor health). In the end, Chen retreated into political exile in the mountains of Sichuan. There, considered an apostate by Nationalists and Communists alike, this once-towering historical figure faded into obscurity. His devoted follower Wang Fanxi described the banished Chen as "a lion returned to his lair to lick his wounds."[98]

In the political wilderness,[99] Chen's belief in democracy as the most civilized form of government did finally reemerge. Especially as Stalin's tyranny darkened and his cynical pact with Hitler made a mockery of the idea of "socialist democracy," Chen's faith in communism waned. In 1940, he spoke to Wang admiringly of democracy as a system in which "no institution apart from the court has the right of arrest; there may be no taxation without representation; the government has no right to levy taxes unless they are agreed by parliament; opposition parties are free to organize, speak, and publish; workers have the right to strike; peasants have the right to till the land, and there is freedom of thought and worship."[100] He had certainly suffered enough by then at the hands of capricious one-party systems to grasp the dangers of government bereft of any regularized checks and balances. But, of course, by then it no longer really mattered what he thought, because no one was listening.

As with so many other early Chinese reformers, in this last stage of his life the recessive Confucian genes in Chen's intellectual genome began to ineluctably express themselves once again. The classical word had through his early training been so deeply made flesh within him that, despite his protracted and determined intellectual revolt, he was never able to completely excise it. Even as a revolutionary, he had not fully been able to cease seeing things through a classically Chinese lens. And like his mentor, Liang Qichao, and his literary comrade, Lu Xun, when the verities and burdens of revolutionary iconoclasm in the real world became too great and life too lonely and alienated, Chen almost involuntarily reached back to the comfort of the very cultural tradition he had fought so hard to overthrow. Like those metal alloys that possess "shape memory"—they bend when heated, only to snap back to their original shape upon cooling—members of this transitional generation were never quite able to escape the intellectual molds of their childhoods. For Chen, this meant returning irresistibly in the end to classical poetry, ancient philology, and other filial devotions that he had spent so much of his life trying to escape. As the Chinese saying puts it, "You can take the monk out of the temple, but not the temple out of the monk."

So, even as Chen and his New Culture rebels sought to jettison the "garbage can" on their backs, an internal struggle made it almost impossible for many of them to ever truly escape their own pasts. Like China itself, traditional culture proved to have a firmer grip on them than they had ever imagined while they were in rebellion, meaning that it would take a far more relentless, even brutal revolt than they themselves had been able to launch to break its stranglehold. In the end, tradition was a kind of haven too familiar and soothing for Chen to completely resist. Here, in China's past, he could continue thinking and

Chen Duxiu in the 1920s

working without either putting his life in constant jeopardy or facing yet more disappointments of the kind that the twentieth century had thrown his way in such abundance.

Toward the end, Chen was a chastened man, filled with regrets and even possessed by a certain fatalism that had been so uncharacteristic during his younger years. He also seemed to lose his belief that China might somehow be able to reform itself and once more arise to become great. "Today is no longer the age of Li Hongzhang," he wrote wistfully in 1942, just before he died, as if those days had become an object of nostalgia. "One should stop dreaming the pleasant dream that [China] could become a rich, strong country at a single leap."[101]

Chiang Kai-shek circa 1920

CHAPTER 8

Unification （统一）

CHIANG KAI-SHEK （蒋介石）

Tea with the Generalissimo

In public, Chiang Kai-shek was the ramrod-straight, self-anointed "Generalissimo," or "G-Mo," proud president of the Republic of China, and leader of the Nationalist Party. In private he was physically far less imposing. Like many Chinese leaders of his generation, he never fully mastered Mandarin and spoke his native Zhejiang dialect in high-pitched, Chinese-opera-like tones at odds with his martial bearing, stern countenance, shaven pate, and disciplined manner.

In the early 1960s, during his long Taiwan exile, Chiang sometimes hosted special "teas" for the handful of foreign scholars and students then studying in Taipei. Held in his presidential palace, a gloomy red-brick edifice built by the Japanese when they colonized the island a half century before, these social events were organized by the Nationalist Party's Save-the-Nation Youth Corps, an official youth group dedicated to the party's sacred mission of *fangong dalu* （反攻大陆）, "counterattacking the mainland," where Mao Zedong then ruled, to *zhengjiu tongbao* （拯救同胞）, "save Chinese compatriots" from the wages of communism. Awaiting the Generalissimo to appear in one of his palace's grand salons, it was not difficult to summon up images of those ambassadorial wives back in the early 1900s as they waited in the Forbidden City for the Empress Dowager to present herself at tea.

Upon arrival, Chiang's presence was riveting. After all, he had been the leader of the most populous nation in the world, even once canonized as a member of the "Big Four," along with Winston Churchill,

Franklin Delano Roosevelt, and Joseph Stalin, by being invited to the
Allied summit in Cairo in November 1943 (which Stalin finally refused
to attend).[1] Now, twenty years later, he was a crownless émigré sovereign banished to an isolated subtropical island. Forced to surrender his
country and his people in 1949, Chiang had been ignominiously chased
by his nemesis, Mao Zedong, into inglorious exile. Here on this island
outpost he reigned over a simulacrum of the nation he had once dominated on the mainland, as China proper was then referred to almost
reverentially in Taipei.

As became evident during those awkward teatimes, the Generalissimo was a man of contradictions, someone who had learned to temper
his passions with martial discipline and neo-Confucian self-control to
balm the indignity of his actual circumstance. Uncomfortable in the
public eye, especially among foreigners, he compensated for his lack of
ease by retreating into a highly stylized imperiousness that seemed calculated to leave an impression of strength. And from a distance there
was a certain power in the posturing. But, from closer up, his rigidity
conveyed more than a hint of insecurity and vulnerability. In his perfectly tailored Sun Yat-sen suit and with his cup of tea raised to his thin
lips, you could feel the effort he put into maintaining a stoic pose of
dignified calm and aloofness that might convey a measure of the full
majesty that he knew his present office lacked. Indeed, it was hard to
repress the thought that even presenting himself before such a ragtag
group of foreign scholars (some of whom had arrived by bicycle!) only
reinforced how far down the global pecking order he had fallen.

One left his palace with a sense of having been in the presence of a
tragic figure, a proud man left to cope with the indignities of having
fallen so far. Like so many other Chinese leaders, Chiang had spent his
life seeking to restore his people to greatness by appealing to them to
"save our country and make China strong and independent, with a
position of equality among the other nations of the world," as he put
it.[2] But here he was, marooned on an offshore island, a living example
of yet another failed attempt to restore wealth and power to China.

To live in Taiwan during those early years of the 1960s was to be in
a land that felt as if it had hit a historical dead end. Students, especially
Americans, were strictly forbidden from crossing the hundred-mile-
wide Taiwan Straits to the "real China." The closest they could get to

that promised land was to take a bus to the coast, and there, camped out near a fishing village, listen surreptitiously to illegal radio broadcasts from Beijing on tiny, battery-powered transistor radios. It was electrifying to lie on the beach under a starry night sky and hear those static-filled propaganda newscasts in the exotic Beijing dialect crackling in over the airwaves. The thrilling historical drama playing itself out with such elusive bravado just on the other side of the Taiwan Straits only lent Chiang and his exiled "government" all the more of an air of has-beens in this grand revolutionary struggle.

The Golden Decade

Six years older than Mao Zedong, Chiang was born in 1887 to a salt merchant family from the town of Xikou, near the busy coastal cities of Zhejiang Province, a region famed for its rich Confucian tradition. As a young man, Chiang was schooled in the classics, and they imprinted on him a deep sense of his responsibility to engage in self-cultivation, maintain self-discipline and decorum, and embrace society's natural hierarchy of obligations to elders and deference to superiors.[3] But in 1905, after a traditional arranged marriage, Chiang cut off his queue as an act of rebellion and departed to study in Japan.[4] Whereas other young Chinese there, such as Sun Yat-sen, Chen Duxiu, Lu Xun, and Liang Qichao, were driven by a quest for new ideas about culture and politics, what interested Chiang was military strategy, tactics, and technology. While they hoped to change Chinese culture and consciousness through new ideas, he studied at Japanese military academies, hoping to master the art of war for the sake of the nation.

After returning home to attend the Central Army School in Baoding, Chiang was back in Japan in less than a year, this time to study at the Shimbu Gakko in Tokyo, a military school offering a course of training specially developed for Chinese exiles.[5] It was here that he began cultivating his lifelong dedication to martial discipline. In the process, through a fellow Zhejiang provincial, Chen Qimei, he was introduced to Sun Yat-sen's Revolutionary Alliance and his republican political movement. In fact, as the Qing Dynasty was collapsing in 1911, Chiang received a telegram from Chen asking him to return to Shanghai to work in the new anti-Qing militia. "This was the real beginning of my revolutionary career," he later recalled.[6] It was during this chaotic and confusing decade, after he had been forced to return again to Japan in 1913, that he first met with Sun Yat-sen in person and began working with him, ultimately even forming a "dare to die" team with Chen to assassinate local officials in Yuan Shikai's government.[7]

When Yuan's agents turned the tables and assassinated Chen Qimei in May 1916, Chiang fell into a spiral of despondency and debauchery.[8] He did, however, keep up his contacts with Sun. In fact, in the kind of bizarre incident that was characteristic of this chaotic period, Chiang, who had been steadily rising in the ranks of Sun's Guangdong Army, was in 1922 urgently summoned to help rescue Sun himself, who was being held on a gunboat on the Pearl River by a rival Canton warlord.[9]

In August 1923, Sun sent Chiang to Moscow to study military and party organization, so that when Sun opened the Russian-funded Whampoa Military Academy near Canton in June 1924, he could appoint him as its commander (and Zhou Enlai as its political commissar). By then, Chiang's life had become intertwined with Sun and his legacy in another important way. Sun had married Song Qingling, one of the three beautiful daughters of the devoutly Christian, American-educated industrialist Charlie Song, who, upon returning to China, had made a fortune selling dried noodles.[10] At a Christmas party in Sun's Shanghai house in 1921, Chiang met Qingling's Wellesley-educated younger sister, Meiling, and was immediately smitten.[11] But since he had already been married several times and was not then even properly divorced, the idea of Meiling becoming betrothed to Chiang was hardly welcome in the straitlaced, Christian Song family. And so began a long courtship, causing the famously shy and austere Chiang to at one point confide to his diary about the shrewd, vivacious, cigarette-smoking beauty: "Recently, night and day, there is nothing in my heart but San Mei [Song Meiling.]"[12]

By finally clarifying his marital status and promising to engage in regular Bible study (among other things), Chiang finally did manage to gain the Song family's consent. He and Meiling were married on December 1, 1927, in double-barreled Shanghai ceremonies—one Christian, the other Chinese—followed by a spectacular reception at the Majestic Hotel's grand ballroom. Chiang's betrothal came just as he was triumphing in his effort to militarily unify the country, and his new marriage now allowed him to also consolidate his relationship with China's new capitalist class and the West.

By the time of Sun's death in 1925, the ambitious Chiang had come to view his life as inseparably intertwined with the destiny of his country. Moreover, by then he had managed not only to inherit the leadership mantle of the Nationalist Party but also to weave together the beginnings of a new, well-trained national military force, which enabled him at age thirty-eight to set out on the Northern Expedition to reunify China. It was telling that upon taking the city of Wuhan from a local warlord, Chiang had an iron tower constructed on a prominent hill and inscribed it with massive characters proclaiming: *Feichu bupingdeng tiaoyue* (废黜不平等条约), "Abolish the unequal treaties."[13] This phase as national unifier would culminate on January 4, 1928, when Chiang was sworn in as chairman of the Political Council for the new Nationalist government, whose capital had been moved to Nanjing.[14]

When Chiang had taken over the Nationalist Party leadership in 1925, the country seemed to be reaching a new low point each year and no one seemed to know how to stop its downward slide. But when in 1926 he launched his new Russian-trained army on the Northern Expedition and, through a combination of military victories, backroom accommodations, and good luck, managed to bring China's patchwork of feudal warlords back into a semblance of national unity, it was a stunning and unexpected triumph.

Given his later fall from power, it is hard to recall just how astonishing Chiang's rise and success actually were at the time. Until it happened, few had had much confidence in China's future. Skeptics such as Lu Xun had found little reason to hope that China would ever pull itself out of its abyss of haplessness. American journalist and scholar Nathaniel Peffer summed up the moment in his 1930 book, aptly entitled *China: The Collapse of a Civilization*: "The picture China presents is shocking. In recent years China has shown an extraordinary capacity for muddling its affairs, a barrenness of leadership and an almost fatalistic instinct for aggravating its own misery. Not for a hundred years has there been any sign of statesmanship or of collective, constructive ability."[15] The challenges confronting Chiang, in historian Lloyd Eastman's words, were "awesome—nothing less than to turn back the tide of national disintegration that, for a century and more, had been washing over the Chinese nation. A central, national government had virtually ceased to exist."[16]

Despite his success, there was one group that, albeit still small in numbers, in Chiang's mind posed a profound threat to his vision of a unified and strengthened China. This was his own party's Communist partners in the so-called United Front set up by Sun just a few years before. "I treat them with sincerity," Chiang declaimed in a 1926 diary entry on his Soviet advisors, "but they reciprocate with deceit."[17]

In April 1927 Chiang shocked the country by launching the "white terror," massacring the very Communist labor leaders with whom his mentor had allied him. The purge—carried out most brutally in Shanghai by his new underground allies, the criminal Mafia-like Green Gang—was grim and bloody. But it was also an expression of Chiang's new confidence that he and the Nationalist Party (which had by then been reorganized along Leninist lines) could now reunify the country without the Communists.

With Communist militants driven underground or into the countryside and the fractious warlords more or less in line, by 1930 Chiang's government drafted plans for its new capital in Nanjing, where Sun's mausoleum was already under construction. Chiang wanted a capital that would be awe-inspiring in its grandeur, a "source of energy for the whole nation," and "a role model for the whole world."[18] With heroic monuments, regal parks, stately new buildings, grand avenues, and other design elements copied from Paris and Washington, D.C., the new Nanjing would, said its planners, "glorify the nation's culture."[19] Such grand pretensions hinted at how important it was to create the kinds of symbols, if not the reality, of prosperity and strength for which so many Chinese continued to yearn.

Next, Chiang began implementing fiscal reforms, masterminded by his Harvard-educated brother-in-law, businessman T. V. Song, and investments in much needed ports, highways, railroads, airports, and even a new legal system. And Chiang undertook this ambitious agenda while the world was in recession, Japan's armies were occupying Manchuria, and Mao was organizing an insurrectionary peasant movement against him in China's vast rural hinterland. With the United Front broken down, Chiang began a series of "bandit suppression" cam-

paigns to confront Mao's guerrilla forces head-on. "Today, we are facing dangers from within as well as without," he said in a 1933 speech,
echoing Feng Guifen's lament about "calamity within and anxiety
without. "Domestically, the brutal, violent bandits [Communists] are
burning and killing every day, and across the sea come the Japanese
imperialists who take over one piece of territory after another. These
imperialists will not be satisfied until they exterminate China as a nation."[20] Comparing the two enemies, Chiang was explicit about which
he viewed as more dangerous. "The Japanese aggression comes from
without and can be compared to a disease of the skin, while the bandit
rebellion, working from within, is really a disease of the heart. We must
cure a disease of the heart before proceeding with the cure of a disease
of the skin, because the heart disease, if not cured, will kill the patient,
while the skin disease will not."[21] In this conclusion, Chiang unwit-
tingly also echoed Prince Gong, who had told the Xianfeng Emperor in
the 1860s, when British and French were sacking the old Summer Palace: "The rebels [the Taiping Rebellion] menace our heart. The British
are merely a threat to our limbs. First of all we must extirpate the
rebels."[22] Nonetheless, by 1936 the Dagongbao, one of China's most
independent newspapers, felt emboldened enough to write about China
under Chiang's leadership, "In the period of the last few months, the
people's confidence seems as though it were revived from the dead."[23]

In a dramatic turn that December, a patriotic warlord leader from
Manchuria, Zhang Xueliang, took Chiang hostage outside the ancient
city of Xi'an and demanded that he resume United Front cooperation
with the Communists and focus on fighting Japan. The Xi'an incident
might have been a humiliation for Chiang. However, after he agreed
and was released, he ended up receiving a hero's welcome back in Nanjing, as hundreds of thousands of people marched in the streets in support of their Generalissimo.[24]

World leaders watching Chiang execute his nation-building efforts
were also impressed, and many concluded that the Chinese had at last
become capable of running their own country again. Although problems still abounded, some even started referring to the early 1930s
in China as the "golden decade."[25] Left-leaning American journalist
Edgar Snow was less sanguine. "Perhaps it glittered for a handful of
foreign businessmen and their native compradors," he wrote cynically,

"[but] it was also a time when there was never a year in which millions did not perish in famines, floods, epidemics and other preventable disasters and when millions of farmers were losing their land. Chiang Kai-shek's Nanjing Government was always announcing plans to remedy these situations, and then always postponing them."[26]

Japan and the Undoing of the "Golden Decade"

This brief period of fragile national renewal and hope was cut short by Japan's imperial ambitions on the Chinese mainland. Like Liang and Sun before him, Chiang had initially held out hope that China and Japan might somehow still agree on a pan-Asian plan of cooperation. But his wake-up call came in 1928 at the city of Jinan, in coastal Shandong Province, where Japan still had not let go of the German concessions it had inherited as a result of the Treaty of Versailles. In fact, the Japanese government had started to quietly amass troops there, so when Chiang sought to take Jinan on May 3, they resisted, even shelling the city. Before the fighting was over, the military clashes and atrocities left many thousands of soldiers and civilians dead.[27]

Outraged by the brutality of the Imperial Army and embarrassed by his own defeat, Chiang now derogatorily referred to Japanese as *wokou* (倭寇), "dwarf pirates."[28] Sure enough, because his resistance had been so weak, Manchuria began slipping out of Chiang's control, with Japan creating a puppet state called Manchukuo in 1931. "We're finished, done for!" Chiang wrote despairingly in his diary on September 18, 1931. "Our only way is to spare nothing in the performance of our duty to the end."[29]

Chiang had decided to reserve his strength to fight the Communists later in central China instead of the Japanese in the north, which meant that the Imperial Army's advance went virtually unobstructed. However, Chiang felt the humiliation of having to endure such an indignity, and again and again wrote of his agony in the pages of his diary. "How can our country mobilize itself with sufficient will to make it strong enough to wash away the humiliation?" he wrote with an air of desperation on April 18, 1934.[30]

Hungry for more pieces of the Central Kingdom, the Japanese now moved to overwhelm the heartland of their still almost supine neighbor. "Events in history have repeatedly proved that if only the Powers combine against China, they can dictate any terms to her," the Japanese emissary to China, Baron Hayashi Gonsuke, cold-bloodedly declared. "The way to deal with China is for the Powers to insist on what they want and to go on insisting until they get it."[31]

A gathering sense of national disgrace was turning more and more Chinese against Chiang's strategy of putting off war with Japan. It was only after the Xi'an Incident and the Japanese attack at Marco Polo Bridge outside Beijing in 1937 that Chiang felt he no longer had any choice but to fight. "The Japanese have challenged us, and we must finally respond with resolution," he confided to his diary. "The time has come!"[32]

War quickly spread as fierce fighting broke out around Shanghai that November 1937, heading toward a horrifying denouement with the Rape of Nanjing in December. Chiang and his wife decided that here, at least, in the new national capital of which they were so recklessly proud, they had to go all out to resist. For several weeks Chinese armies made a heroic effort to defend the capital against a far superior Japanese force. Only when artillery shells started bursting around his presidential palace, did Chiang finally abandon his effort.

As the Japanese occupied the city, hundreds of thousands of Chinese residents were wounded, raped, tortured, or massacred in what became one of the worst atrocities of World War II. "What you hear and see on all sides is the brutality and bestiality of the Japanese soldiers," testified John Rabe, a German Nazi businessman working in the city who sought to protect as many Chinese victims as he could and who today is known as "China's Schindler."[33]

For Chiang, the deeply humiliating loss of his new national capital was a bitter reminder that, whatever its progress, China was still unable to protect itself from marauding foreigners. Like the Empress Dowager in 1860 and again in 1900, Generalissimo Chiang now also had to flee his seat of power for a base deep in the hinterland—the southwestern city of Chongqing. "The war will not be decided in Nanjing or any other city," he defiantly proclaimed. "It will be decided in the countryside of our vast country and by the inflexible will of our people. We shall fight on every step of the way."[34] Yet for seven and a half long years, until their final defeat in 1945, Japanese armies would, despite continued resistance by both Nationalist and Communist forces, rapaciously march back and forth across China with relative impunity, conducting their savage "kill all, burn all, loot all" campaign against the Chinese people.

Japanese occupation of large portions of China was hardly the end of Chiang's trials. Wartime inflation grew worse every year, sinking both rural and urban populations into increasing economic misery. Equally devastating for Chiang, corruption within his own Nationalist Party became epidemic. By the early 1940s, his legitimacy as the country's savior was under serious challenge. As his reputation for incorruptibility plummeted, journalist Edgar Snow likened the Nationalists' temporary capital in Chongqing, far up the Yangtze River, to "Chinese Augean stables" and his government to "a dictatorship of a small clique of Guomindang members, of whom the Generalissimo is the point of focus and the figurehead."[35]

In 1943 Theodore H. White, another well-known, but highly critical, American journalist, left a wartime interview with Chiang "convinced [that] he was not only useless to us . . . but useless to his own people."[36] By the end of the decade, with the Japanese finally defeated, Chiang would suffer his final indignity: lose the civil war to Mao and be driven off the mainland to Taiwan.

The Yin and Yang of Chiang

Such was Chiang's roller-coaster ride as "supreme leader" of China. But what exactly was it that distinguished him as leader, animated his thinking, and conditioned his decision making? Just how did he fit into the larger history of reform efforts to revive his country?

Like the tumultuous age in which he rose, Chiang was a contradictory mixture of past and present, East and West, Confucianism and Christianity, authoritarian instinct and democratic pretension. On one hand, he was a traditionalist who venerated the notion of the Confucian *junzi* (君子) or "gentleman," who gains higher consciousness and leadership ability through self-cultivation. He loved the Chinese classics and centered his conception of leadership around a tireless (some would say tiresome) effort to restore traditional virtues to government and society. He was smitten by Tang Dynasty poetry, was a passably good calligrapher, and faithfully kept a Confucian-style diary of daily self-criticism.[37] He spoke no Western language and, other than his stays in Japan and a short tour of Russia, was largely unacquainted with the outside world. He admired military discipline, control, and order, and he was an ardent patriot and nationalist who strongly identified with China's fortunes in the world. When political life became too intense, he had a penchant for theatrically "retiring" in pique from politics, affecting the manner of a classical scholar to repair to a mountain redoubt in his home province of Zhejiang for a time-honored interlude of Confucian reflection and self-examination.

On the other hand, upon marrying his American-educated, English-speaking, and devoutly Christian wife, Song Meiling, Chiang turned to reading the Gospels, praying daily, and even sprinkling his diary with references to the long suffering of Jesus. But his efforts to straddle the East-West divide presented him with contradictions he was never able to resolve. At the heart of all of these contradictions was the inconvenient truth that even as he saw the West and Japan as tormentors of China, like his mentor Sun Yat-sen, he could never fully separate himself from them, much less give full voice to his sense of indignation over their treatment of his country. Inasmuch as his own wife was so westernized, he was even seen as symbolically married to the West. And when his wartime alliance with the British and Americans left him more dependent than ever on the very countries that had perpetrated the unequal treaty system on China, he found himself in the middle of a painful contradiction, one visually exemplified by his sartorial habits. Whether attired like a Prussian general in trim-fitting, military regalia, complete with epaulets, medals, shiny leather boots, and a sword; in Western-style cape and black fedora; in traditional-style Chinese scholar's robes and cotton-soled shoes; or in high-collared Sun Yat-sen suits, Chiang showed affection for both Eastern and Western wardrobes. Despite all his Confucian pretensions, he would also sometimes accessorize himself with a svelte walking stick—which he justified by reference to the back injury he had sustained while trying to escape his captors during the Xi'an Incident—that lent him the foppish air of a British colonial wannabe with a swagger stick.

Chiang's theatrical dressing habits could not alter the fact that he was a deeply conservative man and felt most comfortable in traditional

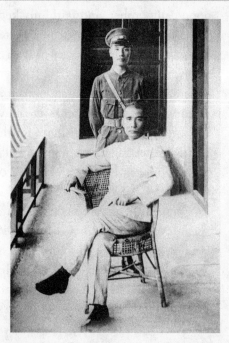

Chiang Kai-shek with Sun Yat-sen at Whampoa Military Academy, 1924

Japanese troops burying Chinese alive during the "Rape of Nanjing," 1937–38

Chiang and wife, Song Meiling, with FDR and Churchill at the Cairo Conference, 1943

Chiang toasting Mao, 1945

Chinese settings. He was also a chauvinist whose patriotism was rooted in a deep sense of wounded national pride. As he saw it, the unequal treaties had "completely destroyed . . . our sense of honor and shame was lost."[38] That this sorry process had culminated on his watch with the Japanese occupation of his country only increased his sense of humiliation.

"Stiff-necked Chinese pride" was "the first quality that came to mind when one reflected on Chiang," wrote Theodore White. "With his people he shared, and shared personally, a century of humiliation that had cut him so sharply it edged every facet of his personality."[39]

Perhaps it was Chiang's inability to remedy the problem of his country's weakness that helped turn him into such a combustible combination of simmering control and uncontrollable outbursts. White remembered that Chiang behaved "with ice-stiff self-discipline—except for the moments when he flew into a tantrum, yelled, threw teacups or plates about, tore up papers and raged out of control."[40] His anger, said White "came in spasms," running the gamut "from casual beatings to killing."[41]

Chiang's fierce pride in the face of foreign slurs and sensitivity to his country's inability to defend itself reflected a sense of hurt national pride that had pooled within him for decades. His was the same sense of inferiority that had inspired the nationalism of the May Fourth Movement and engendered its relentless attacks on old ways of thinking and acting, but in Chiang's case nationalism drew him not against the past, but irresistibly back to tradition in the hope of somehow arousing China's *jiben jingshen* (基本精神), its "fundamental spirit"— a concept Chiang cherished, just as Sun had dreamed of a revival of "national spirit."

Chiang's speeches and writings are replete with passionate exhortations not only to follow Sun's Three People's Principles but also to return to core Confucian virtues as the surest path to national regeneration. He felt little sympathy for the likes of Chen Duxiu, whose student acolytes had flooded the streets of Beijing and other cities attacking "Confucius and sons." He acknowledged that their demonstrations showed "the Chinese people's fighting spirit and patriotism,"[42] but their desire to tear down China's cultural heritage struck him only as nihilistic.

"Does the New Culture Movement mean the overthrow of the old ethics and the rejection of national history . . . the blind worship of foreign countries and indiscriminate introduction and acceptance of foreign civilization?" he asked. "If it does, the new culture we seek is too simple, too cheap and too dangerous."[43]

Chiang was a political revolutionary but a cultural traditionalist. "As members of the revolutionary party, we must dedicate ourselves sincerely to the preservation of the traditional virtues and the traditional spirits," he proclaimed in 1933. "Only by doing so will we be able to revive the highest culture of our nation, to restore our nation's very special standing in this world."[44]

Unequal Treaties and Anti-Foreignism

At the very center of Chiang's grievance lay the "ruthless and powerful unequal treaties"[45] that, in his view, still kept China in "bondage."[46] The treaties, of course, infringed on Chinese sovereignty, but even more abhorrent for him was the "mood of weak surrender"[47] they engendered among the Chinese people.

A smoldering anti-foreignism is everywhere evident in Chiang's writings and utterances. As early as 1925, when more then fifty demonstrating Chinese—including some cadets from his Whampoa Military Academy—were killed by British troops in Canton, he angrily wrote in his diary, "The stupid British regard Chinese lives as dirt. . . . How can we emancipate mankind if we cannot annihilate the English?"[48]

Over and over Chiang heaped blame for China's plight on the unequal treaties, and he was determined to win their cancellation. "The deterioration of China's national position and the low morale of the people during the last hundred years can be largely attributed to the unequal treaties," he wrote, and their implementation "constitutes a complete record of China's national humiliation."[49]

Indeed, once ensconced in Nanjing as president of the Republic, Chiang defiantly proclaimed his intention to renegotiate all extraterritorial rights granted to foreigners before 1930. Alas, his government was still so weak, the West so intransigent, and Japan so implacable that he couldn't completely follow through on his vow.[50] It was not

until 1943 that Britain and America finally did agree to relinquish all
provisions of these agreements and the hated system of forcing Chinese
"to cede territory and pay indemnities" was at last ended.[51]

For Chiang, the humiliation that grew out of these treaties was a
personal loss of face written on a national scale, and it is hard to open
any volume of his writings and not immediately stumble upon his indignation. "Today you can only endure the insults and prepare yourselves for vengeance." Though Chiang had only recently succeeded in
re-unifying China through his Northern Expedition, he had far from
forgotten his country's bitter experience of foreign occupation. As he
wrote, "It will take ten years to train the population in the firm belief
of our forefathers that the lost territories can and must be recovered
and the national humiliation avenged."[52]

In calling for such endurance until vengeance could be exacted,
Chiang identified with the ancient legend of King Goujian, explored in
great depth by historian Paul Cohen. Despite the story's antiquity, Chinese are still familiar with the Monte Cristo–esque tale of how Goujian
lost his kingdom of Yue to a rival king and was taken prisoner, but
nonetheless stoically endured his suffering without wavering in his intention to someday rise again to defeat his rival, restore his own rule,
and wipe out his disgrace. So that he would forget neither his humiliation nor his obligation to seek revenge, Goujian slept on a bed of
brushwood and hung above it a bitter-tasting gallbladder that he forced
himself to lick daily as a way to remain focused on his single-minded
quest to avenge the wrong done him and his kingdom. Goujian's story
gave rise to the still popular aphorism *woxin changdan* (卧薪尝胆), "to
lie on brushwood and taste gall."[53]

Chiang was deeply admiring of Goujian's example of forbearance,
fortitude, and determination. In fact, after Japan's incursion around
Jinan, Shandong Province, in 1928, when he felt most powerless to
resist, Chiang issued a directive to army personnel using the Goujian
aphorism. His defeat so mortified him and he identified so closely with
Goujian's own loss, that from 1928 on, he wrote a special daily diary
entry headed with the term *xuechi* (雪耻), meaning "wipe away humiliation."[54] And so that he would not forget his promise to himself,
he wrote, "From this day on, I will rise out of bed at six o'clock. I will

remind myself of this humiliation and continue to do so until the national humiliation is wiped away completely."[55]

After the Mukden incident in September 1931, when Japanese troops overran that Manchurian city as a prelude to pushing southward, Chiang wrote in his diary, "During Goujian's captivity, not only did he lie on brushwood and taste gall, he also drank urine and tasted excrement. Compared with me today, his ability to put up with hardship and tolerate humiliation was many times greater."[56] After 1949, marooned on Taiwan, Chiang had all the more reason to imagine himself a modern-day version of the ancient hero.[57]

China's Destiny

Chiang Kai-shek's most substantial written work, and the place in which one gets the clearest feel for his political sensitivities, was his book *China's Destiny*, an anti-imperialist call to arms drafted with the help of editor Tao Xisheng and published in 1943 during the darkest days of China's wartime travails. Despite his regime's close alliance with the British and the Americans, this tract brims with contempt for "the poison of foreign economic oppression"[58] and the "dangerous and maliciously ruthless . . . intrigues and methods of the imperialists."[59] With *China's Destiny*, Chiang took the pot filled with nationalism and victimization left simmering by Sun Yat-sen and brought it to a full boil.

"Whenever any foreign aggressor has forcibly broken through the defense lines of our state and occupied territory needed for our nation's existence, the Chinese nation, impelled by a sense of humiliation and the need for survival, has had no alternative but to rise and fight until that territory was restored to us,"[60] Chiang wrote on the first page of his manifesto. "And not until all lost territories have been recovered can we relax our efforts to wipe out this humiliation and save ourselves from destruction."[61] Summarizing the thinking passed on by late Qing self-strengtheners, Chiang observed, "From the Opium War down to the Revolution of 1911, the unanimous demand of the people was to avenge the national humiliation and make the country strong."[62] Indeed, it had been Chiang who, in 1927, established National Humiliation Day, playing on the slogan that had gained currency after Japan's Twenty-One Demands made in 1915: *wuwang guochi* (勿忘国耻), "Never forget national humiliation."[63]

For someone as proud, and fixated on China's weakness as Chiang, to be so beholden to the Americans and British during the war years was not easy. Adding insult to injury, he soon found himself stuck with an American military officer as chief of staff, the U.S. general "Vinegar Joe" Stilwell, who, as war progressed, became increasingly contemptuous of Chiang's reluctance to commit his Nationalist troops to battle against the Japanese. (Chiang, expecting an Allied victory, was in fact still reserving his forces[64] for the civil war against the Communists that he knew would come after the Japanese surrender.) Stilwell referred derogatorily to Chiang as "the Peanut" and openly chastised him as "a stubborn, prejudiced, conceited, despot"[65] surrounded by "yes-men."[66]

If Stilwell infuriated Chiang, the Chinese leader's rhetoric in *China's Destiny* returned the favor. But it also put him in a diplomatic bind. Not surprisingly, those few foreigners who were able to read Chiang's magnum opus in the original Chinese tended to be offended by its truculent, anti-foreign tone. American China hand John S. Service, who had been attached to Stilwell's staff from the U.S. Foreign Service, called the book Chiang's "*Mein Kampf,*" and, because it charged that "foreign aggression is to blame for all of China's troubles and failure," he viewed it as "a bigoted, narrow, strongly nationalistic effort."[67]

Wisely, Chiang's advisors thought better of allowing the book to be translated into English while World War II still raged. In fact, they soon withdrew it from circulation even in Chinese.[68] Reading it today, one gets a clear sense of how deep was Chiang's sense of injustice over China's treatment by the great powers and how powerful was his yearning—like so many Chinese before him—to see his country reunified and restored to a rightful position of power and influence. And, in his view, the key to attaining almost every one of his goals was mobilizing the spirits of nationalism, which Chiang tirelessly extolled as "the most meritorious of all human emotions, because a nation is formed by natural forces, and the consolidation of a nation must depend on the instinctive emotions of man."[69]

Tutelage Redux

While Chiang splattered his speeches and writings with references to "constitutional democracy," "liberty," and "freedom," he did so in much the same way as had Sun, in a rather offhand manner. For him, these were vague, long-term aspirations, nowhere near as important in China's immediate struggle for survival and national rejuvenation as control. Democracy was all well and good, but only in time and only if it promoted his primary goals of unity, wealth, national strength, and international prestige. Otherwise, Chiang was a pragmatist who would use whatever was necessary to create a disciplined Nationalist Party and a strong, centralized government, which he saw as antecedents to independence.

"We must be self-reliant before we can be independent," he wrote in *China's Destiny*. "[And] we must be strong before we can be free."[70] Even though he was well aware that Chinese liberals idealized democracy, he was not about to buy into the luxury of democracy for democracy's sake, as some adherents of "New Culture" had. Instead, he repeatedly and scornfully cautioned against the idea of "wholesale westernization."

Nonetheless, even as he steadfastly maintained that China needed a prolonged stage of "political tutelage," he bristled defensively at any suggestion that he was a "dictator." In the end, his quest for national strength would lead him into a complex ideological world in which nationalism, democracy, Confucianism, Leninism, Christianity, and even a bit of cryptofascism all mingled uncomfortably together.

Confucius Meets Lenin and Mussolini

Because above all else Chiang was focused on maintaining some semblance of order and stability during the unruly process of modernization, he imagined a return to Confucianism as a source of future strength. After all, in the Confucian scheme of things, the ideal family involved a carefully arranged order that relied on each person accepting his or her assigned position in a preordained hierarchy, respecting the authority of parents and elders, and then to acting out prescribed roles in a faithful and disciplined manner. As the Sage famously declared in the *Analects*, "A man who respects his parents and his elders would hardly be inclined to defy his superiors. A man who is not inclined to defy his superiors will never foment a rebellion."[71] Like filial sons in a model Confucian family, good citizens of an orderly nation owed their respect, loyalty, and obedience to their leaders and should thus yield unselfishly to the dictates of paternal state authority, which Chiang saw as being a benevolent moral force. And, of course, he envisioned himself at the helm of such a political patriarchy and thus deeply deserving of devotion, and even obedience. This very traditional view of leadership was not so different from that of all the "Sons of Heaven" who had preceded him during imperial times since time immemorial.

In their enthusiasm to restore neo-Confucian morality, Chiang and Song Meiling even concocted a spiritual/political campaign they called the New Life Movement. She explained the movement's ideology as "rescuing the people from the cumulative miseries of poverty, ignorance, and superstition, combined with the after effects of communistic orgies and natural calamities, and, last but not least, the grave consequences of external aggression."[72] Based on the cardinal virtues of Confucianism, one of which was having a sense of shame, the New Life Movement was also heavily laced with a strong dose of Song's Christian moralism, emphasizing such things as personal hygiene, devotion, modesty, frugality, sexual abstinence, patriotism, and anticommunism. It was a confection that caused *Time* magazine to joke: "There's Methodism in this madness!"[73] It was also an effort all too many educated Chinese dismissed as retrograde and simple-minded. Nor did it ever catch on with the masses, who were struggling just to stay alive.[74]

If warmed-over Confucianism could not sufficiently fortify Chiang's efforts to create a new centralized leadership, there was one other, even stronger remedy available. Like his mentor Sun Yat-sen, Chiang was deeply inspired by Lenin's prescriptions for a tightly disciplined party organization led by a small cadre of highly regimented "professional revolutionaries" all adhering to a centrally determined ideology.[75]

In August 1923, after introducing Chiang as his "most trusted deputy," Sun had sent him as head of a delegation to Moscow to study the political training techniques of Red Army officers and the principles of Leninist party organization. In 1927 when Chiang turned on the Com-

munists in the Shanghai "white terror," the Nationalist Party had ironically already become deeply imbued with these Leninist organizational
ideas and practices.[76] Chiang was even reputed to have said in an off-
the-record 1932 speech, "If we want our revolution [to be] a success,
we must create a party dictatorship."[77]

The first few decades of the twentieth century were a period in Chinese history during which many revolutionaries, Chiang included, were
picking through different systems of global politics and cultures for
whatever might "work." For Chiang in the 1920s, that menu certainly
included Leninism, with its party-building principles of "democratic
centralism." Then, in the early 1930s, he even went through a period
of flirtation with German and Italian fascism. It was his interest in big-
leader *kultur*, as well as his obsession with control, obedience, and
party discipline, that had first drawn him to Leninism and now to fascism. Although he never came close to manifesting, let alone mobilizing, the organizational malevolence of a Hitler, Stalin, or Mussolini, he
was attracted to aspects of those totalitarian systems that fit in with his
own nostalgic version of Confucian traditionalism. Just as fascists in
Germany and Italy had welded traditional patriarchal cultural elements
onto their new ideology to give them more appeal, so Chiang saw a
congruency between fascism and his own desire to emphasize national
culture, order, hierarchy, and orthodoxy. At one point, he was even
reported to have spoken of China's need to *nacuihua* (纳粹化), or "Na-
zify" itself.[78] And he did promote within his Nationalist Party the creation of vaguely protofascist organizations such as the Blue Shirts,
formally known as the Society for Persistent Conduct, a paramilitary
group that was said to be loosely modeled on Hitler's Brown Shirts and
Mussolini's Black Shirts.[79] But Chiang's fascist tendencies were far
more muted than those of his European counterparts. One crucial difference was that his authoritarianism was closer to that of traditional
Chinese secret societies than mass-based political organization.[80] In
this and other ways, Chiang proved incapable of truly promoting mass
political organization, an art in which his rival and nemesis, Mao Zedong, would prove the master.

Chiang's argument for borrowing from these less than democratic
traditions was quite straightforward. He admired the well-organized
and disciplined military forces in Japan and Germany, and in 1934

even welcomed generals Hans von Seekt and Alexander von Falken-
hausen, sent to China as advisors by Hitler. Evoking Sun's famous
"sheet of loose sand" metaphor, Chiang seemed to feel that if protofascist organizations were capable of serving as a binding agent for China,
then that was justification enough. In this metaphoric world, no disag-
gregated element was welcome. As Chiang warned, "Loose grains of
sand cannot be tolerated."[81]

"Chiang Kai-shek wanted absolute power," wrote Edgar Snow. But,
he never managed to become "a great tyrant, only a petty one; he failed
not because he was Caesar or because he killed too few of the right
people; he never understood that his worst enemies were inside his own
camp. Chiang was not resolute, only obstinate; not wise, only obsolete;
not disciplined, only repressed; not original, only a scavenger among
the relics of the past; and not ruthless, merely vain."[82]

The Fall

By the end of World War II, with the legitimacy of Chiang's government badly eroded, the "golden decade" of the 1930s seemed like a
distant memory. When the armistice with Japan in 1945 led to the collapse of the second United Front with the Communists, open civil war
with Mao's People's Liberation Army (PLA) broke out. By 1948, critics
such as Columbia University scholar A. Doak Barnett, who was living
in China at the time, had concluded, "Faith in the Central Government
seems to have vanished."[83]

When Chiang finally fled to Taiwan in 1949 to be labeled "the man
who lost China," leading historians on both sides increasingly began to
view the whole republican era as just one more unsuccessful experiment in China's series of failed efforts to reinvent itself. And when Mao
established the People's Republic of China (PRC) in October that same
year, the notion that, after a chaotic republican dead end, history had
started up again with a hopeful new *dashi* (大事), or "great enterprise,"
as imperial historians once called the founding of new dynasties,
Chiang's tenure on the mainland acquired an even greater imputation
of failure and irrelevance. It was hardly surprising, then, that during his
years in Taipei such an air of disappointment, even tragedy, hung over
his studied efforts to keep up appearances. His lingering Nationalist

Chiang Kai-shek circa 1960

government, like the whole republican experiment itself, seemed to have been run off onto a historical siding and left there to rust away as a cast-off of history.

During Chiang's early years in Taipei, Nationalist Party officials liked to refer to Taiwan as "Free China." Their island redoubt may have been "free" of communism and on the road to prosperity, but it was still ruled by a single Leninist party under an autocratic general— just as Sun's notion of "political tutelage" had called for. However, after Chiang's death in 1975, his son and anointed successor, Chiang Ching-kuo, surprised everyone by ushering in a wholly unexpected new era. Turning more resolutely toward the longer-term goal of con-stitutionalism that Sun had set forth in his Three People's Principles, but which China had never been able to approach while either Sun or Chiang lived, in the 1980s Chiang's son lifted martial law, allowed op-position parties to operate openly, and even allowed Chinese people the first free elections since 1913. As a functioning democracy actually came to life on Taiwan, it provided proof that Chinese were not some-how congenitally incapable of sustaining democratic governance, and thus enabled Chinese everywhere to imagine for the first time how, with further political maturation, perhaps even mainlanders could someday look forward to living in a more open political system.

And who knows? In the future, we may yet find ourselves looking back on that time long ago when Chiang Kai-shek still held his triste tea parties for foreign students in Taipei and see it not as a dead end, but as a period of gestation when those inchoate ideas of democracy that were always so well hidden behind exhortations for strong govern-ment were actually incubating, not just for the enjoyment of people on Taiwan, but for mainlanders as well.

CHAPTER 9

Not a Dinner Party（革命）

MAO ZEDONG（毛泽东）, PART I

A Revolutionary Shrine

By a small pond into which Mao Zedong once threatened to jump as a boy in order to spite his bullying father stands the large brown stucco house with a tiled roof where he was born.[1] It was first designated a historical site in 1961. But when the Cultural Revolution erupted in 1966, spewing Red Guards across China by the tens of millions, the natal place of the Great Helmsman became the premier destination in a whole web of revolutionary shrines spread throughout the country. Ever since, Communist Party faithful have flocked to Shaoshan in southern Hunan Province, turning this once out-of-the-way rural community into a modern-day Chinese Bethlehem. While Mao was still alive, visitors arrived like awestruck pilgrims at a place of worship. There was the kitchen in which Mao's saintly mother cooked family meals, the room where Mao studied, even the figurative manger of this Chinese redeemer, a wooden bed in which he once slept, with mosquito netting rather than swaddling clothes, on display. During tours, the only sounds came from official docents who incanted a memorized hagiography with the breathlessness of true believers.

Mao died in 1976, and during the years that followed, as Deng Xiaoping's reforms set China on the road to Leninist capitalism, the attitude of visitors began to change, and the former godhead came to seem a little less infallible. In the process, both the town and the house evolved from sacred shrine to historical theme park. Restaurants boasting the Mao family name with signs in blinking neon popped up, while

Mao Zedong in 1927

new souvenir shops sold knockoff Mao busts in porcelain and gold, T-shirts proclaiming "Serve the People," cigarette lighters that played "The East Is Red," and chopsticks inscribed with his political quotations. Shaoshan became a Mao-branded marketing opportunity, and visitors arrived not in a spirit of veneration but in one of recreational curiosity. Hushed reverence gave way to a more recreational impulse as hordes of tourists—insouciantly chattering away, stuffing themselves with snacks, and clowning around in front of cell phones and digital cameras—flooded into the village, giving it a strange new commercial feel.

As China's reform program continued to open the country up, it became ever harder to define just what Mao Zedong, like Shaoshan itself, meant to "his people." But to this day Mao's still substantial appeal seems to derive, at least in part, from his ability to project a commanding sense of fearlessness and strength. For better or worse, he was a leader unafraid to exercise authority. If new wealth and global power came to China after his death, under his leadership it at least became a nation that the world could no longer ignore, much less mistreat. Accustomed to being bullied and denigrated, many Chinese found Mao's self-confidence and bravado (even when it morphed into a self-serving swagger) seductive and, in the end, surprisingly reassuring. Being bullied by your own new "emperor" was better than being at the mercy of arrogant foreign powers. And being bullied was something Mao had learned more than a little about at an early age.

Fathers and Sons

Mao was born in 1893 in Hunan Province, a century after the Macartney mission, and a year before the disastrous Sino-Japanese War, just as Qing China entered the final stage of terminal decline. His early years were irrigated by two quite different wellsprings of influence. The first was his experience growing up in a state of struggle, sometimes even physical combat, in the household presided over by a demanding and unyielding patriarchal father. The other was the writing of turn-of-the-century thinkers such as Liang Qichao, Yan Fu, and Chen Duxiu, who helped spark and shape Mao's lifelong passion for political ideas and revolutionary nationalism.

By Mao's own account, from his earliest years he was constantly on guard against the tyranny of his father, who regularly beat him. His father was, said Mao, "a severe taskmaster" and a "hot-tempered man,"[2] making the young Mao's home a place of unending antagonism, menace, and violence, where survival depended on the boy's readiness and willingness to struggle. It is hardly surprising, then, that his fraught relationship with his stubborn, powerful father bred within him a deep-seated antiauthoritarianism. Mao's father, born an illiterate peasant, ended up a prosperous small-town rice trader—later conveniently designated as a "middle peasant" by the Communist Party to relieve him of the class odium of too much wealth. Considered the family scholar because he could read and write, the young Mao was forced to study the Confucian classics, breeding within him a loathing of the monotonous memorization and recitation process. What he adored, instead, was reading "the romances of Old China," as he called them, especially tales of rebellious heroes and bandits, in which his native province, Hunan, historically abounded. Mao reveled in such popular novels as *The Water Margin*, *The Romance of the Three Kingdoms*, and especially *Journey to the West*, which chronicled the endless antics of Sun Wukong, the rebellious Monkey King, who arose from the earth like "wind and thunder" and possessed supernatural powers that enabled him to *danao tiangong* (大闹天宫), "rage against heaven."[3] Chinese traditionally considered monkeys to be the spontaneous and unpredictable personifications of the playful trickster, and throughout his life Mao celebrated the rebellious spirit of the Monkey King. Indeed, he ended a 1961 poem with these lines:

The golden monkey wrathfully swung his massive cudgel
And the jade-like firmament was cleared of dust,
Today, a miasmal mist once more rising,
We hail Sun Wukong the wonder-worker.[4]

In a letter to his third wife, Jiang Qing, written not long before his death, Mao compared himself to the tiger, a symbol of power, but added that he was also "just a monkey." "I have a tigerish nature as my main characteristic," he continued, "and a monkey nature as my subordinate characteristic."[5]

As a boyish tiger-monkey, Mao prided himself on surreptitiously finding creative ways to continue his subversive reading, "devouring everything I could find, except the Classics,"[6] he told Edgar Snow in Bao'an in June 1936 while holed up in the hill caves of Yan'an, with the fate of his Communist revolution still uncertain.[7] The book that resulted from Snow's interviews, *Red Star over China*, published in 1938, proved to be the only comprehensive account of his life Mao would ever give.

"Despite the vigilance of my old teacher, who hated these outlawed books and called them wicked," Mao remembered gleefully to Snow, "I used to read them in school, covering them up with a classic [text] when the teacher walked past."[8] Such insubordination infuriated his teacher and father. Endless altercations followed, such as once when Mao was about thirteen years old and his father had invited a group of guests to their home. "While they were present," recounted Mao, "a dispute arose between the two of us. My father denounced me before the whole group, calling me lazy and useless. This infuriated me. I cursed him and left the house. . . . Thus, I learned to hate him."[9]

Although Mao would later boast about his defiance of paternal authority, in conservative rural Hunan culture such unfilial behavior toward a father would have made any son an object of social scorn. "Never disobey!" was the advice of Confucius to sons.[10] "In serving his father and mother a man may gently remonstrate with them," Confucius taught his disciples. "But if he sees that he has failed to change their opinion, he should resume an attitude of deference and not thwart them."[11]

Mao later dismissed these family battles royal by humorously using Communist Party lingo to describe them, saying, for example, that "the dialectical struggle in our family was constantly developing," or that, he, his two brothers, and their mother, a kindly Buddhist believer whose devotion to Mao probably fortified him with his unusual self-confidence, formed "a United Front" against his tyrannical father. Such struggles, however, were doubtless traumatic experiences.

Adding to the tension, Mao was also in a constant state of rebellion against the other main authority figure in his life, his classics teacher, whom he described as being from "the stern treatment school . . . harsh and severe, frequently beating his students,"[12] much as Chen

Duxiu's grandfather had beaten him. Indeed, on one such occasion, the ten-year-old Mao became so upset that he ran away from school and wandered lost for several days, "afraid to return home for fear of receiving another beating there."[13] To his surprise, however, upon finally going home, far from being punished, Mao found that both his father and his teacher had unexpectedly softened. Perhaps alarmed by the boy's boldness in fleeing, his father was "slightly more considerate," while his teacher became "more inclined to moderation." For Mao, this was an important lesson in the power of defiance. "The result of my act of protest impressed me very much," he recounted. "It was a successful 'strike.'[14] . . . I learned that when I defended my rights by open rebellion, my father relented, but when I remained meek and submissive, he only cursed and beat me the more."[15]

Soon enough, Mao became aware of a far larger oppression—China's treatment at the hands of the great powers. "In this period also I began to have a certain amount of political consciousness, especially after I read a pamphlet telling of the dismemberment of China." He remembered the pamphlet as beginning with the words "Alas, China will be subjugated!" After reading that single line, Mao recalled feeling "depressed about the future of my country." But he also "began to realize that it was the duty of all the people to help save it."[16] This was his *jiuguo* (救国) or "save the nation" moment, something almost every maker of modern China experienced in one form or another.

Mao surely derived much of his later fascination with the dynamics of class and imperialist oppression from his standoff with his father. In fact, the experience of familial struggle seems to have had an almost Darwinian effect on him, challenging him to strengthen himself and evolve as a survival mechanism, a process that could only have taken place on a crucible of actual oppression and revolt. Since Mao had lived the logic of survival of the fittest in his own family, he could later embrace the Marxist notion of class struggle with a well-developed instinct for competition, endurance, and triumph. And in drawing salutary conclusions about the value of struggle, Mao also took a giant step outside the bounds of conventional Confucian thinking. Instead of viewing struggle as a precursor to undesirable disorder and upheaval—which most traditional Chinese political philosophers lumped together under the much-disparaged category of *luan* (乱), "chaos"—Mao came to embrace and even revere them as generators of dynamism and change.

At seventeen years old, just before the Qing Dynasty collapsed, Mao managed to enter the Xiangxiang School, not far from his village.[17] Here, to supplement the traditional classical curriculum, he acquired a smattering of "new knowledge" from the West, largely through the works of progressive intellectuals such as Kang Youwei and Liang Qichao. "I read and reread these books until I knew them by heart," he said. "I worshipped Kang and Liang."[18] It had been Liang who caustically observed that while China was "the first nation to evolve culture on earth," its old system had since caused it "to shun progress, to stagnate, and to be jeered at as an uncivilized nation."[19] Mao adored such unapologetic iconoclasm and became so worshipful of these reformers that when the dynasty did fall, he naively posted a manifesto on the wall of his school calling for a new government with Sun Yat-sen as president, Kang as premier, and Liang as foreign minister, never mind that Sun was irreconcilably opposed to the other two.[20]

In 1912 Mao moved on to Hunan's provincial capital, Changsha, where, after six months in a local republican militia followed by a period of rigorous self-study in the Changsha Public Library, he entered the First Provincial Normal School.[21] Before graduating in the winter of 1918, he studied geography, history, and philosophy, voraciously absorbing new influences and ideas from abroad.[22] It was also during this period that Mao first began putting his own thoughts on paper.

Willpower, Bodybuilding, and Heroism

One of Mao's very earliest literary efforts was a 1912 essay, written when he was only eighteen years old, on the subject of Lord Shang Yang, the founding figure of the Legalist school of statecraft. Unlike Confucianism, Legalism stressed the need for strong leadership, rigid authoritarian controls, strict centralism, and an uncompromising system of laws and punishments, all "to enrich the people and strengthen the state." Almost anything done in pursuit of these basic goals was considered justifiable. It was precisely this pragmatic, whatever-works approach that had drawn Wei Yuan, a self-identified Confucian also born in Hunan Province, to Legalism as a panacea for China's decline a century before Mao.

Commending Lord Shang's draconian system, the teenage Mao noted, "Shang Yang's laws were good laws. If you have a look today at the four-thousand-odd years for which our country's history has been recorded, and the great political leaders who have pursued the welfare of the country and the happiness of the people, is not Shang Yang one of the very first on the list?"[23]

Legalism emphasized the law as a way for the state to control its people, including government officials, through strict punishment, and thereby maintain order and increase their collective wealth and well-being. In the Legalist world, in other words, the rule of law had nothing to do with protecting people's rights against the state. Growing up amid the malaise of the late Qing and the chaos of the early republic, Mao—like Sun Yat-sen and Chiang Kai-shek—was attracted to the promise of strong government and order, writing disdainfully of the abiding "stupidity of the people of our country," which seemed to make them ungovernable.[24] If Lord Shang's harsh prescriptions for governance had brought order and strength to the equally chaotic dawning of imperial China millennia ago, why would Chinese eschew them now, in the empire's twilight? Mao concluded that one way to overcome the kind of "ignorance and darkness" that had brought China "to the brink of destruction" was strong, heroic, willful, sometimes even brutal and violent leadership.[25]

Mao's youthful fascination with the rigors of Legalism soon took a more concrete form. While at First Provincial Normal School, he also became an avid reader of Chen Duxiu's New Youth magazine and soon began writing for it.[26] In his first contribution, a 1917 essay on physical education, he urged Chinese to strengthen their own bodies as a precondition for strengthening their country, and he proposed a self-help course in building both personal character and a stronger nation through physical exercise.[27] Whereas a previous generation had called for a program of "self-strengthening" by building modern schools and arsenals and introducing foreign technical training, Mao now preached national rejuvenation through a proto-twelve-step program that began with bodybuilding. "Our nation is wanting in strength, the military spirit has not been encouraged," he lamented. "The physical condition of our people deteriorates daily. These are extremely disturbing phenomena."[28]

Delving into the interrelationship between an individual's physical strength and a nation's collective strength, Mao derided those who "overemphasize knowledge"[29] and have "white and slender hands,"[30] "flabby" skin, and "small and frail" bodies.[31] Only "when the body is strong," he proclaimed, can one "advance speedily in knowledge and morality and reap far-reaching advantages."[32]

Being a young man of action, he also began taking long mountain hikes, swimming in freezing rivers, and sleeping outside on frosty nights.[33] It was almost as if he had a premonition of the physical ordeals that lay ahead. Already tall, he began going bare-chested to show off his well-sculpted physique, causing his teacher (whose daughter he would ultimately marry) to write in his journal: "It is truly difficult to imagine someone so intelligent and handsome."[34]

As Mao wrestled with China's "want of strength," he concluded that both individual and national strength depended not just on physical effort but on "will" as well.[35] Real strength could only arise, he wrote, through the discipline of endless "drill,"[36] which in turn could only be generated by a will that was "savage and rude" and had "nothing to do with delicacy."[37] Physical education was important, he wrote, because it "not only harmonizes the emotions, it also strengthens the will," which he was coming to see as a precursor of those human qualities he most admired—military heroism, courage, dauntlessness, audacity, and perseverance. All were, he declared, "matters of will."[38]

To a friend, he wrote, "Those who wish to move the world must move the world's hearts and minds." In order to do that, they must possess not only physical strength and willpower but also "ultimate principles" and "the truths of the universe." These muddy notions revealed a young Mao groping his way toward a new understanding of how to become an effective agent for change. "If all the hearts of the realm are moved, is there anything which cannot be achieved?" he asked with naive ebullience. "And, if the affairs of the realm can be dealt with, how, then, can the state fail to be rich, powerful and happy?"[39]

In the end, Mao came to believe that physical prowess and strong leadership were inescapably dependent on strength of will and the ability to act heroically. In this, he was deeply influenced by the romantic historical novels peopled with their larger-than-life martial heroes that had filled his head as a boy. Even after he became a Marxist, his emphasis on the efficacy of individual will would continue to distinguish him from others, and also put him at odds with the economic determinism of orthodox Marxism. After all, the great revelation of Karl Marx's "scientific thinking" was supposed to lie in his discovery that the dynamics of class struggle had an inherent scientific basis of their own and would lead inevitably to the triumph of proletarian revolution through an unstoppable historical process. But as it turned out, the young Mao would prove too impatient to sit passively by and wait for this supposedly inevitable process to unfold on its own.

To the Capital

Upon graduating from Hunan Normal in 1918, Mao packed up and took a job at the new Peking University Library in the capital, then essentially under warlord control.[40] A low-level position, it nonetheless put him near the center of the country's political and intellectual ferment and especially close to the university librarian, Li Dazhao, one of the first Chinese intellectuals to become interested in Marxism. Like Mao, Li viewed "self-conscious group activity" as an essential part of political action, instrumental enough even to "change the tendency of economic phenomena."[41] If class struggle alone did not prove powerful enough to drive the revolution forward, both Li and Mao were ready to jump into the breach, bending their own wills to the task.

Li was also an editor of *New Youth* with Chen Duxiu, which meant that in Beijing Mao now found himself in the orbit of the most exciting intellectual and political currents of his time. But with his thick Hunan accent and provincial ways, he could hardly expect to play more than a bit part on this national stage. "My office was so low that people avoided me," he remembered. "One of my tasks was to register the names of people who came to read newspapers, but to most of them I didn't exist as a human being. Among those who came to read, I recognized the names of famous leaders of the [Chinese] 'renaissance' [New Culture] movement, men . . . in whom I was intensely interested. I tried to begin conversations with them on political and cultural subjects, but they were very busy men. They had no time to listen to an assistant librarian speaking southern dialect."[42] It is not hard to see how Mao, largely ignored by such well-known and haughty intellectuals and kept on the periphery of Beijing's intellectual scene, might have begun to develop the kind of resentment that would express itself decades later in his vitriolic attacks on "the stinking ninth category," those members of the intelligentsia whom he viewed as arrogant and having too much book learning and too little practical experience.

Although Mao left his library post just before the May Fourth Incident erupted in 1919, he was inspired by the demonstrations that followed. They showed that sometimes ideas *can* mobilize people to action and move history. But back in Hunan, he soon found himself pondering a very different kind of social force—the dispossessed peasants of rural China, who had been largely written off by urban intellectuals as an ignorant and inert segment of society, of little use to proletarian Marxist revolution or individualist liberal reform. In a 1919 essay, "The Present State of China's 'Great Union of the Popular Masses,'"[43] Mao was almost alone in raising the provocative possibility of ordinary peasants organizing "a union with others who cultivate the land" and thus becoming an important part of a Chinese revolution.[44] "From Dongting Lake to the Min River, the tide rises higher than ever," he effused. "Heaven and earth are aroused by it, the wicked are put to flight by it!"[45] And "We must all exert ourselves! We must all advance with utmost strength! Our golden age, our age of glory and splendor lies before us."[46]

As naive as Mao's enthusiasm may now sound, such youthful expressions did not go unnoticed elsewhere. While in prison in Beijing, Chen Duxiu found himself uplifted by such writing, which he viewed as exemplary of a new generation of Hunan activism filled with an encouraging "spirit of unrelenting struggle."[47] Reading Mao's essays, Chen professed, "my delight was so complete I nearly shed tears!"[48]

Sometime between 1917 and 1919 Mao inscribed a series of comments into the margins of a translated volume of Friedrich Paulsen's *A System of Ethics*. These surviving notes offer tantalizing hints to his evolving notions about what "the hero" could accomplish in history through the exercise of will, what Mao then called "motive power."

"The great actions of the hero are his own, are expressions of his motive power, lofty and cleansing, relying on no precedent," wrote Mao grandly. "His force is like that of a powerful wind. Arising from a deep gorge, like the irresistible sexual desire for one's lover, a force that will not stop, that cannot be stopped!"[49]

Even just jotting notes in someone else's book, Mao couldn't help preaching. "It is said that one man who scorns death will prevail over one hundred men," he scribbled. "This is because he fears nothing, because his motive power presses forward in a straight line. Because he cannot be stopped or eliminated, he is the strongest and the most powerful."[50] Here was a clear elucidation of the role that Mao saw evolving for himself. He was a born activist and already dreaming of bending Chinese reality to his will.

In a local periodical he edited in Hunan, he wrote a stirring manifesto filled with similar youthful ebullience. It began with a passage that included these lines: "Today we must change our old attitude toward issues that in the past we did not question, toward methods we would not use, and toward so many words we have been afraid to utter. Question the unquestionable! Dare to do the unthinkable! Do not shrink from saying the unutterable. No force can stop a tide such as this; no one can fail to be subjugated by it."[51]

A Party Founder

Mao was working as a local organizer setting up Communist cells in Hunan when on July 23, 1921, during the most brutal period of summer heat, he was summoned to Shanghai to join the underground meeting of the First Congress of the Chinese Communist Party.[52] In truth, Mao's conversion to communism was initially motivated less by a belief in Marxism than by his frustration with the agenda of earlier reformers and revolutionaries, so many of whom had looked to the West for answers, to no avail. In a 1949 tract, "On the People's Democratic Dictatorship," he would explain his ideological transition to communism this way: "From the time of China's defeat in the Opium War of 1840, Chinese progressives went through untold hardships in their quest for truth from the Western countries. . . . Only modernization could save China, only learning from foreign countries could modernize China. . . . [But i]mperialist aggression shattered the fond dreams of the Chinese about learning from the West. It was very odd—why were the teachers always committing aggression against their pupil? The Chinese learned a good deal from the West, but they could not make it work and were never able to realize their ideals. Their repeated struggles, including such a countrywide movement as the Revolution of 1911, all ended in failure."[53]

But then, of course, a new force burst onto the world stage: "The Russians made the October Revolution and created the world's first socialist state," wrote Mao. "Under the leadership of Lenin and Stalin, the revolutionary energy of the great proletariat and laboring people of Russia, hitherto latent and unseen by foreigners, suddenly erupted like a volcano, and the Chinese and all mankind began to see the Russians in a new light. Then, and only then, did the Chinese enter an entirely new era in their thinking and their life. They found Marxism-Leninism, the universally applicable truth, and the face of China began to change."[54] Mao's belief in willful, strong, heroic leadership now converged with Lenin's notion of the "professional revolutionary."[55]

Neither Chen Duxiu nor Li Dazhao had been able to attend the meeting in Shanghai establishing the Chinese Communist Party, which was disrupted by a police raid in which everyone was almost arrested.[56] But Mao, who arrived after a week of travel from Changsha via steamship, was present at the creation, a happenstance that helped endow him thereafter with a unique standing in party circles.[57] Soon, though, he found himself drawn in a very different direction than the kind of urban revolution that the Soviet Comintern, which largely controlled the new Chinese Communist Party leadership, intended.

Not a Dinner Party

As the fledgling Communist Party, led by Li Dazhao in the north and Chen Duxiu in the south, was ordered by Stalin to focus its energies on organizing China's emerging working class in cities along the coast, Mao was back in rural Hunan with those he knew the best, disenfranchised peasants. Surprisingly, they turned out to be the most active political agents in the region. On a monthlong field investigation in 1927 to some of the province's most backward rural areas, he discov-

ered that the peasant masses were far more cocked, loaded, and ready
to revolt than intellectuals or urban workers. In fact, although largely
unheralded in the press, masses of poor peasants had already risen in
revolt to, in Mao's words, "overthrow the feudal power" of the countryside by seizing lands rented to them at usurious rates by wealthy
landlords.[58] Mao's amazement upon discovering this movement would
lead to the next great chapter in his political life, and then to the Chinese Communist Revolution itself.

Mao's simple solution to the problem of making Marxism work in
an overwhelmingly agricultural society was to turn China's greatest
weakness, its rural poor, into its ultimate strength. "As every schoolboy
knows, 80 percent of China's population is peasants. So the peasant
problem of the Chinese revolution and the strength of the peasants is
the main strength of the Chinese revolution," Mao was to write in
1940.[59] "This means that the Chinese revolution is essentially a peasant revolution."[60] Mao seamlessly inverted Marx, as tenant farmers,
rather than factory workers, were made into the standard-bearers of
the Chinese Communist revolution.

Mao articulated this new vision in his forty-page "Report on an
Investigation of the Peasant Movement in Hunan," submitted to the
CCP in February 1927. It was the most incisive, passionate piece of
investigative writing he ever produced over a long and verbose career.
He began his eyewitness account almost like an adventure tale, saying,
"I saw and heard many strange things of which I had been hitherto
unaware."[61] "If you are a person of determined revolutionary viewpoint, and if you have been to the villages and looked around, you will
undoubtedly feel joy never before known," Mao continued breath-
lessly. Calling the spontaneous peasant movement he encountered "a
colossal event," he famously added, "In a very short time, several hundred million peasants . . . will rise like a fierce wind or tempest, a force
so swift and violent that no power however great will be able to suppress it. They will break through all the trammels that bind them and
rush forward along the road to liberation. They will, *in the end*, send
all the imperialists, warlords, corrupt officials, local bullies, and bad
gentry to their graves. All revolutionary parties and all revolutionary
comrades will stand before them to be tested, to be accepted or rejected
as they decide."[62]

Being a peasant himself, Mao was naturally drawn to this vision of revolt in the countryside in a way that few of his revolutionary comrades in the city could understand. He grasped the nature of rural life and its discontents, and on this 1927 expedition he witnessed the brute, inchoate, and defiant power of peasant rebellion. Its energy inspired him, and the force of this incipient popular revolt against the traditional cultural, social, and political corpus that had kept Chinese rootbound for so long undoubtedly also resonated with him personally.

Mao's 1927 report on what he called "a revolution without parallel in history" was almost messianic in tone.[63] "To march at their head and lead them, to stand behind them, gesticulating and criticizing them, or to stand opposite them and oppose them? Every Chinese is free to choose among the three, but by force of circumstances you are fated to make the choice quickly," he wrote, posing the wager with unalloyed prejudice.[64]

Because his experience in Hunan irrevocably enthroned in his mind the importance of peasant rebellion in any future Chinese revolution, this was a critical tipping point for Mao as an incipient revolutionary leader. "What Mr. Sun Yat-sen wanted, but failed to accomplish in the forty years [that] he devoted to the national revolution," wrote Mao, "the peasants have accomplished in a few months."[65] And it was in this report that Mao penned these celebrated lines: "A revolution is not like inviting people to dinner, or writing an essay or painting a picture, or doing embroidery; it cannot be so refined, so leisurely and gentle, so 'benign, upright, courteous, temperate and complaisant.' A revolution is an uprising, an act of violence whereby one class overthrows the power of another. . . . To right a wrong it is necessary to exceed the proper limits; the wrongs cannot be righted without doing so."[66]

The strictures of the old system that had kept China's peasantry in servitude, women in bondage, and youth confined by filial obligations were, at last, under attack from an unexpected quarter: millions of angry peasants rising like "a fierce wind or tempest" as "the privileges the feudal landlords have enjoyed for thousands of years are being shattered to pieces."[67] Observing the unrepentant violence of Hunan's resentful peasantry, Mao drew his own conclusion for the future: "The rural areas must experience a great, fervent revolutionary upsurge, which alone can rouse the peasant masses in their thousands and tens

Mao with his family in Hunan
Province, 1910s

Mao with Zhou Enlai (left) and Bogu (right) in Yan'an, 1937

Mass meeting in Shaanxi Province, 1938

Bust of Mao under construction in Hunan, 2009

of thousands to form this great force," he wrote. "To put it bluntly, it is necessary to bring a brief reign of terror in every rural area, otherwise we could never suppress the activities of the counterrevolutionaries in the countryside or overthrow the authority of the gentry."[68] While chaos and disorder had long been reviled by good Confucians as signs of decay and collapse, Mao was now coming to see them as creative and regenerative motor forces of progress, what he would later describe as "the locomotive of history."[69]

In his 1917 "A Study of Physical Culture," Mao had with youthful zeal written of his longing "to charge on horseback, amidst the clash of arms, and to be ever victorious; to shake the mountains by one's cries, and the colors of the sky by one's roars of anger, to have the strength to uproot mountains."[70] As he became more and more enamored of the creative powers of rebellion, violence, and disorder, his writing became ever more replete with upbeat allusions to storms, upheavals, tornados, tempests, tides, and waves. All were expressions of a raw, natural energy he admired and would seek to unleash in his quest to *fanshen* (翻身), "turn over" China, just as the peasant movement was then turning over rural Hunan.[71] Throughout his life, Mao would return again and again to the language of turmoil, especially during his last great act, the loosing on his country of the Great Proletarian Cultural Revolution. "No need to be afraid of tidal waves," he would write in a 1966 *People's Daily* editorial. "Human society has been evolved out of tidal waves."[72]

Creative Destruction

Mao's developing views on the need for a violent and totalistic uprooting of China's traditional culture and society ultimately would make Liang Qichao, Chen Duxiu, and other early iconoclasts seem like dabblers, especially when it came to reforming, even demolishing, "old society." As he matured, Mao never wavered from the invigorating challenges of such demolition. Indeed, he wanted to do for China what Joseph Schumpeter claimed capitalism did for a strong economy: "The perennial gale of creative destruction incessantly revolutionized the economic structure from within, incessantly destroying the old one, incessantly creating a new one."[73] Schumpeter had written his paean to the notion of "creative destruction."

Mao's first dalliance with this very un-Confucian idea seems to have come from Liang Qichao, who after the failure of the Hundred Days' Reform developed his theory of "destructionism."[74] "Destroy and there will be destruction. Do not destroy and there will also be destruction" (*pohuai yi pohuai, bupohai yi pohuai*, 破坏亦破坏, 不破坏亦破坏), Liang warned, having concluded that England and France achieved modernity only because their revolutions and civil wars had demolished their old feudal systems.[75] If China did not do the same, he concluded, it would never regenerate. While Liang ultimately moved on from his "destructionist" phase, Mao made a career of it.

In his otherwise rather moderate 1940 essay "On New Democracy," Mao delivered this well-known line: "There is no construction without destruction, no flowing without damming and no motion without rest" (*Bupo buli, busai buliu, buzhi buxing*; 不破不立, 不塞不流, 不止不行).[76] Although this aphorism was originally used by the Tang Dynasty philosopher, poet, and statesman Han Yu, Mao adapted it as a slogan of Communist insurrection.

Contradictions

Mao's Hunan report came out just months before Chiang Kai-shek launched his white terror, massacring urban Communist activists and forcing party cells in the cities deep underground. Yet the Communist leadership continued to resist Mao's call to relocate the Chinese revolution to the countryside. Nonetheless, even while his urban partisans were being hunted down by Chiang's Nationalist troops every step of the way, he pressed on, organizing peasants into a revolutionary party in China's remote rural backlands. Driven out of Hunan after the failed Autumn Harvest Uprising, Mao kept on organizing. He occupied the "liberated areas" of the Jinggangshan mountains in Jiangxi Province, until Chiang's "bandit suppression" campaigns finally forced him onto the Long March. A desperate retreat of six thousand miles across some of China's most remote and inhospitable lands, this Chinese hegira was a prolonged rout that reduced the Red Army from approximately eighty thousand to eight thousand.[77] For Mao, however, the march ended as a triumph. At a pivotal leadership meeting in the remote southwestern town of Zunyi in January 1935, he consolidated his leadership position in the CCP and would remain its preeminent leader until his death forty years later.[78]

Mao's experiences in the 1920s and 1930s only confirmed his belief that what drove the whole process of permanent revolution irresistibly forward was the fact that everything in the universe—especially societies and their endlessly conflicting social classes—exists in a state of constant contradiction. As Karl Marx (following philosopher Friedrich Hegel) had pointed out, these contradictions throw everything into a permanent state of dialectical tension in which opposites clash ad infinitum before recombining to form new syntheses, which, in turn, create new antitheses and then clash all over again, even as they generate a cyclical forward motion in history.

"Contradiction is universal and absolute," wrote Mao in his classic 1937 discourse "On Contradiction." "It is present in the process of development of all things and permeates every process from beginning to end."[79] The natural course of historical progress involved the endless triumph of one side of a contradiction over the other and in the serial destruction of the old by the new. Mao believed that out of this ceaseless process of contention and annihilation comes renewal. "The old unity with its constituent opposites yields to a new unity with its constituent opposites, whereupon a new process emerges to replace the old. The old process ends and the new one begins," he wrote. "The new process contains new contradictions and begins its own history of development of contradictions."[80]

Whereas most traditional Chinese thinking esteemed the Confucian adage *heweigui* (和为贵), "There is nothing more precious than harmony," Mao completely rejected this idea. In his view, it was precisely through the struggle between contending sides of a contradiction that higher stages of historical or even personal development were reached. "We often speak of 'the new superseding the old,'" he wrote in "On Contradiction." "The suppression of the old by the new is a general, eternal and inviolable law of the universe."[81]

Mao had viewed China's state of arrested historical development during the nineteenth and early twentieth centuries as both unnatural and unhealthy. He believed that by being so conflict averse, Chinese had opted for stagnation and entropy over a healthy and dynamic, if sometimes chaotic, natural state of historical forward motion in which conflicting forces are always opposing one another. By so emphasizing harmony, traditionalists had denied their country the kind of energy, vigor, and innovation that reformers had come to so admire in the West and Japan. Despite his love of history and the fact that his own writing was strewn with classical allusions, Mao never tired of disrupting the established order with his version of "creative destruction." "Trouble-making is revolution," he would later pronounce with oracular finality to party secretaries from across China just as he was fomenting his last "disorder under heaven," the Great Proletarian Cultural Revolution.[82]

Yan'an

For millennia the dust blowing from the Mongolian steppes across northwest China has slowly deposited itself on the hauntingly barren and desolate loess, or "yellow earth," landscape of Shaanxi Province. It was here among these eroded hills that Mao and the remnants of his exhausted Red Army finally found refuge in 1935 after their Long March. To visit this dusty, hardscrabble county town in the mid-1970s, when Mao was still alive and Yan'an still looked much as it had when he resided here, left it hard to imagine how such an impoverished and uncongenial part of China could have become such a successful haven for his tattered political movement, much less become the cradle of his revolution. But by offering protection from both Nationalist forces and invading Japanese troops, Yan'an's remoteness and inaccessibility served the Red Army well. Its isolation allowed Mao, by dint of his own fierce determination, to help his spent movement claw its way back from near oblivion to both military viability and political triumph.

It was in the walled town of Bao'an, several days' trek from Yan'an, that Edgar Snow met up with the forty-three-year-old Mao in 1936, interviewed him, and wrote his history-making *Red Star over China*. Snow was then a thirty-year-old freelance journalist from Missouri who had already spent seven years in China. Quickly becoming a best-seller, his book became one of the most important building blocks in Mao's mythology.

Snow found Mao "a gaunt, rather Lincolnesque figure, above average height for a Chinese, somewhat stooped, with a head of thick black hair grown very long, and with large, searching eyes, a high-bridged nose and prominent cheekbones." He had a "face of great shrewdness," wrote Snow,[83] who at first found himself smiling "at the extravagance of his [Mao's] claims."[84] However, Snow soon warmed to Mao. "If at first, I found him grotesque," he wrote, his "utter self-belief" slowly began to make an impression. "He had what Mark Twain called 'that calm confidence of a Christian with four aces,'" observed Snow. "Mao knew the physical contours of the land and the people who lived in it better than any political rival of his time."[85] Most notably, he wrote, there was "a certain force of destiny in Mao. It was nothing quick or flashy, but a kind of solid elemental vitality. One felt that whatever there was extraordinary in this man grew out of the uncanny degree to which he synthesized and expressed the urgent demands of millions of Chinese, and especially the peasantry."[86]

During Mao's Yan'an decade, from 1935 to 1945, as the Japanese occupation spread across China and Chiang's Nationalist government was forced to retreat up the Yangtze River to a temporary capital in Chongqing, the CCP's emphasis on simplicity in lifestyle, idealism, and discipline came to contrast sharply with the decadence, cynicism, and corruption that became rife in the Nationalist seat of power. Colonel David Barrett, a Chinese-speaking U.S. military attaché who was sent to Yan'an in 1944 as part of the "Dixie Mission," tasked by the U.S. government with providing a liaison between Mao's Communist forces and the American military's anti-Japanese effort, was impressed by the enormous difference between the two leaders.[87] "When Chairman Mao appeared in public, as he frequently did [in Yan'an], he travelled on foot, or in a battered truck, with enclosed cab, which as far as I ever knew, constituted the Communists' sole motor transport," reported Barrett. "There was no parade of long black cars, often moving at high speed, which one saw in Chongqing when the Generalissimo traversed the streets, and no cordon of guards and secret service operatives such as always surrounded him in public."[88]

John S. Service, another Chinese-speaking American diplomat attached to the Dixie Mission, reported that the Communist leaders
there impressed him as being "men of unmistakably strong conviction"
whose "sincerity, loyalty and determination are patent."[89] He called
them patient, tough, realistic, well-informed, democratic, straightforward and frank.[90] "They are," he said, "a unified group of vigorous,
mature, and practical men, unselfishly devoted to high principles."[91]
Service also reported that Mao was surprisingly eager for closer relations with Washington. "American friendship and support is more important to China than Russian," he reported Mao telling him.[92]
Through the reports of American visitors such as Barrett and Service,
Yan'an began to win a reputation as a place of discipline, austerity, and
equality.

Because a second United Front between the Communists and the
Nationalists had been effected in 1937 to focus the joint war effort
against Japan, Mao and other CCP leaders had agreed to deemphasize
class struggle, and even to embrace what they called "patriotic" members of the bourgeoisie.[93] However, although it was not always evident
at the time to outside visitors impressed by the congenial atmospherics
of Yan'an life, the relaxed surface did not mean that Mao had altered
his long-term commitment to thoroughgoing social revolution, his tendency to divide people into enemies and friends, or his lifelong prejudice that intellectuals were fundamentally unreliable. And since he had
decided that his kind of revolution would ultimately require profound
changes at every level of society, members of the intelligentsia could
hardly expect to remain exempt. Before they could ever become reliable revolutionaries, Mao believed their thinking needed to undergo a
painful process of "rectification."

Rectification

The many idealistic Chinese intellectuals and artists who made the arduous cross-country trip to distant Yan'an in the late 1930s and early
1940s expecting to find a "liberated area" of freethinking and open
discussion quickly had to revise their expectations once they got there.
Despite the appearance of idealism that was so noticeably absent in
Chiang's Nationalist-held territories, the Yan'an reality was more com-

plex. Facing Japanese troops moving down from Manchuria into China proper, new Nationalist attacks, and growing disagreements with his erstwhile Russian backers in Stalin's Comintern, Mao and his movement's other leaders were left feeling vulnerable and in need of a more unified common language, ideology, and purpose.[94] Furthermore, being a Chinese nationalist himself, Mao was determined that his new "mass line" would not just be borrowed from the Russian revolution, but develop out of China's own unique experience. "If you want to know the taste of a pear, you must change the pear by eating it yourself," Mao famously wrote in 1937. He wanted his followers to taste Chinese pears, not Russian ones. "If a Chinese Communist, who is part of the great Chinese people, bound to his people by his very flesh and blood, talks of Marxism apart from Chinese peculiarities, this Marxism is merely an empty abstraction," Mao admonished his followers. Requiring local practice to determine theory was also a clever way of helping free Chinese Communist doctrine from the shackles of the Bolshevik mother ship. As Mao, the alpha Chinese theorist, wrote in 1941, "The arrow of Marxism-Leninism must be used to hit the target of the Chinese revolution."[95] Henceforth, not only would communism in China have to become indelibly Chinese, but it would also have to become "Maoist," and follow whatever ideological twists and turns Mao henceforth might choose.[96]

One important milestone in Mao's consolidation of political power was his 1942 "rectification campaign" (shorthand for "rectification of the three bad work styles" [zhengdun sanfeng, 整顿三风], namely, bureaucratism, subjectivism, and sectarianism).[97] Yan'an party members and other camp followers—often disillusioned and freethinking intellectuals who were flooding into Yan'an—were reminded that, because the party newly prized orthodoxy, manifestations of political thinking deemed "unorthodox" and "incorrect" would henceforth be singled out for special remedial attention.[98] Mao was set on consolidating a more politically disciplined movement from the bottom up, remaking each of his followers in his own image. Just as early on he had focused on the physical health of young activists, now he turned to their ideological health. Thus the Yan'an period came to mark the beginning of the rise of Mao as a transcendent thought leader and, not surprisingly, the beginning also of the canonization of his writings as what would come to be known as "Mao Zedong Thought," which he insisted "united the universal truths of Marxism-Leninism with the practice of revolution and construction in China."[99] Because in Yan'an he had spare time on his hands, not to mention a new staff of party researchers and theoreticians at his beck and call, Mao began writing prolifically, creating a sprawling corpus of texts that became both the ideological foundation of his new "rectification" movement for intellectuals and the scriptural canon for all future measurements of Chinese Communist orthodoxy.

Mao now believed that if China was ever going to become independent, prosperous, and strong, the Chinese people needed a new creed—namely, Mao Zedong Thought—to replace old pieties. And so, during the winter and spring of 1942, he began spelling out his thinking on "rectification" and "correct thinking" in a series of speeches given in and around the General Auditorium at Yangjialing, just then under construction.[100] With its severe white walls, altarpiece-like stage set (adorned with images of Marx, Lenin, Engels, and Stalin), pew-like seats, and stolid stone and brick construction, the hall feels very much like one of the houses of worship built by Christian missionaries that still dot Shaanxi Province. Opened only in 1942, the hall became the party's central meeting place, its administration center, and even the venue for the social dances Mao was fond of attending during his less ideological moments.

In his first broadside, entitled "Correcting Unorthodox Tendencies in Learning, the Party, and Literature and Art," which was delivered on February 1, 1942, Mao took aim at those comrades whom he deemed lacking in the kind of practical experience he most esteemed and were thus detached from the revolutionary reality he most cared about.[101] "Only if those with book knowledge develop in practical spheres will it be possible for them to go beyond their books," he said, adding, "Only then will it be possible for them to avoid the error of dogmatism."[102] For Marxism-Leninism to be relevant to China, he asserted, it must be "derived from objective reality and tested by objective reality."[103] Such language was Mao's indirect way of saying that he neither liked nor fully trusted the flighty urban intelligentsia who were all brain and no brawn.

"Our comrades must understand that we do not study Marxism-

Leninism because it is pleasing to the eye, or because it has some mystical value," he said with thinly veiled contempt. "It seems that right up to the present, quite a few have regarded Marxism-Leninism as a ready-made panacea; once you have it, you can cure all your ills with little effort. This is a type of childish blindness and we must start a movement to enlighten these people. . . . We must tell them openly, 'Your dogma is of no use!' Or, to use an impolite phrase: 'Your dogma is of less use than shit.' We see that [dog] shit can fertilize the fields, and human shit can feed the dog. And dogmas? They can't fertilize the fields, nor can they feed a dog! Of what use are they?"[104]

Mao then addressed the subject of party discipline, calling on members to "eradicate all tendencies towards disunity." The party might need certain kinds of socialist democracy, but "it required centralism even more." He chastised those who had "forgotten the system of democratic centralism in which the minority obeys the majority, the lower ranks obey the higher ranks, the particular obeys the universal and the entire party obeys the Chinese Communist Party."[105] Whereas May Fourth Movement intellectuals such as Chen Duxiu had advocated individualism, free inquiry, open debate, and receptivity to outside ideas and influences, Mao now focused on uniformity and orthodoxy, which were to be reinforced through "thought reform," a new, innovative Maoist idea.

In the Soviet Union thinkers whom the party came to view as heterodox tended to disappear into Stalin's gulag. In Mao's China, however, those accused of "erroneous thinking" were first to be given an invitation by the party to "reform" themselves through a process that came to be known as "criticism and self-criticism." This form of autotherapy had Leninist roots, which, when embellished by Mao, operated on the assumption that if the party suspected a member of harboring "unhealthy" political tendencies, that member, as a good revolutionary citizen, naturally would desire to remedy the malady, and so should be given a chance at self-redemption.

Of course, if the party's invitation to self-reform failed to elicit the "correct" response, additional party pressure always lay in reserve in the form of public criticism, shaming, persecution, prison, or worse. But what was new about Mao's ambitious program to make over both individual and society was that, after fault was found with an individual's ideological views, the refractory person's fate was—initially, at least—remanded back into his or her own hands for resolution.

This new emphasis made for an interesting variation on a preexisting Leninist theme. Elsewhere in the Communist world, party discipline was maintained by external threats and punitive action. But here was Mao placing the onus on individuals themselves for purifying their own thoughts. Such a responsibility system brought into play a powerful set of new psychological self-control mechanisms, including shame, guilt, and a deeply traditional desire to conform to societal norms. Such an expectation exerted enormous pressure on individuals to extirpate their own errant thinking and reform. Moreover, by being invited to heal themselves, wayward comrades were artfully made complicit in the process of their own ideological remolding.

In initiating this program of political self-purification, Mao emphasized that "two principles must be preserved." These were embodied in an ancient Zhou Dynasty aphorism, "Learn from past mistakes to avoid making new ones" and "cure the disease and save the patient." Here, as so often, Mao used an ancient historical allusion (never mind its indelibly "feudal" nature) to clarify the logic of his revolutionary point. "Past errors must be exposed with no thought of personal feeling or face," he explained. "Our object in exposing errors and criticizing shortcomings is like that of a doctor in curing a disease." In an almost avuncular way, he assured his ideological patients, "The entire purpose is to save the person, not cure him to death."[106]

A week later, in his second speech on rectification—this one burdened with the dreary title of "Opposing Party Formalism"—Mao embroidered on his healthcare metaphor. "The first method in reasoning is to give the patients a powerful stimulus, to yell at them, 'You're sick!' so the patient will have a fright and break out in an over-all sweat. Then, they can be carefully treated."[107]

Sounding unctuous and menacing at the same time, Mao said that it was wrong "to have a brash attitude toward diseases in thought." As if he were an all-knowing physician of the soul, he cheerfully reminded party leaders that they had an obligation to adopt "an attitude of 'saving men by curing disease.'"[108] He ended this talk by urging all the young, idealistic revolutionaries sitting in the freezing cold "to consider this speech carefully," even to "consult with your sweethearts, your intimate friends and comrades around you," the better to "cure your own disease thoroughly."[109]

Of course, the "frights" and "cold sweats" Mao's cures might induce could be traumatic, especially when misguided comrades did not have the good sense in "self-criticism sessions" to perceive themselves as being ideologically sick in the first place. The writer Wang Shiwei was one such reprobate who resisted Mao's insistence that intellectuals should give up their independence and consign themselves wholeheartedly over to the party. He made his objections to "rectification" public in a two-part essay, "Wild Lilies," published in *Liberation Daily* by the well-known feminist writer and editor Ding Ling.[110] Such independence got her unceremoniously sent off to labor in the countryside. And Wang, who had not only dared write about finding a new kind of "darkness in Yan'an" and urged the party to listen to young critics and use them "as mirrors with which to look at itself" instead of attacking them, was quickly accused of being a Trotskyite for his efforts.[111] Because he continued being unrepentant and eschewed a helpful Maoist "cure," he ended up not only being tried in a Kafkaesque show trial and imprisoned, but then executed—beheaded, actually—under mysterious circumstances in 1947, in one of the party's more bizarre and gruesome final solutions to impure thought.[112] From the perspective of a "patient" such as Comrade Wang Shiwei, the only problem with Mao's new ideological health care system was that illness was in the eye of the diagnosing caregiver rather than the patient, and as Yan'an's acting surgeon general, Mao, along with his lieutenants, did not usually welcome second opinions. With the advent of the 1942 Rectification Movement, the May Fourth spirit of writers and intellectuals as independent voices was effectively quashed. Henceforth, the intelligentsia was expected to "serve the people," the state, and the party, not themselves.

Serving the People

Continuing his effort to "rectify" the thinking of Communist Party members and promote greater "party discipline," on May 2, 1942, Mao gave the first of several important speeches that later came to be known as "Talks at the Yan'an Forum on Art and Literature."[113] Since spring had now come to Shaanxi, Mao gave the last of his speeches outside, on a flat stretch of land in front of the General Auditorium, in the shadow of the cliffside cave dwellings in which he and many party leaders then lived. Because Mao tended to be nocturnal, the concluding talk did not begin until past midnight.[114] "The moon overhead made the night as bright as day," remembered one starstruck attendee. "Under the moon and the stars, hills nearby and distant were darkly silhouetted. Not far away, the Yen River flowed merrily, its surface shot with silver."[115]

In these Yan'an talks, which Mao gave extemporaneously with only a handful of notes to guide him, he laid out the principles that would define the roles of intellectuals, artists, writers, and journalists in China's future revolutionary society.[116] As a start, he declared that all culture and media were henceforth to be considered property of the new state and party and that the intelligentsia should be a key element in the party's quest to create a "new China." Mao also reminded his select audience that all art had an inescapable class bias. "In the world today all culture, all literature and art belong to definite classes and are geared to definite political lines. There is, in fact, no such thing as art for art's sake, art that stands above classes, art that is detached from or independent of politics. Proletarian literature and art are part of the whole proletarian revolutionary cause; they are, as Lenin said, cogs and wheels in the whole revolutionary machine."[117]

Mao urged those in his audience who remained dedicated to art and literature as a means of personal self-expression to rethink their attitude as being a form of petty bourgeois individualism. "Many comrades place more emphasis on studying the intelligentsia and analyzing their psychology," he said. "Their main concern is to show their side of things . . . instead of guiding the intelligentsia from [their] petty bourgeois background and themselves, as well, towards closer contact with workers, peasants and soldiers."[118] The new challenge for artists, he declared, was to figure out how to serve ordinary people. Mao's answer was unequivocal: "Literary and art workers must gradually move their feet over to the side of the workers, peasants, and soldiers, to the side of the proletariat."[119] In short, he expected literature and art to "become a constructive part of the whole revolutionary machine" so that they could serve "as a powerful weapon for uniting and educating the

Mao Zedong in 1938

people and for crushing and destroying the enemy."[120] And the only way to turn artists, intellectuals, and politicians into reliable "screws" in this enemy-crushing machine of revolution—as Lenin had so graphically put it—was to first subject them to "a solid, serious movement to correct unorthodox tendencies."[121]

These 1942 speeches turned out to be just the opening act of a prolonged series of "rectification" movements that would gather momentum and ferocity over the next three decades. Such an ambitious plan of mass ideological remolding, unprecedented in history, was indeed a form of magnificent madness. But for a leader such as Mao—steeped in ambition, willfulness, and struggle, and convinced that one lone, heroic individual can actually bring about fundamental change, even in refractory China—it all had a cold logic. There was really no way to reconstruct the kind of "new man," "new culture," and "new China" that Mao had been conjuring up in his revolutionary imagination since his youth, short of first being willing to erase the past that lay so stubbornly rooted within each and every Chinese. Only then could they be written upon again "with beautiful new words," as Mao cheerfully put it. Mao's urge was to do nothing less than to reinvent China, filling in the abyss of self-doubt, weakness, and resentment that was the legacy of the Qing Dynasty's demise, imperialist aggression and the May Fourth generation's iconoclasm. And it was on the slope of a hillside honey-combed with cave dwellings on the outskirts of Yan'an that Mao began to piece together the new foundational documents and methods for reformatting the minds of his people, the first step in his Orwellian project of radically reorganizing Chinese society. "This was the first time that a Marxist-Leninist solution was formulated for the problem of the relationship between the writers and the artists of the proletariat and the people they serve," recalled a *Liberation Daily* reporter who attended the talks. "It is valid as a guide for us for all time."[122] In fact, the role that Mao sketched out for artists and writers in revolutionary society that spring would serve as a prototype for the many successive political campaigns that would shake China to the core over the next few decades. And the notion that artists and members of the media should be a megaphone for the party and state is one that still has not been officially amended today.

Mao Zedong in 1949

CHAPTER 10

Creative Destruction（不破不立）

MAO ZEDONG, PART II

The Square

On September 21, 1949, Mao Zedong stood before the Chinese People's Political Consultative Congress in Beijing and told them: "Fellow delegates, we are all convinced that our work will go down in the history of mankind, demonstrating that the Chinese people, comprising one quarter of humanity, have now stood up. The Chinese have always been a great, courageous and industrious nation; it is only in modern times that they have fallen behind. And that was due entirely to oppression and exploitation by foreign imperialism and domestic reactionary governments. . . . Ours will no longer be a nation subject to insult and humiliation."[1]

On October 1 he stepped forward again, this time before tens of thousands of cheering followers, and in his high-pitched, almost lisping Hunanese accent proclaimed the official founding of the People's Republic of China. It was like the finale of a long Peking opera, and the only stage imaginable for such a grand spectacle was atop Tiananmen—the Gate of Heavenly Peace.

During dynastic times, the T-shaped space just in front of the imposing gate had been known as the Imperial Way, leading to Chessboard Street beyond a narrow corridor through which the emperor's retinue left the Forbidden City each time the Son of Heaven ventured into the world beyond. It was one of the few spaces where "the great within," in which the imperial family lived, overlapped with the mortal world outside.[2] Here also the government ministries were situated, imperial decrees were handed down on "cloud trays," criminals were brought to be sentenced for capital crimes, and successful examination candidates had their names posted.[3]

The significance of Tiananmen as a symbol of state power had, however, been transformed by the May Fourth demonstrations. By protesting there, student activists and New Culture intellectuals refashioned it into a place of public remonstration, henceforth a magnet for repeated modern manifestations of populist, nationalistic, antigovernment sentiment. On March 18, 1926, this area was rebaptized not only in remonstration but in blood when students protesting the killing of thirteen of their compatriots in Shanghai by British soldiers were fired on by the troops of Beijing's reigning warlord. Lu Xun memorialized the tragic moment with these unforgettable lines: "This is not the conclusion of an incident, but a new beginning. Lies written in ink can never disguise truths written in blood. And blood debts must be repaid in kind; the longer the delay, the greater the interest."[4]

With the advent of the People's Republic, this space began to take on yet another new persona—as the physical representation of Mao's New China and his obsession with immortalizing himself as its emblem. In the process, he transformed it into the most central symbol of his new revolutionary Central Kingdom. As it happened, these yin/yang aspects of the square's modern identity—as embodiment of both state power and the people's resistance to it—were also dueling aspects of Mao Zedong's own personality. He was in love with spontaneity and upheaval, mass demonstrations and peasant earthiness, but no less fixated on control, discipline, orthodoxy, majesty, and the formal trappings of high office.

While his Tiananmen appearance in October 1949 was a triumphant milestone in the Chinese people's century-long struggle against disunity, inept government, imperialist exploitation, chronic backwardness, and unbearable humiliation, it was not an end marker. In Mao's ideological universe of ceaseless contradictions, protracted struggles, and "permanent revolution," there were never real finish lines, only brief intermissions between periods of struggle. As Mao had cautioned while waging civil war against Chiang Kai-shek's Nationalist government, "A drama begins with a prologue, but the prologue is not the climax."[5] In 1949 there was yet much more drama to come, and

Mao needed an even grander stage on which to enact it. So, upon his move to Beijing from Yan'an, one of the first projects he took up involved turning the space fronting on Tiananmen into a grand public square worthy of the revolution that had just brought him to power. Given Mao's revolutionary pretensions, it was hardly surprising that, like Sun Yat-sen and Chiang Kai-shek before him, he, too, soon had an enormous devotional portrait of himself hung just above the Tiananmen's middle arch.[6] This likeness turned out to be only the beginning of a much larger effort to "rebrand" China and the Chinese Communist Revolution with himself as its grand progenitor and his visage as its logo. It would become one of the best-known trademarks on the planet.

Despite his antifeudal rhetoric, Mao the revolutionary did not hesitate to borrow imperial associations and to reclaim elements of the past to legitimize his new rule. As a start, he moved the new Communist Party leadership into Zhongnanhai, the imperial Lake Palace complex beside the Forbidden City. Built by the Ming and Qing emperors for their exclusive banqueting and boating pleasure, Zhongnanhai was also where the unfortunate Guangxu Emperor had been imprisoned in a pagoda by the Empress Dowager. Just as under the emperors of old, it was here, behind high vermillion walls, far away from "the people," that Mao and his revolutionary cohort sequestered themselves to rule their country. Mao even emblazoned an outline of Tiananmen on China's new national crest.

By the early 1950s, Mao and his Soviet architectural advisors had completed bold plans to expand the Imperial Way and Chessboard Street in front of Tiananmen into a magnificent new parade ground, "big enough to hold an assembly of one billion," he hyperventilated.[7] Mao was so intent on outdoing Moscow's Red Square that Chinese planners soon found themselves outdoing their "socialist younger brothers," their Russian advisors.[8] While Moscow's Red Square was a mere twenty-two acres in size, the new design called for Tiananmen Square to be fifty acres and would ultimately cover a staggering one hundred and nine acres.[9] Size, it turned out, really did matter, especially in the world of competing Communist "big leaders."

"The Chairman's mind, broad as the ocean, flies beyond the confines of the old walls and corridors, and penetrates into the future," proclaimed official Chinese architects in a seizure of ecstatic rhetoric about the new plan.[10] Wanting a site for massive rallies where he could be properly adored in public during his nouveau reign, Mao summarily rejected plans by preservationists such as Liang Qichao's son, the celebrated U.S.-trained architect and planner Liang Sicheng, who pleaded with him to save the old city center.[11] Liang's alternative was to construct a brand-new government complex in the western suburbs, a Chinese equivalent of La Défense or Brasilia, both also built in the late 1950s.[12] "I spent twenty years fighting to get in, now he wants me to leave," said Mao of Liang's plan.[13] The Chairman was set on bulldozing his way into the future through the historic heart of old Beijing.

Ever since, modern Chinese history has featured alternating bursts of destruction and construction, but with neither impulse leaving much room for conservation or preservation.[14] "It would be best if all the old buildings in Beijing . . . were replaced with new ones," Chairman Mao insouciantly declared at a party Central Committee meeting in 1958, when the question of destroying Beijing's magnificent old city wall—built during the Ming Dynasty with a rampart as wide as Manhattan's Fifth Avenue at the top—and various other ancient structures came up for discussion. "There are people who criticize me for being obsessed with grandiose plans," he continued. "They say I suffer violent mood swings and that I have no regard for antiquities. Well, they're right! I do like the grandiose. As for antiquities, well, you can enjoy them, but not too much. It is quite right for people to love relics. [But] if I did, then we'd be having today's meeting at Zhoukoudian!" This was a reference to a prehistoric archaeological site where Peking Man was excavated.[15]

By the time the new Tiananmen Square was completed in the late 1950s, more than sixteen thousand ancient courtyard houses, a host of old imperial buildings, and a significant segment of the old city wall had been demolished.[16] As if the sheer size of the new square would not be sufficiently awe-inspiring in itself, Mao ordered two massive edifices to be raised on either side: the Druidic Great Hall of the People, flanking it on the west, and the elephantine Museum of the Chinese Revolution and the Museum of Chinese History (later merged to form the National Museum) on the east. Both were hastily thrown up in just a year's time to be ready for the grand parade planned by Mao to celebrate the tenth anniversary of the founding of the People's Republic of China.

Then, after Mao died in 1976, the party had a mammoth memorial hall also constructed at the very center of this politically charged public place and laid Mao to rest inside, making the square a full-scale Maoist shrine, a monument to his life and the revolution he led, as well as his necropolis. The stolid Mao Zedong Memorial Hall still displays his desiccated remains in repose, making it a cross between a wax museum and an imperial tomb repurposed as a tourist destination.

Even now, decades after so much of his legacy has been jettisoned, it is impossible to be in Tiananmen Square and not feel it as belonging to Mao himself. To depart from the shaded refuge of the sycamore trees on the east side of this huge plaza and move out onto its flat vastness is to experience the sensation of being set adrift on a giant, becalmed—but somehow still menacing—body of water. Even as one shoreline recedes, landfall on the opposite side remains forebodingly distant. Such expansive emptiness leaves an individual feeling minuscule and exposed, which would seem to be precisely its point.

In constructing such a monumental public space, Mao eclipsed even the grandiosity of the Forbidden City and the two Summer Palaces. Chinese historian Hou Renzhi and architect Wu Liangyong reflected that after the square was completed, the majestic Forbidden City seemed to have "retreated to occupy a secondary position," becoming "something like the 'backyard.' "[17]

Poor and Blank

Once he had declared his "people's republic" and started planning his new square, the task of constructing a new state and society loomed. Because Mao had no doubt that radically dismantling its old society was a necessary prelude to reconstructing a new China, in the 1950s he turned his attention to that superhuman task. If ordinary Chinese were, in fact, like a "blank sheet of paper," as he was wont to describe them, that made it all the easier for a willful Mao to begin imprinting them with his own vision for a completely new society.

"Apart from their other characteristics, China's 600 million people have two remarkable peculiarities," he wrote in a 1958 article for the first edition of the party's theoretical journal, *Red Flag*. "They are first of all, poor, and secondly blank. That may seem like a bad thing, but it is really a good thing. Poor people want to change, want to do things, want revolution. A clean sheet of paper has no blotches, and so the newest and most beautiful words can be written on it. The newest and most beautiful pictures can be painted on it."[18]

"Poor and blank" was a beguiling metaphor, as evocative in its own way as Sun Yat-sen's notion of "a sheet of loose sand." But it was also odd for a Chinese leader, even one as iconoclastic as Mao, to describe a people possessed of so many millennia of history and so steeped in a traditional culture as "blank." As Liang Qichao, Chen Duxiu, and Lu Xun—Mao's youthful heroes—had become painfully aware, the Chinese people were far from blank. In fact, China's history and culture were so deeply engraved upon them that to make them blank, someone would have to become something of a political Shiva, the Hindu "destroyer god," of their old identity. For this monumental task, Mao reached back to his experience with the rectification movement in Yan'an, calling on the power of "thought reform" as an individualized way of deconstructing old China, with each person called on to extirpate his own *fengjian lijao* (封建礼教), or "feudal mind-set." The uniquely Maoist notion to *xinao* (洗脑), "cleanse the mind"— which in the antitotalitarian West became known pejoratively as "brainwashing"—proved to be one of the twentieth century's more innovative, if savage, intrusions into the individual psyche.[19]

Permanent Revolution

No longer a guerrilla insurgent but now a fully enthroned leader who, like his rival, Chiang Kai-shek, viewed China's destiny as his own, Mao needed to make his new revolutionary word flesh—no small matter in a decentralized country with such formidable cultural specific gravity. But as the writer Hu Feng, whom Mao later threw in jail for twenty-five years,[20] wrote in 1950 of the audacious new Chairman:

> Mao stands like an idol,
> Speaks to the whole world,
> Gives orders to time.[21]

As Mao saw it, his dramatic victory in the Chinese Civil War was part of the ineluctable and never-ending process of Marxist dialectics, which continued to dance out its endless but antagonistic pas de deux through history. And so, on the eve of his triumphant entrance into Beijing in 1949, when a normal mortal might have felt entitled to enjoy a few moments of fulfillment, not to say respite, Mao was instead preparing himself—and others in the party—for the next round of struggle in his version of "permanent revolution."

"With victory certain moods may grow within the Party—arrogance, the airs of the self-styled hero, inertia and unwillingness to make progress, love of pleasure and distaste for continued hard living," Mao cautioned the delegates at the Second Plenary Session of the Seventh Central Committee when they met in March 1949 to form a new government. "The flattery of the bourgeoisie may conquer the weak-willed in our ranks. There may be some communists who were not conquered by enemies with guns and were worthy of the name of heroes for standing up to these enemies, who cannot withstand sugar-coated bullets."[22]

Mao saw the institutionalization of a sense of "permanent revolution" as an important way of keeping political zeal at a fever pitch and his adversaries off-balance. So it was not long before he plunged the country into a series of mass political campaigns, each aimed at preventing the formation of new establishmentarian forces by keeping "the people" in a state of ceaseless revolutionary activism. Even the greatest "achievements in socialist construction," he warned in a February 1957 speech on contradictions, should not be construed as meaning "that contradictions no longer exist in our society. To imagine that none exist is a naive idea which is at variance with objective reality."[23]

"Our revolutions," said Mao, "come one after the other,"[24] and in the 1950s Mao set out to keep Chinese society "turning over" with a succession of mass movements: the land confiscation and reform movement, in which at least a million landlords were executed (1950); the Marriage Law, which fundamentally changed the status of women, the Chinese family, and the labor force (1950); the decision to send three hundred thousand Chinese "volunteers" to fight in Korea against the United States (1950); the "Three-Anti" and "Five-Anti" campaigns to ferret out corrupt cadres and unreformed bourgeois elements

(1951–52); the Agricultural Cooperative Movement to push millions of peasants into cooperatives (1952–53); and the Hundred Flowers Movement, when intellectuals were encouraged to speak out, only to be brutally cashiered in the subsequent Anti-Rightist Campaign (1956–57).

These revolutionary outbursts culminated in Mao's Great Leap Forward (1958–61), which communized Chinese agriculture, completely reorganized rural Chinese society, and saw upward of thirty million farmers die from famine. After this catastrophe, for a while it was difficult for Mao to launch new campaigns. Nonetheless, by 1963 he was able to initiate the Socialist Education Campaign, which sought to make all Chinese more proletarian—and which turned out to be a stalking horse for his last and most epic experiment in keeping revolution permanent, the Great Proletarian Cultural Revolution (1966–76), later known as the "Ten Lost Years." Over the course of his lifetime, Mao would evince little interest in gradual, piecemeal improvements. Like an addict in search of the next high, he was always looking to the next campaign or movement, each more relentless, brutal, and exhilarating than the last.

The Great Leap Forward

The Great Leap Forward was one of the most striking examples of Mao actually putting his singular and radical theories into practice. In mid-1958, believing that his revolution was beginning to stagnate and that the "ever-rising political consciousness" of the country's five hundred million peasants was the key to its further development, he pushed a new campaign through a hesitant party leadership. All private farmland, which had been confiscated from landlords and redistributed to the peasants only a few years before in a bloody pogrom, was now to be forcibly abolished and the country's 740,000 agricultural cooperatives reorganized into 26,000 gigantic "people's communes."[25] To make production more efficient in this "higher stage" of collectivized rural life, not only would all land be communalized, but so would all houses, livestock, tools, meals, and even bathing. The plan also called on peasants to become a major source of iron production by forcing them to set up small backyard furnaces. It was a political reverie of unprecedented audacity: to reengineer virtually every aspect of rural life.

Driven by his unique sense of urgency, as well as nostalgia for the raw peasant energy that had so impressed him in Hunan in 1927, and believing that in a single leap he could miraculously transform China from a backward agrarian society into an agricultural and industrial giant, Mao once again sought to "arouse the masses in an entirely uninhibited manner."[26] The communized peasantry, not the country's urban workers, were to be the engine of this new revolution, the ones who would finally, as optimistic posters proclaimed, enable China to "overtake Britain in iron, steel and other major industrial areas of production in fifteen years."[27] Such extravagant aspirations were expressions of a long-frustrated dream, one to which generations of Chinese reformers eager to catch up with the West had clung. Just as Mao had once led the Red Army on an unlikely Long March in an end run around Chiang Kai-shek's far better equipped conventional Nationalist forces, now he would lead the Chinese people in another glorious, unconventional forced march around all the verities of Western developmental theory, the better to attain their own homegrown version of modernity.[28] Filled with dreams of reenacting his guerrilla past, Mao deliriously proclaimed, "We are now witnessing greater activity and creativity of the popular masses on the production front than ever before."[29] With his past successes allowing him to imagine himself as a Chinese Moses, Mao set about single-handedly to lead his peasant nation to the promised land of socialist agrarian liberation.

China scholar Franz Schurmann characterized the move as "the most momentous instance of ideology in action in the brief history of Chinese Communism."[30] Seasoned experts, including economic planner and Politburo member Chen Yun, urged a more "prudent and practical" approach to development that would "slowly gather experience" and only "push ahead gradually."[31] But Mao, convinced that the "masses," inspired by his vision of socialist salvation through upheaval, would make the Great Leap a pathbreaking success, wanted to storm the barricades.

Distrusting almost everyone in the leadership around him, Mao nonetheless evinced an insatiable need for reassurance that the "broad masses" were enthusiastic about his revolutionary vision and that they continued to adore him. His private physician, Li Zhisui, recorded a typical incident on September 19, 1958, just as the Great Leap Forward was beginning, that caught the complicated relationship between Mao and his beloved *guangda qunzhong* (广大群众), "broad masses." That day, hundreds of thousands of people lined the streets of Hefei in Anhui Province, hoping to catch a glimpse of the Great Helmsman as he passed by. "He rode slowly through the city in an open car, waving impassively to the throngs, basking in their show of affection," wrote Dr. Li. "I suspect that the crowds in Hefei were no more spontaneous than those in Tiananmen. . . . These crowds had also been carefully chosen, directed by the Anhui Bureau of Public Security. But the crowds were no less enthusiastic, no less sincere in their adulation, for having been carefully chosen. At the sight of their Chairman, they went wild with delight."[32]

Something in Mao made him want to stubbornly resist the inevitable tendency of political movements, even revolutionary ones, to become routinized upon gaining power. A risk taker, he had little tolerance for the workaday process of orderly nation building, so as he watched his own revolution become more bureaucratized in the 1950s, he felt deeply conflicted. He was terminally beguiled by the idea that agricultural production could be increased simply through dynamic leadership, exhortation, and mass mobilization, rather than through expertise, technology, and capital investment. His dream was to industrialize China with verve and panache via a new "high tide" of socialist fervor that would so inspire his fellow peasants that they would willingly generate the resources needed to finance the country's industrial development. He called this process "putting politics in command," and imagined that new forms of agricultural cooperatives run by the peasants themselves, not large-scale industrial complexes run by well-trained technocrats and bureaucrats, would be sufficient to propel China into the modern world. He even decried what he called *jishu shenbihua* (技术神笔化), "the fetishization of technology," as if technological knowledge were somehow suspect.[33]

Mao's was the ultimate rejection of the old "self-strengthening" model of reform. Mao would not seek technical changes in "use" (*yong*, 用) without revolutionizing the "core" (*ti*, 体). He wanted to remake China from the ground up. His new, self-proclaimed slogan was "greater, faster, better, and more economical results."[34] What is more, he allowed himself to imagine that all this was happening because "the people" were spontaneously organizing themselves into "community dining rooms, kindergartens, nurseries, sewing groups, barber shops, public baths, [and] happy homes for the aged," because they knew it would lead them "toward a happier collective life."[35] The vision of it all was breathtaking in its ambition, one that no other modern thinker or leader had dared even imagine, much less put into practice.

For Mao, there was not a little self-deception involved, a common weakness among leaders who often end up being convinced by the very propaganda they themselves have generated for others. Sets of stunning production figures from allegedly bumper crops—many false—were soon contrived by anxious cadres in the field to lend an incontrovertible sense of "correctness" to Mao's Great Leap Forward policies. What grain local communes did manage to harvest was often sent to state granaries, as local officials competed with each other to meet their "targets" and please the central government, leaving the local peasant who had grown it to starve.[36] The seeming success of the Great Leap Forward convinced Mao that he possessed almost supernatural insights into how the unique energies of the Chinese people could be unlocked by superior leadership. Even as mass famine spread, he allowed himself to believe that his commune movement was, at last, germinating the first "sprouts of communism"[37] that would enable China to "complete the building of socialism ahead of time."[38]

Of course, Mao was also aiming to win the who-will-reach-communism-first race against the Russians, whose revolution he viewed as hopelessly mired in revisionist paralysis, even as the Russians, who still viewed Moscow as communism's Holy See, were not pleased by Mao's supercilious doctrinal challenges to their supremacy. Mao was utterly contemptuous of Soviet leader Nikita Khrushchev, who took over after Stalin's death in 1953. To Chairman Mao, Khrushchev's notions about "peaceful coexistence" and cryptocapitalist "goulash communism" might put a little more food on Russian tables but they lacked all the revolutionary boldness and grandiosity of his experiment. Such modest goals were the antithesis of everything that made Mao's revolutionary heart skip. "All you have to do is to provoke the Americans into military action, and I'll give you as many divisions as you need to crush them," Mao is reported to have said to his Soviet counterpart while they floated together in Mao's Beijing pool in August 1958, the hapless Khrushchev trussed up in a ridiculous pair of water wings because he could not swim.[39]

It was not just the Soviets who had to deal with Mao's imperiousness. When the much-revered Marshal Peng Dehuai, a veteran of the Chinese Revolution and commander of Chinese forces during the Korean War, started noting the increasingly evident catastrophes of mass starvation caused by Great Leap policies and vainly attempted to rein in Mao, even he was summarily dismissed from the leadership. In a long, disjointed speech at the Lushan party conference in July 1959, Mao attacked Peng and other moderates, who were no less interested in fostering China's wealth and power than he was but who were unwilling to put the Chinese people through such suffering. Mao lashed out at his critics. If opposition to him in the party became too severe, Mao belligerently threatened, "I will go to the countryside to lead the peasants to overthrow the government. If those of you in the [People's] Liberation Army won't follow me, then I will . . . organize another Liberation Army."[40] He ended his self-indulgent defense with a characteristically mocking cadenza of earthiness that hardly acknowledged his critical role in all the disasters that had happened. "The chaos caused was on a grand scale," he unconvincingly admitted, "and I take responsibility. . . . [But c]omrades, you must all analyze your own responsibility. If you have to shit, shit! If you have to fart, fart! You will feel much better for it."[41]

Of all Mao's mass campaigns, the destructive Great Leap Forward turned out to have the most widespread and tragic consequences. Mao's grand experiment, which attempted to completely reorganize hundreds of millions of peasants in a year or two, saw widespread crop failures and mass starvation, killing an estimated thirty-six million people, and making "all of China's other famines pale by comparison," as Yang Jisheng writes in his exhaustive account based on Chinese government documents.[42]

"After years of famine, an eerie, unnatural silence descended on the countryside," Dutch historian Frank Dikötter has written in Mao's Great Famine. "The few pigs that had not been confiscated had died of hunger and disease. Chickens and ducks had long since been slaughtered. There were no birds left in the trees, which had been stripped of their leaves and bark, their bare and bony spines standing stark against an empty sky. People were often famished beyond speech."[43] By the time the effects of the famine had fully ended in 1962, Mao really had come close to making his New China truly "poor," if not "blank."

The failure of the Great Leap left so many Chinese leaders alienated from Mao's extreme vision of socialist transformation that by the end of 1960 he had been forced to "retire from the front line" of the leadership. A period of retrenchment ensued as officials who were more pragmatic reintroduced individual incentives, private plots, and rural markets—all adopted again later on as bedrock policies by Deng Xiaoping after Mao's death—to get the economy running again.

A Calm Between Storms

Forced to the sidelines, with the sour taste of failure and tacit rebuke in his mouth, Mao now turned his attention from domestic affairs to China's relations with Russia. Having watched as the USSR turned "revisionist" under Khrushchev, Mao was not about to countenance China falling prey to a similar "capitalist restoration." But soon enough he began regrouping his forces on the home front, and in 1963 he was off again, this time launching his Socialist Education Campaign, the goal of which was to reemphasize socialist values, lest refractory bourgeois elements, which Mao firmly believed were still plotting against his revolution, be allowed to carry out their "class revenge."[44] Despite his setbacks, no one dared to challenge him overtly. Party leaders all remembered what happened to Marshal Peng Dehuai. If he could be purged, who could survive challenging Mao directly?[45]

In 1965, Mao's still-towering ambition expressed itself in his poem "Reascending the Jinggan Mountains," which received wide circulation in the party-controlled press:

I have long aspired to reach for the clouds . . .
Nothing is hard in this world,
If you dare to scale the heights.[46]

Communal kitchen during the Great Leap Forward, 1958

Red Guards waving the Little Red Book in Tiananmen Square, 1966

Mao Zedong and Henry Kissinger, 1973

Mourning Mao, 1976

With such messages, Mao was, in effect, putting rivals on notice that the old tiger-monkey, a patriarch disinclined to forget slights, was far from sleeping. And as it happened, he would soon have a chance to launch one last mass movement of unprecedented scope aimed at the whole panoply of "reactionary" forces he saw as gathering against him: misguided intellectuals, ideologically incorrect adversaries, "feudal-minded" followers of traditional culture, Communist Party cadres who had taken "the wrong path," "capitalist roaders," agents of hostile foreign powers, and revisionist Russians. These antagonistic forces obsessed him, because he feared that he would someday be denounced by such adversaries, just as Stalin had been denounced by Khrushchev. At stake was the very nature of the party, its revolution, and his historical legacy. "The key point of this is to rectify those people in positions of authority within the Party who take the capitalist road," explained Mao in a January 1965 directive. "Some are out in the open and some are concealed."[47] This was Mao's warning to the party's more pragmatic leaders, and particularly the triumvirate of moderates—Party General Secretary Deng Xiaoping; Premier Zhou Enlai; and most especially President Liu Shaoqi—whom Mao viewed as trying to "control the temperature" of his revolution to "prevent excesses."[48]

Soon Mao's latest revolutionary sidekick, General Lin Biao, a fellow Hunanese, was fanning the sparks of a full-blown "cultural revolution" for him. Thanks to Lin's enterprising editorial work, a little red book filled with Mao's choicest quotations and bits of his revolutionary wisdom had already been compiled for use among soldiers in the People's Liberation Army. It proved such a useful tool among soldiers that soon ordinary citizens were urged to study it as well. Before the Great Proletarian Cultural Revolution had run its course, almost half a billion copies of this so-called "little Red Book"—so called because of its red plastic cover—would be printed, and Mao would morph from an atheistic Communist leader into a demigod of liberationist theology.

High Tide

When the Cultural Revolution erupted in full force in early 1966, Mao was already seventy-three. As if to defy the reality that he, too, was subject to the inevitable withering of mortal flesh, he stepped up his attacks on liberal intellectual critics in the cultural establishment and those in the party leadership who had advocated a more pragmatic and "gradualist" approach to revolutionary development. By the spring of 1966, demonstrations by Red Guards—spontaneously organized groups of youths who deputized themselves with red armbands to be Mao's revolutionary vanguard—were erupting across China as purges of moderates swept the party. And Mao was back, egging on those whom he had stirred up with paranoid visions of capitalist and revisionist enemies under every bed. "The representatives of the bourgeoisie who have sneaked into the party, the government, the army, and various spheres of culture are a bunch of counter-revolutionary revisionists," he thundered. "Once conditions are ripe, they will seize political power and turn the dictatorship of the proletariat into a dictatorship of the bourgeoisie."[49]

Soon revolutionary wall posters were springing up on campuses all across the country, encrusting almost every available public surface, as increasingly fanatical Red Guard units attacked anyone they suspected of undermining or slowing down Mao's revolutionary upsurge or of being a "class enemy," even if it meant attacking their own parents and teachers. "Beat to a pulp any and all persons who go against Mao Zedong Thought, no matter who they are, what banner they fly, or how exalted their positions may be!" proclaimed one wall poster at prestigious Tsinghua University in Beijing, a hotbed of Red Guard fervor.[50]

When "work teams," set up by members of the gradualist faction in the party, tried to temper this storm of Red Guard–induced mass hysteria and ideological violence, they too came under attack. As all semblance of order collapsed, Red Guards attacked even such icons as Peking University president Lu Ping, as well as other senior faculty members. "This morning students from all over campus were mobilized to form a boundless ocean of people's war," recounted one Red Guard eyewitness account. "The black gang [the faculty] was swamped like rats, accompanied by shouts of 'Beat them!' . . . The battle of annihilation was like a tempest; those who yielded to it survived, while those who resisted perished." As this Red terror spread, it created a heady sense of chiliasm among protesters. "The black gang trembled with fear and shook with fright," continued this eyewitness, "and the revolutionary teachers and students were filled with joy like never be-fore."[51] On July 7, 1966, Mao met with party leaders and told them that the Cultural Revolution was a test to see "whether we can or can-not dare" to eliminate class distinction.[52]

The next stage in this process would require burrowing into the consciousness of every citizen, he said, and rooting out any "wrong thinking" that was found—removing it violently, if necessary. "With-out this destruction, there cannot be the construction of socialism," he preached, echoing Liang Qichao but with a virulence beyond Liang's imagination. "We must be prepared to have the revolution hit at us. . . . You will have to direct the revolutionary fire towards yourself, ignite it and fan it up. Will you do that? It will burn you!"[53] Admonishing his excited followers to let "the word 'fear' be replaced by the word 'dare,'" Mao concluded with a dire warning: "Anyone who suppresses the student movement will end badly!"[54]

Mao seemed intent on creating "great disorder under heaven"—the delight of the Monkey King, Sun Wukong—as a prelude to restoring "great order under heaven." Such utterances helped give birth to the unlikely slogan "World in great disorder, excellent situation." As one group of admiring students writing in *People's China* put it: "Revolu-tionaries are Monkey Kings, their golden rods are powerful, their su-pernatural powers far-reaching, and their magic omnipotent, for they possess Mao Zedong's invincible thought. We . . . use our magic to turn the old world upside down, smash it to pieces, pulverize it, create chaos, and make a tremendous mess, the bigger the better. We must . . . make rebellion in a big way, rebel to the end! We are bent on creating a tremendous proletarian uproar and hewing out a proletarian new world."[55] It was as if Mao now believed that nation building could be accomplished through nothing but the force of upheaval inspired by his own charismatic leadership.

Although Mao's exhortations were echoing everywhere, he re-mained eerily unseen and evidently unfazed by the growing bedlam. Downplaying the "red terror" he had unleashed, he was reported to have glibly commented in a closed meeting of central leaders, "Beijing is too civilized. I would say there is not a lot of disorder."[56] With much of China spiraling into chaos by the summer of 1966, Mao, the lover of "havoc under heaven," had good reason to be pleased. Deng Xiaoping's daughter Deng Rong would later write, "Mao's most fundamental principle was 'smash first, then build.' He believed that 'only chaos under the heavens can bring stability throughout the land.' "[57] China was now, it seemed, approaching that sublime state.

Two leading experts on the Cultural Revolution, Roderick MacFarquhar and Michael Schoenhals, explain that Mao "craved a measure of catalytic terror to jump-start the Cultural Revolution"[58] and that he "had no scruples about the taking of human life" to do it. In fact, Mao himself even suggested that true revolutionaries sometimes needed to be willing to countenance outright killing. "This man Hitler was even more ferocious," Mao told confidants. "The more ferocious the better, don't you think? The more people you kill, the more revolutionary you are."[59]

During the first half of 1966, it was difficult to know who was in control of China, much less where the whole Cultural Revolution was headed. Even as Mao was exhorting China's youth to make revolution, he remained largely behind closed doors, leaving his loyal premier, Zhou Enlai, to try to maintain some semblance of governance and order. But in a moment of candor, even Zhou confessed his confusion about what was actually going on: "All in all, this is a new thing, a new movement, and we aren't familiar with it, especially those of us who are so old," he said with evident cautiousness.[60]

Creating an air of uncertainty around his intentions, as well as his whereabouts, Mao exercised an elusive power over the rest of the leadership. While many public figures claimed to want to "work toward the Chairman," few were sure how best to do that.[61] As President Liu Shaoqi said to Premier Zhou at one meeting, "Now, as for *how* to carry out the Great Proletarian Cultural Revolution, you're none too clear about it, and [you] don't know too well, so you ask us to do it. I tell you honestly, I don't know either. We're mainly going to be relying on you to make this revolution."[62] Even those willing to pander to Mao's every whim were often at a loss to know how to follow Mao, who seemed to be heeding the advice of Han Fei, a Legalist philosopher from more than two millennia earlier, who advised rulers: "Be empty, still, idle, and from your place of darkness observe the defects of others. See, but do not appear to see; listen, but do not appear to listen; know, but do not let it be known that you know."[63]

On July 16, 1966, Mao did finally make a dramatic corporeal appearance in the central Chinese city of Wuhan. There, he joined some five thousand supporters to swim across the Yangtze River. A decade earlier he had written a poem, "Swimming," that contained these prescient lines:

> Now I am swimming across the great Yangtze,
> Looking afar to the open sky of Chu.
> Let the wind blow and waves beat,
> Better far than idly strolling in a courtyard
> Today I am at ease . . .
> Great plans are afoot:
> A bridge will fly to span the North and South,
> Turning a deep chasm into a thoroughfare;
> Walls of stone will stand upstream to the west
> To hold back Wuhan's clouds and rain
> Till a smooth lake rises in the narrow gorges.
> The mountain goddess, if she is still there,
> Will marvel at a world so changed.[64]

Mao's epic ten-mile swim in the summer of 1966 not only fulfilled his poetic prophecy but harked back to his earliest political stirrings, when he first became interested in physical culture as a fundamental expression of the nation's urge for self-strengthening, and made repeated expeditions into the mountains of Hunan to test his own physical prowess against nature. "The Yangtze is deep and its current is swift," he reputedly told a woman swimming alongside him that summer day. "This can help you train your body and strengthen your willpower."[65] It all had a familiar ring.

Five days after his swim, Mao reappeared in Beijing and abruptly called a leadership meeting at which he began a new barrage of attacks against party officials on his political blacklist. This proved the death knell for President Liu Shaoqi, who was now accused of being "China's Khrushchev" and "a renegade, traitor, and scab."[66] Liu would soon be incarcerated and left to die in detention. Deng Xiaoping was also formally denounced as "the number two person in authority pursuing the capitalist road" and ultimately "sent down" for five years of banishment to a Jiangxi Province military compound as a part-time machinist in a tractor repair facility.[67] If party leaders would not lead where Mao wanted to go, the masses, guided by Mao Zedong Thought, would replace them. Marshal Lin Biao, who uttered the immortal admonition "Carry out Mao's instructions, whether you understand them or not,"[68] soon had his toadying rewarded by being anointed the Great Helmsman's "chosen successor."

While Mao's immediate goal was to vanquish his rivals within the top leadership, his grander ambition was to overthrow the increasingly bureaucratic nature of the party and to irreparably rip China loose from the moorings of its remaining traditional culture. It was to be a radical transformation "by a path that has never been explored" but would, he promised, attain "heights that have never been reached."[69]

In the early stages of this Cultural Revolution, Red Guards organized themselves without official backing. But on August 1, 1966, Mao decided to weigh in on their side by writing an open letter to rebellious students at Tsinghua University, thereby providing them with carte blanche to criticize and attack any authority figure—their teachers, officials, even parents—whom they suspected of harboring bourgeois tendencies. "You say it is right to rebel against reactionaries," wrote Mao. "I enthusiastically support you."[70] The phrase *zaofan youli* (造反有理), "to rebel is justified," quickly became a mantra, electrifying young rebels all across China.

Then on August 5 Mao offhandedly scribbled, "Bombard the headquarters!" on a piece of paper, giving his sanction to attack the Chinese Communist Party itself.[71] His "order" also gave the Red Guards permission to march through the streets arbitrarily singling out for attack any official whom they chose to designate as a "monster or freak" or as members of what they called the "counterrevolutionary black gang."[72]

With Mao now clearly in guerrilla command again, things began to move with frightening rapidity. On August 8 a plenary session of the party Central Committee, which had been usurped by a rump Central Cultural Revolutionary Group of Mao loyalists, passed a document known as "The Sixteen Points," which served as a manifesto for the next phase of struggle.[73] The Cultural Revolution, it began, "has reached a stage that affects human beings even in their souls."[74] It warned that although the bourgeoisie had already been overthrown, stubborn elements had nonetheless "gained a foothold in the Party and have set out on the capitalist path"[75] by trying "to use the old ideas, culture, customs and habits of the exploiting classes to corrupt the masses, capture their minds and endeavor to stage a comeback." The document called on people to "overthrow those persons in authority who are taking the capitalist path."[76] Of course, it insisted that all acts and actions must be guided by Mao Zedong Thought. But the manifesto concluded with a series of "directives" that were bad news for party regulars who naively still imagined that things would soon return to normal. A massive housecleaning of the "underworld kingdom" was, it turned out, just beginning.

On the morning of August 18, 1966, with less than twenty-four hours' notice, more than a million adoring Red Guards assembled before dawn in Tiananmen Square to swear allegiance to Mao's new political line. The event was a climactic coming-out party for his Cultural Revolution, precisely the kind of populist grand spectacle for which he had built the gargantuan square in the first place. When at 5:00 a.m. he appeared on the rostrum atop Tiananmen, the vast throng of young Chinese, who had already been patiently waiting in the darkness for hours, began chanting "Long Live Chairman Mao!" over and over, while thrusting Little Red Books of his quotations into the air like talismans.[77]

Mao did not actually give a speech that day—he left such mundane tasks to Lin Biao and Zhou Enlai—but his cameo appearance sent the signal he wished: the Great Proletarian Cultural Revolution was all his. And when he and Jiang Qing finally stepped down from the heights of the fabled gate into the sea of delirious, chanting, weeping students below, the effect was akin to Zeus and Hera descending from Mount Olympus to the mortal world.

Later, Mao met with a select few students and anointed each with a special silk armband emblazoned with the characters hongweibing (红卫兵), "Red Guard," in his own hand.[78] Such armbands had originally been the insignia of peasant militiamen in Jiangxi and Yan'an in the 1930s, and so summoned up for Mao an emotional connection to his guerrilla past.[79] Through this meeting, Mao made it indelibly clear that he welcomed the support and sanctioned the activities of these "little generals" as they waged revolution against family elders, teachers, and other authority figures, just as he had done as a boy half a century before.[80]

It is hard to know what Mao really thought about these smitten youths who obeyed him with such slavish devotion, but perhaps they awakened in him memories of the youths in Yan'an whom Edgar Snow had described as "red-cheeked 'little Red devils'—cheerful, gay, energetic, and loyal—the living spirit of an astonishing crusade of youth."[81] In any event, the Red Guard rally on August 18 was only the first of eight such mass events held in Tiananmen Square and attended by more than eleven million devotees, who, drawn by the promise of joining Mao's new army, had begun flooding into Beijing from the provinces.[82] By that fall, Red Guard units were ransacking museums, trashing government offices, and looting the homes of educated elites accused of having "taken the capitalist road." Mao truly appeared to be nearing his cryptic goal of engendering "havoc under heaven."

"We're going to carry the Great Proletarian Cultural Revolution through to the end," Mao told the newly formed Central Cultural Revolutionary Group. "If it comes down to it, we'll all go down together."[83] He seemed to revel in the idea of putting himself and the country in circumstances so tumultuous that most other leaders would not dare follow him, and there was an undeniable power in such brinksmanship, especially in the eyes of young Chinese who yearned for a strong and fearless leader. "Don't be afraid of people making trouble," Mao counseled in the summer of 1967. "The bigger the trouble gets, [and] the longer it lasts, the better. . . . It doesn't matter how bad it gets, you must not be afraid. . . . Pustules and bacteria, wherever they are, are bound to burst at some point."[84]

By then the country was, in fact, in real chaos, as fighting between armed factions erupted. Many government offices were closed, and even transportation, strained by the millions of Red Guards making revolutionary pilgrimages around the country, was breaking down. Lin Biao and Jiang Qing, acting on Mao's behalf, egged the rebels on, proclaiming slogans such as "Overthrow everything" and "Wage civil war."[85] Only in the spring of 1967, after Red Guard factions began staging pitched armed battles against each other so that chaos was extreme, did Mao allow Zhou Enlai to call in the People's Liberation Army to restore order. While much of the outright factional warfare then ceased, the Cultural Revolution would not fully end as a political campaign until Mao died on September 7, 1976, almost a decade later.

Its launching had certainly been a stratagem in Mao's larger plan to keep political challengers off-balance. As his early interest in Shang Yang and Legalism indicated, he was always fascinated by ways of staying one step ahead of political adversaries in the game of realpolitik. But, the cost of this last revolutionary hurrah was astonishing: eviscerating the Communist Party; impeding the country's economic development; bringing the Chinese educational system to a standstill; splitting up countless families by sending many millions into rural exile; and causing the deaths of untold numbers by murder, suicide, executions, and even acts of ritual cannibalism.[86] From the perspective of conventional nation builders, these years of revolutionary turmoil represented a lost decade. However, for Mao, in addition to being a way to regain power, they were a time of grand theater when he could act out his visions of permanent revolution and lay the basis for what as early as 1940 he was already referring to as "a new Chinese national culture." As he explained in his essay "On New Democracy," China's revolution had always been about culture: "For many years we Communists have struggled for a cultural revolution as well as for a political and economic revolution, and our aim is to build a new society and a new state for the Chinese nation," he said. "In other words, not only do we want to change a China that is politically oppressed and economically exploited into a China that is politically free and economically prosperous, we also want to change the China which is being kept ignorant and backward under the sway of the old culture into an enlightened and progressive China under the sway of new culture."[87] In his recklessness, Mao doubtless thought of himself as finally realizing the dream of Liang Qichao and Chen Duxiu, however horrified they might have been by his version of revolution, of delivering a coup de grâce to traditional Chinese culture.

The high tide of the Cultural Revolution eventually did ebb, along with Mao's health, as his age advanced. But, before his death, he turned into an isolated, obese, mumbling, drooling dictator, estranged from

his scheming third wife, alienated from most of the veteran revolutionaries with whom he had shared times of travail and glory, and intelli-
gible only to his young mistress and a few other revolving acolytes. His
failure during this period to immediately further advance China's progress toward "wealth and power" did make it appear as if these decades
when he had sought to write himself so boldly in the heavens had come
to very little indeed.

Kissinger in Beijing

As it turned out, before the final historical balance sheet would be
drawn up, *Lao Mao* (老毛), "Old Mao," as the Chinese people came to
call him, had one more card still up his sleeve: the normalization of
relations with the United States, and he would play his last hand for the
highest of stakes.

Curiously, once before Mao had tried to seek a rapprochement with
Washington. On January 9, 1945, he asked members of the U.S. Dixie
Mission in Yan'an to pass word on to the American embassy in Chongqing, and then to President Roosevelt, that both he and Zhou Enlai
were "immediately available either singly or together for an explor-
atory conference at Washington, should President Roosevelt express
desire to receive them at the White House as leaders of a primary Chinese party."[88] Unfortunately, the U.S. embassy in Chongqing, headed
by Ambassador Patrick Hurley, a fiercely anti-Communist Republican
and steadfast supporter of Chiang Kai-shek, never forwarded the message through proper channels to either the president, the Department
of State, or the War Department.[89] Now, twenty-six years later, Mao
would try again, and this time the astute chess master would manage
to move China and the United States toward diplomatic recognition,
via two other fierce anti-Communists, President Richard Nixon and his
national security advisor, Henry Kissinger. In doing so, Mao would finally manage to put China on the road to the kind of prosperity and
global standing that had so long eluded it.

Kissinger, who would meet five times with Mao in Zhongnanhai,
described the Chairman as living "in a style as remote and exalted as
any of the emperors he was wont to deride." He also was being de-

ferred to by those around him with "near religious awe."[90] At their
final meeting, in October 1975, Kissinger reported being "shocked" by
Mao's deteriorating appearance. "He stood, as customary, before the
semicircle of easy chairs in the middle of his study," remembered Kissinger. "But he had declined so alarmingly since I had last seen him two
years earlier that two nurses were required to hold him up. Saliva
dripped from his chin. He had had several strokes and could barely
articulate words."[91] But still, reported Kissinger, "he exuded greater
concentrated willpower and determination than any leader I have encountered."[92] Even in precipitous decline, Mao managed to change the
terms of the global geopolitical game.

When President Nixon met Mao in 1972, he began by appealing to
his vanity, complimenting him for having "transformed an ancient civilization." But Mao dismissively waved away the idea of any such
grand transformation, saying, "I haven't been able to change it. I have
only been able to change a few places in the vicinity of Beijing,"[93] adding that Chinese were "very stubborn and obstinate."[94] Later Kissinger
was moved to observe, "After a lifetime of titanic struggle to uproot
Chinese society, there was not a little pathos in Mao's resigned recognition of the stubborn imperviousness of Chinese culture."[95]

Then there was also the bitter paradox of Mao having waged a lifetime of revolution against the rigid structures of traditional Chinese
culture and society, only to end up running into new, no less rigid structures within his own Communist Party. As Kissinger put it, "Rebelling
against the nightmare that one result of his victory had been to re-
create the Chinese tradition of an all-embracing mandarin class, Mao
launched ever more fierce campaigns to save his people from themselves."[96]

Guerrilla Legacy

Despite Mao's willingness to play the role of destroyer to advance his
revolutionary goals, Chinese culture and tradition had, in the end,
proven remarkably persistent. Like other May Fourth Movement activists, Mao had come of age at a time when the country's intellectual
vanguard viewed tradition as the main obstruction to national prog-

ress. Of course, most members of this generation had also studied the classics, so even in revolt they remained stubbornly and infuriatingly rooted in the very culture they sought to overthrow. In their urge to purge China of its "feudal" past, they inescapably found themselves in a parallel struggle to expunge the taint of that tradition from their own selves. Only Mao, however, wrote this struggle across the nation in such an all-embracing way. Although many reformers and revolutionaries before him had viewed Chinese tradition as lying at the root of China's weakness and had struggled mightily against it, none had been able to imagine going to the extremes that Mao was finally willing to pursue. And it may be this very revolutionary totalism—Mao's calculated, sweeping, and relentless assault on China's old ways of doing things—that ends up becoming his most important, if complicated, legacy.

But there was another, subtler, though nonetheless important, legacy that Mao bequeathed to China, and in particular to Deng Xiaoping. As doctrinaire and unyielding as Mao could sometimes be, the side of his personality that had allowed him to become such a good guerrilla fighter—infinitely able to adjust to the kaleidoscope of ever-changing challenges and dangers to ensure survival—created a new tradition of exceptional tactical flexibility. In a counterintuitive way, Mao's very opportunism—his willingness to do whatever it took to prevail despite the rigid demands of ideological discipline—created and left a curious new space in which Deng's pragmatism would ultimately be able to take root and flourish, as it did in the 1980s, when China finally did begin to approach its dream of wealth and power.[97]

In Mao, China had a leader who managed not only to uproot society from its deeply rooted traditional past but also to inject into it a certain new, dynamic pragmatism that, going forward, allowed it to reimagine and re-create itself in surprisingly innovative ways. To many outsiders, such "innovativeness" looked like nothing more than hypocritical opportunism, which it was. But in the end, Mao's willingness to do whatever was necessary to get where he wanted to go bequeathed to Deng a country that, while traumatized, had come far closer to escaping the drag of its four thousand years of tradition than at any time since the May Fourth Movement. For better or worse, Mao liked to

Mao Zedong in 1966

describe his people as "poor and blank," which was not completely accurate. But perhaps he did so because in the end it enabled him to imagine them finally escaping their past and being imbued with a new ability to adapt to changing circumstances and unexpected uncertainties with agility and innovation.

Deng Xiaoping circa 1920

CHAPTER 11

Black Cat, White Cat（白猫黑猫）

DENG XIAOPING（邓小平）, PART I

Rodeo and Ribs

On a rainy February night in 1979, a limousine turned off a dark country road at a sign announcing: "Simonton, Texas, Rodeo Round-up: Where East Meets West."[1] As it rolled to a stop in the parking lot, several Fort Bend County sheriffs, who had been leaning on hay bales, probing their teeth with toothpicks, and listening to Willie Nelson sing "Whiskey River" over outdoor speakers, snapped to attention and began working their walkie-talkies. When the limo door opened, out stepped the diminutive man who then ruled China, and who was now on a nine-day tour of the United States, Deng Xiaoping.

When Deng entered the indoor rodeo arena, the phalanx of Texans waiting inside, wearing cowboy boots and bolo ties and carrying sagging paper plates heaped with huge slabs of pork ribs, beans, and potato salad, towered over him. Nonetheless, he began pumping their hands like a small-town pol on the campaign trail. Waiting among these oversized Texans was an unlikely sprinkling of Chinese in dour Mao suits. They were members of the delegation that had just arrived in the United States to reestablish formal diplomatic relations between the two countries for the first time since the Chinese Communist Party had taken power three decades earlier.

As soon as the Chinese delegation was seated ringside, young horsewomen galloped into the arena carrying the flags of the United States, China, and the Lone Star State. One reined up in front of where Deng sat, leaned over the pommel of her saddle, and presented him with a ten-gallon cowboy hat. When he waved his new hat in the air, the crowd erupted with cheers and rebel yells. As a symbol of China's new flirtation with the West, donning the Stetson would have sufficed, but Deng then left his seat only to reappear a short while later, this time riding in an old-fashioned horse-drawn stagecoach. As he circled the arena waving like a beauty queen through the coach's open window, the crowd went into another frenzy of adulation.

Through these simple yet theatrical gestures, Deng was not only signaling to Americans that U.S.-China relations were entering a new era, but also sending a message to his own people that their country's recent opening to the outside world and the bold domestic economic reforms that went with it were here to stay. Deng in Texas wearing such an outlandishly American hat confirmed for Chinese back home, watching their first live telecast from abroad, that their world was indeed finally changing, that Mao's political danse macabre was over and Deng's new wild-west rodeo was launched.[2]

As that historic trip hinted, despite Deng's very different political agenda, his goals would be the same: wealth, power, and prestige for his nation. "The purpose of socialism is to make the country rich and strong," Deng told visitors from Romania a year later.[3] And in 1985, at the peak of his policy's initial success, he explained that his new reforms were designed "to lift China out of poverty and backwardness."[4] But his method would be utterly unlike Mao's. Deng was not interested in changing China's identity, or arguing about culture and the political system—what nineteenth-century reformers had called their "core" (ti, 体). Instead, he was hell-bent on transforming the economic "means" (yong, 用) by doing whatever was necessary to strengthen the state and enrich the people.

Because Deng had no fear of borrowing from more advanced countries, Feng Guifen's old idea of self-strengthening through learning from the West became the linchpin of his reform effort. But one thing he did not intend to borrow from the West was its liberal political model. On that score, Deng would prove almost as ruthless as Mao in silencing his critics, most notably the outspoken democracy advocate Wei Jingsheng, who would be tried and imprisoned for "subverting the socialist system" shortly after Deng's trip to the United States ended. Deng dreamed of a postpolitical age in which economic development could proceed undisturbed by either Maoist mass politics or individualistic liberal democracy.

Recognizing that his citizens were weary of Mao's fever of permanent revolution and mass campaigns, Deng steered away from divisive Marxist politics. But once in power, he did not hesitate to foment a new kind of frenzy—for making money. By the mid-1980s, he had named his counterrevolution *gaige kaifang* (改革开放), "reform and opening up." Deng's strange hybrid reform combined Vladimir Lenin's recipe for a disciplined and well-organized state and Milton Friedman's celebration of free market economics. He branded his new "line" with simple new maxims such as "Let some people get rich first," "Markets are good," and "Poverty is not socialism." In place of Mao's severe utopian vision—and China's dystopian reality—of radical egalitarianism, central planning, and ideological mobilization, Deng made economic development the raison d'être of both the Communist Party and contemporary Chinese life.

But Deng was not just an anti-Maoist counterrevolutionary whose templates for reform and opening up reversed the idology of the Cultural Revolution. After all, this was a man who had been helping set the course of twenty-first-century China for decades and was old enough to remember life under the Qing Dynasty. Because he had absorbed firsthand the bitter lessons of all the other failed modernization efforts that littered the Chinese historical landscape, only by looking at the full sweep of his life is it possible to fully understand how Deng's vision for yet another kind of New China evolved.

To Save China

Deng was born deep in southwestern China in 1904, just as the Empress Dowager was belatedly implementing reformist "New Policies" and Liang Qichao was publishing his revolutionary *New Citizen* from a safe haven in Japan. Deng's family counted as local gentry in their village of Guang'an in Sichuan Province, creating a childhood milieu remarkably similar to that of the young Wei Yuan and Feng Guifen.[5] Deng was the eldest son, and his given name, Xixian, or "Hoping for a Sage," reflected the deeply Confucian aspirations placed on him by his father. Yet barely a year after his birth, as the Empress Dowager abolished the imperial civil service examination system, the path to Confucian sagehood suddenly vanished for the young boy. Even so, Deng's family chose to give him a classical education.

By 1918, Deng's father, who had relocated to Chongqing and joined Liang Qichao's Progressive Party, decided his son needed more than the Confucian classics to get ahead in the changing world. Thus Deng was enrolled in an innovative work-study program that sent young Chinese to postwar Europe. On September 11, 1920, Deng sailed from Shanghai on a Messagerie Maritimes ship, the *André Lebon*, bound for Marseilles—leaving just months after Liang Qichao had returned from his Spenglerian grand tour to attend the Paris Peace Conference and survey war-torn Europe.[6] Making this trip abroad set the young Deng on a pathway that Mao had eschewed, and the contrast between the two men would later translate into profoundly different visions for China. Mao's first act of self-definition came through rebellion against his father, and his earliest writings called for revolt against the Confucian social hierarchy and the rigidities of filial piety. Deng, by contrast, bore no such animus against his father, "feudal society," or Confucian patriarchy. Although he refused to marry the girl chosen for him by his parents, and did not see much of his father (who was killed in mysterious circumstances in 1938), he did not come to define himself through struggle against parental authority. Quite the contrary: in a 1926 autobiographical essay, Deng described his boyhood under the care of his mother and father as being "very free and very full."[7] Growing up without the kind of familial strife that had marked Mao's youth, Deng was throughout his life a far steadier person, a family man who, after two short marriages, was deeply devoted to his third wife, protective of his children, and a doting grandfather.

Deng and Mao's dissimilar attitudes toward family reflected their differing orientations toward traditional Chinese culture as a whole. If the self-absorbed Mao was a riot of self-contradiction—an ostentatious aficionado of Chinese classics while militantly demanding that his people liberate themselves from old thinking and feudal values—Deng suffered no such contradictions. His writings and speeches largely ignored the subject of traditional culture and Confucian ideology. The epochal struggle to transform Chinese culture and revolutionize people's consciousness seems in Deng's mind to have been a distraction from the real work that needed to be done: namely, improving material conditions and making China a global powerhouse. Unlike Mao, Deng was neither particularly introspective nor possessed by an overweening narcissistic urge to write himself grandly into Chinese history. As his daughter Deng Rong, who published a two-volume memoir about her father, commented laconically, "Papa never talked about himself."[8] Perhaps at an early age Deng sublimated some basic sense of his own self-development in the service of a larger identification with the nation. Indeed, on the eve of his departure for France, he told his father that he was going abroad to learn how to save the nation. "China was weak and we wanted to make her stronger, and China was poor and we wanted to make her richer," he explained. "We went to the West in order to study and find a way to save China."[9]

Deng arrived in France just in time for the Roaring Twenties, but instead of seeking the secrets of Western civilization in Sorbonne classrooms, the cafés of Montmartre, or the ateliers of artists, he spent five years drifting around working-class areas of postwar France, sweating through stints at a shoe factory in Montargis and a Renault car plant outside Paris. Although he did develop a lifelong fondness for coffee and croissants, he was otherwise immune to the fascinations and temptations of French thought and culture, showing no interest in mastering the language of Proust or becoming a "fake foreign devil" on the Left Bank.[10] Instead Deng passed most of his time in Europe in the company of fellow Chinese student-workers. Politically, they were a pretty radical bunch, driven not so much by a personal quest for the meaning of life as by a utilitarian quest for new ideas that could rescue their nation from its diminished state. Deng's most fateful introduction during these years was to Zhou Enlai, who became like an "elder brother," and through whom Deng was inducted first into the new Chinese Communist Youth League and then the Chinese Communist Party itself.[11] Deng's father may have dreamed of a Confucian sage, but he now had a son who was becoming a dedicated Communist revolutionary.

By the end of 1925, French authorities had grown weary of hosting this out-of-place band of Chinese socialists, and so to avoid arrest, Deng and many of his comrades made their way to the Mecca of international communism—Moscow. Arriving in January 1926, he enrolled in the recently rechristened Sun Yat-sen University for the Toilers of

China, an institution that was a testament to Stalin's support for Sun's United Front, now already under the leadership of Chiang Kai-shek. In fact, one of Deng's classmates in Moscow was none other than Chiang's sixteen-year-old son, Chiang Ching-kuo, who would later lead the democratization of Taiwan.[12]

In Moscow, Deng also met his first wife, Zhang Xiyuan, whom he married in 1928, but who died in childbirth two years later. His other, more lasting Russian romance was with the ideas of Vladimir Lenin, who had died in 1924, but whose posthumous impact on Deng, and other Chinese activists, was profound. Indeed, Leninism became the focal point of Deng's studies in Moscow and the young revolutionary remained forever loyal to the tenets of his organizational theories on the need for a strong, disciplined political party, led by trained revolutionaries, operating on the basis of "democratic centralism." Deng's commencement statement upon leaving Sun Yat-sen University in Moscow demonstrated how deeply he had internalized Leninist dogma. "Henceforth," he swore, "I am ready to absolutely receive the Party's training, obey the Party's command, and always fight for the interests of the proletariat."[13]

Deng would later be attacked by senior party comrades, persecuted by Red Guards, and betrayed by Chairman Mao, yet his loyalty to the Communist Party and Leninism's founding principles never wavered.[14] He may not have been a great ideologue, essayist, or orator, but as a master of the arts of political organization, he possessed skills that the party desperately needed—putting the right people in the right places, keeping machinery running, making appropriate corrections in policy at key times, and enforcing party loyalty. As political scientist Lucian Pye observed, "Whereas Mao and many other Chinese leaders thought Communism's greatest strength was its ideology and its world view . . . Deng [believed] that the supreme imperative was the preservation of the Party's organizational identity and monopoly on power."[15] The seeds of this abiding belief were planted first during his years as a Communist agitator in France and then as a student in Moscow.

After six eventful years in the West, it was time for Deng to make his way home, where he landed a junior staff position at the makeshift Communist Party headquarters in Wuhan. There, he served briefly under party general secretary Chen Duxiu—"China's Lenin"—before

Chen was purged from the CCP leadership at the instigation of Joseph Stalin. Deng also met an up-and-coming Hunanese comrade named Mao Zedong. Then in 1927 he followed his "elder brother" Zhou Enlai to the new underground party headquarters in Shanghai's foreign concessions, which offered a tenuous refuge from Chiang Kai-shek's "white terror." Like Feng Guifen waiting out the Taiping Rebellion back in 1861, Deng lay low in Shanghai for more than a year until the party decided to dispatch him to the remote southern province of Guangxi to foment rebellion.[16]

Mao's Little Fellow

In the hill country of Guangxi, near the Vietnam border, Deng opened the next chapter in his long history of making revolution, this time with a gun in his hand. For most of the next twenty years he served as a "political commissar" in the Red Army—the top civilian officer in his military unit. Although he never distinguished himself militarily like Mao, during these years he built up critically important relationships within the People's Liberation Army and gained a long-standing credibility among its leadership that would serve him well when he came to run the country himself and needed to enforce Mao's dictum that "the Party commands the gun, and the gun must never be allowed to command the Party."[17] Most important, he attached himself to the coattails of the party's newest rising star, Mao Zedong, and halfway along the Long March in late 1934, he became part of Mao's inner circle.

By September 1939, Deng had married for the third time in a Spartan ceremony overseen by Mao in a Yan'an cave. But there would be no honeymoon for him and his bride, Zhuo Lin. Instead, Mao sent them back to a village base area deep in the mountains protecting Yan'an, where Deng was to supervise the anti-Japanese war on the front lines. Despite the Imperial army's brutal tactics, he later described his years there on the front as the happiest in his life—perhaps because three of his children were born during this time.[18]

When Japan abruptly surrendered in August 1945 and full-scale civil war erupted between the Communists and the Nationalists, Deng emerged as the key political commissar in the pivotal fight against Chiang Kai-shek for control of central China. After serving as the chief political officer in the legendary 1948 Huai-Hai Campaign that sealed the Communists' military victory over the Nationalists and sent Chiang running to Taiwan, Deng entered Nanjing with the victorious Red Army. There, in a moment of political theater, just as foreign troops had once posed on the Empress Dowager Cixi's throne after she fled Beijing, so Deng and his comrades now mockingly memorialized themselves on Chiang Kai-shek's "presidential throne," a residual symbol of power from the fleeting "Golden Decade" (1927–37) when Nanjing was the capital of Chiang's Republic of China.[19]

As the Chinese Civil War moved toward its denouement in late 1949, Mao divided the country into six military commands and placed Deng in charge of the vast Southwestern Department, which included his native Sichuan Province as well as Tibet. Here, Deng oversaw the capture of Chiang's wartime capital, Chongqing, and was duly appointed mayor of this sprawling metropolis where he had studied as a teenager. His next critical task was negotiating the "liberation" of Tibet, a delicate assignment that grew out of Mao's determination to see the new government reinstate the expansive boundaries of the multiethnic Qing Dynasty after a century of centrifugal forces had allowed the empire to spin apart. Prioritizing territory over ideology, Deng instructed Red Army officers to go to Tibet "with one eye open and one eye closed." Only socialist revolution would free Tibetans from their poverty and backwardness, he said, but that would have to wait. "Now our main responsibility is to make harmonious relations and to eliminate hatred between nationalities," Deng pragmatically reasoned.[20] He remained in charge of the Southwest Department until 1952, when Mao disbanded the regional command structure, recalling its six powerful heads to Beijing. Deng returned triumphantly to party central to help administer the new nationwide bureaucratic state.

As an old Chinese adage goes, the empire can be conquered from horseback but not governed that way. While Mao clung to the myth of himself as a guerrilla leader, a rebel Monkey King forever disturbing all under heaven, Deng proved far more inclined to administrative work than to guerrilla insurgency. As a result, he effortlessly made the transition from military campaigning to peacetime political governance, and his star rose rapidly in early PRC Beijing. By 1956, he had made it onto the Standing Committee of the Political Bureau of the Central Committee of the Chinese Communist Party, thus becoming one of the six men who ran the country. All this was due to his close relationship with Mao, whom he followed devoutly, even as the Chairman developed his grand plans to foment permanent revolution not only in China but across the Communist world. Mao even brought Deng with him on a tense 1957 visit to Moscow. "See that little fellow over there," Mao told Khrushchev, pointing at Deng. "He's a very wise man, sees far into the future." Khrushchev reported in his memoirs that Mao then "lavished praise on Deng in every possible way as the future leader of China and its Communist Party."[21] Mao's tribute was in fact a kind of warning to Khrushchev, for Deng proved his mettle as Mao's "bull terrier" in the vicious arguments that would soon erupt between the Soviets and the Chinese over who was the true standard-bearer of international communism.

Back home, Deng again proved his indispensability to Mao by orchestrating his 1957 Anti-Rightist Campaign, which Mao had drummed up to punish intellectuals who had criticized the regime too sharply in the preceding Hundred Flowers Movement. Deng would later regret the extremism of this campaign. "Large numbers of people were punished inappropriately or too severely," he ultimately acknowledged. But—ever the party loyalist and staunch Leninist—he never wavered in defending the fundamental legitimacy of the crackdown. "Some people were making vicious attacks," he rationalized. "It would not have been right for us to refrain from striking back."[22]

Yet there were limits to Deng's loyalty, if not to Mao, then to Maoism, and he finally reached these limits when the Great Leap Forward led to catastrophic famine. When faced with the evidence of mass starvation and economic dysfunction, he began to shift his allegiance to moderates such as Liu Shaoqi and Zhou Enlai.[23] After all, if there was one trait that marked Deng's character, it was common sense. Facts trumped ideology and prudence dictated principle. So, Deng became a key player in what Zhou, ever sensitive to not making Mao lose face, euphemistically labeled a period of policy "adjustment." Most important, as a matter of survival, the moderates granted permission for communized farmers to sell some of their surplus privately in local markets, which was heresy in Mao's view of radical agrarian revolution.

It was during this transitional period of the early 1960s, when Mao's radicalism was partially restrained, that Deng went to a Communist Youth League meeting and famously proclaimed: "Speaking about the best system of production, I would support whatever type can relatively easily and rapidly restore and increase agricultural output, and whatever type the masses are willing to implement should be adopted. If it is not yet legal, then it should be legalized. Yellow or white, a cat that catches mice is a good cat."[24] This earthy proverb contained the essential elements of Deng's future approach to political economy—an emphasis on production instead of revolution and on pragmatism instead of ideology. Over time, Deng's proverb became known in shorthand as the "black cat, white cat" approach to economic development. But, soon enough, he would pay a severe personal price for this kind of realism.

Capitalist-Roader Number Two

The ancient Confucian philosopher Mencius claimed that only men who are tested through profound suffering can ever achieve true greatness. "When Heaven is about to confer a great office on any man," he taught, "it first exercises his mind with suffering, and his sinews and bones with toil. It exposes his body to hunger, and subjects him to extreme poverty. It confounds his undertakings. By all these methods it stimulates his mind, hardens his nature, and supplies his incompetencies."[25] Deng's Mencian trial came in the course of his many painful years of political exile during the Cultural Revolution. Even as the humiliations he suffered surely shook him to his core, they also tempered and hardened him for the last, triumphant phase of his long revolutionary career. Demonstrating his gift for understatement, he later acknowledged, "The saddest period I went through is, of course, the Cultural Revolution."[26]

When Mao launched his "last revolution" in the summer of 1966, Deng—the fourth-most-powerful man in the country and Mao's presumed successor—suddenly found himself relabeled China's "Capitalist-Roader Number Two" and cast out of the leadership because of his unwillingness to buy into Mao's extremist policies. He endured the taunts of radical college students invading his courtyard home in Beijing while his children furtively watched the humiliating denunciations of their once all-powerful father. One daughter recounted a Red Guard attack on their home in the summer of 1967:

> The Zhongnanhai [leadership compound] rebels swarmed into our home. They took Papa and Mama out to the garden and surrounded them. Rebels pushed their heads down and forced them to bend at the waist, demanding that they confess. Roars of "Down with them!" shook the air. A string of shouted accusations followed, and a babel of voices yelled questions. . . . Papa was rather deaf. Standing half-bent, he could hardly hear anything, and could answer none of the questions. He tried to offer an explanation, but the words were barely out of his mouth when he was rudely interrupted. The rebels said he had a bad attitude, that he was feigning ignorance to avoid replying.[27]

In 1968, the Central Committee, now flaming Red in its politics, summarily dismissed Deng from all his party and government positions. Labeled a "capitalist-roader" late in 1969, he was sent to a remote corner of Jiangxi Province to rusticate in a backwater tractor repair facility. It looked as if his political career was over. Moreover, in Maoist China, much as in bygone Confucian days, there was no such thing as a lone, culpable *individual*—guilt, like success, was a family affair. Sure enough, Deng's whole family paid dearly for their patriarch's fall from grace, and one of the best-known tragedies of the Cultural Revolution was the sad fate of his son, Deng Pufang, whom Peking University Red Guards hounded into jumping from a four-story building on campus. Because of his father's compromised political standing, limited medical treatment was afforded the young man, leaving him a paraplegic. His father's letter from the distant tractor factory to party central in Beijing begging for mercy for his boy marks the tragic collision between Deng the loyal father and Deng the party loyalist. "From what we understand he is completely paralyzed from the waist down, and still needs help in everything," Deng wrote in his heartbreaking plea. "He can't be improving that quickly. How can we cope if he comes here? We [Deng, his wife, and her mother] are three elderly people. . . . We therefore earnestly request that he continue to be treated in his present hospital. In our situation today, we don't know what to do. We can only beg you to help, beg the Party to help."[28]

Adding insult to injury, Deng himself was compelled to write a self-criticism during the Cultural Revolution, in which one finds strangely prophetic statements hidden among the mindless revolutionary self-flagellation. "My real mistake is that I have not stood on the side of the masses and have opposed the mass movement," Deng wrote in 1966. "In terms of class struggle, I have not, during the Cultural Revolution, stood on the side of the revolutionary proletariat, and have pursued a line which is in absolute opposition to the policies of comrade Mao."[29] In another long self-criticism of his revolutionary career submitted to the party in 1968, he conceded that "because my bourgeois world view was never corrected, I have ended up as the greatest follower of capitalism within the Party."[30] Pathetically, Deng promised to reform himself into a defender of the proletarian masses and begged that "when timing makes it possible, the Party would assign me some small work to do, and give me the opportunity to make amends and start anew."[31] For a grown man to be forced to grovel so obsequiously was doubtless a profound humiliation. Yet, in a way that would have made Wei Yuan proud, Deng managed to find inspiration in his debasement and humiliation. While the Cultural Revolution still raged and he remained sidelined, Deng nonetheless set his will on someday regaining his dignity and power.

In November 1971, Deng learned that General Lin Biao, high priest of Mao's cult and the creator of the Little Red Book, had died in a plane crash as he had tried to flee the country. According to Deng's daughter, Lin's death was an important turning point for her father. "His one aim before Lin Biao's fall was to preserve a last line of political defense," she explained. But after Lin's dizzying fall, Deng regained some hope and ambition to lead his country once again. "He would grasp every opportunity to make a comeback, to work again for the people and the Party. In the past five years he had given a great deal of thought to how China should proceed on the socialist road. If the day came when he could return to office, he would devote all of the knowledge he had acquired during the long stormy years of the revolution to bring order out of chaos."[32]

Deng's chance to "bring order out of chaos" finally arrived not long afterward. Amid the relentless chaos he himself had unleashed, Mao found himself needing to counterbalance the influence of his wife's power-hungry leftist faction. By early 1973 he was urgently in need of some capable leadership to keep the country going, and he unexpectedly summoned Deng back to Beijing that February. Within a couple of months Mao's old comrade was again playing a significant role in the country's foreign affairs. "Mao thought I could again be useful and therefore brought me back from the grave," Deng later explained.[33]

Putting Things in Order

Deng needed to play catch-up. But, after six years in the political wilderness, he was now able to venture forth and see what had actually happened to the country during the upheaval of the Cultural Revolution. Traveling back to the old Communist base in southern Jiangxi Province where he had served as county party secretary in the 1930s, he listened to reports from local officials. "It's much better now than it was in the past," he said afterward. "We've done a lot since Liberation and accomplished a good deal." Nevertheless, he was unafraid to acknowledge the toll taken by the Cultural Revolution and China's relative inferiority. "We're at least 40 years behind the countries in the West," he reported. "We've got to work hard."[34]

Deng was right about the forty-year gap. Mao's self-induced seizures of permanent revolution had left the Chinese people with a low standard of living, technologically backward, and artificially cut off from the outside world. Indeed, to visit Beijing in the mid-1970s was an almost otherworldly experience. Arriving at Capital Airport, which now boasts a vast network of modern runways and a spectacular Norman Foster–designed terminal servicing many hundreds of flights each day, was then like landing at a small regional airport in the American Midwest. When an arriving aircraft parked and pilots finally shut down its engines, a visitor stepping down onto the empty tarmac was immediately enveloped by a profound and eerie silence. And despite its millions of inhabitants, Beijing itself hardly felt like a world capital. Without a single individually owned automobile, private shop, or commercial advertisement (other than the huge and ubiquitous propaganda

placards emblazoned with Mao quotes), and with its populace uniformly attired in "Mao suits" (a garb that genuflected to fashion only
by coming in four regimental colors—khaki, blue, gray, and black),
an outsider found himself in a strangely somnambulant city, a quality
that only deepened after sundown, when it became dark and quiet as
a tomb.

Once back from his political grave, Deng began trying to change all
this. Even as the Cultural Revolution ground on, he quietly piloted a
host of pragmatic new initiatives to revitalize the domestic economy
and repair China's international relationships. In fact, during the spring
of 1974 he made his maiden voyage to the United States to address the
United Nations, to which the PRC had been admitted after Taiwan was
expelled in 1971. Speaking at a conference on economic development,
he deftly embedded his own vision of China's urgent need to begin
"opening up" into a paean to Mao's "three-world" theory, which posited that the new "contradiction" in the global system was between the
developed First and Second Worlds pitted against the developing Third
World. "Self-reliance in no way means 'self-seclusion' and rejection of
foreign aid," Deng declared to the General Assembly, whose members
were enthralled by the novel presence of a Communist Chinese leader
in their midst.[35] Deng later explained what he hoped to achieve in New
York. "Comrade Mao Zedong's strategic idea of differentiating the
three worlds opened up a road for us . . . to make use of capital from
foreign countries and of their advanced technology and experience in
business management."[36]

While in New York, Deng dined with U.S. national security advisor
Henry Kissinger. "He [Deng] articulated no grand philosophy; unlike
Mao, he made no sweeping claims about the Chinese people's unique
destiny," remembered Kissinger, who was immediately struck by the
contrast between Deng and Mao. "His pronouncements seemed pedestrian, and many were concerned with practical details. Deng spoke on
the importance of discipline in the military and the reform of the Ministry of Metallurgical Industry. He issued a call to increase the number
of railway cars loaded per day, to bar conductors from drinking on the
job, and to regularize their lunch breaks."[37] But, what Kissinger described as Deng's "pedestrianism" was actually a signal marking a his-

toric shift, from Mao's utopian politics back to the pragmatism of the late nineteenth century's "self-strengthening" agenda.

Since Deng's trip to the United States was seen as a success back home, he was emboldened to press on, albeit gingerly, with domestic reforms. Now also de facto foreign minister, he used this portfolio to realize his youthful determination to "study the West in order to save China." But he did not need to look as far as Paris or Moscow, since China was surrounded in its own East Asian backyard by "miracle" economies, most notably Japan's, which was once again, as in the latter part of the nineteenth century, giant steps ahead of China. Determined to catch up quickly, Deng pumped the trickle of Japanese visitors to Beijing for information on how their country's leaders had managed to modernize science, technology, and industry.[38]

As Mao and Zhou Enlai succumbed to old age and illness, Deng took on ever more responsibility for managing the economy—or at least what was left of it. As his blueprint, he adopted Zhou's earlier "Four Modernizations," an agenda lofted back in 1964 but ignored since, which called for a fifteen-year "construction phase" to modernize agriculture, industry, science and technology, and national defense. Putting Zhou's Four Modernizations atop China's policy agenda once more, Deng started peppering his speeches with the word *fazhan* (发展), "development," a term that would later become the mantra of party rule.[39]

Although very few outside observers saw their significance at the time, these were carefully designed but audacious symbolic moves. By 1975, Deng was running much of the People's Republic. In January he was given high-level appointments across the trifecta of power centers—the party, the military, and the government—and in his speeches, he began to speak repeatedly about *zhengdun* (整顿), "putting things in order," a euphemism for rolling back the madness of the Cultural Revolution. Although Deng's immediate priorities were "pedestrian" ones, such as professionalizing the military, fixing the railroad system, reviving industry, and mending fences internationally, their combined implications were profound.[40] Rejecting Mao's strict egalitarianism, Deng openly promoted material incentives in the form of increased wages in order to "encourage people's initiative" . . . even if they did create inequalities. "People's contributions do differ," he told his comrades in the leadership. "Shouldn't there, therefore, be differences in remuneration?"[41] In the context of the preceding years of Maoist egalitarianism, these were almost heretical comments.

But Deng also proved his capacity for Leninist ruthlessness in the face of resistance. In the summer of 1975, Muslim villagers in a remote area of Yunnan Province not far from the Vietnam border refused to pay a grain tax until their demands for religious toleration were met. Deng signed an order dispatching PLA troops to "put things back in order," and an estimated sixteen hundred men, women, and children were killed in the twenty-one-day "pacification" operation that followed.[42]

Deng soon discovered, however, that the biggest threats to "putting things in order" were not in recalcitrant, faraway villages but within the party leadership itself. In an attempt to pry open China's insular centralized economy, for example, Deng called for the expansion of imports and exports.[43] But his efforts were constantly undermined and attacked as capitalist apostasy by Maoists. At one nasty leadership meeting, Mao's wife, Jiang Qing, attacked Deng as a "slave to the West" corrupted by a "comprador mentality." Comparing him to those despised nineteenth-century Chinese entrepreneurs who served as middlemen for Western "imperialist capitalists" in the reviled treaty ports, she charged that Deng's cardinal sin was that he wanted to purchase from abroad, rather than build from scratch, better transport ships. "China already has a 10,000-ton vessel!" she indignantly scolded, accusing Deng of a lack of patriotism. Courting political suicide, Deng angrily mocked her ignorance, pointing out that he himself had traveled to France on a 40,000-ton ship—in 1920! A 10,000-ton ship was nothing to brag about.[44]

By the end of 1975, Deng's efforts to jump-start the economy were starting to bear fruit.[45] But his turn at the wheel of leadership was not to last. The Cultural Revolution had still not yet fully run its course, and Mao was not done blockading those whom he viewed as "taking the capitalist road." As Deng proceeded with his practical initiatives, Mao grew increasingly skeptical of his fealty, and in the spring of 1976 an unexpected and spontaneous mass protest indirectly cost Deng his tenuous new hold on power.

The April Fifth Movement

By the mid-1970s many ordinary Chinese, who for years had not dared to think or act independently, began cautiously stirring back to life, even wondering how they had allowed themselves to become so mesmerized by Mao and his long and destructive seizure of political extremism. After Premier Zhou Enlai died on January 8, 1976, Beijing was stunned by how these new sentiments suddenly manifested themselves.

Although they knew Premier Zhou had collaborated with Mao, many Chinese viewed him as someone who had also managed to moderate the Chairman's excesses, quietly protecting innocent people from political attack and saving parts of the country's cultural heritage from Red Guard predation. But no one was prepared for what followed: more than one million Beijingers who, weary of the Cultural Revolution's endless deprivations, spontaneously turned out on the day of Zhou's funeral to pay homage along the nine-mile route to the cemetery. "To us—ordinary Chinese who had suffered much in the decade of madness during the Cultural Revolution—Zhou had become our only hope for rationality," remembers art historian Wu Hong, who worked and lived at the time inside the Forbidden City at the Palace Museum on Tiananmen Square. "Now he was dead. We wailed for him and for ourselves."[46] A few days later, tens of thousands more mourners wearing black armbands and bearing memorial wreaths spontaneously flooded into the square to stand before the Monument to the People's Heroes reading poems and giving memorial speeches.[47]

When Zhou's ashes were finally taken to the Great Hall of the People for an official farewell ceremony (ordinary people were excluded), it was Zhou's "younger brother" from their days in France, Deng Xiaoping, who delivered the eulogy. "He was open and above board, paid attention to the interests of the whole, observed Party discipline and was strict in 'dissecting' himself,'" Deng solemnly eulogized. "We should learn from his fine style—being modest and prudent, unassuming and approachable, setting an example by his conduct, and living in a plain and hard-working way."[48] Mao was tellingly absent from the ceremony, signaling that perhaps his grief over Zhou's passing was not all that deep.

Deng and Mao, 1959

Deng at the United Nations in New York, 1974

Democracy Wall with posters mocking Mao's widow, Jiang Qing, 1979

Wei Jingsheng on trial, 1979

As soon as the official memorial service was over, an unexpected announcement was broadcast over the speaker system in Tiananmen Square: the leadership declared a formal end to all further public expressions of mourning for Zhou. Angered by the peremptoriness of this party diktat, many of the mourners waiting outside felt that they were being denied the opportunity to grieve adequately, even as Zhou's good name was being demeaned by his adversaries. And when, after the eulogy, Deng disappeared from public view, rumors of a power grab by radical Maoists ricocheted around the city.[49] On March 25, when two leftist newspapers in Shanghai published articles derogating Zhou as "a capitalist-roader," demonstrations supporting him and Deng erupted in many cities across China.[50]

Unluckily for the party, there was another occasion coming up soon when ordinary people could honor Zhou and support Deng. Qingming Festival is the day each spring when Chinese traditionally pay respect to the dead by sweeping ancestral graves, and in 1976 this holiday fell on Sunday, April 4. Although grave sweeping had been banned during the Cultural Revolution by the party as "feudal," people now looked to it as an opportunity to be heard. And so, in the lead-up to Qingming, memorial wreaths and poems began once again to appear at the foot of the Monument to the People's Heroes in the middle of Tiananmen Square.[51] Read one:

> The people loved their premier.
> The people's premier loved the people.
> The premier and people shared weal and woe,
> Their hearts were always linked.[52]

Although the government explicitly banned mourning in Tiananmen Square, by early April hundreds of thousands of ordinary Beijingers were defiantly going back into the square to commemorate Zhou and his moderation. "Gone for good is Qin Shihuang's feudal society," read a line of one poem criticizing Mao's Legalist authoritarianism.[53] Other mourners openly derided Mao's wife, Jiang Qing, calling her a latter-day Empress Dowager.[54]

Then, in the early morning of April 5, hundreds of trucks suddenly arrived in the square to remove the drifts of funeral wreaths that had been piling up. When the handful of young people lingering there were also summarily arrested, thousands of supporters poured anew into the square to protest. A loudspeaker truck urged the protesters not to be mislead by "a handful of class enemies," but such announcements only caused the formerly pacific crowd to turn angry, overturn the truck, and burn several other police vehicles. Singing "The Internationale," the crowd then surged toward a small police command center and incinerated it.[55]

At 6:30 p.m. the amplified voice of Beijing mayor Wu De ominously boomed forth, warning the "revolutionary masses" to leave the square at once.[56] Several hours later, Workers' Militia, PLA soldiers, and other security forces appeared and began beating and arresting whomever they could catch. Before the April 5 incident ended, the area around the Monument to the People's Heroes had once again been baptized in repression and blood. Although it has never been officially revealed how many were wounded, died, or were arrested that day, one Hong Kong publication later quoted the vice minister of public security, Yang Gui, as reporting that more than one hundred perished and three thousand to four thousand more were arrested.[57]

As soon as the square was cleared, the so-called April Fifth Movement was branded a "counterrevolutionary" incident and the party Central Committee issued a statement declaring that "the Deng Xiaoping problem has turned into one of antagonistic contradiction." The Central Committee's Political Bureau then also unanimously dismissed Deng from all his posts, allowing him to keep only his party membership "to see how he will behave himself in the future."[58]

Emancipating Minds

This time, however, the triumph of radical leftists proved short-lived. On September 9, 1976, Mao died, leaving his younger Hunanese comrade Hua Guofeng as his chosen successor. (On his deathbed, Mao reputedly whispered to Hua, "With you in charge, my heart is at ease."[59]) But, supported by the military, Hua soon moved against Mao's wife and her coterie of leftists, known as the "Gang of Four," who were arrested three weeks after Mao's death. Hua hoped to hold on to his new status as paramount leader, but he proved no match for Deng, his four-foot-ten-inch-tall adversary, whom Mao had once aptly described as "a needle wrapped in a ball of cotton."[60] Deng had waited his whole life for the opportunity to steer the Chinese ship of state, and now was his chance. When Communist Party polemicist Han Suyin sat down to interview him in 1977, she described him as "lively and agile in his movements, spits copiously, and smokes constantly . . . so absolutely direct, candid and completely unaffected that it is impossible not to like him."[61] Deng's message to her, in what was his first public interview since Mao's death, came straight from the pages of the self-strengtheners: "Only when we recognize that we are backward," he said calmly, "will we progress."[62]

For two years after Mao's death, Deng carefully lined up his supporters among party elders, PLA generals, provincial leaders, and younger technocrats, all the while continuing to tirelessly rally support behind the banner of the Four Modernizations. Against great odds, he and a group of trusted leaders managed to win out in the complicated game of political musical chairs that determined the final post-Mao leadership pecking order. And, in December 1978, Deng's new grip on the reins of both state and party power was finally put on display at an epochal party conference. Deng's great capitalist counterrevolution in the name of "reform and opening" would now spread to all corners of the People's Republic.[63]

On December 13, 1978, Deng gave arguably the most important speech of his life. It was the final day of the Central Work Conference preceding the Third Plenum of the Eleventh Party Congress—a meeting whose bureaucratic nomenclature, as is so often the case in Communist China, disguised its importance. At this historic turning point, Deng called on the Chinese people to "emancipate their minds." Seizing on the language of wealth and power, he proclaimed, "Let us advance courageously to change the backward condition of our country and turn it into a modern and powerful socialist state."[64] "Our fundamental task," he would later explain, "must be to develop the productive forces, shake off poverty, build a strong, prosperous country, and improve the living conditions of the people."[65]

But how? Deng's answer was unequivocal: by relying on the economics of development instead of on the politics of revolution. In place of mass campaigns and class struggle, Deng forcefully asserted, "we must learn to manage the economy by economic means."[66] Blazing this bold path forward would require new skills and new leaders. "We need large numbers of path-breakers who dare to think, explore new ways, and generate new ideas," he proclaimed. "Otherwise, we won't be able to rid our country of poverty and backwardness or to catch up with— still less surpass—the advanced countries."[67]

Deng called for a systematic retooling of Chinese life, a learning process that would have to start at the top: "The Central Committee and the thousands of senior cadres at the central and local levels should take the lead in making an in-depth study of modern economic development," he declared.[68] One of the most direct techniques Deng would use to emancipate the minds of officials was to let them travel abroad. "The more we see," Deng reported, "the more we realize how backward we are."[69] Indeed, during normalization discussions conducted in January 1979, President Jimmy Carter asked him about liberalizing travel restrictions, and Deng stunned Carter by leaning forward, spreading his hands expansively, and replying, "Fine. How many do you want? Ten million?"[70]

Deng was ready as well to reverse a century of resistance to, and ambivalence about, learning from the West that went all the way back to the self-strengtheners' failed study-abroad program in the 1870s. In place of China's long-standing aversion to overseas experience, which reflected a debilitating mixture of arrogance and insecurity, Deng's message was the Chinese equivalent of "Go west, young man." "Have broad contacts, make detailed investigations, and carry on deep research into the issues," he told an economic delegation en route to Europe. "Look at how they manage their economic activities. We ought to study the successful experiences of capitalist countries and bring them back to China."[71] And when these foreign travelers did come home, they were now looked upon as valuable assets. One of them, a young man named Xi Jinping—a staff member on a military delegation to the Pentagon in 1980 and then a member of an agricultural delegation to Iowa in 1985—is now the president of the country and secretary general of the CCP.[72]

Deng made his stunning volte-face plain as day at the historic Third Plenum in 1978: "From this day forward, we renounce class struggle as the central focus, and instead take up economic development as our central focus," the CCP promised.[73] With that single sentence, Deng summarily canceled two decades of Maoist policy. The cause of the disastrous Cultural Revolution, he explained to Italian journalist Oriana Fallaci in a 1980 interview, was the "taint" of "thousands of years of feudalism," which in the end corrupted the party itself, "as manifested in such things as the personality cult, the patriarchal ways or styles of work, and the life tenure of cadres in leading posts."[74] The bureaucratic scourge of "feudalism" that so many had struggled against before Deng had at last infected even the core of the Revolution itself.

To escape the trap of "feudal values," however, Deng did not intend to start yet another struggle against Chinese culture, nor was he intent on reformatting China's national identity. His strategy for ridding China of feudal tendencies was simply to build on top of them. Deng charged a small group with rewriting CCP history that acknowledged the errors of the late Mao era, while affirming the party's destiny as savior of the Chinese nation. He was closely involved in this history's drafting, and personally ordered numerous revisions. The resulting document, "Resolution on Certain Questions in the History of Our Party Since the Founding of the PRC," was a kind of collective self-criticism by the party itself, which, while taking responsibility for marginal mistakes, insisted on its overall correctness. The resolution reflected an unofficial verdict Deng himself had already offered: Mao Zedong was 70 percent correct and 30 percent wrong (the same rating Mao had once given himself, and, ironically, the same grade that Khrushchev had given Stalin).[75] It was a deft way to express criticism of the past without risking the dangers of totally rejecting a former leader or line, much less the party's fundamental "correctness."

The most important message of the resolution was that Deng would not let China remain obsessed with the past. This was a profound departure from both the self-strengtheners, who sought to salvage traditional culture through limited reform, the May Fourth Movement, which hoped to replace traditional culture with New Culture, and Mao, who had sought to destroy tradition through total revolution. Deng was the first modern Chinese leader to suggest that there was no further payoff to be had in the twentieth-century obsession of Chinese intellectuals with culture. The old temple had been destroyed; it was time to raise a new one in its place. After revolutionary destruction must come construction. In a revealing discussion on the topic of "eliminating feudalism," Deng chided his comrades. "We should not think that we have only to 'put destruction first' and construction will follow automatically," he said.[76]

Because Deng did not suffer from Mao's insecurity complex about intellectuals, one of his first acts was to "reverse the political verdicts" on nearly three million party cadres and intellectuals who had been branded as "class enemies" and persecuted during the previous political movements.[77] This much-welcomed release of erstwhile "enemies of the state" was a symbolic gesture of how serious Deng was about "opening up," and it won him many friends among the political and intellectual elite. At the same time, the mass rehabilitation of so many well-educated people with technical skills also provided his government with a vast new reservoir of talent and expertise, at just the moment it most needed the help. After all these decades, Deng was ready to turn to Mr. Science (if not Mr. Democracy). And, in the choice between "Reds" and "experts," Deng was ready to take the experts. "How can we dismiss nearly 10 million of China's intellectuals with one stroke?" he asked rhetorically in 1977.[78] Indeed, his newest, and not very orthodox, slogans—"Practice is the sole criterion of truth" and "Seek truth from facts"—enhanced a sense that he was turning irrevocably from ideological faith to empirical reality.

One of the people Deng expressly brought along on his 1979 trip to the United States and the rodeo outside of Houston (where he also toured NASA's Johnson Space Center) was Fang Yi, his new vice premier and minister of science and technology. As Fang said in an interview just before an unlikely tour of Disneyland, "We want to absorb those things from you which are good and advanced, and try our best to avoid the unsuitable aspects." When asked if he was worried about the side effects of a mass importation of technology from the West, Fang replied, "These were fears when China was very weak. That's no longer true."[79]

Democracy Wall

Echoing his self-strengthening predecessors, Deng had insisted in 1977, "We must recognize our backwardness, because only such recognition

offers hope."[80] This meant that China could not be too proud to acknowledge weakness—something Mao always had trouble doing—and
then must be willing to borrow heavily to redress the imbalance. One
thing Deng was *not* keen on borrowing, however, was the West's political system. This, he felt, would weaken China—and the party.

As it happened, just as he was consolidating his grip on the leadership, a spontaneous popular movement was bubbling to the surface on
the streets of Beijing, picking up where the May Fourth and April Fifth
Movements had left off, demanding a reprise not just of Mr. Science
but also of Mr. Democracy. The movement's most prominent voice was
a fearless worker-intellectual named Wei Jingsheng, who challenged
not only the ghosts of Maoism but also the new spirit of Deng's Leninism. This movement of political dissent began in the late fall of 1978
around an unprepossessing gray brick wall that enclosed a public bus
yard and a dusty playing field in a drab Beijing neighborhood marked
by stolid structures of Stalinist design. It began with a few handwritten
posters containing poems, essays, quotations, and political exhortations posted on the wall because of its proximity to well-trafficked
streets near Tiananmen Square, but very soon it began to look like one
of the poster-covered walls of the Cultural Revolution. However, instead of exhorting people "never to forget class struggle" or "bombard
the headquarters," the posters called on Chinese leaders to reevaluate
the April Fifth Movement, promote democratic thinking, and liberate
themselves from the oppression of the "lost decade" of the Cultural
Revolution.[81] Because of the political nature of most of the posters, this
brick enclosure was soon dubbed "Democracy Wall."

During the winter of 1978–79, the crowds of onlookers and gawk-
ers at the wall grew exponentially, sometimes even marching down the
Avenue of Eternal Peace into Tiananmen Square chanting, "We demand democracy!" or "We demand freedom!"[82] It was a feeling of
delighted surprise that swept the city when, on November 15, the party
announced that it was revising the verdict on the April Fifth Movement, reclassifying what had happened not as counterrevolutionary
but as "a revolutionary act of the masses."[83] And when all those who
had been arrested during the 1976 movement were exonerated, the
sense of surprise turned to relief, especially among those gathered

around the wall. One April Fifth Movement demonstrator, Guiyang poet Huang Xing, reappeared to write ecstatically of a new "world ruled by light and warmth":

O torch, you extend a thousand shining hands,
Open up ten thousand shining throats.
Awaken the great road, awaken the square,
Awaken all members of this whole generation.[84]

Deng was becoming the darling of China's new incipient democratic movement. "Putting heaven and earth in order, opening the doors, establishing order, discipline, and great democracy, Vice Premier Deng is open-minded, humble, and honored by the entire world," waxed one enthusiastic poster on the wall. Under his leadership, it proclaimed, "the nation will be rich and strong and the economy will be pushed ahead."[85]

Being in the final stages of his power struggle with Hua Guofeng, Deng at first was, in fact, magnanimously tolerant of the upwelling of new democratic public sentiment. He insouciantly told a Japanese visitor on November 26, 1978: "We should not check the demands of the masses to speak."[86] A few days later he observed, "Sometimes it is necessary for us [the leaders] to be urged along by them [the masses]." Then, as if he wished to encourage more activity at Democracy Wall, he pointed out that the right to put up wall posters had been guaranteed by China's constitution during the Cultural Revolution.[87] Although Deng's encouragement was indirect, for any Chinese leader to support such public dissidence was electrifying. When Deng told the American columnist Robert Novak that Democracy Wall was *haoshi* (好事), "a good thing," the news caused still larger crowds.[88]

But it was Deng's historic speech on "emancipating the mind" at the party conference on December 13 that really got people's attention. In it he proclaimed, "In dealing with ideology problems we must never use coercion," and "We must firmly put a stop to bad practices such as attacking and trying to silence people who make critical comments."[89] Upon hearing these words, China's small but growing number of reform-minded democrats experienced a frisson of genuine optimism.

And when posters started popping up on other walls around Beijing, and the Democracy Wall phenomenon even began to spread to other cities, it seemed that China's dark political winter was thawing at last.[90]

The Fifth Modernization

On a cold morning in early December, a small and unobtrusive poster entitled "The Fifth Modernization—Democracy, Etc." appeared on Democracy Wall. It was signed Jin Sheng, the pen name of Wei Jingsheng, an electrician at the Beijing Zoo, who brazenly wrote his address on his poster so that anyone could contact him.[91]

Wei had been up all night writing what was to become one of the most lucid and provocative documents of the Deng era.[92] Its title, "The Fifth Modernization," was meant to be a pointed riposte to Deng's call for the Chinese people to implement the Four Modernizations. While Wei supported the new openness, he diverged from Deng in his belief that if the leadership focused only on seeking to modernize agriculture, industry, science and technology, and defense without including an essential "fifth modernization," namely, democracy, China would never become a truly modern and stable society.

Like Deng, Wei dressed simply, had a no-nonsense bearing, and almost always had a cigarette between his nicotine-discolored fingers. Wei's stained teeth and short-cropped, tufted hair suggested as little attention to the niceties of appearances as did Deng's utterly plain demeanor and sartorial habits. And both men were marked by a determination that bordered on obstinacy. But Deng and Wei's ideas could not have been more different. "To achieve modernization, the Chinese people must first put democracy into practice and modernize China's social system," wrote Wei. "Without democracy, society will become stagnant and economic growth will face insurmountable obstacles. Judging from history, therefore, a democratic social system is the premise and precondition for all development, or what we can also call modernization. Without this precondition, not only is further development impossible, but even preserving the level of development already attained would be very difficult. . . . When democracy defeats dictatorship, it always brings with it the most favorable conditions for accelerating social development."[93]

In Wei's view, democracy was China's "only choice," because if China ever hoped to modernize its economy, it must first modernize its people.[94] On this point Wei was in accord with the Chinese utilitarian reformers of the past who saw democracy as a practical means of attaining wealth and power. But Wei differed from them in also seeing democracy as an end in itself, and he was utterly contemptuous of the view that what the majority of ordinary Chinese most needed from their government was better economic times and stability without self-government. "To such people I would like to say, with all due respect: We want to be the masters of our own destiny. We need no gods or emperors and we don't believe in saviors of any kind. We want to be masters of our universe; we do not want to serve as mere tools of dictators with personal ambitions for carrying out modernization. . . . Democracy, freedom and happiness for all are our sole objectives in carrying out modernization. Without this Fifth Modernization, all other modernizations are nothing but a new lie."[95]

Wei held an almost Manichean view of the "battle" that he now saw taking shape over the soul of China: "Democracy Wall at Xidan has become the first battlefield in the people's fight against the reactionary forces," he wrote. "There may be bloodshed and sacrifice, and people may fall prey to even more sinister plots, yet the banner of democracy will never again be obscured by the evil fog of the reactionary forces."[96] Here was a gauntlet thrown down before Deng.

Cardinal Principles

By February 1979, when Deng returned from his successful trip to the United States, his domestic power base was secure. He had, however, ordered the PLA to invade Vietnam to teach Hanoi a lesson about siding with the Soviets and daring to overthrow the Beijing-backed Khmer Rouge regime in Cambodia, and the brief war did not go well for China. In this tense atmosphere, and given the increasingly critical tone of the voices on Democracy Wall, Deng was beginning to lose patience. It was not long before he dispatched state workers to remove every poster from Democracy Wall.[97] But Wei Jingsheng was not yet done. On March 25, he posted an unrepentant attack headlined "Do We Want Democracy or New Dictatorship?" In it, he accused Deng by name of "metamorphosing into a dictator."[98] He was arrested four days later. "So much for democratic freedom under the Chinese government," wrote his coeditors at their new journal, *Exploration*. "What brutal hypocrisy!"[99]

The state-owned *Beijing Daily* countered with its own editorial: "The kind of democracy we need is socialist democracy, or democracy enjoyed by the overwhelming majority of people. We don't want bourgeois democracy, which enables a handful of people to oppress the majority of people."[100]

On March 30, Deng gave another defining speech to a group of ranking officials, this time on the *limits* to "emancipating the mind." In it, he focused on upholding the "Four Cardinal Principles" that were to become the foundation of Deng's future leadership: adherence to socialism, people's democratic dictatorship, party leadership, and Marxist-Leninist-Maoist thought. The democracy movement, said Deng, had now "gone too far" and was no longer in the interest of "stability, unity, and the Four Modernizations."[101] "Can we tolerate this kind of freedom of speech which flagrantly contravenes the principles of our constitution?" he asked. His answer was an emphatic no. "We practice democratic centralism," he declared, reminding everyone of his and the PRC's Leninist roots, "not bourgeois . . . individualist democracy."[102]

Six months later, when Wei was finally brought to trial on October 16, 1979, he appeared in court wearing prison garb, his head shaven. No foreigners—and only a small number of carefully selected party officials—were allowed to attend the trial, but Wei not only stubbornly refused to plead guilty, he also insisted on defending himself. The most serious charge against him centered on allegations that, because he had discussed China's January 1979 attack on Vietnam with a Reuters correspondent, he had "betrayed his fatherland."[103]

It was true that as the notoriety of Democracy Wall spread, participants had for the first time in decades begun speaking openly with members of the foreign press corps based in Beijing. Although Wei spoke no foreign language, "he immediately saw the usefulness of getting to know foreigners," remembered Agence France-Presse reporter Marie Holzman. "Whatever you did on Democracy Wall, it wouldn't go very far," she recalled. "People saw it and that was that, whereas if you got things printed in the foreign press, then it would go round the world and come back to China."[104] Admitting at his trial that he had discussed China's Vietnam war effort with a foreign correspondent, Wei insisted that because he had no access to any state secrets, he had "nothing at all" to supply the nation's enemies.[105]

In his defense, Wei gave a ringing endorsement of free expression. "The Constitution grants citizens the right to criticize their leaders, because their leaders are human beings and not gods. It is only through the people's criticism and supervision that those leaders will make few mistakes, and only in this way that the people will avoid the misfortune of having their lords and masters ride roughshod over them."[106] But Wei also tried to evoke the mainstream of utilitarian pragmatism that had defined so much of modern Chinese reformist thinking by insisting to the court that the purpose of his journal *Exploration* was "making China more prosperous and powerful," adding that he believed that "only by free, unrestrained and practical exploration is it possible to achieve this purpose."[107]

In the end, it didn't really matter how Wei positioned his defense. The party understood the fundamentally antagonistic nature of his critique—that all human beings had an innate right to basic freedoms—and, despite his efforts to give it a patriotic, utilitarian spin, the party was implacably opposed to it. Wei was found guilty of "supplying a foreigner with military intelligence and openly agitating for the overthrow of the government of the dictatorship of the proletariat and the socialist system in China," and was sentenced to fifteen years in prison.[108]

By putting Wei on trial, Deng had hoped to "scare the monkeys by killing a chicken," thereby ensuring that the party could get on with its new program of making China prosperous, unopposed by stubborn and troublesome critics like him. In fact, by January 1980 Deng himself had started complaining that certain "factors of instability" were impeding the progress of his Four Modernizations, including the "so-called democrats and dissidents who openly oppose the socialist system and the CCP leadership, such as Wei Jingsheng and his ilk." Acknowledging that the party had "made serious mistakes," Deng insisted that these same mistakes have always been "corrected by the party itself."[109] In other words, his conception of reform required no checks and balances and no outside criticism such as those lofted by Wei, and certainly no Western-style democracy. Deng would not let Wei and his fellow liberal democratic dissenters stand in the way of his vision for transformation of post-Mao China.

To Get Rich Is Glorious

As Deng solidified his position as paramount leader, he made a revealing choice of science and education as the two issues he wished to position at the very center of his new policy portfolio. "Backwardness must be recognized before it can be changed," he proclaimed in a 1978 speech to a national meeting of scientists. "One must learn from those who are more advanced before one can catch up with and surpass them. . . . Independence does not mean shutting the door on the world, nor does self-reliance mean blind opposition to everything foreign."[110]

The most important type of scientific and educational expertise that Deng needed, however, was economic. Ironically, this man who would go down in history as the architect of China's extraordinary economic rise could claim no economic expertise himself. "I am just a layman in the field of economics," Deng confessed. "I have proposed China's economic policy of opening to the outside world, but as for the details or specifics of how to implement it, I know very little indeed."[111] Nonetheless, he managed to clearly identify, instate, and then defend certain new core economic principles. For example, Deng wanted to incentivize productivity and efficiency by allowing individuals and households to earn and retain any surplus profits they made. He was also willing to make room for private entrepreneurialism, and he was ready to decentralize economic decision making.[112] Although such notions were anathema to Maoist economists, Deng defended them with the courage of his convictions. In this sense, he was not so much the architect of China's new economic reforms as the project director with the political clout to *hire* the architects, namely, talented men like Zhao Ziyang in the 1980s and Zhu Rongji in the 1990s, who later became premiers (and in Zhao's case, party general secretary as well). Deng was able to recognize that they had the skills and ability to turn his vision into reality.

Deng was convinced that what he called a "socialist market economy" could be China's salvation. As he told American visitors in 1979, "Of course we don't want capitalism, but we don't want socialist poverty either; what we want is socialism that is advanced, that develops productive forces, and that makes our nation wealthy and powerful."[113] To goad his people onward to this goal, Deng latched on to more slogans and catchphrases, such as "Socialism does not exclude a market economy," that he hoped would help further emancipate thinking.[114] Although he faced substantial conservative resistance within the party, he hoped most ordinary Chinese would not need much convincing to follow him. And follow him they did. Indeed, a foreign visitor accustomed to Mao's China walking through Chinese cities in the early 1980s had to process a dizzying array of new phenomena: individual merchants setting up private street stalls almost everywhere; women starting to get their hair done and to use lipstick and makeup; clothing that reflected ever greater fashion-consciousness; the reappearance of private cars; recrudescence of nightclubs, discos, and even prostitution; newspapers that featured bold new pieces of "investigative literature" (*baogao wenxue*, 报告文学); colorful ads beginning to clutter the pages of new, glossy magazines; black-market money changers; and the reappearance of long-banned private pedicab drivers, who had been considered irredeemably "feudal" just a few years before. After a decade of castigating anyone with the slightest bourgeois affectation as a "capitalist-roader," now the popular slogan "To get rich is glorious" was widely touted by the party itself.

Economic Democracy

Deng did not try to micromanage the changes he was unleashing. Instead, he gave local officials the freedom to experiment with new alternative economic models. He even labeled his reforms "economic democracy" and then followed through by remanding ever more economic control to lower levels of government.[115] Indeed, Deng *demanded* that local officials experiment boldly. "Under our present system of economic management, power is over-concentrated," he said. "So it is necessary to devolve some of it to the lower levels without hesitation, but in a planned way."[116] These local experiments were sometimes technically illegal, but Deng nonetheless gave provincial leaders the go-ahead to try new things and let them succeed or fail on their own merits.

The first of these local breakthroughs was the decommunalization of agriculture. In 1977, a new party secretary arrived in Anhui Province to discover grinding rural poverty almost everywhere he looked. He came up with a six-point proposal based on a truly counterrevolutionary proposition: he wanted to take control away from the "people's communes" and collectivized production teams, and instead let individual peasant households manage their own plots of land and be allowed to sell their surplus at private markets. Deng supported this Anhui model of a "household responsibility system" (*baochan daohu*, 包产到户) even though these proposals directly contravened national policy.[117] Agricultural productivity skyrocketed, and within a few years communes throughout China were a thing of the past.

The next pathbreaking local experiment was a new species of business organization called *xiangzhen qiye* (乡镇企业)—"town and village enterprises," or TVEs. This new kind of "collective" disguised what were essentially private enterprises in the form of local public-private joint ventures. Fueled by the release of pent-up entrepreneurial energy, TVEs spread from the Yangtze Valley like wildfire across the countryside in the 1980s, creating an unprecedented surge of grassroots capitalism. Amazingly, many of the winners in these new businesses came from the poorest segments of society: China's more than seven hundred million peasant farmers, the same people who had first helped catapult the Communists to power. Soon these experimental businesses had fostered a new kind of vibrant countryside capitalism that was lifting tens of millions out of poverty so successfully that some economists began labeling the phenomenon as "reform without losers."[118]

By the mid-1980s, collectivized agrarian socialism was withering away, while rural standards of living and household incomes were improving dramatically.[119] Deng had made good on his slogan "Poverty is not socialism."[120] He had liberated people from the rigidities of Maoist egalitarianism, arguing from the beginning that it was necessary to "allow some regions, enterprises, and people to become better off sooner than others."[121] In 1983 he was even blunter, stating: "Some people in rural areas and cities should be allowed to get rich before others. It is only fair that people who work hard should prosper."[122] Yet the most remarkable, and perhaps most unexpected, outcome of this rapid economic growth was that the gap between rich and poor began to shrink.

A third local motor of new growth—the one closest to Deng's heart—was China's famed Special Economic Zones, or SEZs, piloted in 1980 in Shenzhen, Zhuhai, and Shantou, near the bustling colonies of Hong Kong and Macau, and in Xiamen, across from Taiwan's "tiger" economy. These were manufacturing and industrial zones governed by special protocapitalist legal regulations and tax benefits designed to attract outside investment. Deng modestly defined them as "a medium for introducing technology, management and knowledge"[123] into China. But it would have been more accurate to describe them as experiments in reverse-engineering the much reviled system of treaty ports. This time around, however, Deng hoped to make a growing foreign presence in coastal trade enhance China's wealth and power without undermining its sovereignty.

The first proposal for a new kind of trade zone came from Guangdong Province governor Xi Zhongxun—father of future president and party secretary Xi Jinping. Xi was a war hero from the anti-Japanese resistance of the 1930s, famous for helping to establish the base area—originally called a "special zone" (tequ, 特区)—that protected Mao's guerrilla capital in Yan'an. Deng, evoking his and Xi's personal authority from having fought the Japanese, proposed that their new experiment in Guangdong also be called a "special zone."[124] The choice of label also hinted at the linkage in Deng's mind between "enriching the people" and "strengthening the state."

To oversee this bold new project, Deng tapped Sichuan party secretary Zhao Ziyang, whose tenure in the province had made it one of the guinea pigs in both rural marketization reform and in separating party management from the daily running of industrial enterprises. Zhao became premier in 1980 and would serve as the country's economic czar for the rest of the decade. Much later, in his secretly recorded memoirs, he testified to the depth of Deng's commitment to opening up. "Xiaoping believed in bringing in large-scale foreign investments," said Zhao. "He believed it was difficult for a developing economy like

China's to take off without foreign investment. Of course, he only dealt with major issues and didn't intervene much as to how this might be brought about. But he supported all of it: preferential loans, non-preferential loans, joint ventures."[125]

At the time, these reforms were so shocking in their boldness and so defied every Maoist notion of development that many feared they would never survive. Deng had, after all, broken free of the paralyzing fears of "imperialist monopoly capitalism" that Communist doctrine had codified as the ultimate enemy ever since Lenin wrote *Imperialism: The Highest Stage of Capitalism* during World War I. He knew full well the momentousness of his experiment, even audaciously comparing it to one of Mao's greatest contributions to the triumph of the Communist revolution—his strategy of "encircling the cities from the countryside."[126] And he expected opposition.

Sure enough, intense and stubborn resistance arose within the party leadership, and SEZs remained highly controversial throughout the 1980s. The leading oppositional figure was the party's economic guru, Chen Yun, who had cautiously defended some market mechanisms in the age of Mao but became a defender of central planning in the age of Deng. Chen was Deng's only equal in the leadership when it came to party seniority and gravitas, and on economic issues his views carried special weight. He was not fond of Deng's Special Economic Zones, because he saw them as harkening back to the hated foreign concessions in the treaty ports of China's shameful "semifeudal, semicolonial" past. In fact, when Chen launched a Strike Hard Campaign in 1983, ostensibly against corruption, he was actually going after those promoting Deng's initiatives for "economic crimes." This counterattack very nearly took Deng's reform movement down. "It was not easy for China to carry out the Reform and Open-Door Policy," Zhao Ziyang disclosed later. "Whenever there were issues involving relationships with foreigners, people were fearful, and there were many accusations made against reformers; people were afraid of being exploited, having our sovereignty undermined, or suffering an insult to our nation."[127]

It was a familiar litany of reasons to fear "borrowing," but Deng persisted. "Don't be afraid," he reassured anxious colleagues, whom he chided as being "always worried that if we open up, undesirable things may be brought into China."[128] Or, as he once put it more vividly, "When you open the window for fresh air, some flies get in."[129]

In 1984, pushing back against conservative resistance, Deng backed Premier Zhao's proposal for a whole new "coastal development strategy," one that called for the creation of fourteen additional "open ports." When he visited Guangdong Province that winter, Deng was bowled over by the explosive growth of the Shenzhen SEZ. Where once there had been a sleepy fishing village, now there was a city buzzing with construction. Soon a huge sign went up in downtown Shenzhen proclaiming a profoundly un-Maoist motto: "Time is money, efficiency is our life."[130]

Xiaoping Ninhao!

Deng's faith in such experiments was based on the lessons he took from what he called "our long history" of seeking and often failing to strengthen China by borrowing from the West. It was a history he himself had been living since that maiden voyage to France in 1920. In his speech opening the 1982 party congress, he defended his new initiatives this way: "Both in revolution and in construction we should also learn from foreign countries and draw on their experience, but mechanical application of foreign experience and copying of foreign models will get us nowhere. We have had many lessons in this respect. We must integrate the universal truth of Marxism with the concrete realities of China, blaze a path of our own and build a socialism with Chinese characteristics—that is the basic conclusion we have reached after reviewing our long history."[131]

There was a strange kind of inner logic to the fact that Deng had arrived at a position not so different from the one Feng Guifen had proposed over a century before: to graft Western methods onto a Chinese core. But in a country that was post-Confucian, post-Maoist, and post-Communist, it was no longer clear exactly what that essential core was. China had become a welter of contradictions created by the way its revolt against tradition was fusing with its revolt against revolution. The only real constants were the yearning for a strong, prosperous, respected nation, and the faith that it could be achieved through strong leadership and a strong party, as well as a more open China. "No coun-

Deng Xiaoping at Simonton Texas rodeo in 1979

try can now develop by closing its door," Deng told party leaders in October 1984. "Isolation landed China in poverty, backwardness and ignorance."[132]

Deng and his reforms reached a crescendo of popularity at the celebration of the thirty-fifth anniversary of the founding of the People's Republic of China on October 1, 1984. With a billion Chinese watching a televised parade through Mao's beloved Tiananmen Square, Deng revealed his self-strengthening colors by proudly proclaiming, "The Chinese people are now stronger and wealthier!"[133] As he stood in an open-roofed Red Flag limousine to review troops as they marched by, a ragtag group of Peking University students danced by, holding aloft a handmade sign that read 小平您好 (Xiaoping ninhao), "Hi, Xiaoping!". The spontaneity and intimacy of this exchange between ruler and ruled was utterly foreign to the imperial and Maoist traditions of political theater in Tiananmen Square. As captured in a photo snapped by a Xinhua reporter, the informal, heartfelt banner symbolized not official ritualistic leader magnification, but a nation's warm gratitude, tinged with relief, at being at last led out of the political wilderness of the Mao years. But this honeymoon of good cheer was not fated to last long. Not everyone in China was so grateful to Deng for simply not being Mao.

Deng Xiaoping in 1984 driving through Tiananmen Square

CHAPTER 12

Turmoil (动乱)

DENG XIAOPING, PART II

Mr. Science Demands Democracy

The year 1984 proved a turning point, the high-water mark of Deng Xiaoping's popularity and legitimacy. Based on the initial success of reform and opening, the party found the moment propitious to change its policy focus from rural to urban reform, from villages to cities, from farms to factories, and from the landlocked hinterlands to the export-driven coastal regions. But this next phase of reform did not go as smoothly as the first. The price of daily goods began skyrocketing, throwing urban households into a state of economic insecurity. To make matters worse, party cadres started taking advantage of the difference between state-set prices and market-based prices to line their own pockets. "Red envelopes"—the elegant Chinese term for bribes— became an increasingly standard operating procedure for getting things done in the new economy. From setting up an enterprise or making an investment to getting a favorable article in the press or securing a loan, corruption became endemic. How to deliver urban, industrial growth in China's cities without triggering inflationary spirals and systemic corruption increasingly vexed Deng and his reformist allies. In the meantime, a mushrooming number of university graduates faced bleak job prospects, while their underpaid professors and anxious parents grew increasingly critical of the party. More and more citizens began pointing to a more fundamental problem—the lack of transparency, accountability, and democracy in the political system.

Probably the most influential political critic to emerge in this mid-

1980s transition period was the country's most famous astrophysicist, Fang Lizhi. Born in 1936, Fang had been expelled from the party during the 1957 Anti-Rightist Campaign but rehabilitated in 1978, once Deng came back to power. As the youngest full professor and then vice president of one of the nation's leading science institutions, the University of Science and Technology of China, Fang emerged in the tumultuous 1980s as an electrifying champion not just of academic freedom but also of freedom of speech, human rights, and democracy. The Western press inevitably proclaimed him "China's Sakharov," in honor of the physicist and father of the Soviet atomic bomb, who had become a Russian dissident and won a Nobel Peace Prize in 1975.[1]

Chinese students got a taste of Fang's alternative vision of reform during a free-ranging, sometimes humorous talk he gave at Peking University on November 4, 1985, in which he encouraged them to embrace social concerns and political activism—and to look to the West for new models of intellectual commitment. Addressing the perennial question of China's backwardness, he told his student audience that to be truly productive, they must be willing to "break the bonds of social restraint." Echoing a question raised by Feng Guifen more than a century earlier, Fang asked: if "foreigners are no more intelligent than we Chinese, why, then, can't we produce first-rate work?" He answered not in the mode of the self-strengtheners but in that of the May Fourth Movement activists: "The reasons for our inability to develop our potential lie within our social system." He urged his audience to "be open to different ways of thinking . . . and willing to adopt the elements of those cultures that are clearly superior. A great diversity of thought should be allowed in colleges and universities. For if all thought is narrow and simplistic, creativity will die. At present there are certainly some people in power who still insist on dictating to others according to their own narrow principles. . . . We must not be afraid to speak openly about these things. In fact, it is our duty."

Peking University students had never heard a respected, senior faculty member speak publicly this way before. Soon Fang was traveling the university circuit, spreading his message of human rights and democracy from campus to campus. In Beijing, Hefei, Hangzhou, Ningbo, and Shanghai—wherever he showed up—students flocked to hear him, often transcribing his talks by hand so that they could send copies via mail to friends and other student groups elsewhere in China.

Appearing at Tongji University in Shanghai in November 1986, for instance, Fang roused a crowd to repeated rounds of applause with his argument that political liberties are universal, innate, and foundational, rather than simply means to an end: "Human rights are fundamental privileges that people have from birth, such as the right to think and be educated, the right to marry, and so on. . . . But we Chinese consider these rights dangerous," he told these Shanghai students. "Although human rights are universal and concrete, we Chinese lump freedom, equality, and brotherhood together with capitalism and criticize them all in the same terms. If we are the democratic country we say we are, these rights should be stronger here than elsewhere, but at present they are nothing more than an abstract idea. . . . [In China] democratization has come to mean something performed by superiors on inferiors." Then, to cheers, he added, "Our government does not give us democracy simply by loosening our bonds a bit. This gives us only enough freedom to writhe a little."

The party repeatedly urged Fang to tone down his political evangelism, but he proved deaf to their entreaties. When asked what he thought of Deng's sacrosanct Four Cardinal Principles, he impishly replied that although they were "articles of faith among the political leadership," he preferred four different principles, namely, "science, democracy, creativity, and independence."

Unfit for Democracy

Fang Lizhi's vision of a democratic China, with its echoes of Wei Jingsheng's "fifth modernization," was precisely what Deng was convinced the country did *not* need. On the few occasions when Deng even hinted at the possible virtues of democratic governance, he had been quick to add, as had so many before him, that the Chinese people were not yet ready for it. Had not the United States needed two hundred years to realize the principle of one man, one vote? he asked a visiting American official in 1987.[2] "Because," he said on another occasion, "we have one billion people, and their educational level is not very high, conditions are not yet ripe for direct elections."[3] Perhaps after another half century of political tutelage China would be ready. Deng might talk about "political reform," but as his protégé Zhao Ziyang explained, what he really meant was "administrative reform," not "political modernization and democratization."[4] Yes, the bureaucracy should be streamlined and economic decision making decentralized, but the party's political monopoly over government appointments should remain sacrosanct.[5]

Like the CEO of a large corporation, Deng was a results-driven leader with an urge to improve government efficiency. As Mao astutely observed, Deng's defining characteristic was being "very decisive."[6] And democracy, as Deng saw it, would only create indecisiveness and inefficiency. Multiparty elections and institutional checks and balances would complicate decision making at the very moment when China had no time to lose in catching up with the West. Indeed, Deng openly praised dictatorships for being able to act quickly, mocking the United States for having "three governments" (executive, legislative, and judicial) in one, which collectively often rendered it incapable of dealing with serious problems in a timely and decisive manner.[7] Maybe an advanced economy could afford political gridlock, but not China. "We cannot adopt the practice of the West," he told a visiting Yugoslavian comrade. "The greatest advantage of the socialist system is that when the central leadership makes a decision, it is promptly implemented without interference from any other quarters. When we decided to reform the economic structure, the whole country responded; when we decided to establish special economic zones, they were soon set up. We don't have to go through a lot of discussion and consultation, with one branch of government holding up another and decisions being made, but not carried out. From this point of view, our system is very efficient."[8] In other words, his dream was to perfect Lenin's concept of democratic centralism, but in the context of an increasingly capitalistic China.

For Deng, the cardinal virtue of rule by the CCP was stability. "The United States brags about its political system," he told a visiting American professor. "But politicians there say one thing during a presidential election, another after taking office, another at mid-term elections and still another with the approach of the next presidential election. . . .

Compared with its policies, ours are very stable indeed."[9] Unfortunately, this stability would soon be seriously challenged in the gravest threat Deng would face to his power and his policies. Just like during the May Fourth Movement in 1919, the epicenter of revolt was to be university campuses, which started erupting in protest in the winter of 1986.

Beginning at Fang Lizhi's own University of Science and Technology in Hefei, Anhui Province, on December 5, 1986, twenty major Chinese cities were soon racked by demonstrations in which students demanded a speed-up of political reform. Tens of thousands of protesters flooded the streets carrying placards and banners emblazoned with such slogans as "No Democratization, No Modernization" and "Government of the People, by the People, and for the People."[10] Shocked by this upsurge of student demonstrations and outraged over public attacks by liberal intellectuals, Deng bluntly told the party leadership in a closed-door meeting, "This proves that you cannot succeed without recourse to methods of dictatorship."[11]

One enormous lesson Deng had drawn from watching China's earlier failed modernization drives was that it could not afford disorder, and he saw democracy as an invitation to a new kind of "anxiety within." For him, the main lesson of the Cultural Revolution was that an "excess of democracy" leads to the anarchy, violence, and the demagoguery of mass politics. "During the Cultural Revolution we had what was called mass democracy," Deng recalled, no doubt thinking of his own ordeal. "In those days people thought that rousing the masses to headlong action was democracy and that it would solve all problems. But it turned out that when the masses were roused to headlong action, the result was civil war. We have learned our lesson from history."[12] And the long course of Chinese history taught one other lesson: when the sparks of rebellion were not promptly snuffed out, it was not long before the rulers in Beijing were burned.

The efflorescence of democratic spirit in Fang Lizhi's rousing speeches, as in Wei Jingsheng's wall posters, only reinforced the same dangerous lesson for Deng: an excess of free speech can easily morph into open subversion of the state. As the modern-day embodiment of Chen Duxiu's call for the fusing of Mr. Science and Mr. Democracy in a single force for change, Fang Lizhi quickly came to be viewed by

Deng as a serious threat, endangering his leadership and vision for the country. "If today we tried to achieve democracy by kicking aside the party committees, isn't it equally clear what kind of democracy we would produce?" Deng had asked. "The four modernizations will vanish into thin air."[13] As he saw it, Fang was a cancer that had to be excised from the body politic. "I have read Fang Lizhi's speeches. He doesn't sound like a Communist Party member at all," Deng told a Central Committee meeting on December 30, 1986. "Why do we keep people like him in the Party? He should be expelled, not just persuaded to quit."[14]

Less than two weeks later, Fang was, in accordance with Deng's writ, forced to step down as vice president at the University of Science and Technology. The following day, Deng again raised Fang's case, but without bothering to mention him by name: "Certain individuals have made exceedingly pernicious statements, trying to incite people to action," he said. "They oppose Communist Party leadership and the socialist system, they call for total westernization of China and adoption of the whole capitalist system of the West. These instigators are well-known persons, and we have to do something about them."[15] Less than a week later, Fang was unceremoniously expelled from the party. "We put Wei Jingsheng behind bars, didn't we?" Deng reportedly said. "Did that damage China's reputation? We haven't released him, but China's image has not been tarnished; in fact our image improves day by day."[16]

That same month, an even greater political lightning bolt struck when Deng purged his own chosen successor, president and party secretary Hu Yaobang, for being insufficiently tough on liberal critics and student demonstrators. Over the course of a five-day party meeting, the top leadership initiated a humiliating group criticism of Hu. By the time Hu had finished making his own obligatory self-criticism, he had been reduced to a whimpering shell of his former self.[17] Although Deng promoted the liberal-leaning Zhao Ziyang to replace him, he also put hard-liner Li Peng in the role of premier as balance.

Dissenting intellectuals such as Fang and his discontented students, however, continued to push for democratic reforms, even as they were receiving deeply ambivalent signals from the party leadership about just how far they would be allowed to go. One curious sign of just how unsettled things were occurred in the fall of 1987, when Fang was introduced to the NBC *Nightly News* anchor Tom Brokaw, who happened to have just interviewed Zhao. When Brokaw offered to show Fang a tape of the interview (which was not scheduled to be shown on Chinese television), Fang bizarrely found himself seated in an NBC screening room in Beijing watching his country's head of state essentially speak directly to him, China's number one dissident. "Recently some Communist Party members were expelled from the Party, while others were persuaded to leave the Party," Zhao told Brokaw amiably, taking periodic swigs from a glass of Tsingtao beer perched on a table beside him. "Maybe some people in the U.S. view this as a crackdown, as oppression against intellectuals. I do not agree. I think probably you are already familiar with the name of Mr. Fang Lizhi." As Zhao spoke his name, Fang sat bolt upright, a slight smile on his lips. "Over the last few years he has made many remarks and speeches and written articles criticizing the Chinese government and the policies of our Party. Sometimes he has even referred to the leadership in our country. . . . [S]ince he has such beliefs, he could no longer remain a Communist Party member. . . . I think the Party itself should have the freedom to decide whether someone should remain in or not. But when intellectuals leave the Party, they will still be respected and will still be able to play their own roles in their own [professional] capacities. I don't think you could call this a crackdown."[18]

Zhao was right, albeit for reasons he did not yet fully grasp. The real crackdown was yet to come, and he would soon end up joining Fang as its most prominent victim.

Turmoil at Tiananmen

To stand atop Tiananmen Gate in the spring of 1989 at the spot where Mao had waved to his adoring masses forty years earlier as he proclaimed the founding of the People's Republic of China was to take in an unexpected new reality. Instead of rows of uniformed soldiers, sailors, and well-ordered party acolytes with resolute socialist smiles marching in lockstep past the fabled gate, the square was now roiling with hundreds of thousands of disheveled freethinkers, boisterously challenging the leadership of the party that Mao had founded and Deng had so painstakingly rebuilt. An atmosphere of unalloyed spontaneity and jubilance prevailed as wave after wave of protesters spilled chaotically down both sides of the Avenue of Eternal Peace with banners flying and megaphones blaring. Like two turbulent rivers meeting in a vast lake, the twin currents of demonstrators from the east and west halves of the city converged in Tiananmen Square, where they swirled and eddied in ever-changing kaleidoscopic configurations. So many people filled the vastness of Mao's great square that the din of this ecstatic multitude could be heard even in the surrounding *hutong* alleyways of Beijing, like the roar of some distant cataract.

When Deng contemplated these "masses" haphazardly camped out and protesting at the symbolic center of the country, what he saw were not idealistic young patriots bravely exercising their democratic rights in the best May Fourth tradition, but his worst nightmare: the specter of disorder and instability. Whereas Mao looked at "chaos" (*luan*, 乱) as an essentially positive force in the process of bringing about "creative destruction," what Deng saw was irredeemably negative "turmoil" (*dongluan*, 动乱), the Cultural Revolution reborn and transposed to his newly prospering China. Consequently, his eventual decision to order armed PLA soldiers to restore order—even to fire on the people if necessary to clear the square—was almost inevitable. In retrospect, the real puzzle was not that Deng and the party leadership cracked down so hard, but rather that this great eruption of democratic protest gained as much momentum as it did before being put down.

As with Zhou Enlai in 1976, the demonstrations began after the death of a leader, in this case the dismissed liberal party general secretary Hu Yaobang. Again, Chinese came spontaneously to the square to honor in death a man whom they had not been able to honor fully in life. They arrived quietly at first on April 15, 1989, bearing commemorative funeral wreaths, which they heaped with solemnity around the Monument to the People's Heroes at the center of the square. But as the crowds swelled over the days that followed and no police moved in to stop them, the atmosphere grew less and less funereal and more celebratory. Banners, placards, and speakers that initially asked the party to "reassess the verdict" on the purged Hu soon widened their list of grievances.

"Seventy years have passed since the May Fourth Movement and still we have no freedom and democracy," proclaimed one speaker, to wild applause from onlookers.[19] A biology student, perhaps also with 1919 on his mind, observed, "Hu Yaobang's death has the potential to start a student movement!"

"We were almost drunk with success," one participant later remembered of those heady, early days. "We had spent our lives heeding authority, and our parents were always warning us that insubordination would spell disaster. Then we found ourselves protesting against the government in the middle of Tiananmen Square and out in front of Zhongnanhai as if we owned the place. . . . And, we were able to get away with it! Everything seemed suddenly so different that it was hard to imagine ever becoming obedient again."[20]

Soon, self-appointed student leaders called for a sit-in before the gate leading into the Zhongnanhai leadership compound. When on the night of April 19 some members of the sit-in were beaten as police dispersed them, the movement only gained more strength.[21] By the time of Hu's official state funeral three days later, despite the party's attempts to keep them away, more than a hundred thousand people assembled in the square. When senior officials arrived for the funeral service but ignored student demands for dialogue, an intrepid band of protesters ostentatiously kowtowed before the Great Hall of the People with reform petitions rolled up in scrolls and held forth in outstretched arms in a classic position of supplication. By invoking traditions of remonstrance dating back to the imperial era, in the same place where Liang Qichao and Kang Youwei had first organized fellow scholars to protest against the humiliating Treaty of Shimonoseki ending the Sino-Japanese War in 1895 and where the May Fourth Movement had erupted in 1919, students in 1989 implicitly now mocked the party leadership for its still "feudalistic" refusal to "talk to the people."

Deng, however, was in no mood for talking. On April 26, egged on by party conservatives including Li Peng, he signed off on a hard-line lead editorial in the state-run *People's Daily* that labeled the students' actions "a planned conspiracy and a turmoil" that jeopardized "the great aspiration of the revitalization of China cherished by the whole nation."[22] In impugning their patriotism, Deng seemed to have forgotten the nature of protest movements in modern Chinese history. Since their first outrage over the Treaty of Shimonoseki, hypersensitive patriotism invariably lay at the radioactive core of youth disaffection. So when Deng implied that Hu Yaobang's mourners lacked patriotism, he stepped on the third rail of Chinese protest politics—nationalism—and he would pay a bitter price for it.

Feelings for Democracy

The day after Deng's incendiary editorial, tens of thousands more indignant students poured back into the streets of Beijing, marching from the far northwest suburb of Haidian—Beijing's university quarter—to Tiananmen Square. Residents and shopkeepers along the way cheered them on like fans at a marathon, passing out water and snacks to the boisterous procession. There was a feeling of festive elation that sunny spring day, as if the students' noble intentions and proud association with their May Fourth predecessors conferred a certain indestructible historical destiny on them. And when, astonishingly, they managed to peaceably break through several cordons of police trying to block their passage to the square, they became all the more intoxicated with their righteousness, even invincibility.

All that May, students and sympathetic citizens would occupy the square by staging a nonstop drama of protest. As the days and then weeks passed and people became less and less fearful of a crackdown, an increasingly festive, even carnival-like atmosphere took hold, drawing tens of thousands more onlookers into the square just to see what was happening, if not to express their own solidarity with the students and their desire for more democracy. As waves of chanting protesters flooded into Tiananmen from almost every conceivable work unit in the city and then began spending whole days and even nights there, the square was transformed into a semipermanent, living community. Walking through the crowds past rows of colorful tents was like traversing a massive bazaar filled not with merchants hawking wares but with students trading ideas, waving placards, arguing, and debating, but also struggling to take care of the increasingly complex needs of the massive but inchoate social organism that had spontaneously become this new, bustling, instant city-within-a-city. Gazing out over the million people in the square from the top of Tiananmen made it seem impossible to imagine how the party could ever reverse this tide, much less restore itself to full authority.

Meanwhile, inside the halls of power, the unity of the party's central leadership was fracturing. Zhao Ziyang, who had been in North Korea when Deng approved the fateful *People's Daily* editorial, believed that a softer line might quell the demonstrations. And, upon his return to Beijing he took a more conciliatory posture than Deng toward the students, setting off a "two-line struggle" within the party between moderates like himself and hard-liners such as Premier Li Peng.

On May 12, student leaders declared a hunger strike until party leaders responded in a meaningful way to their demands—which now called not just for a reassessment of the verdict on Hu Yaobang but also for permission to conduct mass political campaigns, more effective measures to halt official corruption, greater official dialogue between the government and students, and greater freedom of the press.

The hunger strike turned what had been a festival of freedom into a life-and-death drama. Areas of the square became sectioned off into zones designated for different functions, with one shaded by tent flies reserved exclusively for the hunger strikers. There was also a hospital area, staffed by scores of volunteer doctors and nurses in white smocks; a propaganda area, where materials could be printed; a finance area, where all the contributions from supportive citizens could be tabulated and disbursed; and a commissary section, for the collection and distribution of all the donated food and drink that was now flooding in, with residents of Hong Kong even chartering planes to carry their donations to Beijing. Students carved out "lifeline" routes through the crowds so that ambulances and emergency workers could gain easier access to any fasters who needed to be taken to the hospital. And the sense of drama was only heightened by the fact that the country at large was now watching each day's events unfold live via state television, which had become almost completely uncensored.

Like the turning point in a Greek tragedy, events soon took on an international dimension thanks to a long-planned visit to Beijing by Soviet leader Mikhail Gorbachev. His arrival on May 14 was supposed to mark a historic milestone in Deng's campaign to normalize China's foreign relations with Russia as another step forward in opening up the country to the world. It was, after all, the first such meeting between Russian and Chinese leaders in Beijing since Khrushchev's ill-fated trip in 1958. Deng hoped his summit with Gorbachev would be

Beijing students with "Hi, Xiaoping!" banner in Tiananmen Square, 1984

Fang Lizhi and his mentor, 1989

Zhao Ziyang in Tiananmen Square (with aide Wen Jiabao), 1989

Deng Xiaoping billboard in Shenzhen Special Economic Zone

the equivalent for him of what Nixon's 1972 visit to Beijing had been for Mao—a strategic breakthrough in international relations of the highest order.

Gorbachev was impressed by Deng's fresh thinking, despite the Chinese leader's way of sometimes cloaking his views in "phrases typical of times past."[23] For Deng, however, the Gorbachev visit turned out to be an unmitigated disaster. Hundreds of television reporters and print journalists who had been invited from around the world to cover the historic summit were now focused not on the triumph of China's reconciliation with the Soviets but on the humiliation of the Chinese Communist Party by thousands of its best and brightest youth in the middle of Tiananmen Square. Even more mortifying, by the middle of May hundreds of thousands of ordinary citizens had joined in, and the whole spectacle was being beamed around the world live on CNN, which had been granted special dispensation for a satellite feed to cover Gorbachev's visit.[24] Tiananmen Square had turned into a giant sound stage for one of the century's most protracted, spellbinding, and epic live dramas of political protest. The revolution was being televised globally! For Deng, it was a devastating loss of face.

The party central finally agreed to engage in direct dialogue with student leaders. In a high-ceilinged conference room in the Great Hall of the People, Premier Li Peng found himself sitting stiffly opposite a pair of young students: Wang Dan, a Peking University freshman majoring in history, and Wu'er Kaixi, a flamboyant young Uighur from Beijing Normal University who managed to stage a mini-masterpiece of political theater by showing up to the meeting in his hospital gown and dragging an oxygen tank. The premier had hardly begun the meeting, in his predictably patronizing manner, when Wu'er cut in. Like a boxer punching above his weight, he exploited his weakened state from fasting for dramatic effect, and quibbling with Li over who had invited whom to the meeting, prevented the flummoxed premier from making any headway with the determined, self-righteous students. When the premier graciously extended his arm to shake their hands at the end, none of them would reach out to reciprocate.[25] Making the confrontation even more painful for the party was their prior agreement with the students that the entire encounter would be aired live on national television.

Li Peng's report to Deng on the meeting sealed the movement's fate. Deng and his colleagues, except Zhao Ziyang, were so deeply offended that they promptly agreed to declare martial law. "Do not yield to the feelings for democracy," Deng had once told Zhao. "Democracy is only a means [to an end]."[26] But Zhao, yielding to the euphoria of people power—and maybe also seeing the demonstrations as a potential means to defeat his conservative rivals—now decided to ally himself with the students. On May 19, in the last public appearance of his life, he made an impromptu visit to the square. Surrounded by students, his eyes welling with tears, he stammered out through a hand-held bullhorn the Shakespearean line: "We have come too late." A photographer caught an image of Zhao squeezed into a van filled with disheveled hunger strikers. At his side, hauntingly, was the now familiar face of Wen Jiabao, who was then an aide to Zhao but would one day become premier, staring expressionlessly out into the square.

It was indeed "too late," at least for Zhao. He had failed to heed the lesson of the Guangxu Emperor and Liang Qichao's failed Hundred Days' Reform a century earlier: he had hoped to encourage a new wave of reform but had not laid the necessary political groundwork within the party, and as a result ended up being isolated. He had been relying on a think tank of bright young minds to develop new approaches to reform, much as the Guangxu Emperor had relied upon Kang Youwei and Liang Qichao. Zhao's idealistic brain trust, the Chinese Economic Structure Reform Research Institute, had been pushing a theory they called "new authoritarianism," asserting, unremarkably enough, that what China really needed was a strong central leadership to guide the country toward democracy via further economic development. But to now call for sweeping changes without first developing a firm political base left Zhao in the same no-man's-land that had doomed Liang and the Guangxu Emperor. Under the circumstances, it was not difficult for his rivals to convince Deng that Zhao himself, not Deng, was supposed to be the "new authoritarian." Deng's response, made the day after Zhao visited the square, was curiously similar to Empress Dowager Cixi's. She had imprisoned her nephew in a tower on an island in the imperial compound. Deng removed Zhao from power and locked him up in his home in Beijing (without trial or further punishment) until his death in 2005. There Zhao spent the last sixteen years of his life under de facto house arrest, infrequently allowed to leave his small courtyard home, located—a final irony—at Number 6 *Fuqiang hutong* (富强 胡同), "Wealth and Power Alley."

Massacre

Having eliminated the closest thing to a liberal within the party leadership, Deng now moved to crush the democracy movement itself. On May 20 the government declared martial law and dispatched troops to secure the square. But tens of thousands of ordinary people promptly and nonviolently spilled into the streets to block the progress of the People's Liberation Army as they tried to enter the city. As humiliating as this was, for the government, the most painful part of the tragedy was yet to come.

As citizens proffered flowers and food to PLA tank captains and soldiers, some units engaged in a military version of passive resistance: rather than struggling against the crowds, they simply yielded to them, and then finally retreated. A few officers were even reported to have openly sided with the protesters, making it appear as if the PLA might even balk at the party's orders to end the protest.[27] But Deng's grip on the military—going back to his days in the 1930s and '40s as a "political commissar" in the Red Army and then strengthened by an extensive network of military relationships thereafter—did finally prevail. On June 2, he gave new orders to clear the square, by force if necessary. This time the gun obeyed the command of the party.

On June 3, a second wave of armed troops began to close in around the city, starting from various points on the outskirts of Beijing and working inward like a noose closing around the center. By the time these troops reached Tiananmen Square in the darkness of the early morning on June 4, most of the killing had already taken place in the city's periphery as soldiers had to battle their way through numerous citizen-erected barricades. All that was left was to dislodge the last remaining students, bedraggled and fearful, from their refuge around the Monument to the People's Heroes.

Untold hundreds, perhaps thousands were killed or wounded that hellish night. In the eyes of the international community, Deng had hit a nadir. Yet there is no suggestion that he was unduly tormented over

"6/4," as the Beijing Massacre came to be known. He appeared in public for the first time five days later unapologetically to address his PLA commanders and commend those few soldiers who had died as "martyrs" to the cause of restoring order to the capital. Led by a handful of rebels who "tried to subvert our state and our Party," Beijing's democracy spring was a "disturbance" that had been bound to happen, Deng asserted.[28] But, thanks to the efforts of the party, the PLA, and the people, China had managed to weather the turmoil.

In Western scholarship, the demonstrations of spring 1989 loom, like the May Fourth Movement, as a milestone in what was presumed to be China's ineluctable historical path toward greater openness, if not full-scale multiparty liberal democracy. But for Deng, as for Sun Yat-sen, Chiang Kai-shek, and Mao Zedong, such non-party-sanctioned demonstrations were milestones to nowhere—or, worse, way stations to a poorer and weaker China.

Exiling Dissent

Fang Lizhi had not even gone to Tiananmen Square during the weeks of protest. "I am sure what I have been doing and saying has had a strong influence on what the students think and, of course, we support what they are doing," Fang said just before martial law was declared. "But neither they nor I want to give the government any pretext for saying that I am the hand-in-the-glove."[29]

After the mayhem of June 4, he and his wife, fearing for their lives, sought shelter in the American embassy. By taking advantage of this residual diplomatic shoal of extraterritoriality, the Fangs reenacted a familiar drama, as when Feng Guifen had hidden from Taiping rebels in Shanghai in 1861, Liang Qichao had fled the Empress Dowager's arrest warrant to the Japanese embassy in Beijing in 1898, and Deng himself had once hid out in the foreign concessions of Shanghai in the 1920s. The Fangs were also blazing a trail that would be followed again almost a quarter of a century later when the blind legal activist Chen Guangcheng also sought refuge in the American embassy in Beijing in 2012.

Fang hoped his stay would be temporary, but after the White House unexpectedly announced that he had "sought sanctuary," China's Public Security Bureau branded him a "black hand" who had helped to create the "counterrevolutionary rebellion" that had just been suppressed. It also issued warrants for the arrest of him and his wife, charging them both with committing crimes of "counterrevolutionary propaganda and incitement." While other Tiananmen Square political activists and student leaders were either already in prison or desperately trying to slip out of China, Fang and Li suddenly found themselves trapped in a diplomatic no-man's-land. Because the Chinese government did not know exactly in which of the U.S. embassy's compounds the two were sequestered, they surrounded all of them with cordons of unsmiling Chinese soldiers armed with assault rifles. With Beijing still under martial law and a hostile climate existing between the United States and China, some U.S. diplomats even feared that if Chinese security forces learned exactly where the two were hidden, they might be tempted to storm the embassy, Boxer Rebellion style, to seize them. In fact, their whereabouts were so secret that, with the exception of the U.S. ambassador himself and several ranking diplomats, other embassy officials had no idea where in their midst the two Chinese dissidents were hidden. As the months drifted by, Fang and his wife remained in their strange limbo, while the Chinese government charged the U.S. government with harboring criminals and traitors.

Calling their crowded quarters—several small rooms that had served as a clinic in back of the ambassadorial residence, with windows that were now completely covered—his "black hole," Fang joked that he was the only astrophysicist in the world who could not see the stars. But during his long confinement, he kept his spirits up by reading materials friends sent him through the U.S. diplomatic pouch and continuing to write scientific papers. For a year Fang and his wife remained inside the embassy as the Chinese government pressed its propaganda campaign against him and other dissidents, going so far as to call Fang "scum of the intelligentsia." At first, Chinese officials insisted he be handed over and "dealt with according to Chinese law." They insisted that only if he made a public admission of guilt, which he refused to do, would they consider letting him leave the country. But once the first anniversary of June 4 passed without further incident, they started recalculating. Perhaps it was more in their interest to resolve the bedeviling matter so that China's relations with the outside world, especially the United States, could start being normalized again. And so their position began to soften.

In May 1990 Fang reported some minor heart palpitations, which ultimately turned into a face-saving way to resolve the standoff. Although a Western embassy physician found no serious medical problem and Fang himself dismissed the chest pains as the result of "too much coffee," news that he had been "stricken" was leaked in Washington. On June 25, 1990, he and his wife were finally allowed to leave Beijing on humanitarian medical grounds via a U.S. Air Force plane sent by President George H. W. Bush.

"If circumstances allow, I will go immediately back to China to make whatever contributions I can, because I can only function there," Fang said upon arrival in exile. Asked about his being forced to leave his motherland, he replied: "It is a victory in the sense that the Chinese government finally had to let me out, because they were under pressure. But it can also be seen as a failure because I have left my own country, my colleagues, and also many of my acquaintances and friends, and naturally my effectiveness will now be marked by this."[30] Henceforth, exporting critics would become a regular party strategy. Dissidents would be given the choice of incarceration or exile; if they chose the latter, there would be a brief period of bad press that the party had to endure, but most would soon sink into political oblivion thereafter.

Deng in Retreat

The legitimacy of the party and Deng went into free fall after June 4, and his bold domestic reform process was stopped dead in its tracks. Western governments announced a wave of sanctions that also jeopardized his hopes for a continued "opening up" to the world. Backpedaling in the face of this latest example of "anxiety within and calamity without," Deng instinctually returned to his Leninist roots, blaming the "Western imperialists" and their "rule of international monopoly capital" for destabilizing China, and denouncing the West's imposition of sanctions for human rights violations as an insult to the Chinese nation and the developing world.[31] Developed countries' "talk about human rights, freedom, and democracy is only designed to safeguard the interests of the strong, rich countries [*qiangguo fuguo*, 强国富国],"

complained Deng.[32] Not surprisingly, he also fell back on the meme of
the nation's historical humiliation by the great powers. "Since the
Opium War, when they began to invade China, how many Chinese
people's human rights have they violated?" he asked.[33]

As antidote to all that had happened, Deng also approved a "patriotic education campaign," an effort to inoculate the next generation of
potentially insubordinate students against the heresies of "wholesale
westernization." Given new Western sanctions against China, the idea
of a "century of humiliation" was reprised in this new propaganda
campaign, which focused on the issue of "national pride" and extended
from kindergarten to university.[34]

This more conservative, nationalist ideological agenda was fine by
Deng, but he urgently wanted economic policy exempted from any
similarly regressive drift. However, conservative rivals, led by Chen
Yun and Li Peng, seized the post–June 4 moment to reassert socialist
economic orthodoxy. Like Mao, sidelined after the disaster of the Great
Leap Forward, Deng now suddenly found himself no longer in direct
control of key matters in domestic policy, and again, like Mao, he had
to bide his time as he pondered a countermove.

Deng was also alarmed by the way the geopolitical map of the
world was being redrawn after the Chinese Communist Party's near-
death experience in Tiananmen Square. In Poland, the non-Communist
opposition party Solidarity had—on June 4, 1989, of all days—won
national elections. The Berlin Wall fell that November, and soon Communist Party–run and Soviet Union–dominated states were unraveling
one after another all across Eastern Europe. Most disturbing was the
violent end of Romania's Communist dictator, Nicolae Ceauşescu,
whose three-decade rule was terminated with his unceremonious exe-
cution on Christmas Day 1989. Finally, on Christmas Day two years
later, the mother ship of communism, the Union of Soviet Socialist Republics itself, simply disappeared into history, fracturing into dozens of
independent states in a manner all too suggestive of what could happen
to China if similar centrifugal forces in Tibet, Xinjiang, Inner Mongo-
lia, Hong Kong and Taiwan were ever unleashed. What is more, throughout China's East Asian backyard, a succession of democratic, "people
power" movements had been toppling authoritarian governments—
Communist and capitalist alike—while the region's capitalist "tigers"

were posting double-digit economic growth rates. As Deng warned, China "must forge ahead or be swept downstream."[35]

Watching the socialist bloc collapse amid the conservative backlash following the trauma of June 4 had the curious effect of goading Deng on to even bolder decision making. Nearing his ninetieth birthday, he seemed to have concluded that if he was going to save the nation, something audacious needed to be done. If the Chinese Communist Party was to survive and reimbue itself with legitimacy in a socialist world that was disassembling around it, the party needed to start delivering, quickly and in a big, new way. Unfortunately, the party was no longer at Deng's bidding. In fact, when he bluntly warned Central Committee members in 1990 that to survive socialism they must rely equally on markets and planning, imploring his fellow comrades, "Don't be afraid of taking a few risks," they spurned his call.[36]

Early in 1991, he set out for Shanghai in a last-ditch attempt to get his message out. A pseudonymous article placed in Shanghai's *Liberation Daily* at the bidding of his ally Mayor Zhu Rongji made Deng's agenda clear: "Reform and opening is the only path to making the nation wealthy and the people strong."[37] But the national media refused to reprint the article, a sign of the countervailing strength of the conservative opposition in Beijing. "There is no other option open to us," Deng is reported to have warned at a leadership meeting in Beijing during the fall of 1991. "If the economy cannot be boosted, over the long run, we will lose people's support" and "will be oppressed and bullied by other nations throughout the world. A continuation of such a situation will only lead to the collapse of the Communist Party."[38]

Finally, in January 1992, brittle in body but still hardy in spirit, Deng made his move. He embarked on a historic one-month trip, visiting the original Special Economic Zones of Shenzhen and Zhuhai in Guangdong Province and again swinging by Shanghai. The term used to describe his sojourn, *nanxun* (南巡), "the southern inspection tour," evoked the grand imperial expeditions made by early Qing emperors when China was at the height of its power and prosperity in the eighteenth century. Deng's task, as he saw it, was single-handedly to reignite the fire in the party's belly for rapid economic development. In essence, Deng told his party and the nation, China had to develop—or die. "If China does not continue with socialism, reform and opening, and economic development to improve the livelihood of the people, whatever other road we might take will be a dead end," he warned his audience in Guangdong, jabbing his finger in the air as he spoke.[39]

Unbound Feet

The word Deng kept incanting on his southern tour was *boldness*. "In order to make socialism superior to capitalism," he proclaimed in Shenzhen, "we must boldly take heed of, and absorb, all accomplishments of every civilization achieved by the human race . . . including those of the developed capitalist countries."[40] Borrowing a metaphor that Mao had used to launch the collectivization of agriculture back in the mid-1950s, Deng scolded conservative colleagues: "We should be bolder than before in conducting reform and opening to the outside and have the courage to experiment. We must not act like women with bound feet."[41]

For Deng, it was time to grow again, even faster, by opening even wider to the world economy. "Development is the absolute principle," Deng insisted.[42] Drifting by boat past a Qing Dynasty customs house on the Pearl River near where the Opium War had begun, he commented darkly, "Those who are backward get beaten. . . . We've been poor for thousands of years, but we won't be poor again,"[43] and, like his predecessors, he remained wary of the "imperialist threat." During negotiations with British prime minister Margaret Thatcher over the return of the crown colony of Hong Kong, he griped that he would not become another Li Hongzhang.[44] However, the only way to overcome that threat once and for all was to make China strong and prosperous, which, ironically, required foreign capital. So on his southern inspection tour Deng defiantly proclaimed: "China cannot close its doors and just defend its borders. It should be open to the outside world."[45] Throughout the 1980s, he had worked hard to pry open China's back doors. Now in the 1990s he wanted to fling open the front gate as well. Since he still retained control over major foreign policy initiatives, he was already moving to improve relations with Taiwan, normalize relations with South Korea, and create the necessary conditions to attract major flows of new foreign investment back into China. In 1991 he even normalized relations with Vietnam—the country he had ignominiously invaded in 1979. He made peace overtures to India, with which China had fought a war in 1962 and had had border scuffles throughout the 1980s. In the early 1990s, Deng explained his approach to his grand strategy with the Delphic dictum that China must *taoguang yanghui* (韬光养晦): "avoid the limelight."[46] China saw its challenge as becoming more wealthy and powerful without alarming other nations about its rise.

The effect of the tour was not instantaneous. With the exception of a lone newspaper, the *Special Economic Zone News* in the boomtown of Shenzhen, his message continued to be shut out of the national media. Undeterred, Deng pressed on until he finally managed to get his utterances out to the country at large through notes of his Shenzhen speeches released by the branch offices of the Chinese Communist Party.[47] Soon provincial and city leaders, especially along the eastern seaboard, began rallying to his flag and then one by one other leaders in Beijing began defecting from Chen Yun's policy of caution to Deng's boldness on the question of further openness and marketization. Finally, in June, his "new line" was embraced in a *People's Daily* editorial and formally adopted at the Fourteenth Party Congress in October 1992 as official dogma.[48] "Our policy of reform and openness will not change for one hundred years," Deng promised emphatically.[49]

Dead Ancestor

Under Deng Xiaoping, two trails long-explored by China's political and intellectual elite since the nineteenth century came to a crossroads. The idealistic search for democracy ended tragically with the Tiananmen massacre, even as the quest for prosperity opened up one of the most explosive and sustained bursts of economic growth in all of history. Thanks to this boom, the Communist Party managed to begin restoring much of its diminished legitimacy, especially at home. By his death in 1997, Deng had brought his country to the brink of exactly the kind of wealth and power so ardently sought by generations of reformist thinkers and revolutionary leaders.

In his decades of revolutionary struggle, Mao Zedong had sought to free Chinese from the past to realize a utopian Communist future, and in a certain grim way he did succeed in emancipating Chinese society

Deng Xiaoping on his "southern tour" in 1992

from the tyranny of the past that had so obsessed the May Fourth generation. Paradoxically, Mao's savage revolution did prepare the ground for Deng to build not the proletarian paradise imagined by his predecessor, but a strong and prosperous, if unequal, nation in which the Chinese people at last could take pride.

"Deng has never come to see me about anything," Mao complained in the 1960s. "He respected me but kept away from me, treating me like a dead ancestor."[50] Indeed, Deng was the first reformer since the beginning of the nineteenth century to also treat the question of Chinese culture and identity like a dead ancestor. He had escaped the magnetism of tradition, perhaps in no small measure due to the monumental efforts of Mao and those who had come before him, even if he saw those Sisyphean efforts as largely wasted energy. But Mao's revolution did help free Deng, the deracinated Leninist, to deal pragmatically with the present. Rather than having to dwell on the past in an endless joust with Confucius and sons, or dreaming unrealistic dreams about pie-in-the-sky communism, Deng was freed to focus on making China more prosperous.

And just as Deng preferred to leave the issues involving the core of Chinese tradition and cultural identity to others, he demanded that the core of China's new political system—Communist Party rule—be left untouched. If he surrendered socialism's dreams of egalitarianism and social welfare, he defended the political core of Chinese Leninism: single-party dictatorship. He saved China from the deadly elixir of Maoism with a heady cocktail of neo-authoritarianism and state-led capitalism.

Deng died on February 19, 1997. On May 2, his ashes were scattered over the ocean, in accordance with Mao's proposal that there would be "no tombs built" for party leaders—except, that is, for himself in the form of the Mao Zedong Memorial Mausoleum in Tiananmen Square.[51] Deng's cremation, by contrast, was in keeping with his overall attitude of self-effacement and party discipline. Grand sepulchers may have been built to inter the sacred remains of the Ming emperors, the Empress Dowager Cixi, Sun Yat-sen, and Mao, but for those wishing to posthumously venerate Deng Xiaoping, there would be no place to go. His monument was China's restoration to wealth and power.

Zhu Rongji in the early 1980s

CHAPTER 13

Entering the World（入世）

ZHU RONGJI（朱镕基）

Opening Up

In June 1998, when U.S. president Bill Clinton landed in Beijing for an official state visit, the nightmare of the June 4 massacre was fading, the successes of Deng's southern tour were already beginning to manifest themselves, and Deng's heirs, President Jiang Zemin and Premier Zhu Rongji, were firmly in command. Back in May 1989, before the final denouement in Tiananmen Square, Deng had summoned Jiang, then Shanghai's party secretary, to Beijing and made him CCP general secretary to replace the deposed Zhao Ziyang. In 1991, he summoned Shanghai mayor Zhu Rongji as well and put him in charge of the economy for the rest of the decade as premier. Not having been at the center of Beijing power politics, the two men were unlikely candidates, but both proved stalwart Deng supporters, and with impressive speed they managed to get China back on the development track. In fact, by 1998 things had so improved under their leadership that President Clinton—like Presidents Carter, Reagan, and Bush before him—was willing to visit the Central Kingdom to, in effect, signal that the past was the past.

For anyone with a sense of recent history, it was a strange experience to be on the bank of stone steps leading up to the Great Hall of the People's intimidating main entranceway on the west side of Tiananmen Square awaiting the arrival of presidents Clinton and Jiang, as if Tiananmen Square were not a place haunted by hungry ghosts. After all, it was in this exact spot that in 1989, students had knelt in supplication during Hu Yaobang's memorial, proffering a petition for redress of grievances to their leaders. And it was down these same steps that squadrons of troops had spilled before dawn on June 4 to clear the square of the last protesters after the People's Liberation Army had earlier committed what was perhaps the most humiliating self-inflicted wound of China's twentieth century: firing on their own people. At the time, it was hard to imagine how Tiananmen Square would ever be cleansed of such memories, much less how the CCP would regain control of China and restore healthy relations with the horror-stricken outside world. Yet here on a bright sunny day in June nine years later, the two smiling presidents arrived, cheerfully greeted each other, and then amid the pomp and ceremony of this state visit ascended the staircase to participate in a joint press conference in the Great Hall itself.

The attending officials and foreign correspondents were still seating themselves inside one of the hall's many imposing salons when a stunning announcement was made: Jiang, whose habit of singing songs such as "O Sole Mio" or "Home on the Range" and of reciting bits of the Gettysburg Address at diplomatic events suggested a somewhat overexuberant urge toward showmanship, had decided that the press conference, at which both presidents would field spontaneous questions from the international press corps, would be broadcast live across China on both radio and television. If discussion strayed inopportunely into sensitive political territory, there would be no last-minute way for censors to sanitize the record. The gesture was a dramatic example of Jiang and Zhu's attempts to make Chinese interactions with other countries more open and in conformity with the way other world leaders allowed themselves to be subject to a freer flow of exchange.

Indeed, animated by President Clinton's good-ol'-boy bonhomie, the press conference proceeded with a congenial and unscripted air of give-and-take. In fact, as Jiang rose to the podium, he seemed charged with a real enthusiasm to try and hold his own next to this American master of spontaneous dialogue. As if he could hardly wait to get things rolling, as soon as each had concluded their initial formal statements Jiang took charge and piped up: "Now President Clinton and I are prepared to take your questions." After an initial question on the Asian financial crisis, when the topic turned to the sensitive issue of human rights, Jiang did not miss a beat. After defending China's record, he cheerfully continued, "I'd like to know whether President Clinton will have anything more to add."

The irrepressible Clinton promptly launched into a discourse on human rights, adding, "If you are so afraid of personal freedom, because of the abuses, that you limit people's freedom too much, then you pay, I believe, an even greater price in a world where the whole economy is based on ideas and information and exchange and debate, and children everywhere [are] dreaming dreams and feeling they can live their dreams out."

Unprompted, Jiang then jumped right back into the exchange. "I am sorry to have to take up an additional five minutes," he said, bursting into a smile that suggested he had actually started to enjoy the back-and-forth himself. "I'd like to say a few words on [the] Dalai Lama." Jaws dropped, as Tibet and its exiled religious leader were not exactly topics Chinese leaders usually welcomed discussing anywhere, and especially not before live TV cameras. After a boilerplate disquisition on Tibet, Jiang announced that he would now like to pose a question to Clinton: "During my visit to the U.S. last year, I found that although education in science and technology has developed to a very high level and people are now enjoying modern civilization, but still quite a number believe in Lamaism," he declared, "I want to find out the reason why."

But then, as if he had suddenly thought better of wading any further into this incredibly sensitive and treacherous topic, he hastily added, "I think President Clinton is a strong defender of American interests, and I am a strong defender of Chinese interests. But despite that, we have friendly exchanges of views and discussions. I think that is democracy. . . . If you agree, we will finish this."

By then, however, Clinton was having far too much fun to stop. "I agree, but you have to let me say one thing about the Dalai Lama, since you brought it up," he interjected. A ripple of laughter, at once mirthful and uneasy, spread across the room. "For us the question is not fundamentally religious, it is political. That is, we believe that other people should have the right to fully practice their religious beliefs, and that if he in good faith presents himself on those terms, it is a legitimate thing for China to engage him in dialogue." Unable to resist continuing, and all the while beaming almost affectionately at Jiang, Clinton added: "And let me say something that will perhaps be unpopular with everyone. I have spent time with the Dalai Lama. I believe him to be an honest man, and I believe that if he [the Dalai Lama] had a conversation with President Jiang, they would like each other very much."[1]

It would be some time before such a collegial atmosphere between the leaders of the two countries would again reignite. Even more telling, however, this effort toward openness gave a strong indication of the direction in which Jiang Zemin as president and Zhu Rongji as premier were trying to lead their country. What Jiang was attempting, somewhat awkwardly, to do in that press conference in terms of international politics—namely, show a more open, even "democratic," China—Zhu Rongji was then also quietly accomplishing with extraordinary results in the economic realm. He was making his country "the factory of the world," thereby ensuring that Deng's vision of reform and opening up would outlive Deng himself.

Pudong

Although Jiang was the top-ranking official of the "third generation" (after Mao and Deng) of party leaders and was thus afforded the most exposure at the Clinton summit, the more important figure shaping China's quest for prosperity in the 1990s was the number two man, Premier Zhu Rongji, whose odyssey to national prominence also began in Shanghai in the late 1980s.

In the spring of 1988, needing someone to go to Shanghai and fight for his vision of China's future, Deng tapped Zhu, then a senior central planner with decades of experience at the State Planning Commission in Beijing. Thus a relatively unknown central government economic bureaucrat became mayor of this celebrated city, which was slated to become the newest experiment in Deng's version of capitalism, then euphemistically referred to as "socialism with Chinese characteristics." In its myriad reincarnations, the city was the perfect representation of China's chameleon-like passage through modern times. Shanghai had become, in serial fashion, the archetype of China's shameful "treaty port" past, an outpost of cosmopolitanism in the days of Chiang Kai-shek, a symbol of humiliation under Japanese puppet government occupation, and most recently a hotbed of Maoist radicalism and the launching pad for the Cultural Revolution. If Deng had his way, it would—with Zhu's help—now be reborn yet again, this time as a boomtown megalopolis and a lustrous new financial Pearl of the Orient.

Once there, Zhu immediately positioned himself as the city's supreme local economic developer. He quickly adopted the bold, visionary thinking of a venture capitalist who looked on Shanghai as a giant start-up opportunity. The Huangpu River ran through the heart of downtown, and along its western bank was the mythic Bund, that famed strip of art nouveau banks, hotels, and trading houses built back when Shanghai was a boomtown under foreign dominion. The rest of the city spread out from there, stretching north over Suzhou Creek through the neighborhood where Lu Xun lived in the 1920s, and westward past the former British and French concessions where Feng Guifen wrote his *Dissenting Views* and where Chen Duxiu, with an assist from Mao, helped found the Chinese Communist Party in 1921. But in the area known simply as Pudong, or "East of the Huangpu River," there was still virtually nothing. And where others still saw vacant, uninviting mud flats, Zhu saw future prosperity. Like an artist contemplating an empty canvas, he had spotted an empty space that begged for an epic development project.

All Zhu lacked was the foreign capital to make his grand vision a reality. To attract it he built huge scale models to tantalize foreign capitalists. One such prospective investor was an erudite Dutch count, Hugh von Kryenhoff, from a global investment company, the New Perspectives Fund. Visiting Shanghai in the early 1990s to scout out the city's new investment climate, the count was brought before an enormous model of the planned Pudong development. Gazing at the staggeringly ambitious rendition, which called for scores of new high-rise office buildings, stock markets, banks, hotels, parks, and performance halls, von Kryenhoff uttered a single exclamation: "Terrifying!" He was right. It was not easy to imagine how those unprepossessing Pudong mud flats, which sat mostly undisturbed across the river from the bustling Bund, might ever be reborn according to this grandiose model.

To make his vision a reality, Zhu created the Shanghai Foreign Investment Commission and endowed it with unprecedented authority to streamline the approval process for foreign investment, with no more interminable waits or need to grease the palms of countless bureaucrats. Soon enough the foreign business community had nicknamed the new mayor "One-Chop Zhu."[2] This Hunanese native, who had built his career in Beijing, confidently and forcefully began turning Shanghai upside down, lashing out at corruption among cadres even as he was pushing for faster growth and greater openness to foreign capital. He had clearly drunk Deng's Kool-Aid: what China needed was better economics, not politics; development, not class struggle; Western capital, not anti-imperialist rhetoric.

Then came the storm of mass protest during the spring of 1989. Shanghai's spring under Zhu Rongji, however, played out very differently than the carnage unleashed in Beijing on June 4 under Deng. In Shanghai, the mass demonstrations reached their zenith on the evening of June 8 but then subsided without violence . . . after Zhu boldly appeared live on television to calm the situation. It was his deft handling of an explosive situation that soon helped catapult him into the central leadership.

Such a peaceful outcome was by no means preordained. After all, Shanghai had historically been an epicenter of protest and violent repression. In 1989 it had the second-most-active student movement and the largest public demonstrations outside Beijing. During those nerve-racking weeks, the burden of managing the situation fell squarely on the shoulders of Mayor Zhu, especially after Party Secretary Jiang Zemin was suddenly called to Beijing to replace party general secretary Zhao Ziyang. Zhu's instincts were, in fact, similar to those of the conciliatory Zhao Ziyang. Like him, Zhu was ready to engage the youthful demonstrators in dialogue. When student leaders at Shanghai University of Posts and Telecommunications wrote him a letter of protest, he immediately wrote back promising to hear them out. They proudly posted that letter on campus and students promptly stopped marching. And Zhu telegraphed a message of tolerance to other protesters as well by subtly altering the language of decrees from Beijing, changing Deng's references to "political turmoil" (*zhengzhi dongluan*, 政治动乱), which suggested treasonous, criminal behavior and outraged the students in Beijing, to less inciteful phrases such as "chaos" (*hunluan*, 混乱).[3]

Immediately after the massacre in Beijing, when the streets of Shanghai were seething with outraged protesters, Zhu continued to seek ways to resolve the crisis that would not further agitate student demonstrators. On the night of June 6, for example, he released an "open letter" to the citizens of Shanghai, again leaving out party central's inflammatory language about demonstrators being bent on "subverting socialism and overthrowing the Communist Party." He wrote, instead, only that "a handful of bad people" had incited some students to "excessive behavior," resulting in "the grave situation in Shanghai." And even during those stressed times he tried to keep the focus on economic growth, warning that continued demonstrations would jeopardize the local economy.[4]

Still the city threatened to boil over. However, when millions of Shanghainese turned on their TV sets at 11:00 p.m. on June 8, they saw their mayor deliver an extraordinary address. Zhu naturally appealed for calm and order, but rather than simply condemning the protesters, he took a measure of personal responsibility for what was happening. "My heart is burning with anxiety," he said in almost pleading tones. "As mayor of Shanghai, I have felt very sorry and guilty in recent days because I could not protect the personal safety of my people."[5] Despite what he acknowledged was mounting pressure to do so, he vowed not to call on the army. And he added an ingeniously ambiguous comment that the students and protesters heard as a coded statement of solidarity: "Things that occurred in Beijing are history," said Zhu. "No one can conceal history. The truth will eventually come to light."[6] The next day Shanghai was quiet. Soon after that, it was open again for business.

Zhu's was a masterful performance, a seamless pivot from political crisis back to economic opportunity. Despite China's pariah status after the June bloodletting, by year's end Zhu had helped attract over $400 million in foreign direct investment (FDI) and secured a $3 billion loan from the World Bank to expand housing and transportation in Shanghai.[7] *New York Times* correspondent Nicholas Kristof even profiled Zhu as the ultimate Chinese "pragmatist," noting his local popularity in Shanghai and his growing national prominence.[8] Zhu had rendered his city an oasis of exactly the kind of reform that Deng had hoped to see before the rude interruption of Democracy Spring in 1989.

Back in Beijing, as we have seen, things were quite different. Deng's economic reform efforts were being embargoed by the media and constrained by a resurgent conservatism in the central leadership. "Nobody is listening to me now," Deng complained. "If such a state of affairs continues, I have no choice but to go to Shanghai to issue my articles there."[9] Here, Deng was taking a leaf out of Mao's playbook: the Great Helmsman had turned to Shanghai radicals in 1965 to ignite the Cultural Revolution when he, too, was embargoed by the Beijing party establishment and media. Now Deng was choosing the same strategy, but with an agenda that Mao would have considered indelibly counterrevolutionary.

In February 1991 when Deng visited Shanghai, Zhu rolled out the red carpet for him, ensuring that Shanghai newspapers did what national papers in Beijing were not: publish his call to kick-start the economy back into high gear with new market reforms and a greater quotient of openness.[10] By helping Deng in his 1991 trial run for his 1992 southern tour, Zhu positioned Shanghai—and himself—to surf the crest of the country's upcoming growth tsunami. Indeed, by 1993 the city's FDI had skyrocketed to over U.S. $3 billion, and from there it kept rising, reaching $15 billion in 2010. But Zhu himself was not slated to remain in Shanghai to enjoy the surge of growth and investment that he had sparked. Instead, just a month after Deng's 1991 visit, he became a vice premier with primary responsibility for the national economy, leapfrogging into the high command to preside over the largest economic transformation of modern times.

Deng's Heir

Having failed spectacularly with his previous picks (Hu Yaobang and Zhao Ziyang) as chosen successors, Deng was choosing especially carefully this time. And he chose well. Zhu's unusual background and political trajectory had uniquely equipped him to carry out Deng's plan for achieving national prosperity. Quite like Deng, despite having suffered during the Mao era, Zhu was a fierce patriot, deeply attached to the nation and the party. He was also determined to realize the dream of wealth and power. "Our goal now," Zhu would proclaim in 2000, "is to build a strong and prosperous country with socialist democracy and a socialist legal system—we can achieve this goal."[11]

Born in 1928 in the city of Changsha, the Maoist heartland of Hunan Province, Zhu lost both his parents at a young age. He met his future wife in middle school, and in college found something that perhaps filled the void of parental authority and protection: the Communist movement. Zhu's university, Tsinghua, was the country's premier science and engineering school. He enrolled in 1947 as the civil war between the Communists and Nationalists was gathering momentum, and although he studied electrical engineering, his real passion was literature, both Chinese and foreign. In fact, his role models were the great writers and essayists who were on the Tsinghua faculty, Wen Yiduo, Zhu Ziqing, and Wu Han, all of whom became noted for their dissenting views.[12] In October 1949, the month Mao declared the founding of the People's Republic from atop Tiananmen Gate, Zhu joined a Communist Party cell at Tsinghua and was elected president of the student union. Upon graduation, his formidable talents were put to work at the State Planning Commission—the brain, as it were, of China's new Soviet-style planned economy.

In 1957, at the height of the Great Leap Forward, thirty-year-old Zhu spoke out against what he viewed as unrealistic production targets. For this he was labeled a "rightist" and in April 1958 was expelled from the Communist Party.[13] He never openly discussed what form of punishment he suffered over the next few years, but he finally resurfaced in 1962 back at the State Planning Commission, where he was allowed to continue his economic work. But then in 1970 he was purged again, this time for evincing a lack of revolutionary zeal during the Cultural Revolution. After five years of "reeducation" at a May Seventh Cadre School in rural China, in 1975 he was allowed to return to his desk at the planning office. Finally, in 1979, thanks to Deng's new policies of reversing political verdicts, Zhu was fully rehabilitated and readmitted to the party. After what had been a political roller-coaster ride, his ascent to the highest echelon of power would henceforth be steady.

When Deng surprised officials at the Shenzhen Special Economic Zone in 1992 with his injunction that "reform and opening up require boldness and courageous experiments . . . they must not proceed like a woman with bound feet," it was Zhu who carried Deng's fight forward.[14] "Before we used to worry whether inviting foreign capital and speeding up should be named 'capitalism' or 'socialism,'" Zhu chided Shanghai representatives to the National People's Congress just a month after Deng's trip. "Comrade Deng Xiaoping liberated us from that kind of thinking. If you introduce foreign capital, technology, advanced management, like planting flowers in socialist soil—the result is socialist, not capitalist."[15] The late Qing reformer Yan Fu had used a similar transplanting metaphor a hundred years earlier when he wrote how the reforms that had made Europe "rich and strong" had failed when tried in China, "like a good orange tree on the bank of the Huai River which, after it is transplanted, produces thick-skinned oranges."[16] This time Zhu was confident that Deng's efforts would succeed.

Cultivating investment from Hong Kong magnate Li Ka-shing and welcoming a Japanese firm's proposal for a new airport, Zhu followed with unreserved enthusiasm Deng's injunction to open up his city's development process. "Comrade Deng Xiaoping's talks suddenly helped us see the light that we have to boldly experiment and maneuver, take the good things of capitalist countries and graft them onto our socialist system," he explained.[17]

What he instinctively grasped was the implicit new post-1989 social contract Deng was seeking to draw up between the party and the people: if the party would help the people create wealth, the people would let the party keep power. On a visit to Guangdong, China's most open and reformist province, Zhu sketched out his version of this compact. "If we can increase the speed of economic construction, and continually raise the people's living standards," Zhu preached to a crowd of local cadres, "then the Party will be trusted and respected, and the people will support us."[18] The days of the Chinese Communist Party seeking legitimacy through class revolution and ideological purity had now morphed into something quite new and pragmatic. Legitimacy was to be derived almost entirely from delivering on the promise of prosperity.

A Great Centralizer

Deng was pleased with his new vice premier, describing him at one point as "one of the few cadres who really understands how the economy works."[19] For his part, Zhu always spoke reverentially of Deng, and wept uncontrollably at his funeral in 1997.[20] But what made Zhu such a formidable figure was his unique ability to also win over the support of Deng's main rival, Chen Yun, the one party elder strong enough to go toe-to-toe with Deng on economic matters. Born in 1905 (less than a year after Deng), by the 1990s these two octogenarian revolutionaries embodied the opposing economic philosophies and political poles that would make the reform process so complex, but also give it a certain hybrid vigor. While Deng was a bold experimenter, Chen was a cautious planner. While Deng wanted rapid growth, Chen was fearful of growth that was too fast—especially what Deng called "economic democracy," which Chen saw as a gateway to hyperinflation and chaos. Where Deng wanted to feed the local hunger for development by giving provinces, cities, and Special Economic Zones a freer hand, Chen wanted to ensure that someone in Beijing was coordinating the process and in control. Market reform should occur within the traditional bounds of the planned economy—or, as Chen famously liked to describe it, it should grow up like a capitalist bird in a socialist cage.[21]

Chen had initially been skeptical of Zhu, even making oblique references in the fall of 1991 to him as a Chinese Yeltsin—the Soviet Union's first democratically elected president, who presided over both the marketization of the Russian economy and the collapse of the Soviet Union.[22] As time passed, however, Chen came to appreciate that Zhu, despite being Deng's protégé, shared some of Chen's own reservations about unfettered, rapid growth. Zhu, after all, had spent most of his career as a Beijing technocrat planning a Soviet-style national economy. Just as in the late 1950s he had called the growth targets of Mao's Great Leap Forward "irrational," now in 1992 Zhu described the sizzling 12 percent GDP growth as "crazy."[23] So Chen approved when, in 1993, Zhu acted decisively to cool down the economy, even while Deng, in his last days, was still calling on him to speed development up. And when in 1994 Zhu tightened China's money supply and brought the economy back from the brink of hyperinflation, he was hailed as an economic sage for managing a "soft landing."[24] He turned out to combine the strengths of both Chen and Deng, and his hybrid skills were delivering stunning results.

Finally, the new man in the driver's seat of the Chinese economy seemed to understand how to use both the accelerator and the brakes.[25] By combining the boldness of Deng's rapid local growth with the prudence of Chen Yun's central coordination, Zhu found a balanced formula for realizing what had eluded past reformers for so long. From tax revenues to bank lending, capital markets to foreign trade, even as he gave the economy room to breathe and grow, Zhu used the reform process to aggressively recentralize China's economic system, putting limits on Deng's trademark technique of what Susan Shirk, then Deputy Assistant Secretary of State for East Asian and Pacific Affairs, called "playing to the provinces"—letting local governments control the revenues they generated via new market-based growth.[26] Zhu's genius was that he managed to centralize without strangling the economy.

During the pivotal period after the Tiananmen massacre, Zhu personally dominated the reformist life of the nation by building an innocuously named planning body, the State Council Economic and Trade Office, into a "super-ministry with overall responsibility for managing the economy."[27] And when a financial crisis hit Asia in late 1997, he exploited the opportunity to further centralize economic authority through more institutions of his own making. He was, as Richard McGregor of the *Financial Times* put it, the Chinese economy's "great centralizer."[28]

A trademark of Zhu's leadership style was heavy reliance on economic experts who were, especially by Chinese standards, technically sophisticated, worldly, and daring. As he declared in his first speech as premier, "If everyone in this government acts like 'yes men,' we do a disservice to the people."[29] His protégés were rising stars with PhDs in economics, such as Lou Jiwei, Zhou Xiaochuan, Guo Shuqing, and Li Jiange—all of whom would go on to posts at the commanding heights of public finance.[30] As Zhu and his aides crafted hard-driving reforms, they stuck to Deng's most essential principle: economic methods were in need of constant, structural transformation, while the political core—the system of one-party political control—should be left alone. As a leading expert on Chinese economic reform, Barry Naughton, has observed, "Zhu Rongji's policies were consistently associated with stronger, more authoritative government institutions and more decisive policy making."[31]

State Capitalism

The way Zhu saw things, the true essence of Deng's vision was not just rapid growth but continuous reform. "Without reform," he asked, "how can development continue?"[32] There were two major thrusts to Zhu's reformist campaign. One was to rationalize and centralize the fiscal and financial systems—taxes, banks, and capital markets. The other was to streamline and strengthen the state sector. These two gargantuan efforts constituted the heart of Zhu's work, and their unlikely success marked a grand historical turning point in China's long road to wealth and power.

Zhu's first item of business was to regain central control over the country's burgeoning yet dangerously decentralized tax revenues. Despite the overall growth of the economy, state resources were still insufficient when he took the reins in the early 1990s. In 1993, local government revenues increased a remarkable 35 percent. At the same time, however, the central government revenues shrank by 6.3 percent.[33] A pair of visiting Chinese scholars at Yale University, Wang Shaoguang and Hu Angang—themselves modern-day "self-strengtheners"—produced an influential study, "Report on State Capacity," warning that Deng's "economic democracy" was threatening to splinter the economy, leaving a landscape filled with a wild assortment of disconnected provincial and local projects without any central nervous system to guide the process.[34] Zhu agreed with their diagnosis and warned darkly in a published article that "unless the fiscal and taxation systems are reformed, the state itself will face the day when its very survival will be endangered."[35] As a result, he went in person to each province in China to sell a new "tax sharing" idea modeled on the U.S. federal tax system—another sign of his fearlessness in borrowing helpful foreign ideas.[36] Under the new scheme, revenue from the provinces would go first to Beijing, and only then would a portion be returned. As a result, the central government's cut of total revenue increased by over 20 percent in a single year, balancing the central budget and putting Beijing's resources on track to increase dramatically in the years to come.[37]

At the same time, Zhu was also bringing China's highly decentralized banking system more closely under Beijing's control. He did so,

Jiang Zemin charms the Clintons, 1998

Protests at the U.S. embassy in Beijing after Belgrade bombing, 1999

Shanghai's Special Economic Zone of Pudong

People's Bank of China, center of Zhu Rongji's financial reforms in 1990s

ingeniously enough, by appointing himself governor of the central bank, the People's Bank of China, with jurisdiction over monetary policy and financial regulations. Then, in another deft move, he brought in two younger men with intimate connections to the seniormost conservative technocrats, Chen Yun's son Chen Yuan and First Vice Premier Yao Yilin's son-in-law Wang Qishan.[38] Finally, Zhu summoned to Beijing the heads of all the People's Bank branches across China and gave them three months to report all illegal loans on their books.[39]

"Almost immediately, Zhu's position of vice premier and his forceful style gave him the authority to appoint and remove the heads of the People's Bank branches in each province and major municipality," wrote economist Nicholas Lardy. "This earned him the enmity of provincial government and party officials, who had previously counted on pliant central bank officials in their jurisdictions to ensure that adequate bank credit was available to fund their favorite enterprises and infrastructure projects."[40] In a second wave of reform that also borrowed directly from an American model (the U.S. federal banking system), Zhu dissolved the thirty-two provincial branches of the People's Bank of China and replaced them with nine regional branches.[41] The aggressive maneuvers worked. "Zhu's centralization effort deprived local officials access to cheap credit from banks, drastically increasing their dependence on the central bureaucracy for funding," concluded Chinese finance expert Victor Shih.[42]

Next he turned his attention to the rescue of the "dilapidated" state sector of nearly eighty thousand state-owned enterprises (SOEs) run by government bureaucracies, lumbering remnants of China's Stalinist legacy of the 1950s.[43] While new private companies now accounted for roughly half of China's GDP, most of China's largest and most important economic sectors—banking, energy, transportation, and heavy industry—were still largely occupied by SOEs, many of which were not only inefficient and unprofitable but also heavily reliant on loans from state banks for survival.

Buoyed by the new muscle that increased central tax revenues gave him, Zhu geared up for his next massive undertaking: cleaning China's four colossal state-owned banks of billions of dollars in nonperforming loans accumulated due to profligate local lending to unprofitable SOEs. By quarantining these bad loans in newly created "asset-management companies," Zhu was able to recapitalize the banks through government bonds in a restructuring strategy again modeled explicitly on a "bourgeois capitalist" technique from the United States—the savings-and-loan cleanup in the 1980s.

Zhu's brazen willingness to borrow from abroad even led to the creation of China's first modern investment bank, a joint venture with the Wall Street firm Morgan Stanley. And so the China International Capital Corporation (CICC) was born from the union of Morgan Stanley and the China Construction Bank, one of China's largest state-owned banks, and went on to handle China's initial public offerings that put one giant state-owned company after another on global stock exchanges. They included China Telecom, PetroChina, Industrial and Commercial Bank of China (ICBC), and, in 2010, the Agricultural Bank of China, in what was the largest IPO in history, with a market cap of over $22 billion.[44] Zhu had stayed involved every step of the way, even keeping a telephone hotline open during the $2.9 billion IPO for PetroChina in 2000. CICC was run by Zhu's protégé Wang Qishan until his own son, Levin Zhu (Zhu Yunlai), became CEO in 1998.

Joseph Schumpeter would have approved of Zhu's performance. Even as he created novel financial institutions such as CICC, he also allowed others to fail. A shock wave coursed through the financial world in 1999, for instance, when he announced the bankruptcy of the gigantic state-owned Guangdong International Trust and Investment Corporation (GITIC), which had buried itself in over $4 billion of debt.[45] Foreign investors cried foul, demanding that the Chinese government provide a sovereign guarantee of their stakes—some $2 billion in lost capital. But Zhu was implacable, insisting it was their own fault for making risky investments. He preferred a little bad press on Wall Street to the moral hazard of bailing out GITIC, considering that every province had an ITIC of its own with similar debt issues.

But an even greater challenge still faced Zhu: reforming China's massive, bloated state-owned sector itself, whose eighty thousand SOEs soaked up the lion's share of China's indigenous investment capital and bank loans. The preeminent reform economist Wu Jinglian, an advisor to Zhu, defined what they were up against as deeply rooted "vested interests" in the state-controlled system. "As late as 1993, most scarce economic resources were still in the hands of the government and SOEs, despite the fact that the state sector accounted for less than half of GDP," Wu explained.[46] In other words, China was suffering from a hugely wasteful misallocation of capital.

After his promotion to premier in 1998, Zhu was ready to take on more of these vested interests. While he did save the biggest SOEs, he allowed thousands of other small and medium-sized firms and factories to go under, betting that new growth in the private sector could absorb any surge in unemployment, causing tens of millions of workers to lose their "iron rice bowl" guarantees of cradle-to-grave employment, health care benefits, and pensions. Zhu also challenged the "iron wage" principle, freeing managers to base salaries on performance and market competitiveness. Perhaps most controversially, he tried to destroy the notion of the "iron chair" that allowed incompetent officials to hold on to management positions once they got them. Now, profitability and productivity, not just party loyalty, longevity of service, or cronyism, were to help determine managerial and executive promotions. Of course, Zhu's reforms of state-owned enterprises risked triggering revolts from both the bottom and the top—from the vested interests running factories and the laborers working in them. But Zhu did not blink, and his gamble paid off, as most sidelined workers did find new jobs and better-quality management did turn around many faltering enterprises.

At the time, Western onlookers celebrated such reforms as evidence of China's inevitable economic liberalization. After all, this was happening during that fleeting "end-of-history" moment after the Cold War when capitalism and democracy appeared all-triumphant. Wholesale privatization and marketization were not, however, what Zhu and his fellow Chinese reformers actually had in mind. Indeed, when former president George H. W. Bush met with Zhu in London in 1998 and started their conversation with a friendly inquiry: "How is the privatization program in China coming along?" Zhu remembered being "taken aback." "I told him, 'Mr. Bush, China isn't privatizing. We're creating a shareholding system, and a shareholding system is only one of many forms of public ownership.'"[47] The ultimate goal of these reforms, in other words, was not to dismantle the state sector, but to streamline it and thereby make it a stronger element in Deng's new form of marketized socialism.

Zhu was categorical on this point. He had watched SOEs implode in the former East Germany under the pressures of "shock therapy," he explained to a German correspondent. "We won't go down this road, nor will we adopt a policy of privatization. We can allow state-owned enterprises to sell shares to individuals, but the majority of shares must remain under state control."[48] Indeed, investment in the state sector accelerated in the 1990s, and Zhu stopped his reforms short of legalizing private banks and liberalizing interest rates.[49] The West may have sniggered when Deng announced that he would pursue "socialism with Chinese characteristics," as if he were selling them snake oil, but in Zhu's hands the slogan was actually proving to mean something: growing wealth and power for the nation-state under the firm grip of the Communist Party, just as Lenin had taught.

Belgrade

As Deng's economic heir, Zhu was keenly aware that progress toward the long-elusive restoration of Chinese greatness required two tracks—not just reform but also opening. "Opening up to the outside is a fundamental state policy," Zhu repeatedly insisted, "and practice has long since proven that the earlier we open up, the more rapid will be our development."[50] Yet even as foreign capital poured into the country, efforts to continue opening up often proved an uphill climb. Because he was allowing heresies—such as permitting the giant U.S. insurance company AIG to open a branch in China for the first time, and, even more controversially, was trying to meet Washington's demands for entry into the World Trade Organization (WTO)—critics accused Zhu of "selling out" China and of being a "traitor."[51] Not surprisingly, his ease among foreigners—his affable references to "my good friend" Dr. Kissinger and "an old friend of mine," Alan Greenspan, and his praise for liberal economist Paul Krugman—caused unease among more cloistered Politburo colleagues.[52] These underlying tensions erupted in the spring of 1999, a tumultuous and traumatic year for Zhu Rongji and for China.[53]

Around dawn on May 8, 1999, U.S. Air Force B-2 stealth bombers fired five GPS-guided missiles at a target in downtown Belgrade, but they slammed not into the alleged Serbian arms trading outfit the CIA said it was targeting but into the Chinese embassy. Three people were killed and twenty injured.[54] Within hours, Zhu was sitting in an emergency session called by the Chinese leadership. Not one party leader accepted the CIA's claim that its maps were outdated. (The Chinese embassy, whose location was not classified, had moved three years before the bombing.) Instead, Zhu and his colleagues assumed that the Belgrade bombing was retaliation for Beijing's veto at the UN Security Council of a resolution authorizing military action in Yugoslavia. They surmised that the Belgrade strike was designed to teach China a lesson, test its nerve, and perhaps even spark domestic instability. Feelings were raw, and specters were raised of the predatory and humiliating past. President Jiang Zemin promptly charged Washington with reverting to "absolute gunboat diplomacy."[55]

Zhu nonetheless valiantly argued that confronting the United States, while perhaps satisfying the desire for vengeance, was a dangerous distraction from China's real mission. "We must first maintain stability and continue our economic development," he told his colleagues, just as Deng had urged after 1989. "We must not throw our plans into confusion. This was a deliberate action by the United States. Its purpose is to see China's reaction. . . . If we plunge into confusion, it will have attained its initial aim. Hence the most important thing for us is to persist in our development and construction, and, at the same time, to speak out with a stronger voice."[56]

Foreign Minister Qian Qichen agreed that the country was not yet far enough down the road to "wealth and power" to handle a direct confrontation with the United States. "We must not enter into frontal military conflict with the United States," he warned. "Only when the country is prosperous and the people are strong will we have the strength to back our words with actions."[57] Qian and Zhu appeared to be rigorously trying to heed Deng's post–Cold War foreign policy dictum to "avoid the limelight" until the country was ready for it.

Shell-shocked by Washington's seeming aggression, yet unnerved by the prospect of a serious rift in Sino-U.S. relations, that first day Zhu and Jiang decided not to make a public statement. As popular anger grew, they instead sent their youngest colleague in the top leadership, Vice Premier Hu Jintao, to be China's spokesman. But this half measure only fed public anger and led to further accusations of sacrificing national honor and international prestige just to maintain good relations with Washington. University students in Beijing—docile since 1989—suddenly began putting up sardonic posters mockingly comparing Jiang Zemin to a "turtle that pulls in its head" and the Empress Dowager Cixi. In a replay of May Fourth–era nationalistic sentiment, popular hunger for revenge began to boil over as thousands of angry Chinese demonstrators rallied in Beijing outside the U.S. embassy and ambassadorial residence, chanting and hurling rocks. In a telephone interview with CBS's *Face the Nation*, U.S. ambassador James Sasser described the situation as being like hostages.[58]

Letters of protest expressing solidarity with those killed in Belgrade poured into Chinese newspapers, especially Beijing's *Guangming Daily*, which had lost two journalists in the bombing. As one letter to the editor bluntly put it, "We will only avoid being insulted, if we strengthen ourselves."[59]

It was a mini Opium War moment, and Zhu Rongji was on the hot seat. After all, he had just returned from a controversial trip to Washington, where he had tried, and failed, to secure U.S. agreement on the terms of entry for China into the WTO. One Communist Party leader even compared the Clinton administration's WTO expectations to Japan's notorious Twenty-One Demands, implying that Zhu was an appeaser in the shameful tradition of Yuan Shikai, who had so abjectly yielded to the Japanese.[60] Another open letter from an outraged computer science student, addressed directly to the premier, laid bare his quandary: "Premier Zhu . . . Our government's weak stance has created a distance between itself and the people. . . . You are so capable. . . . But without the 'people's confidence,' how can you lead China's economic construction?"[61]

Such commentary undoubtedly stung, because despite his cosmopolitanism, Zhu was himself an ardent nationalist. He had been born before "liberation" in 1949, and his worldview had been forged on the century-old anvil of victimization and humiliation. "The history of modern China is a history of threats and invasions by imperialist powers," he once said, a remark that could as easily have been made by Sun Yat-sen, Chen Duxiu, Chiang Kai-shek, or Mao Zedong. "We were always the ones being bullied!"[62] It did not take much to revive these incompletely buried memories. "We Chinese all remember that since the Opium War of 1840, the history of modern China has been a history of humiliation and subjugation by foreign invaders," the Iron Premier declared at one party congress press conference. "Think back to when China was so utterly poor and weak—even then, we still shouted 'Arise! All who refuse to be slaves,' and struggled heroically without flinching. When the [Sino-Japanese] war broke out, I was only nine years old, yet even now I clearly remember how I cried whenever we sang songs about saving our country. I felt a surge of emotion and was ready to die for my country."[63]

Zhu, in other words, was every bit as nationalistic as the angry youth throwing rocks at the U.S. embassy and criticizing him. The difference was that he believed that the only way forward was to first ensure that China became simply too significant a global economic powerhouse ever to be humiliated again—a status attainable only through persistent reform, opening up, and further economic development. But since that time had not yet arrived, Zhu now set out to use the Belgrade fiasco as a lever to negotiate better terms for China's entry into the WTO. Susan Shirk was part of the team that engaged in the "harrowing" negotiations in Beijing that fall as a member of the Clinton administration. As she recalled, "The Chinese claimed their pound of flesh for the April humiliation by retracting a number of previous commitments," she reported. "Several times our team members packed our bags and prepared to leave. And, one surreal night, the Chinese trade officials locked the gate to stop us from leaving the ministry." But, remembered Shirk, it was Zhu Rongji who finally broke the impasse "by mustering the support of Jiang and other Politburo Standing Committee members for the critical compromises and a final agreement."[64] After thirteen years of tedious and sensitive negotiation, China finally joined the WTO in December 2001, setting the stage for a decade of even faster growth, fueled by an exponential rise in its global trade and investment. Zhu's vision had finally and emphatically won out.

Achilles' Heel

Widely seen as someone who refused to bow to either patriotic youth in the streets, archconservatives in the party leadership, vested interests in the bureaucracy, or corrupt cadres in the provinces, Zhu established a reputation for fairness and toughness. He laughed off a news report that "my skills consist of nothing but banging on tables, hitting chairs and glaring at people. . . . If I can't glare, wouldn't I be brain dead?" On one point, however, he was deadly serious: "I've never intimidated ordinary citizens. I only intimidate corrupt officials."[65]

As his term neared an end, however, some critics charged that he had not been intimidating enough, and, as a result, that the fruits of his reforms were disproportionately benefiting only a small segment of the population. In the spring of 2000, a local official in the backwater province of Hubei wrote an open letter to the premier that stirred the conscience of the nation.[66] In it he detailed the dire conditions that still existed in rural China, and he placed the blame directly on Zhu's reforms. Investigative writers Chen Guidi and Wu Chuntao expanded that official's complaint into a *cahier de doléance* of rural misery in their native Anhui Province. Their bestselling (and banned) book, *China Rural Survey*, blamed peasant poverty and powerlessness on the premier's acclaimed tax-sharing reforms. They concluded that Zhu's success in recentralizing the economy was, in fact, deepening rural misery. "Income tends to flow up to the central government, while expenses get passed down to the local government," they wrote. "Spending on basic public services such as education, family planning, veteran's pensions and so on were all relegated to the local level." According to them, the peasants' burden was once again beginning "to spiral out of control."[67]

There was no question that in rural China, as in the urban areas, class disparities were widening and that this threatened to become the Achilles' heel of the new development model. As the time for a handoff of power to the next generation of leaders approached, Zhu himself began to express increasing anxiety over the inequality, injustice, and indigence he saw building around him. Indeed, by the time China was finally admitted to the WTO, he was hardly in a mood to celebrate. "Everyone is happy," he commented wryly; "I'm the only one who isn't happy." He feared greater global market integration might drive down farmers' incomes even more and reverse decades of progress in the very regions where Deng's reforms had so successfully begun.[68] His frustrations only intensified when President Jiang Zemin began pushing for yet more high-speed growth, seemingly ignoring these worrisome trends. Calling at the 2002 party congress for the creation of *xiaokang shehui* (小康社会), "a moderately well-off society," Jiang launched what looked to be a new financial free-for-all. Local investment and lending in booming coastal cities surged, while the well-being of the six hundred million people living in the rural hinterlands continued to lag.[69] Jiang was fixated on promoting rapid coastal development, even if it meant bringing the burgeoning class of nouveau riche right into the party itself. Indeed, his new pet theory of *sange daibiao* (三个代表), "the Three Represents," ultimately did formally welcome the wealthy right into the Communist Party as full-fledged members of the revolutionary classes. Suddenly the party was to represent the interests of entrepreneurs and capitalists, a shift that was little short of mind-boggling for a revolutionary party that had come to power with the support of the dispossessed and then spent the intervening decades trying to prevent the reemergence of a bourgeois class of "capitalist-roaders."

Zhu, on the other hand, appeared increasingly to identify with the other 99 percent. "I earn just around 800 yuan a month," he reportedly said. "How come I'm paying taxes and they [the nouveau riche] don't? Why is it that the super-rich pay the least taxes?"[70] Zhu had always wanted to believe that China's "socialist market" economic model would guarantee greater equality. "A market economy is a more efficient method of allocating resources," he argued back in 1993, "but a system of primarily public ownership is better for protecting social justice and realizing common prosperity."[71] Now, though, as he belatedly began to discern just how unequal wealth creation had become in the 1990s, his faith that state ownership would ensure "common prosperity" seemed far less certain.

Strong State, Prosperous People

Zhu's historical end game was the very one that began our story—the quest to remold China back into a strong state with a wealthy populace. By previous standards, he had made unprecedented room for private enterprise, which left many foreign investors with the illusion that they were being invited into an economy in the process of being liberalized piece by piece. However, that was never Zhu's end goal. He saw his reforms in much the same way that the self-strengtheners of the previous century had—as selectively borrowing Western methods and techniques in pursuit of wealth and power but on Chinese terms. It was an old story, but with a new ending. The party-state's ultimate ownership rights of the national economy and the total monopoly of political power were no more to be changed, or even tinkered with, than the basic tenets of the Confucian construct were to be altered by the early self-strengtheners a century ago.

Zhu himself put it this way: "I've always believed that socialism can be successful in China. Our goal now is to build a strong and prosperous country with socialist democracy and a socialist legal system—we can achieve this goal."[72] He promised as well that a newly wealthy and powerful China would be good not just for its own people but for the rest of the world as well: "What we want to do is work for the people's welfare and build China into a strong and prosperous country with democracy and rule of law," he proclaimed. "We absolutely won't engage in hegemony or power politics as some other countries do, because we've suffered enough from these. What good can come from bullying and oppressing others? We can become rich and strong through our own efforts, and we won't bully others."[73]

In his decade at the helm, Zhu's success in establishing central coordination over explosive local growth was a remarkable achievement. Yet he never sought to touch the radioactive core of the new economic reactor bequeathed him by Deng—the political system. Perhaps he had learned a lesson from the fate of his predecessor Zhao Ziyang, still under house arrest at No. 6 Wealth and Power Hutong, a stone's throw from Zhu's own office. So he stuck strictly to methods and techniques (*yong*) and left challenges to the core (*ti*) of China's Leninist political system to dissidents and exiles such as Wei Jingsheng, Fang Lizhi, and Liu Xiaobo, who had, in effect, decided to opt out of the political system as it existed.

When pressed by nagging foreign journalists on the sluggish progress of political reform, Zhu would bob and weave. On a visit to New York in 1999, for example, he reprised the standard argument that the Chinese people were still not yet ready for democracy. "You must understand that China is different from the United States," he tried to explain. "China has a feudal history that lasted for more than two thousand years. It's only been fifty years since the People's Republic of

China was founded. Our people's standard of living is much lower than that of your people. Their educational level is also much lower. To adopt your style of democracy in a country such as ours is simply impossible." But Zhu did like to emphasize the importance of the rule of law. "We're not afraid of democracy, we're not unwilling to implement the rule of law, and we certainly don't want to infringe on human rights," he insisted. "But based on conditions in China, we need to gradually do better and gradually turn China into a country that is completely under the rule of law."[74]

He flatly rejected, however, the relevance of liberal democracy to China, saying that the problem was not just that the Chinese people were unready for democracy, but rather that democracy had *never* been, and would *never* be, suitable for China. "We absolutely will not copy the Western model as we reform our political system," said Zhu defensively in 2001. "That is, we won't have different political parties taking turns running the government, nor will we have a bicameral legislature."[75] Zhu was unbowed and unyielding: "China isn't carrying out its political reforms according to the Western model," he reminded critics. "We're not disappointed by China's political reforms. On the contrary we're full of confidence."[76]

Zhu's biases were evident in his handling of the largest-scale direct challenge to party-state power during his tenure in office. On April 25, 1999, more than ten thousand practitioners of an exercise and meditation cult called Falun Gong surrounded the Zhongnanhai leadership compound's main entrance on the Avenue of Eternal Peace in an eerily sudden and silent protest. They had, they claimed, come to protest state harassment. But many in the central party leadership saw them through a very different historical lens, as a reincarnation of the kinds of mystical populist groups—such as the White Lotus, Taipings, and Boxers—that had since time immemorial helped dethrone dynasties with chiliastic rebellions. Nonetheless, as with the Shanghai students in 1989, Zhu sought to engage the demonstrators in dialogue. His message was conciliatory yet evasive. "I understand you people, and I ask you to understand me," he said to the five Falun Gong representatives with whom he met. But he added, "Maintaining stability is in the highest interests of the country and the people. Without stability, nothing can be done. Please ask everyone conscientiously to uphold social sta-

Zhu Rongji in 2011

bility, as this is in the interests of the whole."[77] In other words, it is in the national interest for everyone just to go back to work and stop demonstrating.

According to leaked government files, "Zhu said that the sect's popularity was a reflection of the difficulties of economic transition and should be treated with more understanding."[78] But Jiang Zemin nonetheless chose to ban, even brutally suppress, the organization. And there is no evidence that Zhu went out of his way to defend the rights of Falun Gong members to remonstrate. Asked in 2001 about the crackdown, he answered tersely: "Falun Gong is an antihuman, antisocial, and antiscientific cult that the Chinese government has banned in accordance with the law. It exercises mental control over its devotees, ruins lives, and destroys families. No responsible government could ignore a cult like the Falun Gong."[79]

While Zhu was a man of enormous energy who understood that China's successful development in the modern world depended on innovatively embracing major economic reforms, and even on accepting certain aspects of the rule of law, this did not include the protection of social organizations whose power base was independent of the party. He would not defend those who dared to question the core principles of the system. In this sense, too, he was the loyal heir to Deng Xiaoping. But, thanks to Zhu's hard-driving management of the economy, Deng's blueprint for reform and opening up was given a second life after the disaster of 1989. Zhu ensured that China would enter the twenty-first century poised to advance ever more rapidly toward the consummation of wealth, power, and greatness to which it so devoutly aspired.

CHAPTER 14

No Enemies, No Hatred（没有敌人）

LIU XIAOBO（刘晓波）

Black Horse

In 2010, when he won the Nobel Peace Prize while still locked in a Chinese prison cell, the writer and activist Liu Xiaobo became a living global symbol for the lineage of Chinese thinkers who have viewed democracy and human rights as a matter of principle, rather than merely as tools in their country's search for renewed greatness. Liu is, in fact, only the most recent representative of that long strain of thinking that has arced through modern Chinese history from May Fourth Movement figures such as Chen Duxiu, Lu Xun, and Hu Shi to more recent democracy advocates such as Wei Jingsheng, Fang Lizhi, and Ai Weiwei. It is perhaps fitting to conclude the story of China's quest for a formula to restore wealth, power, and national greatness and respect with a figure who questions the entire party-sponsored modern Chinese narrative of traveling the *fuxing zhilu*（复兴之路）, or "road to rejuvenation." Why? Because although the ideals of thinkers like Liu Xiaobo have not been the main motor force of Chinese history to date, it is impossible to know how they might ultimately come to play themselves out in the future. They are, at the very least, like a reserve bank account ready to be drawn upon if and when needed. What is more, their mere existence fortifies the possibility that at some future time this fund of ideas and thinking may acquire a new and more practical relevance.

In the spring of 1989, Liu Xiaobo was a thirty-four-year-old profes-

Liu Xiaobo in 1989

sor of literature and philosophy at Beijing Normal University with a keen interest in political ideas, who when demonstrations broke out, quickly became a habitué of Tiananmen Square. Having written a doctoral thesis on the topic of aesthetics and human freedom, he was a prolific if acidic writer, a loner and iconoclast who believed that the most worthy role of intellectuals was to "enunciate thoughts that are ahead of their time" and to strive for a vision that is able "to stretch beyond the range of accepted ideas." He believed that a truly autonomous intellectual must be "adventurous" and "a lonely forerunner" whose true worth would be discovered "only after he has moved on far ahead."[1] A uniquely independent thinker whose signatures were close-cropped hair, an addiction to cigarettes, and a fondness for aviator glasses, Liu rejected the fundamental premises of one-party rule, which he felt had corrupted the ability of most Chinese to think for themselves. Party rulers, he later said, "bribe us with small favors, threaten us with the lash, entertain us with songs and dances, and use lies to poison our souls."[2] For those intellectuals who too easily accommodated the party, Liu had little but contempt. "And China's so-called intelligentsia," he wrote, "is, for the most part, the dictator's conspirator and accomplice."[3]

An admirer of nonviolent leaders such as Vaclav Havel, Mohandas Gandhi, and Martin Luther King Jr., Liu prided himself on his intolerance for cant, groupthink, and political pandering.[4] "The Chinese love to look up to the famous, thereby saving themselves the trouble of thinking," he wrote before the 1989 demonstrations began. That's why they "rush into things en masse. Occasionally someone stands out from the crowd and lets out a shout: Everyone is astounded. What I'm saying is that there are too few people with their own minds, their own ideas."[5]

Born in 1955 into an intellectual family in the northern Manchurian city of Changchun, Liu was "sent down" to the countryside to work on an agricultural commune during the Cultural Revolution in the late 1960s. Admitted to the Department of Chinese Literature at Jilin University when it reopened in 1977, he went on to receive his PhD in 1988 before becoming a lecturer at Beijing Normal University in the capital.[6] During these years, he began writing Lu Xun–like *zawen* (杂文), "miscellaneous essays" in which he subjected everything and everyone he wrote about to withering critical scrutiny. In 1988, for instance, he lit into Chinese attitudes toward the West:

> From the beginning of the Opium Wars, all Chinese reforms have been carried out in an atmosphere of admiration for and fear of the West. But the Chinese will never admit to themselves that they are hopelessly backward, that their culture is senile. Instead, they are constantly engaged in a quest to find some source of national pride with which to console themselves. When the Chinese admit the material superiority of the West, in the same breath they belittle Westerners for their lack of spiritual life. At the same time that they recognize the West's scientific superiority, they opine that it is morally decadent. . . . Confronted with the powerful culture of the West, the Chinese search for a spiritual crutch in the ancient culture that once made them proud.[7]

By being mercilessly irreverent and critical toward anyone he considered fatuous, Liu quickly gained a reputation as an enfant terrible of the intelligentsia, earning the moniker "Black Horse."[8] This put him in an almost constant state of confrontation with party watchdogs and censors, whose utterances he openly disdained. But his iconoclasm also put him on a collision course with many members of the literary and academic establishment whom he viewed as spineless. Because Liu always seemed to be attacking someone, he alienated many and was distrusted by many more.

"In Beijing," wrote Australian sinologist and colleague Geremie Barmé, "his coarse stuttering harangues during academic meetings, public lectures or even at sedate dinner parties in which he would assault every aspect of conventional wisdom left few people, either Chinese or foreign, kindly disposed to the fiery critic." He soon became, says Barmé, "notorious in Beijing as an abrasive and ill-mannered figure."[9] In fact, during the early 1989 demonstrations, Liu even criticized fellow dissident Fang Lizhi, belittling the logic of his refusal to appear in the square, lest by association he compromise the student movement's independence and "purity."[10] Liu justified his provocative manner by insisting, "There should be room for my extremism; I certainly don't demand of others that they be like me."[11] A lodestone for confrontation, he sometimes seemed like a hyperintellectualized version of jailed dissident Wei Jingsheng. Despite their un-Maoist democratic beliefs, both seemed drawn to contradiction and conflict in a way not so dissimilar from Mao himself.

Perhaps because of his stammer, Liu did not come across as a pugnacious person with a chip on his shoulder. Instead, what he radiated was a certain lack of social grace, almost ineptness. His wife, Liu Xia, once described him as "an awkward and diligent poet."[12]

As the demonstrations of 1989 gathered momentum, what distinguished Liu were his constant presence in Tiananmen Square and his close relationship with student protesters. Most other academic colleagues tended to appear only intermittently, usually in groups with other well-known professors and intellectuals, and even then often with an air of grand self-importance. This behavior conformed to Liu's view of the older generation of academics as self-centered, with a superior attitude that made them want to "caress and suckle" less well-known scholars in a manner calculated "to possess, co-opt, and finally asphyxiate" them.[13]

Believing, as he did, that intellectuals must be willing to act on their thinking, Liu participated more fully in the drama of the square than many of his colleagues, and he did so without much pretension or fanfare, even living with younger Beijing Normal University students.[14] With his pockmarked face, a cigarette eternally in hand, and scruffy shirt that had not been changed in days, Liu became a familiar sight around the square. He even became an advisor to the most outspoken and brash student leader, Wu'er Kaixi, a Muslim Uighur from his own university. Their closeness reflected Liu's hope of transcending the barriers that the hierarchies of age and position traditionally imposed on Chinese, especially in intellectual circles.

Ironically, Liu had not been initially supportive of the protests. When the demonstrations broke out in mid-April 1989, he had just arrived in New York City as a visiting scholar at Columbia University and was skeptical that the new movement would amount to anything. Calling the reaction to Hu Yaobang's death "hysterical," he wondered why heroic status should be conferred only on relatively liberal party leaders like him, while true dissidents were ignored. How could someone like Hu, who had stayed in the party system, constantly trimming his jib to match its endless political demands, qualify as a truly independent Chinese intellectual, much less a hero? "Why do the Chinese constantly reenact the same tragedy?" he asked in a 1989 essay, "The Tragedy of the Tragic Hero." "Why do the Chinese mourn as tragic heroes people like Zhou Enlai, Peng Dehuai and Hu Yaobang, while they forget such tragic figures as Wei Jingsheng . . . ? How many of China's intellectuals have thought about asking after Wei Jingsheng's family as he sits rotting in jail?"[15] It was almost as if Liu had a presentiment that one day he, too, would suffer a similar fate.

Despite his initial skepticism about the demonstrations, Liu quickly sensed that this time something different might be afoot, and the thought of missing out on a historic moment in his country's political progress helped focus his attention. So, on the spur of the moment, he gave up his coveted U.S. fellowship, jumped on a plane, and returned to Beijing. Upon his arrival at Tiananmen Square, he was surprised to find himself truly inspired by what he found: a new sense of *gongmin yishi* (公民意识), or "civic consciousness"—a phrase that could have come straight from the pages of Liang Qichao or Chen Duxiu. Soon Liu had become far more involved than he had imagined. Before the Beijing Spring had ended, this acerbic, borderline nihilistic thirtysomething professor had become concerned with building up as well as tearing down.

One senses his change of heart in "Our Suggestions," a statement he largely penned that was released a few days after Deng Xiaoping authorized martial law in May. "Each stage in the expansion and escalation of this student movement and its development into a civic movement has been prompted by the government's political folly," it read. "We must attempt to change the government's long-standing inability to listen to the voice of the people and its ideology of privilege that denies the people the rights to demonstrate, strike, and establish popular organizations. We must teach the government to accept the people's desire to use the powers accorded them in the Constitution to supervise the government and express their demands. We must teach the government how to rule the country democratically."[16]

The Hunger Artist

By the beginning of June, the protest movement had lost much of its effective leadership and momentum. In hopes of helping it regain some of its earlier élan, Liu and three other activists—rock singer Hou Dejian, former Beijing Normal University newspaper editor Gao Xin, and Peking University sociology researcher Zhou Duo—decided to camp in the middle of Tiananmen Square at the base of the Monument to the People's Heroes beneath a banner proclaiming, "No Other Way."[17] They also issued a somewhat histrionic declaration: "We are going on a hunger strike! We protest! We appeal! We confess!" They called on other intellectuals and students to "end their weak-kneed behavior of all talk and no action, passed down for several thousand years," and to "protest martial law and call for the birth of a new political culture." As to why they were fasting, they explained, "We want to use peaceful means to display the strength of our democratic forces in civil society and to smash the undemocratic order maintained only by bayonets and lies."[18]

The four iconoclasts also took on Deng directly. "Chinese society has been living in a vicious cycle of a new emperor replacing an old emperor," they proclaimed. "History has proven that the stepping down of some unpopular leader and the assumption of power by some very popular [new] leader cannot solve the essential problems of Chinese politics. What we need is not a perfect savior, but a perfect democratic system."[19]

Liu and his fellow fasters also criticized the way that student leaders had been running the protest movement, noting its "disorderly internal organization" and "excessive sense of privilege and inadequate sense of equality. . . . The key lies in recognizing mistakes and correcting them." Student leaders may have been democratic in theory, they said, but in handling concrete problems they had shown "too much emotion and too little rationality."

Finally, Liu and his three fellow fasters proclaimed their "Four Basic Slogans":

1. We have no enemy! Don't let hatred and violence poison our wisdom and the process of democratization!

2. We all need to examine ourselves. China's backwardness is everyone's responsibility!
3. We are first and foremost citizens.
4. We are not looking for death, but are seeking a true life![20]

Their refusal to acknowledge an enemy was meant to be a rejection of Mao's notion of "antagonistic contradictions" and of his reliance on unending violent struggle as a process. Their challenge to resist hatred hinted at a Christian influence, while their call for self-examination of personal shortcomings had distinctively Confucian overtones. Their third slogan, affirming "citizenship," was an attempt to realize, at long last, Liang Qichao's dream of a country populated by "new citizens" capable of enough political consciousness to govern themselves without an emperor, dictator, or Leninist party. And their final slogan was a gentle reprimand to those student leaders who had become fascinated with blood, death, and self-sacrifice as signs of patriotic devotion to "the Chinese Motherland" not to get too carried away by such melodrama.[21] Indeed, just before the Goddess of Democracy, a towering white plaster sculpture that looked like a sibling of the Statue of Liberty, was erected by Central Academy of Fine Arts students in front of Mao's portrait in Tiananmen Square, protest movement "general commander" Chai Ling had famously proclaimed, "The next step is bloodshed. Only when the Square is washed in blood will the people of the whole country wake up."[22] In the typically overwrought language of the moment, students pledged, "I will devote my young life to protect Tiananmen and the Republic. I may be beheaded, my blood may flow, but the people's square will not be lost. We are willing to use our young lives to fight to the very last person."[23]

As the drama built on that last fateful night of June 4, at about 4:00 a.m. after many students and citizens of Beijing had already sacrificed their blood and lives as the People's Liberation Army besieged the city, Liu Xiaobo and Hou Dejian managed to secure an agreement from soldiers surrounding the square for peaceful retreat of the remaining demonstrators. With the deal in hand, they rushed back to the monument to plead with students to save themselves by voluntarily leaving. "Blame me if you want, just leave!" Hou begged. A few, who had resolved to die, derided Hou and Liu as "capitulators." But in a chaotic voice vote, a majority of the exhausted, frightened students seemed to agree.[24]

"We have achieved a big victory!" Hou proclaimed. "We have made our point! We are not afraid to die . . . but it is our duty to fight and regroup elsewhere."[25] And in fact, unlike the avenues leading into the square, where the carnage had been great that night, the heart of the Central Kingdom was finally cleared without any known loss of life. In a strange twist of fate, it was thanks to Liu and Hou's efforts that the government could later claim that "no one was killed in Tiananmen Square."

Serial Arrests

As a reign of virtual terror descended on Beijing after June 4, Liu did not go into hiding or flee the country like so many others. Late on the night of June 6, as he was openly taking a friend home on his bicycle, an unmarked van pulled up alongside them; several men jumped out, threw the two into the van, and drove away. Not until June 24 did the Chinese government officially announce Liu's arrest, accusing him of being one of the "black hands" behind the "counterrevolutionary riot."[26]

Although he remained in detention for almost twenty months, on January 26, 1991, he was released from jail far earlier than other offenders.[27] Undoubtedly this was an acknowledgment of the unusual role he had played in preventing a bloodbath in that most symbolic of spaces, Tiananmen Square. The Chinese state would nonetheless find reason to lock Liu up again on numerous other occasions over the coming years.

As was the case for so many others of his generation, Liu found that his experience in the square became a defining point in his life, one that continues to haunt him even today, as can be gleaned from his book of poetry, *June Fourth Elegies*. When in 2002 the U.S.-based Chinese Democracy Education Foundation gave Liu its annual award for "outstanding activism," the Chinese government refused to let him go to Los Angeles to accept it. In a speech delivered in absentia, he revisited his 1989 experience, evincing a continuing sense of survivor's guilt.

I receive this award today, May 31, 2003, only four days before the anniversary of that bloody morning in June fourteen years ago. I do not know whether my work has been worthy of the people who died and cannot claim to deserve this award. I can understand the honor only as a tribute to those who continue to speak the truth inside a system built on lies as an offering to the souls of the dead, delivered through me, of memory that refuses to be erased. I feel that those who perished that day are looking down on me from above. They look down on a person privileged still to be alive . . . and I am haunted by the grave responsibility of being still alive.[28]

What gave Liu's writing about the 1989 massacre such resonance was his humanistic perspective, which he had acquired in part from reading China's greatest twentieth-century writer, Lu Xun. Like Lu in his time, Liu was bent on probing uncomfortably deep into the most sensitive interstices of China's psychosocial identity. "Most depressing is this," Liu wrote in 2006. "Behind the superficial, arrogant nationalism lies a national ethic that is disconnected from civic values. It is more nearly a primitive jungle ethic of master and slave. In front of the strong, people act like slaves; in front of the weak, like masters."[29] Here he was evoking well-known lines of Lu Xun, who had written in *Random Thoughts Under the Lamp* in 1925, "The simplest and most adequate way of describing the history of China would be to distinguish between two types of periods: 1/ The periods when people wished in vain to enjoy a stable slave condition; and 2/ The periods when people managed to enjoy a stable slave condition. The alternation of these two states is what old scholars called 'the cycle of chaos and order.' "[30]

For Liu, the master-slave dynamic, the lack of values, and the excess of patriotism had all been exposed by his 1989 experience. In a rumination on the June 4 massacre, he cited another Lu Xun essay, this one written in 1926 after forty-seven student protesters were killed in front of Tiananmen. "In China a few brief lives count for nothing," Lu had forlornly concluded. In his own memorial essay after 1989, Liu added: "The so-called elites of our country have made no progress at all since Lu Xun's day. It is hard to find any shame or guilt in us. We have yet to learn to draw spiritual meaning from our encounters with suffering, how to live in human dignity, or how to feel concern for the suffering of actual ordinary people."[31]

Liu's sense of unshirkable responsibility for what had happened did little to soften his attitude toward the party, and even his own colleagues. While he was in detention, several of his earlier essays had been published in Hong Kong, and in them he excoriated fellow intellectuals for their continuing subservience to officialdom. "Why is it," he asked, that Chinese intellectuals "in the end always remained the 'prostitutes' and 'tools of emperors'?" Why were they able to oppose an occasional corrupt or incompetent leader but never turn on the despotic system itself, which gave such leaders their legitimacy? Liu's answer was that historically they had been bought off by being given a seat at the official table and, by trading "obedience for the purpose of achieving their own vested interest," had grown accustomed to enjoying its privileges. Even though they well understand the dangers of autocracy, he said, such intellectuals "either sing its praises, contrary to their convictions or remain silent." And, for Liu, silence was the most reprehensible of all responses because, even when "seething with discontent," silent intellectuals do nothing "to weaken evil forces."[32] As he would explain several years later in a letter to fellow dissident Liao Yiwu, "One of the main reasons for the silence and amnesia that enshrouded China in the years after the massacre is that no inspiring moral leader stepped forward to be a symbol" of opposition.[33]

As if to step directly into that role, Liu went right back to writing once he was released from prison—never asking, as his English translator Perry Link puts it, "How should I couch things? What topics should I touch on? What indirection should I use?"[34]

The Universality of Human Rights

In terms of his basic political philosophy, Liu was very much the heir of Fang Lizhi's vision of democracy and human rights as values that transcend their utilitarian benefit to a country's development. For both men, liberal values were part of a universal humanistic legacy that was just as much Chinese as it was French or American. Fang's belief in human rights grew out of his training in science, an intellectual world in which reason and logic were considered universals. In this sense he was indeed the latter-day incarnation of those two esteemed gentlemen, Mr. Science and Mr. Democracy, called for by May Fourth Movement activist Chen Duxiu. Unlike Fang, however, Liu derived his convictions not from scientific rationalism but from a humanistic spirit that left him contemptuous of the impulse to use Western culture "merely as a tool with which to regenerate the Chinese nation." He called on Chinese to instead adopt the West's tradition of employing a "critical attitude toward everything."[35] He was concerned with his country's international status, but in a way quite unlike those leaders who put "wealth and power" before all else. "China's present condition, in international comparison, is just too outmoded, too degenerate, too fossilized, and too senile," he wrote in 1989, just before leaving New York. "It *needs* challenge, even 'menace,' from another civilization; it *needs* a vast and surging, boundless sea to pound it out of its isolation, its solitude and its narrow-mindedness."[36]

As Premier Zhu Rongji and President Jiang Zemin pushed forward their own program of reforming and opening up China's economy in the 1990s, the only place they could imagine for a person as relentlessly outspoken and implacable as Liu Xiaobo was prison. As a result, throughout the decade he was in and out of jail. Indeed, his plight exemplified Chen Duxiu's 1919 observation about the experiential benefits of youth alternating time between school and prison. ("Only the civilization that comes out of these two places," he had said, "is the true civilization, a civilization that has life and value."[37])

During one of his intermittent periods of freedom in May 1995, Liu released a provocative petition entitled "Learn from the Lesson Written in Blood and Push Democracy and Rule of Law Forward: An Appeal on the Sixth Anniversary of Tiananmen." He was quickly rewarded with another stint in prison for his efforts. After seven more months in jail he was again freed, only to let loose with yet another broadside, this one on the ever-sensitive topic of Taiwan. Rearrested in October 1996, he was sent away again, this time via an extrajudicial procedure known as "reeducation through labor" that required neither formal charges nor trial.[38]

Released three years later, Liu now found himself jobless and without any means of support, save what he could earn freelancing for overseas Chinese-language publications. But after so many years of imprisonment, he had become a changed person. Though he remained unrepentant, he was less arrogant and less inclined to launch ad hominem attacks on fellow intellectuals. His experience of deprivation and travail seemed to have tempered him with a new generosity of spirit, an appreciation, perhaps, of how difficult it is for anyone to remain truly human under such trying circumstances. His long periods of incarceration had acquainted him with what it means to suffer and wrestle with one's conscience, even one's soul. In "A Poem to St. Augustine," he wrote of "discover[ing] the cruelty and mystery of time."[39] Indeed, he appeared to have experienced a spiritual epiphany that would be reflected again and again in his writings, especially his love poems to his wife, Liu Xia, which became filled with allusions to martyrdom, guilt, repentance, confession, atonement, forgiveness, and salvation through love. These suggestively Christian themes were possibly due to the influence of his close friend Yu Jie, the novelist, who had converted to Christianity in 2003, before being forced into exile.

Through intense personal struggle Liu seemed to have rid himself of much of his earlier egotism and pettiness, concluding, "Hatred only eats away at a person's intelligence and conscience" and can "poison the spirit of an entire people (as the experience of our country during the Mao era clearly shows). It can lead to cruel and lethal internecine combat, can destroy tolerance and human feeling within a society, and block the progress of a nation toward freedom and democracy. . . . I hope that I can answer the regime's enmity with utmost benevolence and use love to dissipate hate."[40] As he acknowledged in his 2009 courtroom self-defense, June 1989 was a turning point in his life, engendering a new philosophy, which he summed up in these words: "I have no enemies and no hatred."[41]

The China Miracle

When Liu Xiaobo walked out of prison in 1999, he stepped into the middle of one of the most extraordinary bursts of economic growth that China, or any country on the planet for that matter, had ever seen. For the next decade, the attention of the whole world turned in astonishment to the Chinese economic "miracle," which, near the end of his term, President Hu Jintao could extol as the Chinese people's "glorious pursuit of prosperity and strength."[42] Even in 2008, when the U.S. subprime mortgage crisis turned into a global financial contagion and demand for exports flagged, Beijing managed to drum up a stimulus package massive enough to keep China's economy from faltering. In 2009 the country overcame Germany to become the world's largest exporter. The next year China's economy surpassed Japan in total size to become second only to that of the United States. It seemed that Lenin's warnings about the dangers of international finance monopoly capitalism were being inverted. After decades of struggle against the hostile, reactionary forces of international capitalism, the Chinese Communist Party had become not only the darling of Wall Street but banker to the world. On Hu Jintao and Wen Jiabao's watch, the nation's foreign exchange reserves—denominated heavily in U.S. debt—ballooned to over $3 trillion, causing Beijing to look for ways to diversify its foreign holdings away from U.S. Treasury bills. This led to the creation of a sovereign wealth fund, China Investment Corporation, with an initial pool of $200 billion. After over a century of being a debtor nation, in the 2000s China suddenly found itself not only awash in surplus foreign currency but in the unprecedented and enviable position of becoming a global lender and investor.

Hu's "glorious pursuit of prosperity" seemed, from a distance, to have been executed with great acumen, winning over businessmen, tourists, and development experts, all astonished by the towering new urban skylines, magnificent airports, and ultramodern high-speed rail, highway, tunnel, and bridge networks, as well as all the new high-concept museums, opera houses, government centers, and corporate headquarters.

Only a few voices wondered whether the "China miracle" was not in some ways a mirage. Foremost among them was Liu Xiaobo. As the economy flourished, he wrote in a 2008 essay, "Behind the China Miracle," "powerful officials saw an opportunity to make sudden and enormous profits. Their unscrupulous pursuit of profit became the engine of the ensuing economic boom."[43] The prosperity generated by such crony capitalism had "stirred a nationwide popular fever to get rich quick," he charged, allowing a few "to amass huge fortunes." "Growth rates of over 9 percent annually were called a 'miracle,' and, indeed they were, in a way." But, because the "privatization" that followed "was neither legal nor ethical," in Liu's view it had led to "a robber baron's paradise, a free-for-all."[44]

As Liu saw it, the party's elite was using the economic boom to keep the intellectual elite "atomized, scattered and isolated."[45] "First they terrorized them with a bloody crackdown, then they seduced them with material rewards," he said. "After a few years the intellectuals had been transformed into a pack of complacent cynics. In their hearts, many of them still reject the regime's ideology and feel contempt for its actions. But the lure of material benefit on one side and the threat of political persecution on the other have channeled them into alignment with the regime. . . . They no longer feel embarrassed at defending what the power elite does, and are often willing to serve as cosmeticians for the new capitalist-Communist regime."[46]

Whereas many inside China and elsewhere extolled the way the standard of living for hundreds of millions had risen to unprecedented levels and an incomparable new national infrastructure was being built in record time, Liu saw a descent into a morass of craven selfishness that was morally crippling the nation even as it was materially building it up and out. "This is what lies behind the economic miracle: the miracle of systematic corruption; the 'miracle' of an unjust society; the 'miracle' of moral decline; and the 'miracle' of a squandered future," he wrote caustically. "The damage—to the economy, to human rights, to the entire society—is incalculable. Will we ever be able to recover? If so, *that* would be the miracle!"[47]

Although they might not dare to put it so bluntly, many mainstream Chinese economists agreed with Liu, at least in part. Even Premier Wen Jiabao warned of "unsteady, unbalanced, uncoordinated, and unsustainable" growth.[48] The gap between rich and poor that Zhu Rongji had fretted about as he left office had only grown larger. Like continental plates inching inexorably apart toward an earthquake-like rupture, China's Gini coefficient, the standard measure of economic inequality, already exceeded 0.4 by 2001, the last year that the government released an official number. And by 2010, the index was thought to be as high as 0.6, making China one of the most unequal major economies in the world.[49] In 2010, even though up to five hundred million people continued to live in grinding poverty on less than $2 a

Liu Xiaobo and fellow hunger strikers in Tiananmen Square, 1989

Beijing Summer Olympics opening ceremony, 2008

Hu Jintao at the Olympic torch-lighting ceremony in Tiananmen Square, 2008

Nobel Peace Prize ceremony with Liu Xiaobo's empty chair, 2010

day, China earned the dubious distinction of boasting more billionaires than Russia.[50]

And, sure enough, as inequality increased, so did social instability. The number of officially reported "mass incidents" of local protest rose from thousands to tens of thousands a year until 2006, at which point the government stopped releasing annual statistics.[51] But according to leading researchers on social stability, by the end of the Hu Jintao era the number was well over a hundred thousand, some thought fast approaching two hundred thousand.[52]

With instability on the rise, party leaders turned to an ancient formula—the Confucian emphasis on he (和), "harmony"—for an ideological salve. Liu saw Hu Jintao's counterintuitive decision to reembrace the party's former ideological enemy, Confucianism—what Hu called "China's vast and rich culture [that] embodies the profound spiritual aspirations of the Chinese nation"[53]—as an utterly cynical act. Never mind that such a move would have confounded May Fourth intellectuals and disgusted Mao; the party was now shamelessly trying to revive a pop version of Confucianism, to use it like fire retardant to extinguish hot spots of social instability, lest they build into full-fledged conflagrations. Liu had a particular revulsion for the kind of sophistry involved in such popularizers as Yu Dan, the Confucian televangelist who hawked a watered-down version of the Sage's beliefs for the masses, complete, as Liu wrote, "with a sales pitch that combines tall tales about the ancients with insights that are about as sophisticated as the lyrics of pop songs."[54]

Living in Truth

Compelled to live in a society that would not countenance the public expression of dissenting views, Liu wrestled with a dilemma: How could he stay true to his beliefs under such repressive circumstances? He particularly admired former Czech president and playwright Vaclav Havel as one of those rare human beings who, even while living in totalitarian circumstances, had somehow found "the strength in himself to express solidarity with those whom his conscience commands him to support," and who, by stepping beyond "living within the lie," had managed to find a way "to live within the truth."[55] Or, as dissident artist Ai Weiwei described the choices in a 2012 tweet, one can decide "to be true, or to lie. To take action, or be brainwashed. To be free, or to be jailed."[56]

"We need not demand of ourselves any extraordinary courage, nobility, conscience, or wisdom," wrote Liu, echoing Havel. "We need not ask ourselves to risk prison or to go on hunger strikes or carry out self-immolations. All we need to do is to eliminate lies from our public speech and to give up the use of lies as a tactic of dealing with the threats and enticements of the regime. . . . To refuse to lie in day-to-day public life is the most powerful tool for breaking down a tyranny built on mendacity."[57] This might be considered the third refusal in Liu's developing life philosophy—no enemies, no hatred, no lies.

Twenty-First-Century Nationalism

For Liu, one of the most unforgivable forms of state mendacity was when officials used nationalist sentiment to excite citizens over imagined foreign threats in order to distract them from real problems at home. Lacking the deep visceral feeling of so many other reformers and intellectuals that above all else they must first help erase China's "century of shame," Liu, like Fang Lizhi, spoke contemptuously of the party's efforts to promote what he considered a toxic mixture of traditional culture and modern patriotism. Liu felt China's challenge was to regain a sense of national pride by learning how to govern itself justly and treating its own people humanely, rather than by impressing the world through demonstrations of brute wealth and military power. He worried more about "a mentality of world domination" characterized by a "thuggish outlook." "What these traits have actually brought to the common people of China, past and present, has not been peace, success, honor, health, or a vigorous society," he warned in 2002, but "bloodshed, defeat, ruin, humiliation, dismal lives and societal collapse."[58]

What Liu found most humiliating was not China's weaknesses, but the embarrassing way its leaders had historically presumed its citizenry to be incapable of participating in the process of self-government. "During the last century of China's history the nation has fallen victim to cycles of self-abasement and self-aggrandizement, and this is because we have never been able to escape the clutches of the demon of nationalism," he wrote in a provocative 2002 essay, "Bellicose and Thuggish: The Roots of Chinese 'Patriotism' at the Dawn of the 21st Century." Seeing modern Chinese history as an epic of serial catastrophes leading to ever greater levels of failed nerve and collapsed national confidence, he cautioned against reacting with a mixture of arrogance and self-deprecation. "From 'Our technology is not as good as other people's' to 'Our political system is not as good as other people's,' and on to 'Our culture is not as good as other people's' Chinese reflections on our own defects probed ever deeper," he wrote. "But the primary mind-set that guided the probing was neither 'liberation of humanity' or even 'enriching the people,' but rather a sense of shame at China's loss of sovereignty and other national humiliations."[59] Liu particularly feared that China would move from being a weak country that had been bullied to a strong country that would bully both its own people and those of other countries. And he wanted nothing to do with a reform effort that sprang from such "narrow nationalism" or from striving for "goals of enriching the state and strengthening the military [that] took precedence over ideas that could lead to human freedom."[60]

As Liu saw it, China faced a choice between a crude nationalism that could create the impression of strength, on one hand, and universally accepted humanistic values that could create a more just society and real strength, on the other. "When a population gives its majority support to narrow nationalism in preference to the universal values of human freedom and dignity," wrote Liu, "it turns 'patriotism' into an argument for despotic government, military adventurism and thuggery."[61]

The Opium of Gold Medalism

For Liu, one such tawdry manifestation of "thuggery" was the 2008 Summer Olympic Games in Beijing, where "the love of gold medals among Party officials and the patriotic set" quickly reached a point that Liu saw as "pathological."[62] Such an "obsession" with the medal count, he wrote, was devoid of "any traces of the 'Olympic spirit' or human values." It was just another primitive way for the government "to channel popular nationalism into support of its dictatorship."[63]

Of course, Liu already viewed the Chinese leadership's long-standing fixation on "overtaking the West" as also being pathological. "The excitement that gripped the whole country at being number one in gold seemed to forecast a brilliant prospect of China's overtaking America in every other respect and becoming the number one nation in the world," he wrote.[64] But, he concluded, "a nation obsessed with gold medals will never turn into a great, civilized nation."[65]

In many ways Liu agreed with dissident artist Ai Weiwei, who, although he had helped design the giant National Stadium—better known as the Bird's Nest—had come to view the Olympic Games as "an extremely strange and surreal nightmare."[66] For Ai, the Games were like "a fake smile, an elaborate costume party with the sole intention of glorifying the country," as he told the *Guardian*. "From the opening to the closing ceremony, from the torch relay to the cheers for gold medals—these all displayed the might and the desperation of a totalitarian regime."[67]

Needless to say, the party leadership, as well as many ordinary Chinese, saw the Olympic Games in a very different light. Indeed, hosting them was one of Deng Xiaoping's last unfulfilled dreams. In the wake of the events of 1989, he had hoped that by winning a bid to host an Olympic Games, China could repair some of the damage to its international prestige. When in the 1993 competition to win the 2000 Summer Games Beijing lost to Sydney by one vote, party propagandists portrayed the decision—which had been influenced by global human rights concerns—as a national affront, alleging that China's enemies had blocked its bid as part of an ongoing international campaign to deny the country its rightful place in the world. When Beijing won the International Olympic Committee vote in the 2000 competition for the 2008 Games, the decision triggered wild celebrations of joy.

As the 2008 Games approached, Beijing hoped that they would be able to highlight China's *heping jueqi*, and *hexie shehui* (和平崛起, and 和谐社会), "peaceful rise" and "harmonious society." But then trouble suddenly erupted in Lhasa, Tibet. On March 10, the Dalai Lama released a statement on the anniversary of the 1959 Tibetan uprising against Chinese Communist rule, the failure of which had sent him into permanent exile in India. "China is emerging as a powerful country due to her great economic progress," he wrote. "This is to be welcomed, but . . . the world is eagerly waiting to see how the present Chinese leadership will put into effect its avowed concepts of 'harmonious society' and 'peaceful rise.' For the realization of these concepts, economic progress alone will not suffice. There must be improvements in observance of the rule of law, transparency, and right to information, as well as freedom of speech."[68]

That same day a few hundred monks from Drepung Monastery in Tibet marched toward Lhasa to protest restrictions on their cultural and religious life. The next four days saw an escalating cycle of monastic protests and police suppression, until on March 14 the movement grew violent: Tibetan residents in Lhasa exploded into an orgy of rioting and ethnic retribution, rampaging through the streets of the city, reserving a special brutality for Chinese business owners.[69]

For President Hu Jintao, the news from Lhasa must have sparked a sense of déjà vu. In early 1989 when monks, students, and commoners had engaged in an earlier round of mass protest against the Chinese government, he was a rising star in the party, a liberal-leaning technocrat serving as the senior provincial official in the Tibetan Autonomous Region, and he had quickly ordered martial law, forcefully suppressing the demonstrations. His tough line won many admirers in Beijing, including Deng Xiaoping, who put him in line to be selected top leader in 2002. Given Hu's background, it was not surprising, then, that when protests again erupted on his watch in March 2008, his response was to deploy overwhelming force once more. Tibet was put under severe security lockdown, and reports of mass detentions, even executions, were soon filtering out of the region. Members of the foreign press were barred from reporting there, and Chinese officials angrily denounced the Dalai Lama—an internationally respected Nobel Peace Prize laureate—as a "wolf in sheep's clothing." Many in the international community began wondering aloud if it had been such a good idea to award Beijing the right to host the Olympic Games after all.

The violence in Tibetan areas turned the upcoming Olympics into a lightning rod for criticism of the Chinese government on a global scale. To generate excitement for the Games, Beijing had planned the longest Olympic torch relay in history, extending eighty-five thousand miles and touching down in all quarters of the globe. But instead of ending up symbolizing a "journey of harmony," as Beijing had hoped, the torch relay soon degenerated into scenes of acrimonious and sometimes violent confrontations between foreign human rights protesters scuffling with patriotic pro-China counterprotesters. The worst moment came in early April, when a wheelchair-bound Chinese Olympian named Jin Jing was accosted by pro-Tibet demonstrators along the banks of the Seine River in Paris. When Jin used her body to try to defend the torch, nationalist Chinese netizens immediately dubbed her the "Smiling Angel in a Wheelchair," a proud, heroic defender of Chinese dignity pitted against a hostile world still trying to humiliate China.

As the August start of the Games approached, the mood in Beijing felt increasingly like the spring of 1999, when students outraged over the Chinese embassy bombing in Belgrade had hurled rocks at the U.S. embassy. In that volatile moment it had been Hu Jintao, then heir apparent, who had appeared on TV to denounce the "criminal" and "barbarous" act perpetrated by a "U.S.-led NATO."[70] Now, in 2008, Hu was once more under pressure to defend the nation's dignity. But again there was a contradiction: the deep desire for the kind of international prestige and recognition conferred by a successful Olympic Games was in direct conflict with the feelings of insult from the anti-China protests that had so marred the torch's "journey of harmony" around the world. If China was to pull off the feat of successfully hosting the Games—which were, after all, supposed to be a symbol of world peace—leaders in Beijing would have to resist lashing out, for the moment at least, and focus instead on dazzling the world with an Olympic celebration of China's progress.

And dazzle they did. With billions watching worldwide, Beijing put on a spectacle befitting a great-power-to-be. Pyrotechnic artist Cai Guoqiang designed a radiant fireworks show that lit up the night sky over the capital, and the ninety thousand spectators in the Bird's Nest stadium feasted their eyes on an extravaganza produced by legendary film director Zhang Yimou at a cost of over $100 million. In the ceremony's dramatic opening sequence, 2,008 drummers festooned in the robes of ancient warriors took their places on the stadium field, their bodies forming the single Chinese character that President Hu had chosen to define his era: he (和), "harmony."

The Games represented an emphatic victory for China, helping put

1989 behind it, repairing much of the damage of the disastrous torch debacle, erasing the memories of the Tibetan revolt, and projecting instead a gleaming image of a rising power espousing ancient values. But the price of this harmony was paid domestically through further controls on "unharmonious" elements. State security budgets swelled in order to pacify Tibetan areas, while nationwide, police and domestic security agents installed tens of thousands of new surveillance cameras and Web monitoring devices, made "house calls" to the homes of dissidents, and stepped up other kinds of oversight programs to ensure that there would be no surprises. And even after the Games, these enhanced security measures remained in place, "turning the Olympic experience into a lasting mechanism," as the minister of public security put it, in rather Orwellian language.[71] The new buzzword became *weiwen* (维稳), or "stability maintenance," a euphemism for a vast new array of ongoing public security measures on which the government expended close to $100 billion in 2011—reportedly more than on national defense.[72] Perhaps the most prominent victim of this new push to ensure that there were no discordant voices to challenge the party's triumphant narrative of strength and prosperity was Liu Xiaobo.

Blogging the Truth

Already in 2002, in the wake of the Color Revolutions in the Ukraine and Georgia, President Hu had signed off on new crackdowns against political dissent, including yet another detention order for Liu Xiaobo.[73] The state's campaign "to harmonize society" was resisted by civil rights groups, public interest lawyers, and activist intellectuals, who formed a loose-knit movement that came to be known as *weiquan yundong* (维权运动), "rights defenders," and led to public campaigns to defend the physically disabled, AIDS victims, and fellow political dissidents. Those who became too outspoken were simply arrested or disappeared— like the blind legal activist Chen Guangcheng in 2005, the lawyer Gao Zhisheng in 2006, and the community organizer Hu Jia in 2007. But, the biggest new battlefield in Hu Jintao's campaign to impose harmony on an increasingly outspoken and freewheeling society was online.

During the first decade of the twenty-first century, the number of Chinese Internet users exploded, doubling from around thirty million to nearly sixty million in just the first year of Hu's reign alone.[74] A decade later, China had more than half a billion people online, three hundred million of whom were obsessively microblogging their daily lives and thoughts for all the world to see. In order to "maintain order" over this sprawling, hyperconnected virtual China, the party engineered a system in which data coming in from the outside world had to flow through a certain limited number of gateways that were relatively easy to monitor and control via packet sniffing of their content. This online censorship regime, officially called the "Golden Shield" but criticized as the "Great Firewall of China," enabled the party to keep certain ideologically unacceptable sites that resided on servers abroad beyond the reach of most Chinese users. At the same time, tens of thousands of surfing Internet police were employed to warn or simply shut down sites and users who crossed the line of what was acceptable to the party. What the party essentially aspired to create was a Chinese Intranet, one that could be disconnected from the rest of the world as necessary. In this game of online cat-and-mouse, Chinese netizens came up with a playful term to describe having a post deleted or website blocked: they called it *bei hexie* (被和谐), "being harmonized."

Despite the compromised state of the Internet in China, however, a new online revolution was taking place that had a profound effect on Liu Xiaobo and his work. Although he spent much of the last two decades in prison, he never stopped writing. (Indeed, his hundreds of essays and poems now fill some seventeen volumes.)[75] Yet because of official censorship, his work could not be published or distributed in print inside China. Fortunately, the brave new world of the Internet created for him, and other dissident writers, a whole new global outlet, one that has also proven deeply unnerving to the party.

"The Communist regime, always obsessed with media control, has been frantic to keep up with Chinese web users," explained Liu in a 2006 essay, "Long Live the Internet." "Dictators always fear open information and freedom of speech, and the political possibilities of the amazing Internet can be terrifying to them. . . . It is no wonder that controlling what gets onto the Internet has moved to the very top of the regime's agenda in ideological matters."[76]

By 2013, the ballooning number of Chinese online had created a new reality, a powerful tool for dissident writers and political activists previously shut out of state-controlled media outlets. As Liu wrote in a second Internet essay in 2008, "China has a rich tradition of persecuting people for their words. Victims are strewn across Chinese history, from the First Emperor of Qin and his famous 'burning of books and live burials of scholars' "[77] . . . [but] the Internet is like a magic engine, and it has helped my writing erupt like a geyser. Now I can even live off what I write!"[78]

Liu was amazed by the new diversity that the Internet injected into Chinese life. Whereas previously "there was only one avenue to public prominence in Communist China, and that was through the official Party-state system," now the Internet was capable of generating " 'stars' outside the Party-state system," such as Han Han, an immensely popular and opinionated blogger in Shanghai who had millions of followers.[79] The costly effort the government made to erect the Great Firewall was only further proof of the Web's powers. And, as Liu discovered in 2008, one of its new powers was that it enabled people like him to organize and then solicit signatories for political petitions and open letters.

"Before the Internet," it "took a lot of work to organize them," explained Liu. "As a veteran of those efforts, I look now at the computer screen before me, on which I do emails so easily, and sigh to remember what I used to have to go through."[80]

Charter 08

In 2008 Liu became involved in just such an open letter, and its repercussions on his life would be profound. As he watched the Tibetan uprising, the Olympic Games, and "stability maintenance" campaign unfold, Liu and a group of like-minded liberal critics went public with a straightforward critique of China's system of one-party governance in a document they called "Charter 08."

Modeled on Charter 77, the declaration spearheaded by Václav Havel and Jan Patočka in 1977 that helped bring about the Velvet Revolution ending communism in Czechoslovakia, Charter 08 was launched on the occasion of the sixtieth anniversary of the Universal Declaration of Human Rights with the goal of spelling out the reforms necessary to end one-party domination and establish the rule of law in

China. Liu quickly became one of the most active members of the loosely federated group that called itself Chinese Human Rights Defenders. Needless to say, the call for an end to one-party rule was not welcomed by China's leaders, who denied its organizers all access to mainstream media outlets. So the group turned to the Internet. Posted there on December 10, Charter 08 garnered more than twelve thousand supporting signatures, which was a substantial feat in a country where signing anything of a controversial political nature has grave consequences.

For the party, December 2008 was supposed to mark a grand celebration of the spectacular success of thirty years of "reform and opening up" and of national rejuvenation. But for the drafters of Charter 08, China's economic boom had only papered over the failure of political reform and a concomitant debasement of social values. "A hundred years have passed since the writing of China's first constitution," the Charter 08 document began. "We are approaching the 20th anniversary of the 1989 Tiananmen Massacre of pro-democracy student protesters. The Chinese people, who have endured human rights disasters and uncountable struggles across these same years, now include many who see clearly that freedom, equality and human rights are universal values of humankind and that democracy and constitutional government are the fundamental framework for protecting these values. By departing from these values, the Chinese government's approach to 'modernization' has proven disastrous. It has stripped people of their rights, destroyed their dignity, and corrupted normal human intercourse."[81]

Warning that China's "future hangs in the balance," Charter 08 went on to declare, "For China the path that leads out of our current predicament is to divest ourselves of the authoritarian notion of reliance on an 'enlightened overlord' or an 'honest official' and to turn instead toward a system of liberties, democracy and the rule of law."[82] It concluded, "Unfortunately, we stand today as the only country among the major nations that remains mired in authoritarian politics. Our political system continues to produce human rights disasters and social crises, thereby not only constricting China's own development, but limiting the progress of all human civilization. . . . The democratization of Chinese politics can be put off no longer."[83]

In its uncompromising directness, the language of Charter 08 was vintage Liu Xiaobo. "I think my open letter is quite mild," he protested to *The New Yorker*'s Evan Osnos. "Western countries are asking the Chinese government to fulfill its promises to improve the human-rights situation, but if there's no voice from inside the country, then the government will say, 'It's only a request from abroad; the domestic population doesn't demand it.' I want to show that it's not only the hope of the international community, but also the hope of the Chinese people to improve their human-rights situation."[84]

In the end, it didn't really matter how Liu explained his effort; the message of Charter 08 was simply too bold and too antithetical to the strategy for modernization that the party's leadership had adopted.

The Trial

Late on the night of December 8, 2008—two days before Charter 08 was posted to the world on the Internet—police arrived at Liu's apartment, seized his books, papers, and computer files, and detained him yet again. This time he was accused of using "rumor mongering and slander to incite subversion of state power and overthrow of the socialist system."[85] Faced with a trial, Liu, like Wei Jingsheng, insisted on defending himself, hoping to use his court appearance as a pulpit to continue his attack on one-party rule.

Liu's trial did not begin until a year later, leaving him plenty of time to draft his self-defense. In it, he explained to the court that he wanted to leave behind "the fullest possible historical record of what happens when an independent intellectual stands up to a dictatorship."[86] "Criticism is not rumor-mongering and opposition is not slander," he argued defiantly. "Over the past two decades, from 1989 to 2009, I have consistently held that China's political reform should be gradual, peaceful, orderly and under control. I have always opposed the notion of sudden radical leaps, and have opposed violent revolution even more stoutly."[87] And he stubbornly defended freedom of speech, which, he declared, had disappeared after 1949, when "the entire country fell into a tawdry chorus of enforced uniformity."[88] He reminded the court that "treating speech as crime not only runs counter to the modern trends in world history, but more deeply, abuses humanism and human rights in a fundamental moral sense. This is true regardless of whether we are speaking of ancient times or modern, of China or the world."[89]

About himself, he said: "Merely for expressing different political views and for joining a peaceful democracy movement, a teacher [i.e., Liu] lost his right to teach, a writer his right to publish and a public intellectual could no longer speak openly. Whether we view this as my own fate or as the fate of China after thirty years of 'reform and opening up,' it truly is a sad fate."[90]

Liu continued to express hope that whatever the outcome of his trial, he could "rise above my personal fate and contribute to the progress of our country and to changes in our society. I hope that I can answer the regime's enmity with utmost benevolence, and can use love to dissipate hate." But he also evinced defiance. "No force can block the thirst for freedom that lies within human nature, and someday China, too, will be a nation of laws where human rights are paramount. . . . I hope that I will be the last victim in China's long record of treating words as crimes. Free expression is the base of human rights, the roots of human nature, and the mother of truth. To kill free speech is to insult human rights, to stifle human nature, and to suppress truth."[91]

Not surprisingly, the court found Liu's closing statement too much of an affront, and the presiding judge unceremoniously cut him off after fourteen minutes, claiming (contrary to Chinese legal procedure) that a defendant should take no more time in defending himself than the prosecutor took in putting forth the state's accusations.[92]

Then Liu was sentenced to eleven more years in prison.

Nobel Redemption

When Liu's wife, Liu Xia, visited his Manchurian prison to inform her husband that he had won the 2010 Nobel Peace Prize, he wept, declaring, "This is for those souls of the dead."[93] As he had said in his self-defense, "Twenty years have passed since 1989, but the aggrieved ghosts of those who were massacred that year are still watching us."[94]

Of course, he could not travel to Oslo to accept his award, making him only the fifth prize recipient in history unable to attend the ceremony in person. The Chinese government denied his family and friends exit permission to attend the ceremony. At the same time, the Ministry of Foreign Affairs launched a tirade against the Norwegian Nobel Prize Committee. "Liu Xiaobo is a criminal who violated Chinese law," a spokesman declared. "It's a complete violation of the principles of the prize and an insult to the Peace Prize itself for the Nobel committee to award the prize to such a person."[95] Then, Chinese diplomats began aggressively pressuring other governments not to send their ambassadors in Oslo to the ceremony, canceled a fisheries conference scheduled with Norway, and even put Norwegian smoked salmon exports to China on hold.

In praising the Nobel Committee's choice, Fang Lizhi, then living and teaching in Arizona, wrote that the prize committee had "challenged the West to re-examine a dangerous notion that has become prevalent since the 1989 Tiananmen massacre: that economic development will inevitably lead to democracy in China. . . . Regardless of how widely China's leaders have opened its market to the outside world, they have not retreated even half a step from their repressive political creed."[96]

For China, a country that had for so long coveted a Nobel Prize, Liu's award was a bitter slap in the face. Just as many Chinese feel a fierce patriotic urgency to "catch up to the West," so they have also passionately yearned to have a PRC citizen living in the motherland win a prize. But now when the long-awaited moment had at last arrived, the recipient had disappointingly turned out to be incarcerated as an enemy of the state. (Finally, in 2012, a Chinese citizen neither in exile nor in prison, writer Mo Yan, did win the Nobel Prize for Literature.)

In 1988, just before his first trip to the United States, Liu had written his friend Geremie Barmé: "Perhaps my personality means that I'll crash into brick walls wherever I go." But, he wrote, "I can accept it all, even if in the end I crack my skull open."[97] During the two decades since, Liu did indeed hit a few brick walls. What made his predicament so intractable was not just that he was unyielding on matters of principle but that for him human rights had no class or national character, as prescribed by Marx, Lenin, and Mao. For him, human rights could not be eschewed, even if one wished to do so. They were something everyone just had by dint of being human. "Human rights," said Liu,

Liu Xiaobo, undated

"are not bestowed by a state."[98] Like democracy, they were for him immutable, not simply tools that could conveniently be taken up or set aside by a reformer or a government depending on their functionality at a given moment.

Whether in the very end Liu will be pushed to the side of Chinese history, like Wei Jingsheng and Fang Lizhi (the latter dying in exile in Arizona in April 2012), or whether he might someday reemerge from prison a hero and play a prominent role in his country's political future, like Nelson Mandela, Václav Havel, Lech Wałęsa, Kim Dae-jung, and Aung San Suu Kyi, is still uncertain. However, one thing that is certain, at least for the moment, is that most of the things for which Liu Xiaobo sacrificed his freedom remain antithetical to China's current political leaders and that his ideas have represented a parallel, but less urgent, stream of thinking about China's modernization that has flowed quietly alongside the torrent of words from thinkers and leaders questing after revitalization of the nation's wealth, power, and honor.

In contemplating the future, it is always important to remember that, despite all its rigidities and infirmities, the Chinese Communist Party has repeatedly surprised the world with its ability to change course and prevail, including its most recent feat of steering China into the twenty-first century as a nascent superpower. Indeed, in doing so, it has upended both Marxist orthodoxy and the common wisdom of Western experts about how countries develop and whether free markets have an intrinsic and necessary relationship to democracy. But these two streams of thought—one in search of wealth and power, the other reaching for democracy—may well yet converge in the future. And if they do, the voices of people such as Wei Jingsheng, Fang Lizhi, and Liu Xiaobo will doubtless become more important. Of course, when and how this might come to pass is still an unanswerable question.

CHAPTER 15

Conclusion

REJUVENATION (复兴)

If any of the makers of modern China who agonized over their country's enfeebled state and dreamed of better times during the past century and a half could have visited Beijing's Pangu Plaza today, they would hardly believe their eyes. Pangu's preening thirty-nine-story office tower, capped by a massive figurative dragon head in stone, stands high above the fourth ring road, like the king on an oversized chessboard, looming over three luxury apartment buildings and a hotel. Each apartment building is crowned with four ultramodern courtyard-style houses with roofs that open mechanically to the sky. And the lavish Seven Star Hotel at the end boasts inlaid Italian marble floors, personalized butler service, and a vast underground parking garage chock-full of Aston-Martins, Ferraris, Rolls-Royces, and Bugattis. Just across the street lies the sprawling Olympic Park, with its translucent National Aquatic Center changing colors at night like a giant pinball machine, and the National Stadium, better known as the Bird's Nest, whose sinuous metallic superstructure is also illuminated after dark to look like a fantasy from another planet. It was here that the Chinese government kicked off the 2008 Summer Olympic Games with an opening ceremony as spectacular as any in history, the stuff of reveries such as neither Liang Qichao nor Lin Yutang could ever have dreamed. Yet here it was in granite, steel, and light, a manifestation in spectacular form of the People's Republic of China's new wealth and power. And, Pangu Plaza is only one small piece of the ever-startling tableau of progress that has issued forth from Deng Xiaoping's bold blueprint for "reform and opening up." It was he, the grand progenitor of this new affluence, who struck the spark that lit this latter-day capitalist prairie fire by telling his people in the 1980s that it was "all right for some people to get rich first" and even that "to get rich is glorious."

When Jiang Zemin inherited the status of paramount leader from Deng upon his death in 1997, he emphasized not just "development" (*fazhan*, 发展) but also China's need to "rejuvenate" (*fuxing*, 复兴), the latter a freighted word that harked back to Sun Yat-sen's call in 1894 to "reinvigorate" (*zhenxing*, 振兴) the country and even further back to Feng Guifen's hope in the 1860s that the Qing Dynasty would enter a period of "mid-dynastic revival" (*zhongxing*, 中兴).[1] As Jiang summed up the logic of modern Chinese history for delegates to a meeting celebrating the seventieth anniversary of the CCP in 1991, "All endeavors by the Chinese people for the 100 years from the mid-twentieth century to the mid-twenty-first century are for the purpose of making our motherland strong, the people prosperous, and the nation immensely rejuvenated."[2]

Jiang's successor as president and party secretary during the 2000s, Hu Jintao (also handpicked by Deng), carried forward the torch illuminating the way to national wealth and power. "History and reality tell us that 'Backwardness incurs beatings by others,'" he told visitors from Taiwan's New Party in 2005, citing an old Chinese saying, *luohou jiuyao aida* (落后就要挨打).[3] "China was bullied by foreign powers in modern times," he said. "A major reason for that was that China was chronically poor and weak during that period. Since then, the great rejuvenation of the Chinese nation has become the unswerving goal that each Chinese generation has striven to realize."[4]

And when Xi Jinping finally took to the stage in the Great Hall of the People in 2012 to face the cameras as head of the new Politburo Standing Committee—the seven men who would rule 1.35 billion people for the next five years—he proclaimed, "Since its founding, the Communist Party of China has made great sacrifices and forged ahead against all odds. It has rallied and led the Chinese people in transforming the poor and backward Old China into an increasingly prosperous and powerful New China, thus opening a completely new horizon for the great renewal of the Chinese nation."[5]

A fortnight later, Xi and the rest of the new Standing Committee went on a high-profile pilgrimage to view an exhibition at the National Museum, on the east side of Tiananmen Square, called "Road to Rejuvenation" (*fuxing zhi lu*, 复兴之路), which tells modern history as a morality tale, with China rising from the humiliations of the nineteenth century to a restoration of greatness in the twenty-first century. Xi used the occasion to pledge that he would do his part to continue the realization of this "Chinese dream" (*Zhongguo meng*, 中国梦). As the state press agency, Xinhua, reported: "Citing a sentence from one of Mao Zedong's poems . . . Xi said the Chinese nation had suffered unusual hardship and sacrifice in the world's modern history. 'But the Chinese people have never given in, have struggled ceaselessly, and have finally taken hold of their own destiny and started the great process of building the nation,' he emphasized. 'It has displayed, in full, the great national spirit with patriotism as the core.' "[6] As Xi, echoing his precursors down through the decades, later elaborated, "To realize the great revival of the Chinese nation, we must preserve the bond between a rich country and a strong military, and strive to build a consolidated national defense and a strong military."[7] And when he was also appointed state president in March 2013, Xi return to this idea of a "Chinese dream" that now he described as belonging to "the whole nation as well as every individual." And to realize this long-cherished dream, he said, the country must take "the Chinese way," which he proclaimed as being "socialism with Chinese characteristics."[8]

Like a set of genes that is firmly implanted on a genome and is then faithfully transmitted from generation to generation thereafter, DNA coding for this dream to see China restored to greatness and a position of respect has been reexpressing itself over and over since Confucian scholars with Legalist tendencies such as Wei Yuan first began fretting over the Qing Dynasty's early nineteenth-century decline. And it began to be articulated with even greater urgency as reformers like Yan Fu first left for Europe. Upon arriving in London in 1877 to study British thinkers and unravel the riddle of the West's superiority and China's backwardness, Yan wrote home from London with wonder: "It is no exaggeration to say that more has been accomplished [here] in a hundred years than in the previous millennium. As the states have become daily richer, their defenses have become ever more formidable. . . . The power or weakness of a state depends on various sources of wealth, and if one wishes to enrich the state, one must expand the people's knowledge and improve its economic system."[9] Alas, at the time the increasingly desperate warnings of men like Yan Fu fell largely on deaf ears.

Today, however, after weathering a century and a half of "domestic rebellion and foreign aggression," China has finally learned how to borrow effectively from the West. With the skylines of the Central Kingdom's countless boomtowns bristling with high-rise buildings, China now boasts the world's second-largest economy and a rapidly expanding military, and its diplomats increasingly throw their weight around the world. Power has at last begun to flow in wealth's trail eastward. Instead of being forced to sign humiliating "unequal treaties" and endure endless foreign exploitation, Chinese are forging plans of their own abroad in which they are the initiators and financiers of projects across all Africa, Latin America, and even North America. At home, they are putting astronauts in space, launching aircraft carriers, building supercomputers . . . the list is long and keeps growing.

After the collapse of the Soviet Union, when China was still recovering from the aftereffects of 1989, Deng Xiaoping cautioned the next generation of leaders to "avoid the limelight." But today there is wealth to consume and power to wield, and not a few Chinese are both pleased and proud to have the opportunity to be at last tempted by the prospect of joining in on this long-withheld "great power" exercise.

Creative Destruction to Construction: Mao to Deng

A few intrepid historians are now beginning to wrestle with the question of why, after so many generations of failure, China's period of economic dynamism only began when it did, and has now been as successful and durable as it has. Curiously, one of the most interesting and paradoxical explanations originates with the very person who is deemed also to have had such a destructive effect on China's earlier progress, namely, Mao Zedong.

First, by seeking to raze the edifice of old China as relentlessly as he did, the argument goes, Mao may have actually helped clear the way for Deng Xiaoping's subsequent reforms, thereby playing a role in China's rebirth that he never could have quite imagined while alive. No leader in twentieth-century China was more totalistic and unrelenting in attacking traditional culture than Mao, and under his leadership China's inherited Confucian heritage and old social value system, which so many reformers before him saw as China's major impediment to progress, was subject to a series of assaults unequaled in history.

A few early reformers such as Liang Qichao and Sun Yat-sen had recognized that the first steps in China's modernization process would necessarily require destruction of the old to make way for the new. But none of Mao's predecessors had been able—or really willing—to muster the same ideological boldness, much less the organizational fortitude and leadership ruthlessness, to challenge China's thousands of years of continuous culture and history aggressively enough to finally neutralize their drag on modernization. Early on Mao was a disciple of both Liang and Sun, but he turned out to be made of far sterner stuff, and ultimately came to embrace a far more extreme and tectonic form of revolution, one that insisted on constant, violent upheaval. As he had predicted in 1927, first the rural dispossessed and then the urban masses would rise up in a manner that "no power however great will be able to suppress."[10]

So, where others succeeded only in muting the influence of China's ancient culture, Mao came close to extirpating its very roots and thus its hold on several subsequent generations of Chinese. By doing so, he all but severed the bonds of tradition that had fixed father over son, husband over wife, master over student, family over individual, past over future, and continuity over change, bonds that had so tormented earlier reformers, including Chen Duxiu and Lu Xun. Lu had written with anguish about the "odious thoughts that the ancients recorded in their works," which he was "constantly rediscovering in myself."[11] What depressed him even more was the prospect that, despite the efforts of the May Fourth generation, this culture of oppression might also be passed on to China's youth. In near desperation, he cried out, "Let the conscious man assume the heavy burden of tradition, let him arch his back under the gate of darkness to allow his children to escape into the free space and light where they may spend their days in happiness and lead a truly human life."[12] Indeed, so powerful did the hold of the past prove to be, that later in their lives the first generations of reformers like Liang, Sun, Chen, and Lu all finally ended up being irresistibly drawn back into the very "gate of darkness" of traditional values and culture from which they had once so energetically sought to escape. Seen through such a historical lens, the wrecking ball of Mao's revolution can appear in a somewhat different light, as an instrument necessary to clear the way for whatever might follow.

It is true that Mao's final two decades—from the Anti-Rightist Campaign and Great Leap Forward through the Great Proletarian Cultural Revolution—were to a horrifying degree "lost" years for China. As Chen Yun, a comrade-in-arms from the early days of the Long March, was quoted as saying in the newspaper *Ming Pao* in 1979, "Had Chairman Mao died in 1956, there would have been no doubt that he was a great leader of the Chinese people. . . . Had he died in 1966, his meritorious achievements would have been somewhat tarnished, but his overall record was still very good. [But,] since he actually died in 1976, there is nothing we can do about it."[13]

Looked at through the cold eye of history, however, it may have been precisely those periods of Mao's most uncompromising nihilism that finally managed to bring about what no previous reformer or revolutionary had been able to, namely, a forceful enough demolition job on China's "old society" to finally free Chinese from their traditional moorings. Seen this way, Mao's brutal interim was perhaps the essential, but paradoxical, precursor to China's subsequent boom under Deng Xiaoping and his successors, the antecedent to the Chinese people being able to free themselves at last from their past and catapult themselves into their present single-minded and unrestrained pursuit of wealth and power.

Even the founder of modern Chinese studies in America, Harvard's John King Fairbank, by no means a Mao enthusiast, could appreciate the purgative virtue of the Chairman's permanent revolution. "In the old society teachers were venerated by students, women were submissive to their husbands, and age was deferred to by youth," wrote Fairbank. "Breaking down such a system took a long time because one had to change one's basic values and assumptions accepted in childhood. The times called for a leader of violent willpower, a man so determined to smash the old bureaucratic establishment that he would stop at nothing. He had to side with the common peasant, live his hard coarse life, and hate the bureaucratic establishment."[14] For better or worse,

Mao was such a man—modern China's "perennial gale of creative destruction," a leader willing to "carry out harsh rule, and with iron and
fire forge and temper our countrymen for twenty, thirty, even fifty
years," as Liang Qichao once put it.[15]

Mao launched the Cultural Revolution to prevent China from "taking the capitalist road," yet ironically his efforts ended up having
precisely the opposite effect. "A common verdict is, 'no Cultural Revolution, no economic reform,'" declare Roderick MacFarquhar and
Michael Schoenhals, leading historians of the period. "The Cultural
Revolution was so great a disaster that it provoked an even more profound cultural revolution, precisely the one that Mao intended to fore-
stall."[16]

By force-marching Chinese society away from its old ways of doing
things, Mao presented Deng with a vast new construction site on which
the demolition of old structures and strictures had already largely been
completed, making it shovel-ready for Deng's own "great enterprise"
of reform and opening up. Mao's epic destructiveness, which was supposed to prepare China for his version of utopian socialism, ended up
instead preparing the way for China to be transformed into exactly
the kind of cryptocapitalist economy that he most reviled during his
lifetime.

With the advantage of historical hindsight, another group of scholars now argues that Mao also bequeathed one more sublimely ironic
but equally critical legacy to Deng: his unique brand of guerrilla opportunism. At first blush, Mao's vision of class struggle and permanent revolution would seem separated by an unbridgeable chasm from
Deng's more pragmatic, open, marketized, and stable China. Indeed,
it is hard to think of another world political leader who managed to
transmigrate a whole society between two such opposite ideological
poles as Deng. Contemplating this unlikely passage, Elizabeth Perry
of Harvard University and Sebastian Heilmann from the University
of Trier have tried to solve the riddle of what they call the CCP's
unexpected "puzzling vigor" and "surprising resilience and adaptabil-
ity."[17] After all, weren't Leninist political parties supposed to be rigid
and lacking in innovative spirit, they ask, and thus ill-equipped to
survive in the freewheeling global marketplace? What happened to
the "end of history"? How has "Red China" managed to benefit more

than any other country from the past few decades of global market integration?

Perry and Heilmann's fascinating conjecture is that perhaps, despite all its false starts, reversals, and self-induced catastrophes, under Mao the CCP succeeded in evolving a strong survival instinct. This grew not just out of the Communists' need as guerrillas to dodge Nationalist and Japanese troops in China's mountainous interior, but also from their conception of "policy-making as a process of ceaseless change, tension management, continual experimentation, and ad-hoc adjustment."[18] No matter how self-serving, doctrinally inconsistent, or savagely destructive his actions might seem, Mao learned through his guerrilla experience to value flexibility and agility over rigidity and stability, and then to apply the same pragmatic style to party policy formation after establishing the PRC in 1949.[19] He "favored continued experimentation and transformation (or 'permanent revolution') over regime consolidation," say Perry and Heilmann.[20] And "over the course of the revolution, continuous improvisation became a defining feature of Chinese Communist tactics."[21]

Although, when it proved useful, Mao did embrace Leninist discipline and rigid principles of party organization, he was first and foremost a survivor who knew that one has to be willing to evolve through trial and error, or perish. Such opportunism allowed him to make experimentation a core aspect of his and the CCP's opportunistic operating system, and thus to pioneer a form of "unexpectedly adaptive authoritarianism." While such inconsistency did in the end help delegitimize socialism, it also helped the PRC to endure—first to survive the end of the socialist bloc and then to take advantage of post–Cold War economic globalization to such stunning effect.[22] But whether what Columbia University's Andrew Nathan calls "resilient authoritarianism" is the end of the China story is far less certain.[23] When all is said and done, it may prove less of a long-term durable model than an effective short-term strategic adjustment.

The Mirage of 1989

There was, of course, one agonizing interruption in the astonishing boom of the Deng era, and that was the sturm und drang of 1989, which for the subsequent decade exerted a powerful influence on Western views of China and thus the direction in which we assumed Chinese history to be unfolding. But as the 1989 memories of the Tank Man blocking the progress of PLA tanks on the Avenue of Eternal Peace and the Goddess of Democracy going up before Mao's portrait on Tiananmen Square faded, and as the success of "authoritarian resilience" and CCP-sponsored capitalist growth became more evident, Westerners were forced to rethink their views on China's progress, especially whether democratization was always an essential partner to market-driven growth and national development.

As part of his unique role in establishing the field of modern China studies, Harvard's Fairbank helped develop a legendary survey course on Asia that his many students affectionately dubbed "Rice Paddies." Three times a week he would stride into the lecture hall of the Harvard-Yenching Institute and patiently guide his mesmerized—and often overwhelmed—acolytes through one more chapter of China's four millennia of history, all delineated in its infinite and intimidating complexity on a foldout dynasty chart that was regulation issue to all comers.

On one occasion, as the cataclysm of the Great Leap Forward was enigmatically unfolding in that vast and strange Communist land to which Americans could not then travel, Fairbank found himself confronted by an unusually persistent student who kept pushing him to explain the logic of Mao's revolution. Finally, like a Zen master reluctantly delivering a shocking koan to an initiate, he smiled and said, "Just remember: Mao Zedong didn't make the Chinese Communist revolution for you!"

Fairbank was a gentleman, and his reply was not meant to put down his inquiring student. His point was simply that Chinese history as a whole had its own unique patterns, ones often difficult to divine in Western terms. "China still confronts us with a separate tradition and a radically different modern revolution," he wrote in his summa historica, *East Asia: The Modern Transformation*. "Acknowledgment of our ignorance is the necessary beginning of wisdom."[24]

Later generations of sinologists—many of them Fairbank's protégés—would criticize his approach for its Eurocentric reliance on the framework of "Western challenge/Chinese response" to explain modern China. Particularly scholars who came of age during the Vietnam War era were keenly aware of America's tendency to see Asia as Americans wanted it to be, rather than as it really was. They were in a sense using Fairbank's warning to critique Fairbank's own framework, and moved the field of Chinese historical studies toward a more "China-centered" approach.[25]

Fairbank's warning that China's history is indelibly Chinese took on a renewed relevance when democracy demonstrations erupted on a massive scale in Beijing and other Chinese cities in 1989. The temptation once again was to see twentieth-century China in a triumphalist Western paradigm, as moving inevitably from the "democracy and science" protests of the May Fourth Movement in the 1920s to the liberal democratic aspirations of students in the 1980s. Like lava that keeps erupting through vents in the earth's crust to reveal molten evidence of the core of hot magma hidden beneath, each new upwelling of democratic protest in the streets of China seemed to suggest an irrepressible underground current that would inevitably spew forth again to sweep China onto "the right side of history." And when the Chinese Communist Party's near-death experience in 1989 was followed by the collapse of the USSR and most of the Communist bloc, it was all the more tantalizing to imagine that the teleology of the liberal West would soon universalize itself in that last redoubt, Red China.

Indeed, anyone who experienced the heady months of spring 1989 in Tiananmen Square found it almost impossible not to imagine that China was at a historical milestone. For a while, at least, the correctness of Western assumptions about the inevitability of democracy spreading Enlightenment values around the world, even to China, seemed irrefutable. Francis Fukuyama captured this post–Cold War zeitgeist with his notion of the "end of history," "an unabashed victory of economic and political liberalism" in which "the triumph of the West, of the Western *idea*" was realizing itself "in the total exhaustion of viable systematic alternatives to Western liberalism."[26]

When he considered China, Fukuyama seemed especially enthralled by the thought that finally the Central Kingdom, too, might be on the verge of turning toward the universal fold. "The power of the liberal idea would seem much less impressive if it had not infected the largest and oldest culture in Asia, China," he wrote, confidently prophesying that soon the PRC could "no longer act as a beacon for illiberal forces around the world."[27]

China scholars themselves were not immune from such Western predilections and hopes. Although the crackdown following the 1989 protest movement was viewed as retrograde motion, many China watchers assumed that in the long run China would still prove unable to resist the tendency to evolve toward a more liberal, democratic form of governance. Writing just after the demonstrations in 1989, the great Belgian sinologist Pierre Ryckmans, alias Simon Leys, described Chinese as "a populace thirsting for freedom." Of Deng Xiaoping and the party leaders who had been involved in ordering troops and tanks to crush the demonstrations, he wrote, "They know that they are facing the irrepressible surge of the tidal wave which is going to sweep them away tomorrow, together with the last remains of Chinese communism. . . . The collapse of the present government is ineluctable."[28]

Having guided the reader through centuries of Chinese history, Yale's Jonathan Spence concluded in his magisterial *The Search for Modern China*, "There was not the faintest reason to believe, despite the Chinese government's intellectual and political repressions, that the protests of 1989 would be the last. . . . There would be no truly modern China until people were given back their voices."[29]

In the final part (aptly titled "The Boom") of *Mandate of Heaven: The Legacy of Tiananmen Square*, one of the authors of this book noted that "China's next upheaval might be triggered by economics rather than politics, it might erupt in the provinces rather than Beijing, and it might be led by workers rather than students, but if the past was any guide, sooner or later the aftershocks would reverberate back into 'the Square.'"[30]

If the initial romance and ultimate tragedy of 1989 tended to once more encourage Westerners to see Chinese history as unfolding in a Western teleological manner toward a more democratic future, it also helped obscure what most Chinese thought their leaders had actually been driving toward all the previous decades. As the dramatis personae of this book abundantly illustrate, China's modern thinkers and leaders, smarting from the humiliation of precipitous decline and foreign incursion, had their own more immediate and urgent goal, namely, the restoration of national wealth, power and greatness. Although democracy did appear on the Chinese scene in the early twentieth century, did generate a significant following, and might yet come to flourish, the democratic impulse during the twentieth century remained relatively weak compared to the forces of nationalism and the overriding desire to see China become prosperous, strong, and honored in the world. And we easily forget that, Chen Duxiu's love of Mr. Science and Mr. Democracy notwithstanding, May Fourth demonstrators were also intensely patriotic, as were most students during the spring of 1989. Nationalism, it turned out, was fed by stronger and more inexhaustible tributaries of sentiment than was constitutionalism or democracy, and they bubbled up from deep wellsprings of emotions generated by China's painful historical experience.

For a people possessed of such an abiding sense of pride and face, China's fall in the nineteenth century from a place of such centrality and dominance was a special ignominy, and it engendered a very strong and enduring counterreaction. Through a strange alchemy, based on the old Confucian idea that "humiliation stimulates effort," the shame that stemmed from weakness and defeat also generated a steely determination to become strong again. So what might have been a purely enervating force was transmuted into a galvanic one, a source of energy that ultimately enabled Chinese to start righting what they saw as the wrongs of history.

China had suffered, but like the ancient hero King Goujian, through indomitable Sisyphean endurance it also became determined to turn its defeat and humiliation into victory. Far more powerful than any democratic urge during this twentieth-century interregnum was a utilitarian impulse that propelled Chinese in sequential fashion toward republicanism, anarchism, Marxism, Christianity, and even fascism—whatever ism of the time seemed to offer the best restorative promise. And as even a short visit to China's booming cities now confirms, this pragmatism did finally did pay off for the nation, or at least for many of its citizens. However one chooses to explain it, after generations of abject failure, China's hard-nosed but restless quest for wealth and power finally met with demonstrable material success.

A New Consensus?

Does this mean that Chinese leaders have managed to confect what some have tried to dub a "Beijing Consensus," a new model in which free-market economic development becomes divorced from political liberalization, and capitalism delinked from democracy?[31] While not proclaiming such a model per se, in 2010 Premier Wen Jiabao, echoing so many of the voices in this book, did suggest that one of the reasons Chinese authoritarianism had been so successful was that it allowed leaders "to make decisions efficiently, organize effectively, and concentrate resources to accomplish large undertakings."[32]

New consensus or no, what should be acknowledged is that, despite all its obvious shortcomings and defying most predictions, the CCP has managed to create three decades of rapid growth under a relatively stable political system, and it has brought China closer than ever to building the *xiaokang shehui* (小康社会), or "moderately well-off society," to which Deng Xiaoping aspired. This promise has helped many Chinese make a bargain with the party: as long as they are allowed to enjoy growing wealthier and to pursue a better life, and as long as their country is edging ever closer toward wealth, power, and a modicum of greatness in the world, they will not seek to challenge authoritarian rule.

Since Wei Yuan first began puzzling over China's falling state of grace almost two centuries ago, this has been a dream that has goaded one Chinese patriot after another onward. As a prelude to whatever else may follow, the successful conclusion of this particular quest has undeniably now given Chinese new grounds to take pride in their country's accomplishments. It has also provided the kind of middle-class foundation on which a stable democratic future finally becomes even imaginable. But now that China has made a landfall on the shores of wealth and power, the logical question is: What's next? Do leaders and people feel they have been delivered to those promised shores for which they have so long yearned and where no further extreme exertions are required?

Not really. One of the pieces still missing is the kind of self-confident mind-set that would finally allow Chinese to feel that they have arrived and thus deserve to feel comfortable in their new global skin.

Respect

Although the words "respect" and "status" do not explicitly appear together in the age-old couplet of characters *fuqiang* (富强), signifying "wealth and power," they are everywhere implicit in China's struggle for these long-sought-after goals. The urge to prosperity and strength, after all, had its origins in the humiliation of nineteenth-century defeats by the imperialist powers—and thus regaining the respect of those great powers has always been an essential ingredient in any cure. However, to win real global "respect" (*zunzhong*, 尊重)—a term endlessly bandied about in China's diplomatic parlance—a nation must not only attain wealth and power but also successfully cultivate other, more ineffable qualities capable of eliciting such admiration.

It is true that China can no longer be bullied. But, to the great perplexity of many Chinese (especially officials), their country's extraordinary progress toward "wealth and power" has not in itself managed to deliver the full degree of admiration that they once imagined these heroic accomplishments would automatically confer, and which they fiercely feel to be rightfully theirs. Like those Americans who grew up in the Great Depression and for whom no amount of subsequent wealth was ever enough to slake their innate sense of insecurity, the confidence levels of many Chinese, even after all the successes of their economic miracle, still lag behind their actual achievements in curing their historical sense of inferiority. Indeed, it may yet take another generation or so before confidence levels become better aligned with achievements. But then, a major readjustment of any nation's psychology often lags substantially behind changing reality. It is this anomalous situation that may help explain why, despite China's enormous progress, a humiliation complex still remains, nationalism is still on the rise, and Chinese still so easily tend to feel victimized.

So far the kind of global respect that Chinese have long sought has remained a far more elusive laurel than many reformers and revolutionaries ever imagined. As contemporary "soft-power" gurus explain, genuine esteem for a country does not automatically emanate from extravagant riches or brute strength alone. It comes, instead, from other, subtler kinds of accomplishment that often have more to do with the attractiveness of a country's culture, the virtues of its civic life, or the responsiveness of its political system. From the West, at least, admiration has not gravitated to societies marked by exaggerated systems of state control and "stability maintenance." Instead, it has often been those societies that are culturally open, tolerant, welcoming of heterodox influences, and even a little unpredictable that have ended up being able to produce the most innovative and seductive forms of soft power, and thus won the most global admiration and respect. And such societies have excelled in liberating exactly those forms of individual self-expression that the Chinese Communist Party has felt least comfortable allowing, much less encouraging, which have been embodied in creative misfits such as Ai Weiwei, searing critics such as Liu Xiaobo, headstrong reformers such as Chen Guangcheng.

China's dazzling new infrastructure and all the other studied efforts to cultivate a new image of grandness and confidence are, of course, impressive. And such things as the 2008 Summer Olympic Games, 2010 Shanghai World Expo, and elaborate National Day parades have, in fact, succeeded in eliciting a kind of respect. But as impressive as these self-conscious, government-sponsored model projects are, they are not in the end the stuff from which the deepest kinds of soft power attraction and admiration are born.

"Soft power bespeaks a nation's ability to influence the behavior of others to attain the outcomes it desires," notes the grand theorist of this somewhat intangible kind of power, Joseph Nye, in *Soft Power*, a book that has become immensely popular in China since its publication in 2004. "A country may obtain the outcomes it wants in world politics because other countries—admiring its values, emulating its example, aspiring to its level of prosperity and openness—want to follow it." He adds, "Seduction is always more effective than coercion, and many values like democracy, human rights, and individual opportunities are deeply seductive."[33]

Tellingly, even Chinese themselves seem not to quite know what their nation's most fundamental values now are. After decades of serial cultural and political cancellations and self-reinventions, China has jettisoned the cardinal virtues of its traditional and Maoist cultural incarnations, and thus sometimes does irredeemably seem to be a kingdom of means alone, a society and nation largely defined by its ardent pursuit of techniques, but without many answers to the question: Toward what end?

In statements to the world, Chinese leaders constantly emphasize their "core interests," and they considered it something of a diplomatic triumph when President Obama formally agreed that "respecting each other's core interests is extremely important to ensure steady progress in U.S.-China relations."[34] Yet when it comes to "core values," China's leadership is both lost and somewhat deaf and mute, neither wanting to accept the West's democracy and human rights as the birthrights of all people, nor having any other "universal values" of their own to now offer as an alterative.

The Empty Chair

On visits to twenty-first-century China, one can easily become awed by the sheer scale of that country's recent material progress, and even begin to wonder if authoritarian capitalism is not exactly what the country needed; whether economic rights should not sometimes be allowed to trump individual rights in the interest of society at large; and whether democracies are, in fact, always the most effective forms of governance (especially for developing countries). However, just as these illiberal question marks are presenting themselves, an incident will detonate and serve as a reminder of the weaknesses of authoritarianism and the reasons outside respect is afforded so grudgingly to countries like the PRC, even when they become economically successful. Such occasions also usually end up being embarrassing and galling to China's official image makers. Recent examples include the awarding of the Nobel Peace Prize to jailed dissident Liu Xiaobo in 2010; the blind legal activist Chen Guangcheng's flight into the U.S. embassy in Beijing after a daring escape from house arrest in 2012 just as Secretary of State Hillary Clinton was arriving in Beijing; and the announcement in early 2013 that the hundredth young Tibetan protesting Beijing's coercive policies in their homeland had immolated himself. Needless to say, such self-inflicted humiliations have severely undercut China's bid for soft power, acclaim, and global respect.

Back in the days of Liang Qichao and Lin Yutang, when China's long odyssey to wealth and power was still a matter of unrealizable daydreams or science fiction, it was possible to maintain the belief that attainment of these very concrete goals might in themselves be enough to confer that measure of acceptance that Chinese felt so necessary to heal the wounds left by their "century of humiliation." But as that once distant shoreline now actually emerges on the horizon, it is increasingly evident that something else is also going to be required to slake this abiding Chinese thirst. But, at the same time, most Chinese also find it difficult to define exactly what that "something else" might be.

Often overlooked within China today is the fact that throughout this century there have been indigenous voices hinting that wealth and power alone would be insufficient to the dream of the kind of "great rejuvenation" that Xi Jinping revived immediately upon taking office. Critics such as Wei Jingsheng, Fang Lizhi, and Liu Xiaobo—and before them Chen Duxiu, Lu Xun, and Liang Qichao—understood that China's desire for affirmation could not be completely satisfied by wealth and power alone, that the respect deficit was not simply due to the fact that the Chinese state lacked sufficient riches and strength to compel foreigners to treat it in a more respectful manner. In their various ways, these voices from the margins all suggested that a significant part of China's self-esteem problem arose not just from how foreigners treated Chinese, but from how the Chinese government treated its own people. Alas, such voices were often largely unheeded or silenced.

Even for those not blinded by patriotic pride or nationalism, recognizing that China's main problem now lies as much within as without is difficult and painful. It depends, first, on an ability to see—despite a history of foreign incursion, unfair treatment by the great powers, and the elaborate culture of victimization that governments from Sun Yat-sen's and Chiang Kai-shek's to Mao Zedong's and Hu Jintao's have woven out of this bitter reality—that foreign imperialism is no longer the primary cause of China's afflictions. It depends, second, on an ability and willingness to see that the missing tiles in the mosaic of respect that Chinese still so ardently seek now revolve more around the question of the Chinese government's own ability to nurture a more open, transparent, tolerant, just, and even democratic society living under the rule of law than anything else.

Despite the episodic emergence of brilliant and courageous liberal dissenters, their demands for democracy have not ended up being the main motive force of modern Chinese history, at least so far. The far stronger driver would appear to have been the urge to restore China to wealth and power. But as these goals now become realized, will not more and more Chinese demand to enjoy their newfound affluence in a more open and law-abiding society where they have a greater role in deciding who leads them and how they are governed? Is it not also probable that the yearning of Chinese leaders for international respect will end up being just as strong a magnet drawing them, too, toward a more consultative, if not democratic, form of governance?

The PRC has managed to make impressive strides toward establishing the preconditions of just such a future evolution. By opening itself up to foreign investment, world trade, and domestic reform, it has brought about one of the most dynamic surges of economic development in world history. And what is interesting is that it has done so by following the path first laid out by Sun Yat-sen a century ago, then adopted by Chiang Kai-shek, and finally subscribed to, in one variation or another, by most subsequent leaders since: namely, by prescribing some vague kind of democracy as a long-term goal, but deferring its implementation until a protracted period of authoritarian "tutelage" could consolidate China's sovereign power, enrich the nation, and prepare the people for a more direct exercise of their liberties.

If much remains opaque about China's future, one thing is clear: after three decades of Deng Xiaoping–inspired economic reform, China's development drama is approaching its next act. Indeed, as the Eighteenth Party Congress unfolded in November 2012 and Xi Jinping was enthroned as party general secretary and then president in March 2013, there was a palpable fin de siècle feel in the air. The fact that a script for the next act had not yet been written and that nobody knew just who might do so left Chinese steeped in no small amount of uncertainty and anxiety. What is more, because they also understood that their new leaders were now likely to rule in a more consensual manner, with no single leader in a dominant position to boldly plot a new way forward, there was also a worry about rudderlessness. Of course, most people yearned to find grounds for continued hope and optimism, even if few could see a clear pathway forward that warranted such hopefulness.

On his historic "southern tour" in 1992 to Shenzhen, Deng Xiaoping famously proclaimed that any road other than continuing with socialist reform and opening would be a "dead end,"[35] and lead irrevocably away from national rejuvenation. Against no small adversity after 1989, he did finally manage to successfully coax China back to the path of reform and opening.

Several decades later, as Xi Jinping ascended the political stage, the country again found itself in need of finding a new pathway forward. Interestingly, one of the first trips he made as party general secretary was also to Guangdong Province. The visit was an homage to Deng, but also a calculated symbolic effort to suggest that Xi, too, now wished to blaze an equally new and bold trail forward. Having signaled his intention to keep pressing forward with more economic reform, Xi then toured several army and navy bases, where he added a more muscular military dimension to the notion of a new "Chinese dream" that he had raised at the National Museum. "This dream can be said to be a dream of a strong nation; and for the military, it is a dream of a strong military," he told commanders of the Guangzhou Military Region in Huizhou. "We must achieve the great revival of the Chinese nation, and we must ensure there is unison between a prosperous country and a strong military."[36]

But having touched on economic and military strength, there was still an important piece left missing in this evolving new Chinese dreamscape, the question of political reform. Particularly in Beijing and other large cities, there was a growing recognition, articulated among members of the Chinese intelligentsia, that the only realistic pathway forward to a comprehensive and long-lasting "revival" now lay in greater openness, the rule of law, and even constitutionalism. But, this part of Xi Jinping's slowly pixilating dream for the future was left tantalizingly blurry.

Almost a century ago, during a much darker time when China possessed not even the military power to defend itself, never mind wealth, the great writer Lu Xun also found himself worrying about how his country would ever manage to find a hopeful pathway out of the bleakness that then confronted him. "As I think about it," he wrote in 1921, "hope can neither be said to exist or not to exist. It's like the roadways on our earth. Originally there were not even paths. And it was only after many people passed by that such pathways became actual roadways."[37]

And now, after traveling a very long and hard stretch of "roadway," China finds itself in a position far more enviable than Lu Xun could have ever imagined. Having been through a century of "political tutelage"—an interim that Sun Yat-sen had foreseen as unavoidably preceding a final stage of "constitutional government" giving "the people" a chance "directly to exercise their political rights"—China was now at last closer than ever before to this goal that Sun said would "mark the completion of reconstruction and the success of the revolution."[38]

History is rarely fond of final resting places, especially in a country as dynamic and volatile as China. With its surging wealth and growing middle class, as Xi Jinping took the reins as paramount leader, China, at last, now found itself better positioned than ever—should it choose to do so—to follow in the footsteps of other nearby Asian, post-Confucian, and post-colonial societies such as Taiwan, Hong Kong, and South Korea, which had all made similar passages from authoritarianism to constitutionalism. But, because as the new Chinese leadership assumed power in 2013 there was still such trepidation about straying from the socialist path and rocking the political boat in any way, such progress was not a foregone conclusion. In fact, Xi was also reported to have given another set of "secret speeches" cautiously warning party leaders about the dangers of China following in the dreaded footsteps of the former Soviet Union.[39]

"We should overcome our fears," Deng Xiaoping, who led the last great act in China's development drama, had once insisted. "Everything has to be tried first by someone—that's the only way new trails are blazed."[40] And perhaps the easiest way for China's new leaders to start blazing a new political trail forward was by simply starting to enforce their country's existing constitution—something that Chinese intellectuals were already calling for with increasing intensity. For example, during the 2013 New Year, the progressive Canton newspaper *Southern Weekend* wrote an editorial entitled "The Dream of Constitutionalism," which proclaimed, "Only if constitutionalism is realized and powers checked can citizens loudly voice their criticisms of power," and "only then can every person believe in their hearts they are free to live their own lives." Unfortunately, editors quickly ran afoul of

Guangdong Province's party Propaganda Department, which delayed the editorial's publication until they had had a chance to completely rewrite it so that, instead of advocating the need for greater constitutionalism, it ended up extolling the status quo, causing the paper's staff not only to go on strike, but precipitating several days of unprecedented public demonstration among average Chinese in solidarity with the defiant journalists.[41]

But then during his first press conference as premier in March 2013, Li Keqiang proclaimed that the new leadership would "be true to the constitution." It was a tantalizing beginning to his tenure in office.[42]

But, even with this new generation of leaders at China's helm, the question of what kind of rejuvenation they really desired remained very murky. Equally unclear was how, as China continued to become stronger and more prosperous, they would come to act out the consequences of their new wealth and power on the world stage. Would they march under the standard of Deng Xiaoping's admonition to "avoid the limelight" and champion the more recently minted idea of a "peaceful rise"? Or would they want to flex their new economic and military muscles, as retired rear admiral Yang Yi suggested they might when he urged his country's leaders to use the country's new military power to cow neighbors into obedient submission? "We should tell people how many aircraft carriers we're going to build," he was reported as saying. "That will put the great powers at ease and crush the small countries' hopes [that they can provoke us]."[43]

In the nineteenth century, when Chinese reformers first became fixated on their country's deficit of prosperity and national strength, they had looked toward their ultimate attainment largely in defensive terms, as a means of protecting and defending their country from outside incursion. But after a century of relying on patriotism and nationalism as binding agents to congeal Sun Yat-sen's proverbial "sheet of loose sand," there was always the danger of a new sentiment—one not unknown among those once acquainted with oppression—arising: the temptation to do unto others what has been done unto them.

Whether the attitude of China's new leaders toward projections of national strength as international power, especially military force, might morph into something more aggressive than what those nineteenth- and twentieth-century thinkers chronicled in this book yearned for, is one of the unanswered questions challenging new leaders, not just in China, but around the world. But, if the idea of wealth and power did become more assertive, even aggressive, China would doubtless find that the kind of soft power they so eagerly sought would remain elusive in a way that no amount of propaganda or PR would be able to remedy. Moreover, exactly that kind of global respect for which the Chinese people have yearned and labored for so long—and which had, in fact, at last begun to accumulate—would then likely evanesce before their eyes.

However, should China's leaders succeed in resisting such a siren song and instead seek accommodation in disputes with its neighbors, as well as evolving a domestic political system based increasingly on the rule of law, transparency, and accountability of rulers to the ruled, then the People's Republic of China stands a good chance of finally winning the long-dreamed-of title of a truly modern and great country, not just a great power.

Acknowledgments

This book is part of a larger project undertaken by the Center on U.S.-China Relations at the Asia Society in New York City documenting different aspects of China's dramatic reform movement and transition to modernity. It is also a follow-up—and in a sense a prequel—to our already completed China Boom Project (chinaboom.asiasociety.org), which involved video interviewing close to one hundred scholars, officials, diplomats, businessmen, bankers, NGO leaders, and journalists to archive their insights on how it came to pass that China, after over a century of repeated failures, finally managed to transform itself into the economic powerhouse of today. As part of this larger Asia Society project, our book was ably supported by a team of extremely thoughtful and talented people. Andrew Smeall, who was a key player on the China Boom Project, has made an enormous contribution to our efforts both as an intellectual colleague and as our in-house fact-checker. He has also assumed primary responsibility for designing the book's companion website (Chinawealthpower.com). Wang Bo has been our tireless photo editor, doing intensive archival work to identify relevant photos in both the United States and China for the book and the website, and then taking on the grueling process of gaining permissions. Ouyang Bin has provided invaluable assistance with Chinese-language research, not least of which was finding the right calligraphy for the jacket design. Orville's father-in-law, Liu Depeng, has been tireless in his willingness to search out obscure Chinese-language sources. Our other colleagues at the Asia Society have also all put their shoulders to this wheel in different ways: Leah Thompson, Laura Chang, Susan Jakes, Sara Segal-Williams, Jonathan Landreth, Michael Zhao, David Barreda, and Sun Yunfan all deserve our thanks.

Several university colleagues around the country, indeed the world, have also been extremely generous with their time, affording us invaluable counsel. Andrew Nathan of Columbia University took the time out to read our work-in-progress and deliver an enormously thorough and thoughtful critique that helped us recalibrate some of our own thinking. Joseph Esherick of the University of California, San Diego, also read through a draft of the manuscript from head to toe, providing an invaluable list of comments and points for us to reconsider and correct. His UCSD colleague Susan Shirk was a prized sounding board for all the years this book has been in gestation, helping both of us think through our interpretations of different interludes in modern Chinese history and comparing past with present. In that same vein, Roderick MacFarquhar, Barry Naughton, Bill Rowe, Jonathan Spence, and Ezra Vogel have helped inspire and inform our thinking in direct conversation, but even more through their seminal published writings. It was Timothy Garton Ash from Oxford University who suggested the deceptively simple conceit of our book, namely, that we explain our ideas about modern China's progress through chapter-long profiles of iconic thinkers and leaders. He also indulged Orville in many hours of enjoyable and inspiring historical discussion.

Yonsei University provided a stimulating and serene environment for John to carry out his half of this project, thanks to the camaraderie of faculty at the Graduate School of International Studies and Underwood International College. And Yonsei students—the brightest minds in Korea—subjected themselves to "taking" our manuscript as a class, and in ways beyond what they could realize helped shape the final product. Emily Brill, a master's student at the time, in particular deserves thanks for truly Herculean efforts to chase down every stray fact that needed checking, even making the pilgrimage to Yale's Sterling Library for some last elusive sources. Librarians Tang Li in Yale's East Asia collection and Nancy Hearst at Harvard's Fairbank Collection also deserve our special thanks for assistance with sources. Finally, Peking University—a formidable force of its own in modern Chinese history—hosted John as a visiting professor for a summer of intensive research and writing. Professor Peng Xiaoyu not only made that possible, but also through many conversations comparing East and West opened up new perspectives on modern China. Also at PKU, Chen Changwei, Lei Bo, and Yu Jinghui helped in ways big and small with our research and thinking.

To Tom Engelhardt, who over the many years of editing Orville's work has come to know what it is that he is trying to say—sometimes better than he does himself—we offer our profoundest thanks for once again rallying to the cause. To Jonathan Jao, our very able and patient editor at Random House, thanks for putting up with a manuscript that did not quite know where it was going until it got there. Molly Turpin, also at Random House, has been a crucial and always helpful partner in the laborious process of publication. And to Binky Urban, the alpha and omega of this and so many other books, our deepest appreciation. You bring the notion of being an agent to a new plateau!

We could have neither completed nor enjoyed this project without our families supporting and distracting us every step of the way. Baifang, Ole, Sebastian, and Sasha indulged Orville with their patience during the many years it took to incubate this book, and Jeong-eun, Senna, and Sean, as well as Baltimore, California, and Pungnapdong, were John's rock.

Last, but most certainly not least, we want to express our gratitude to the Arthur Ross Foundation, which has been a critical player in sustaining the Asia Society's Center on U.S.-China Relations and, by extension, this book. Our thanks to both Arthur and Janet Ross; all that they have done by way of supporting the work of the center from its very beginning is boundless. And finally, a genuflection is most certainly in order to the memory of Ambassador Richard Holbrooke, who is the reason the Center for U.S.-China Relations exists, and whose spirit hovers eternally over everything we have done there since. Nor before closing can we resist the temptation to tip our hats to an anonymous patron, friend, gadfly, and sage, without whom we never would have dreamed up the idea for this book in the first place, much less ever been able to bring it to fruition.

THE AUTHORS

Works Cited

Ai, Weiwei. "China Excluded Its People from the Olympics. London Is Different." *Guardian*, July 25, 2012.

———. "A Dissident's Tips for Survival." *Wall Street Journal*, December 29, 2012.

———. "The Olympics Was a Strange, Surreal Nightmare." *The China Boom Project.* http://chinaboom.asiasociety.org/period/overdrive/0/155 (accessed February 28, 2013).

Anderlini, Jamil. "AgBank IPO Officially the World's Biggest." *Financial Times*, August 13, 2010.

Arkush, R. David, and Leo Ou Lee. *Land Without Ghosts: Chinese Impressions of America from the Mid-Nineteenth Century to the Present.* Berkeley: University of California Press, 1993.

Ba Jin. *Random Thoughts*. Hong Kong: Joint Publishing, 1984.

Backhouse, Edmund. *Décadence Mandchoue: The China Memoirs of Sir Edmund Trelawny Backhouse.* Ed. Derek Sandhaus. Hong Kong: Earnshaw Books, 2011.

Barmé, Geremie. *The Forbidden City.* Cambridge, MA: Harvard University Press, 2008.

Barmé, Geremie, and Linda Jaivin. *New Ghosts, Old Dreams: Chinese Rebel Voices.* New York: Times Books, 1992.

Barnett, A. Doak. *China on the Eve of Communist Takeover.* New York: Praeger, 1963.

Barnett, Robbie. "Thunder from Tibet." *New York Review of Books*, May 1, 2008.

Barnett, Suzanne Wilson. "Wei Yuan and Westerners: Notes on the Sources of the Hai-kuo t'u-chih." *Ch'ing-shih wen-t'i* 2, vol. 4 (1970): 10–14.

Barrett, David D. *Dixie Mission: The United States Army Observer Group in Yenan, 1944.* Berkeley: Center for Chinese Studies, University of California, 1970.

"Battling the Censors." *Economist*, January 12, 2013.

Baum, Richard. *Burying Mao: Chinese Politics in the Age of Deng Xiaoping.* Princeton, NJ: Princeton University Press, 1994.

Becker, Jasper. *City of Heavenly Tranquility: Beijing in the History of China.* Oxford: Oxford University Press, 2008.

Bergère, Marie-Claire. *Shanghai: China's Gateway to Modernity.* Stanford, CA: Stanford University Press, 2010.

———. *Sun Yat-sen.* Stanford, CA: Stanford University Press, 1998.

Bickers, Robert A. *The Scramble for China: Foreign Devils in the Qing Empire, 1832–1914.* London: Allen Lane, 2011.

Bickers, Robert A., and R. G. Tiedemann. *The Boxers, China, and the World.* Lanham, MD: Rowman and Littlefield, 2007.

Bland, J. O. P., and E. Backhouse. *China Under the Empress Dowager, Being the History of the Life and Times of Tzu hsi.* Boston: Houghton Mifflin, 1914.

Bol, Peter K. *Neo-Confucianism in History.* Cambridge, MA: Harvard University Asia Center, 2008.

Boulger, Demetrius Charles. *The Life of Gordon, Volume I.* London: T. Fisher Unwin, 1897.

Brahm, Laurence J. *Zhu Rongji and the Transformation of Modern China.* Singapore: John Wiley and Sons (Asia), 2003.

Brandt, Conrad. *Stalin's Failure in China, 1924–1927.* Cambridge, MA: Harvard University Press, 1958.

Brandt, Conrad, Benjamin I. Schwartz, and John King Fairbank. *A Documentary History of Chinese Communism.* Cambridge, MA: Harvard University Press, 1959.

Brook, Timothy. *Quelling the People: The Military Suppression of the Beijing Democracy Movement.* New York: Oxford University Press, 1992.

Buckley, Chris. "Vows of Change in China Belie Private Warning." *New York Times,* February 14, 2013.

Burns, John F. "Deng Asserts Ties to West Are Vital to Fight Poverty." *New York Times,* January 2, 1985.

Butterfield, Fox. "Apathy Replaces Marxist Idealism Among Chinese." *New York Times,* December 30, 1980.

Cadot-Wood, Antoine. "Striving Toward a Lovable Nation: Nationalism and Individual Agency in the Writings of Chen Duxiu." B.A. thesis, Wesleyan University, 2010.

Cantlie, James, and Charles Sheridan Jones. *Sun Yat Sen and the Awakening of China.* New York: Fleming H. Revell, 1912.

Carl, Katharine A. *With the Empress Dowager of China.* New York: Century, 1905.

Cassel, Pär Kristoffer. *Grounds of Judgment: Extraterritoriality and Imperial Power in Nineteenth-Century China and Japan.* Oxford: Oxford University Press, 2012.

Chandler, Clay. "Wall Street's War for China." *Fortune,* May 17, 2006.

Chang, Chih-tung [Zhang Zhidong]. *China's Only Hope: An Appeal.* Trans. Samuel Isett Woodbridge. New York: Fleming H. Revell, 1900.

Chang, Hao. "Intellectual Change and the Reform Movement." In *The Cambridge History of China,* vol. 11: *Late Ch'ing 1800–1911, Part 2,* ed. John King Fairbank, 274–338. Cambridge: Cambridge University Press, 1978.

———. *Liang Ch'i-ch'ao and Intellectual Transition in China, 1890–1907.* Cambridge, MA: Harvard University Press, 1971.

Chao, Anne Shen. "Chen Duxiu's Early Years: The Importance of Personal Connections in the Social and Intellectual Transformation of China, 1895–1920." PhD dissertation, Rice University, 2009.

Chen, Duxiu. *Chen Duxiu's Last Articles and Letters, 1937–1942.* Ed. Gregor Benton. Honolulu: University of Hawaii Press, 1998.

Chen, Guidi, and Chuntao Wu. *Will the Boat Sink the Water?: The Life of China's Peasants.* New York: Public Affairs, 2006.

Ch'en, Jerome. *Mao.* Englewood Cliffs, NJ: Prentice Hall, 1969.

———. *Mao and the Chinese Revolution.* London: Oxford University Press, 1965.

———. *Mao Papers: Anthology and Bibliography.* London: Oxford University Press, 1970.

———. *Yuan Shih-k'ai.* Stanford, CA: Stanford University Press, 1961.

Chen, Qitai, and Lanxiao Liu. *Wei Yuan pingzhuan.* Nanjing: Nanjing daxue chubanshe, 2005.

Chen, Xulu. "Guanyu jiaobinlu kangyi [On Dissenting Views]." *Xin Jianshe* 2 (1964): 85–92.

Cheng, Pei-kai, Michael Elliot Lestz, and Jonathan D. Spence, eds. *The Search for Modern China: A Documentary Collection.* New York: Norton, 1999.

Cheng, Zhongyuan, and Xingzhen Xia. *Deng Xiaoping yu 1975 nian zheng dun [Deng Xiaoping and the Reconsolidation of 1975]*. Beijing: Renmin chubanshe, 2004.

Chi, Hsin. *Teng Hsiao-ping: A Political Biography*. Hong Kong: Cosmos Books, 1978.

Chi, Wen-shun. *Chinese-English Dictionary of Contemporary Usage*. Berkeley: University of California Press, 1977.

Chiang, Kai-shek. *Jiang Jieshi riji jiemi*, [Revealing the Secrets of Chiang Kai-shek's Diary], Ed. Zhang Xiuzhang. Beijing: Tuanjie chubanshe, 2007.

Chiang, Kai-shek, and Philip Jaffe. *China's Destiny and Chinese Economic Theory*. New York: Roy, 1947.

Chiang, Kai-shek, and May-ling Soong. *General Chiang Kai-shek: The Account of the Fortnight in Sian When the Fate of China Hung in the Balance*. Garden City, NY: Doubleday, 1937.

Chin, Annping. *Confucius: A Life of Thought and Politics*. New Haven, CT: Yale University Press, 2008.

Chin, Hsin. *Teng Hsiao-ping: A Political Biography*. Hong Kong: Cosmos Books, 1978.

The Chinese Repository. Canton, 1832–1851.

Chinoy, Mike. *China Live: People Power and the Television Revolution*. Boston: Rowman and Littlefield, 1999.

Chow, Tse-tsung. *The May Fourth Movement: Intellectual Revolution in Modern China*. Cambridge, MA: Harvard University Press, 1960.

Chu, Henry, Maggie Farley, and Anthony Kuhn. "Chinese Attack U.S. Missions as Protests Intensify." *Los Angeles Times*, May 10, 1999.

Chu, Samuel C., and Kwang-Ching Liu, eds. *Li Hung-chang and China's Early Modernization*. Armonk, NY: M. E. Sharpe, 1994.

Chung, Sue Fawn. "The Image of the Empress Dowager Tz'u-hsi." In *Reform in Nineteenth-Century China*, ed. Paul A. Cohen and John Schrecker, 101–10. Cambridge, MA: East Asian Research Center, Harvard University, 1976.

Cohen, Paul A. *Between Tradition and Modernity: Wang T'ao and Reform in Late Ch'ing China*. Cambridge, MA: Harvard University Press, 1974.

———. *Discovering History in China: American Historical Writing on the Recent Chinese Past*. New York: Columbia University Press, 1984.

———. *History in Three Keys: The Boxers as Event, Experience, and Myth*. New York: Columbia University Press, 1997.

———. *Speaking to History: The Story of King Goujian in Twentieth-Century China*. Berkeley: University of California Press, 2009.

Confucius. *The Analects*. Trans. D. C. Lau. New York: Penguin Books, 1979.

Conger, Sarah Pike. *Letters from China: With Particular Reference to the Empress Dowager and the Women of China*. Chicago: A. C. McClurg, 1910.

Cooper, James C., and Kathleen Madigan. "China: The Year of the Inflation Dragon." *Bloomberg BusinessWeek*, October 9, 1994.

Crozier, Brian. *The Man Who Lost China: The First Full Biography of Chiang Kai-shek*. New York: Scribner, 1976.

Dai, Qing. *Wang Shiwei and "Wild Lilies": Rectification and Purges in the Chinese Communist Party, 1942–1944*. Ed. David E. Apter and Timothy Cheek. Trans. Nancy Liu and Lawrence R. Sullivan. Armonk, NY: M. E. Sharpe, 1994.

Dalai Lama. "2009 (Forty-Ninth Anniversary)." Central Tibetan Administration. tibet .net/2008/03/10/statement-of-his-holiness-the-dalai-lama-on-the-forty-ninth -anniversary-of-the-tibetan-national-uprising-day-10-march-2008 (accessed February 28, 2013).

Dardess, John W. *Blood and History in China: The Donglin Faction and Its Repression, 1620–1627*. Honolulu: University of Hawaii Press, 2002.

Daubier, Jean. *A History of the Chinese Cultural Revolution*. New York: Vintage Books, 1974.

"DCI Statement on the Belgrade Chinese Embassy Bombing." Central Intelligence Agency. https://www.cia.gov/news-information/speeches-testimony/1999/dci_speech_072299 .html (accessed February 23, 2013).

de Bary, William Theodore. *Sources of Chinese Tradition,* vol. 2. New York: Columbia University Press, 2001.

Deng, Rong. *Deng Xiaoping and the Cultural Revolution.* Beijing: Foreign Languages Press, 2003.

———. *My Father Deng Xiaoping: The War Years.* Beijing: Foreign Languages Press, 2008.

Deng, Xiaoping. *Deng Xiaoping tongzhi de "Wo de zishu"* [Comrade Deng Xiaoping's "Autobiography"]. Manuscript collection, Harvard University, Cambridge, MA, 1972.

———. *Deng Xiaoping wenxuan* [Selected Works of Deng Xiaoping]. Beijing: Renmin chubanshe, 1994.

———. *Deng Xiaoping zishu* [Deng Xiaoping in His Own Words]. Ed. Zhang Liangcun. Beijing: Jiefangjun chubanshe, 2004.

———. *Selected Works of Deng Xiaoping.* Beijing: Foreign Languages Press, [1984] 1994.

———. *Speech by Chairman of the Delegation of the People's Republic of China, Teng Hsiao-ping, at the Special Session of the U.N. General Assembly, April 10, 1974.* Beijing: Foreign Languages Press, 1974.

Deng Xiaoping sixiang nianpu [Chronology of Deng Xiaoping Thought]. Beijing: Zhongyang wenxian chubanshe, 1998.

Der Ling. *Two Years in the Forbidden City.* New York: Moffat, Yard, 1917.

Devichand, Mukul. "Millions 'Left Behind' in Rural China." BBC News, May 12, 2010.

Dikötter, Frank. *Mao's Great Famine: The History of China's Most Devastating Catastrophe, 1958–1962.* New York: Walker, 2010.

Ding, Wenjiang, and Fengtian Zhao. *Liang Qichao nianpu changbian* [Draft Biography of Liang Qichao]. Shanghai: Shanghai renmin chubanshe, 2009.

Dong, Zonglin. *Li Hongzhang de waijiao shengya* [Li Hongzhang's Diplomatic Career]. Beijing: Tuanjie chubanshe, 2007.

Dunstan, Helen. *Conflicting Counsels to Confuse the Age: A Documentary Study of Political Economy in Qing China, 1644–1840.* Ann Arbor: Center for Chinese Studies, University of Michigan, 1996.

Eastman, Lloyd E. *The Abortive Revolution: China Under Nationalist Rule, 1927–1937.* Cambridge, MA: Harvard University Press, 1974.

———. "Ch'ing-i and Chinese Policy Formation During the Nineteenth Century." *Journal of Asian Studies* 24, no. 4 (1965): 595–611.

———. "Political Reformism in China Before the Sino-Japanese War." *Journal of Asian Studies* 27, no. 4 (1968): 695–710.

———. *Throne and Mandarins: China's Search for a Policy During the Sino-French Controversy, 1880–1885.* Cambridge, MA: Harvard University Press, 1967.

Eastman, Lloyd E., Jerome Ch'en, Suzanne Pepper, and Lyman P. Van Slyke. *The Nationalist Era in China, 1927–1949.* Cambridge: Cambridge University Press, 1991.

Eckholm, Eric, and Seth Faison. "China's New Premier: Fast Riser Who Tamed Economy in Chaos." *New York Times*, March 16, 1998.

Editorial. *Financial Times* (London), January 8, 2013.

Elliott, Mark C. *Emperor Qianlong: Son of Heaven, Man of the World.* New York: Pearson Longman, 2009.

Elman, Benjamin A. *Classicism, Politics, and Kinship: The Ch'ang-chou School of New Text Confucianism in Late Imperial China.* Berkeley: University of California Press, 1990.

———. *A Cultural History of Civil Examinations in Late Imperial China.* Berkeley: University of California Press, 2000.

————. "Naval Warfare and the Refraction of China's Self-Strengthening Reforms." *Modern Asian Studies* 38, no. 2 (2004): 283–326.

Esherick, Joseph W. "Cherishing Sources from Afar." *Modern China* 24, no. 2 (1998): 135–161.

————. *The Origins of the Boxer Uprising*. Berkeley: University of California Press, 1987.

Evans, Richard. *Deng Xiaoping and the Making of Modern China*. New York: Viking, 1994.

Fairbank, John King, ed. *The Chinese World Order: Traditional China's Foreign Relations*. Cambridge, MA: Harvard University Press, 1968.

————. Foreword to Ruth Earnshaw Lo and Katherine S. Kinderman, *In the Eye of the Typhoon*. New York: Harcourt Brace Jovanovich, 1980.

————. *Trade and Diplomacy on the China Coast: The Opening of the Treaty Ports, 1842–1854*. Cambridge, MA: Harvard University Press, 1953.

Fairbank, John King, Edwin O. Reischauer, and Albert M. Craig. *East Asia: The Modern Transformation*. Boston: Houghton Mifflin, 1965.

————. *East Asia: Tradition and Transformation*. Boston: Houghton Mifflin, 1973.

Fairbank, Wilma. *Liang and Lin: Partners in Exploring China's Architectural Past*. Philadelphia: University of Pennsylvania Press, 1994.

Fang, Lizhi. *Bringing Down the Great Wall: Writings on Science, Culture, and Democracy in China*. Ed. and tr. by James Williams. New York: Knopf, 1991.

————. "Liu Xiaobo and Illusions About China." *New York Times*, October 11, 2010.

Fathers, Michael, and Andrew Higgins. *Tiananmen: The Rape of Peking*. London: Independent, 1989.

Fay, Peter Ward. *The Opium War, 1840–1842: Barbarians in the Celestial Empire in the Early Part of the Nineteenth Century and the War by Which They Forced Her Gates*. Chapel Hill: University of North Carolina Press, 1975.

Feigon, Lee. *Chen Duxiu: Founder of the Chinese Communist Party*. Princeton, NJ: Princeton University Press, 1983.

————. *Mao: A Reinterpretation*. Chicago: Ivan R. Dee, 2002.

Fenby, Jonathan. *Chiang Kai-shek: China's Generalissimo and the Nation He Lost*. New York: Carroll and Graf, 2004.

Feng, Guifen. *Jiaobinlu kangyi* [Dissenting Views from a Hut near Bin]. Taibei: Wenhai chubanshe, 1971.

Ferlanti, Federica. "The New Life Movement in Jiangxi Province, 1934–1938." *Modern Asian Studies* 44, no. 5 (2010): 961–1000.

Feuerwerker, Albert. *China's Early Industrialization: Sheng Hsuan-huai (1844–1916) and Mandarin Enterprise*. Cambridge, MA: Harvard University Press, 1958.

————. *The Chinese Economy, 1870–1949*. Ann Arbor: Center for Chinese Studies, University of Michigan, 1995.

Fewsmith, Joseph. *China Since Tiananmen: From Deng Xiaoping to Hu Jintao*. New York: Cambridge University Press, 2008.

————. "'Social Management' as a Way of Coping with Heightened Social Tensions." *China Leadership Monitor* 36 (2012).

Fitzgerald, John. *Awakening China: Politics, Culture, and Class in the Nationalist Revolution*. Stanford, CA: Stanford University Press, 1996.

Flannery, Russell. "China's Billionaire Boom." *Forbes*, October 27, 2010.

Fogel, Joshua, ed. *The Role of Japan in Liang Qichao's Introduction of Modern Western Civilization to China*. Berkeley: Center for Chinese Studies, University of California, 2004.

Franz, Uli. *Deng Xiaoping*. Boston: Harcourt Brace Jovanovich, 1988.

Fraser, John. *The Chinese: Portrait of a People*. New York: Summit Books, 1980.

Freeman, Will. "The Accuracy of China's Mass Incidents." *Financial Times*, March 2, 2010.

Fukuyama, Francis. *The End of History and the Last Man.* New York: Free Press, 1992.
———. "The End of History?" *National Interest* 16, Summer 1989, 1.
"Full Text of Hu Jintao's Speech at CPC Anniversary Gathering." Xinhua, July 1, 2011.
Fung, Allen. "Testing the Self-Strengthening: The Chinese Army in the Sino-Japanese War of 1894–1895." *Modern Asian Studies* 30, no. 4 (1996): 1007–31.
Gao, Xin, and Pin He. *Tiemian zaixiang: Zhu Rongji da zhuan* [Iron-Faced Prime Minister: A Biography of Zhu Rongji]. Hong Kong: Mirror Books, 1998.
Garnaut, John. "China's Elite Fail to Share Fruits of Growth." *The Age* (Melbourne), October 1, 2007.
Garside, Roger. *Coming Alive: China After Mao.* New York: McGraw-Hill, 1981.
Gasster, Michael. "Reform and Revolution in China's Political Modernization." In *China in Revolution: The First Phase, 1900–1913*, ed. Mary Clabaugh Wright, 67–96. New Haven, CT: Yale University Press, 1968.
Gentzler, J. Mason. *Changing China: Readings in the History of China from the Opium War to the Present.* New York: Praeger, 1977.
Gilley, Bruce. *China's Democratic Future: How It Will Happen and Where It Will Lead.* New York: Columbia University Press, 2004.
———. *Tiger on the Brink: Jiang Zemin and China's New Elite.* Berkeley: University of California Press, 1998.
Goldin, Paul R. "Persistent Misconceptions About Chinese 'Legalism.'" *Journal of Chinese Philosophy* 38, no. 1 (2011): 88–104.
Goldman, Merle. *From Comrade to Citizen: The Struggle for Political Rights in China.* Cambridge, MA: Harvard University Press, 2005.
———. *Literary Dissent in Communist China.* New York: Atheneum, 1971.
———. *Modern Chinese Literature in the May Fourth Era.* Cambridge, MA: Harvard University Press, 1977.
Goldstein, Melvyn C. *A History of Modern Tibet.* Berkeley: University of California Press, 2007.
Gorbachev, Mikhail Sergeevich. *Memoirs.* New York: Doubleday, 1995.
Gordon, David B. *Sun Yatsen: Seeking a Newer China.* Upper Saddle River, NJ: Prentice Hall, 2010.
Graham, A. C. *Disputers of the Tao: Philosophical Argument in Ancient China.* La Salle, IL: Open Court, 1989.
Granqvist, Hans. *The Red Guard: A Report on Mao's Revolution.* New York: F. A. Praeger, 1967.
Gray, Jack, and Patrick Cavendish. *Chinese Communism in Crisis: Maoism and the Cultural Revolution.* New York: Praeger, 1968.
Grieder, Jerome B. *Hu Shih and the Chinese Renaissance: Liberalism in the Chinese Revolution, 1917–1937.* Cambridge, MA: Harvard University Press, 1970.
Gries, Peter Hays. *China's New Nationalism: Pride, Politics, and Diplomacy.* Berkeley: University of California Press, 2004.
Guan, Zhong. *Guanzi: Political, Economic, and Philosophical Essays from Early China.* Trans. W. Allyn Rickett. Boston: Cheng and Tsui, 2001.
Hahn, Emily. *China Only Yesterday: 1850–1950, a Century of Change.* Garden City, NY: Doubleday, 1963.
Halper, Stefan A. *The Beijing Consensus: How China's Authoritarian Model Will Dominate the Twenty-First Century.* New York: Basic Books, 2010.
Han, Fei. *Han Fei Tzu: Basic Writings.* Trans. Burton Watson. New York: Columbia University Press, 1964.
———. *Han Feizi jijie.* Beijing: Zhonghua shuju, 1998.
Harrison, Henrietta. *The Man Awakened from Dreams: One Man's Life in a North China Village, 1857–1942.* Stanford, CA: Stanford University Press, 2005.

Hart, Robert. *The I.G. in Peking: Letters of Robert Hart, Chinese Maritime Customs, 1868–1907.* Ed. John King Fairbank, Katherine Frost Bruner, and Elizabeth Mac-Leod Matheson. Cambridge, MA: Belknap Press of Harvard University Press, 1975.

Havel, Václav. *Václav Havel: Living in Truth.* Ed. Jan Vladislav. Boston: Faber and Faber, 1990.

Hayter-Menzies, Grant. *The Empress and Mrs. Conger: The Uncommon Friendship of Two Women and Two Worlds.* Hong Kong: Hong Kong University Press, 2011.

Headland, Isaac Taylor. *Court Life in China.* New York: F. H. Revell, 1909.

Heilmann, Sebastian, and Elizabeth J. Perry. *Mao's Invisible Hand: The Political Foundations of Adaptive Governance in China.* Cambridge, MA: Harvard University Asia Center, 2011.

Hevia, James Louis. *Cherishing Men from Afar: Qing Guest Ritual and the Macartney Embassy of 1793.* Durham, NC: Duke University Press, 1995.

———. *English Lessons: The Pedagogy of Imperialism in Nineteenth-Century China.* Durham, NC: Duke University Press, 2003.

Hicks, George L., ed. *The Broken Mirror: China After Tiananmen.* Chicago: St. James Press, 1990.

Hille, Kathrin. "Return of Warlike Rhetoric from China." *Financial Times*, January 23, 2013.

Horner, Charles. *Rising China and Its Postmodern Fate: Memories of Empire in a New Global Context.* Athens: University of Georgia Press, 2009.

Horowitz, Richard S. "Breaking the Bonds of Precedent: The 1905–6 Government Reform Commission and the Remaking of the Qing Central State." *Modern Asian Studies* 37, no. 4 (2003): 775–97.

Hsia, Tsi-an. *The Gate of Darkness: Studies on the Leftist Literary Movement in China.* Seattle: University of Washington Press, 1968.

Hsiao, Kung-chuan. *A History of Chinese Political Thought.* Trans. Fred Mote. Princeton, NJ: Princeton University Press, 1979.

———. *A Modern China and a New World: K'ang Yu-wei, Reformer and Utopian, 1858–1927.* Seattle: University of Washington Press, 1975.

Hsu, Immanuel C. Y. *China's Entrance into the Family of Nations: The Diplomatic Phase, 1858–1880.* Cambridge, MA: Harvard University Press, 1960.

Hu Jintao. "Adhering to the Socialist Cultural Development Path with Chinese Characteristics and Striving to Build a Country with a Strong Socialist Culture." *Qiushi Journal Online—Leaders, Politics, Economics, Culture, Society.* http://english.qstheory.cn/leaders/201204/t20120401_149158.htm (accessed February 28, 2013).

———. "China's Response." *PBS NewsHour*, May 9, 1999.

Huang, Hong. *Ying daoli: nanfang tanhua huimou* [The Absolute Principle: Retrospective on the Southern Talks]. Jinan: Shandong renmin chubanshe, 2002.

Huang, Kang. "An Unforgettable Night in Yanan." *Chinese Literature* 9 (1977): 91–95.

Huang, Max K. W. *The Meaning of Freedom: Yan Fu and the Origins of Chinese Liberalism.* Hong Kong: Chinese University Press, 2008.

Huang, Philip C. *Liang Ch'i-ch'ao and Modern Chinese Liberalism.* Seattle: University of Washington Press, 1972.

Huang, Renyu. *Cong da lishi de jiaodu du Jiang Jieshi riji*, [Reading the Diaries of Chiang Kai-shek from the Perspective of History]. Beijing: Jiuchuan chubanshe, 2010.

Huang, Yasheng. *Capitalism with Chinese Characteristics: Entrepreneurship and the State.* Cambridge: Cambridge University Press, 2008.

Hummel, Arthur W. *Eminent Chinese of the Ch'ing Period (1644–1912).* Washington, DC: Library of Congress, 1943.

Hung, Chang-tai. *Mao's New World: Political Culture in the Early People's Republic.* Ithaca, NY: Cornell University Press, 2011.

Hurd, Douglas. *The Arrow War: An Anglo-Chinese Confusion, 1856–1860.* New York: Collins, 1967.

"International Reaction to Liu Xiaobo Nobel Peace Prize." *BBC News,* October 28, 2010.

Iriye, Akira. *After Imperialism: The Search for a New Order in the Far East, 1921–1931.* Cambridge, MA: Harvard University Press, 1965.

Itō, Hirobumi. *A Maker of New Japan: Marquis Ito's Experience.* Trans. Teizo Kuramata. Nagasaki: Gwaikokugo Kyojusho, 1904.

Itō, Hirobumi, and Miyoji Ito. *Commentaries on the Constitution of the Empire of Japan.* Tokyo: Chu-o Daigaku, 1906.

Jacobs, Andrew, and Jonathan Ansfield. "Well-Oiled Security Apparatus in China Stifles Calls for Change." *New York Times,* February 28, 2011.

Janku, Andrea. "Preparing the Ground for Revolutionary Discourse: From the Statecraft Anthologies to the Periodical Press in Nineteenth-Century China." *T'oung Pao* 90 (2004): 65–121.

Jansen, Marius B. *The Japanese and Sun Yat-sen.* Cambridge, MA: Harvard University Press, 1954.

——. *The Making of Modern Japan.* Cambridge, MA: Belknap Press of Harvard University Press, 2002.

Jones, Andrew F. *Developmental Fairy Tales: Evolutionary Thinking and Modern Chinese Culture.* Cambridge, MA: Harvard University Press, 2011.

Judge, Joan. *Print and Politics: "Shibao" and the Culture of Reform in Late Qing China.* Stanford, CA: Stanford University Press, 1996.

——. "Public Opinion and the New Politics of Contestation in the Late Qing, 1904–1911." *Modern China* 20, no. 1 (1994): 64–91.

Kagan, Richard C. "Chen Tu-hsiu's Unfinished Autobiography." *The China Quarterly* 50 (1972): 295–314.

Kahn, J. F. "Better Fed than Red." *Esquire,* September 1990.

Karl, Rebecca E., and Peter Gue Zarrow. *Rethinking the 1898 Reform Period: Political and Cultural Change in Late Qing China.* Cambridge, MA: Harvard University Asia Center, 2002.

Karol, K. S. *The Second Chinese Revolution.* New York: Hill and Wang, 1974.

Kaufman, Alison A. "One Nation Among Many: Foreign Models in the Constitutional Thought of Liang Qichao." PhD dissertation, University of California, Berkeley, 2007.

Khrushchev, Nikita Sergeevich. *Khrushchev Remembers.* Ed. Edward Crankshaw and Jerrold Schechter. Trans. Strobe Talbott. New York: Little, Brown, 1974.

——. *Memoirs of Nikita Khrushchev,* vol. 3: *Statesman, 1953–1964.* Ed. Sergei Khrushchev. University Park: Penn State University Press, 2007.

Kissinger, Henry. *On China.* New York: Penguin, 2011.

——. *Years of Renewal.* New York: Simon and Schuster, 1999.

Kristof, Nicholas D. "Shanghai's Mayor Gains Credit as Pragmatist." *New York Times,* November 5, 1989.

——. "No Praise, Please! He Wants to Be the Premier." *New York Times,* August 25, 1992.

Kuhn, Philip A. *Origins of the Modern Chinese State.* Stanford, CA: Stanford University Press, 2003.

——. *Rebellion and Its Enemies in Late Imperial China: Militarization and Social Structure, 1796–1864.* Cambridge, MA: Harvard University Press, 1970.

Kwong, Luke S. K. "Imperial Authority in Crisis: An Interpretation of the Coup d'État of 1861." *Modern Asian Studies* 17, no. 2 (2008): 221–38.

——. *A Mosaic of the Hundred Days: Personalities, Politics, and Ideas of 1898.* Cambridge, MA: Council on East Asian Studies, Harvard University, 1984.

Lai, Jiancheng. *Liang Qichao de jingji mianxiang* [Liang Qichao's Views on Economics]. Hangzhou: Zhejiang daxue chubanshe, 2010.

Lam, Willy Wo-Lap. *Chinese Politics in the Hu Jintao Era: New Leaders, New Challenges*. Armonk, NY: M. E. Sharpe, 2006.

Lampton, David M. *The Making of Chinese Foreign and Security Policy in the Era of Reform, 1978–2000*. Stanford, CA: Stanford University Press, 2001.

Landler, Mark. "Bankruptcy the Chinese Way; Foreign Bankers Are Shown to the End of the Line." *New York Times*, January 22, 1999.

Lanza, Fabio. *Behind the Gate: Inventing Students in Beijing*. New York: Columbia University Press, 2010.

Lardy, Nicholas R. *China's Unfinished Economic Revolution*. Washington, DC: Brookings Institution, 1998.

Larsen, Kirk W. *Tradition, Treaties, and Trade: Qing Imperialism and Choson Korea, 1850–1910*. Cambridge, MA: Harvard University Asia Center, 2008.

Lau, Lawrence J., Yingyi Qian, and Gerard Roland. "Reform Without Losers: An Interpretation of China's Dual-Track Approach to Transition." *Journal of Political Economy* 108, no. 1 (2000): 120–43.

Lenin, Vladimir Ilyich. *The Lenin Anthology*. Ed. Robert C. Tucker. New York: Norton, 1975.

Leonard, Jane Kate. *Wei Yuan and China's Rediscovery of the Maritime World*. Cambridge, MA: Council on East Asian Studies, Harvard University, 1984.

Levenson, Joseph Richmond. *Liang Ch'i-ch'ao and the Mind of Modern China*. Cambridge, MA: Harvard University Press, 1959.

Levine, Marilyn A. *The Found Generation: Chinese Communists in Europe during the Twenties*. Seattle: University of Washington Press, 1993.

Leys, Simon. *The Burning Forest: Essays on Chinese Culture and Politics*. New York: Holt, Rinehart, and Winston, 1985.

———. *Broken Images: Essays on Chinese Culture and Politics*. London: Allison & Busby, 1979.

Li, Cheng. *China's Leaders: The New Generation*. Lanham, MD: Rowman and Littlefield, 2001.

Li, Zhisui. *The Private Life of Chairman Mao: The Memoirs of Mao's Personal Physician*. Ed. Anne F. Thurston. Trans. Hung-chao Tai. New York: Random House, 1994.

Liang, Qichao. *Intellectual Trends in the Ch'ing Period*. Trans. Immanuel C. Y. Hsu. Cambridge, MA: Harvard University Press, 1970.

———. *Liang Qichao quanji* [The Complete Works of Liang Qichao]. Beijing: Beijing chubanshe, 1999.

———. *Liang Qichao wenxuan* [Selected Writings of Liang Qichao]. Ed. Wang Defeng. Shanghai: Shanghai yuandong, 2011.

———. *Liang Qichao zishu* [Liang Qichao's Autobiographical Writings]. Ed. Cui Zhihai. Zhengzhou: Henan renmin chubanshe, 2005.

———. "My Autobiographical Account at Thirty." *Chinese Studies in History* 10, no. 3 (1977): 4–34.

———. *Wuxu zhengbian ji* [Record of the Coup of 1898]. Guilin: Guangxi shifan daxue chubanshe, 2010.

Lifton, Robert Jay. *Thought Reform and the Psychology of Totalism: A Study of "Brainwashing" in China*. New York: Norton, 1961.

———. *Revolutionary Immortality: Mao Tse-tung and the Chinese Cultural Revolution*. New York: Random House, 1968.

Lin, Yüsheng. *The Crisis of Chinese Consciousness: Radical Antitraditionalism in the May Fourth Era*. Madison: University of Wisconsin Press, 1979.

Lin, Yutang. *Between Tears and Laughter*. New York: John Day, 1943.

Liu, Kwang-Ching. "The Ch'ing Restoration." In *The Cambridge History of China*, vol. 10: *The Late Ch'ing, Part 1*, ed. John K. Fairbank, 409–90. Cambridge: Cambridge University Press, 1978.

Liu Xiaobo. *June Fourth Elegies*. Trans. Jeffrey Yang. Minneapolis: Graywolf Press, 2012.

———. *No Enemies, No Hatred: Selected Essays and Poems*. Ed. E. Perry Link, Tienchi Martin-Liao, and Liu Xia. Cambridge, MA: Belknap Press of Harvard University Press, 2012.

Loti, Pierre. *The Last Days of Pekin*. Trans. Myrta L. Jones. Boston: Little, Brown, 1902.

Lo, Ruth Earnshaw and Katharine Kinderman. Introduction by J. K. Fairbank. *In the Eye of the Typhoon*. New York: Harcourt, 1980.

Lovell, Julia. *The Opium War: Drugs, Dreams and the Making of China*. London: Picador, 2011.

Lu Xun. *Call to Arms*. Beijing: Foreign Languages Press, 2010.

———. *The Real Story of Ah-Q and Other Tales of China*. Trans. by Julia Lovell. London: Penguin Books. 2009.

———. *Selected Works of Lu Xun*, vols. I–IV. Beijing: Foreign Languages Press, 1957.

———. *Xiaoshuoji*, [The Short Stories of Lu Xun]. Hong Kong: Datong Shuju Chuban, 1959.

Macartney, George. *An Embassy to China; Being the Journal Kept by Lord Macartney During His Embassy to the Emperor Ch'ien-lung, 1793–1794*. London: The Folio Society, 2004.

MacFarquhar, Roderick. "Deng's Last Campaign." *New York Review of Books*, December 17, 1992.

———. *The Origins of the Cultural Revolution*, vol. II, *The Great Leap Forward, 1958–1960*. New York: Columbia University Press, 1983.

———, ed. *The Politics of China: The Eras of Mao and Deng*. 2nd ed. New York: Cambridge University Press, 1997.

MacFarquhar, Roderick, and Michael Schoenhals. *Mao's Last Revolution*. Cambridge, MA: Belknap Press of Harvard University Press, 2006.

MacPherson, Duncan. *Two Years in China*. London: Saunders and Otley, 1843.

Maddison, Angus. *Chinese Economic Performance in the Long Run*. Paris: OECD, 1998.

Makito, Saya. *The Sino-Japanese War and the Birth of Japanese Nationalism*. Tokyo: International House of Japan, 2011.

Manela, Erez. *The Wilsonian Moment: Self-Determination and the International Origins of Anticolonial Nationalism*. Oxford: Oxford University Press, 2007.

Mao Zedong. *Mao Papers*. Ed. Jerome Ch'en. London: Oxford University Press, 1970.

———. *Mao Tsetung Poems*. Beijing: Foreign Languages Press, 1976.

———. *Mao Zedong xuanji*, [The Selected Works of Mao Zedong]. Beijing: Renmin chubanshe, 1961.

———. *Mao's Road to Power: Revolutionary Writings, 1912–1949*. Ed. Stuart Schram. Armonk, NY: M. E. Sharpe, 1992.

———. *Quotations from Chairman Mao Tse-tung*. Beijing: Foreign Languages Press, 1966.

———. *Selected Works of Mao Zedong*. Beijing: Foreign Languages Press, 1969.

Martin, Bernard. *Strange Vigour: A Biography of Sun Yat-sen*. Port Washington, NY: Kennikat Press, 1970.

Martin, W. A. P. *The Siege in Peking: China Against the World*. New York: F. H. Revell, 1900.

McAleavy, Henry. *A Dream of Tartary: The Origins and Misfortunes of Henry P'u Yi*. London: G. Allen and Unwin, 1963.

———. *The Modern History of China*. New York: Praeger, 1967.

McClain, Charles J. *In Search of Equality: The Chinese Struggle Against Discrimination in Nineteenth-Century America*. Berkeley: University of California Press, 1996.

McDougall, Bonnie S. *Mao Zedong's "Talks at the Yan'an Conference on Literature and Art": A Translation of the 1943 Text with Commentary*. Ann Arbor: The University of Michigan. 1980.

McGregor, Richard. *The Party: The Secret World of China's Communist Rulers*. New York: Harper, 2010.

Mei Zhi. *HuFeng's Prison Years*, trans. Gregor Benton. New York: Verso, 2013.

Meisner, Maurice. "Cultural Iconoclasm, Nationalism, and Internationalism in the May Fourth Movement." In *Reflections on the May Fourth Movement: A Symposium*, ed. Benjamin I. Schwartz and Charlotte Furth, 14–22. Cambridge, MA: Harvard University Press, 1972.

———. *Li Ta-chao and the Origins of Chinese Marxism*. Cambridge, MA: Harvard University Press, 1967.

Mencius. *Mencius*. Trans. D. C. Lau. New York: Penguin, 1970.

Miles, Steven B. *The Sea of Learning: Mobility and Identity in Nineteenth-Century Guangzhou*. Cambridge, MA: Harvard University Asia Center, 2006.

Milton, David, and Nancy Milton. *The Wind Will Not Subside: Years in Revolutionary China, 1964–1969*. New York: Pantheon Books, 1976.

Min Tu-ki. *National Polity and Local Power: The Transformation of Late Imperial China*. Ed. Philip A. Kuhn and Timothy Brook. Cambridge, MA: Council on East Asian Studies, Harvard University, 1989.

Mishra, Pankaj. *From the Ruins of Empire: The Intellectuals Who Remade Asia*. New York: Farrar, Straus and Giroux, 2012.

Mitchell, Peter M. "The Limits of Reformism: Wei Yuan's Reaction to Western Intrusion." *Modern Asian Studies* 6, no. 2 (1972): 175–204.

Miyazaki, Ichisada. *China's Examination Hell: The Civil Service Examinations of Imperial China*. Trans. Conrad Shirokauer. New Haven, CT: Yale University Press, 1981.

Mo Shaoping et al. "Criminal Defense in Sensitive Cases." In *Liu Xiaobo, Charter 08, and the Challenges of Political Reform in China*, ed. Jean-Phillipe Béja, Fu Hualing, and Eva Pils, 61–78. Hong Kong: Hong Kong University Press, 2012.

Mokros, Emily. "Reconstructing the Imperial Retreat: Politics, Communications, and the Yuanming Yuan Under the Tongzhi Emperor, 1873–74." *Late Imperial China* 33, no. 2 (2012): 76–118.

Montgomery, Walter G. "The 'Remonstrance' of Feng Kuei-fen: A Confucian Search for Change in 19th-Century China." PhD dissertation, Brown University, 1979.

Mosca, Matthew. *From Frontier Policy to Foreign Policy: The Question of India and the Transformation of Geopolitics in Qing China*. Stanford, CA: Stanford University Press, 2013.

Mufson, Steven. "Economic Pragmatist to Be China Premier." *Washington Post*, March 5, 1998.

Musgrove, C. D. "Building a Dream: Constructing a National Capital in Nanjing, 1927–1937." In *Remaking the Chinese City: Modernity and National Identity, 1900–1950*, ed. Joseph W. Esherick, 139–60. Honolulu: University of Hawaii Press, 2000.

———. "Monumentality in Nanjing's Sun Yat-sen Memorial Park." *Southeast Review of Asian Studies* 29 (2007): 1–19.

Naquin, Susan. *Millenarian Rebellion in China: The Eight Trigrams Uprising of 1813*. New Haven, CT: Yale University Press, 1976.

Nathan, Andrew. "Authoritarian Resilience." *Journal of Democracy* 14, no. 1 (2003): 6–17.

———. *Chinese Democracy*. New York: Alfred A. Knopf, 1985.

Nathan, Andrew J., and Bruce Gilley. *China's New Rulers: The Secret Files*. New York: New York Review of Books, 2002.

Naughton, Barry. "China's Economic Think Tanks: Their Changing Role in the 1990s." *China Quarterly* 171 (2002): 625–35.

———. *The Chinese Economy: Transitions and Growth*. Cambridge, MA: MIT Press, 2006.

———. *Growing Out of the Plan: Chinese Economic Reform, 1978–1993*. New York: Cambridge University Press, 1995.

Nye, Joseph S. *Soft Power: The Means to Success in World Politics*. New York: Public Affairs, 2004.

Ogden, Suzanne, Kathleen Hartford, Lawrence Sullivan, and David Zweig, eds. *China's Search for Democracy: The Student and the Mass Movement of 1989*. Armonk, NY: M. E. Sharpe, 1992.

Orlik, Tom. "Unrest Grows as Economy Booms." *Wall Street Journal*, September 26, 2011.

Osnos, Evan. "Liu Xiaobo Wins the Nobel Peace Prize." *New Yorker*, October 10, 2010.

Paine, S. C. M. *The Sino-Japanese War of 1894–1895: Perceptions, Power, and Primacy*. New York: Cambridge University Press, 2003.

Pantsov, Alexander, and Steven I. Levine. *Mao: The Real Story*. New York: Simon and Schuster, 2012.

Peffer, Nathaniel. *China: The Collapse of a Civilization*. London: George Routledge and Sons, 1931.

Perdue, Peter C. *China Marches West: The Qing Conquest of Central Eurasia*. Cambridge, MA: Belknap Press of Harvard University Press, 2005.

Perry, Elizabeth J. *Rebels and Revolutionaries in North China, 1845–1945*. Stanford, CA: Stanford University Press, 1980.

Peterman, Erika. "Beijing Halts Rights, Arms Talks." *Chicago-Sun Times*, May 11, 1999.

Platt, Stephen R. *Autumn in the Heavenly Kingdom: China, the West, and the Epic Story of the Taiping Civil War*. New York: Alfred A. Knopf, 2012.

———. *Provincial Patriots: The Hunanese and Modern China*. Cambridge, MA: Harvard University Press, 2007.

Polachek, James M. *The Inner Opium War*. Cambridge, MA: Council on East Asian Studies, Harvard University, 1992.

Pomeranz, Kenneth. *The Great Divergence: China, Europe, and the Making of the Modern World Economy*. Princeton, NJ: Princeton University Press, 2000.

Porter, Jonathan. *Tseng Kuo-fan's Private Bureaucracy*. Berkeley: Center for Chinese Studies, University of California, 1972.

"Premier: China Confident in Maintaining Economic Growth." *Xinhua*, March 16, 2007.

Pye, Lucian W. *Mao Tse-tung: The Man in the Leader*. New York: Basic Books, 1976.

Rabe, John. *The Good Man of Nanking: The Diaries of John Rabe*. Ed. Erwin Wickert. Trans. John E. Woods. New York: Alfred A. Knopf, 1998.

Rabinovitch, Simon. "'Strong Army' Xi: The Other Side of China's Reformer." *Financial Times*, December 12, 2013.

Ramo, Joshua Cooper. *The Beijing Consensus*. London: Foreign Policy Centre, 2004.

Rankin, Mary Backus. "'Public Opinion' and Political Power." *Journal of Asian Studies* 41, no. 3 (1982): 453–84.

Reynolds, Douglas Robertson. *China, 1898–1912: The Xinzheng Revolution and Japan*. Cambridge, MA: Council on East Asian Studies, Harvard University, 1993.

Rhoads, Edward J. M. *Manchus and Han: Ethnic Relations and Political Power in Late Qing and Early Republican China, 1861–1928*. Seattle: University of Washington Press, 2000.

———. *Stepping Forth into the World: The Chinese Educational Mission to the United States, 1872–81*. Hong Kong: Hong Kong University Press, 2011.

Rice, Edward E. *Mao's Way*. Berkeley: University of California Press, 1972.

Richard, Timothy. *Forty-five Years in China: Reminiscences*. New York: Frederick A. Stokes, 1916.

Rosenthal, Jean-Laurent, and R. Bin Wong. *Before and Beyond Divergence: The Politics of Economic Change in China and Europe*. Cambridge, MA: Harvard University Press, 2011.

Rowe, William T. *China's Last Empire: The Great Qing*. Cambridge, MA: Harvard University Press, 2009.

———. "Money, Economy, and Polity in the Daoguang-Era Paper Currency Debates." *Late Imperial China* 31, no. 2 (2010): 69–96.

Ruan, Ming. *Deng Xiaoping: Chronicle of an Empire.* Trans. and ed. Nancy Liu, Peter Rand, and Lawrence R. Sullivan. Boulder, CO: Westview Press, 1994.

Salisbury, Harrison E. *The New Emperors: China in the Era of Mao and Deng.* Boston: Little, Brown, 1992.

Schell, Orville. "China's Andrei Sakharov." *Atlantic Monthly*, May 1988.

———. *Discos and Democracy: China in the Throes of Reform.* New York: Pantheon Books, 1988.

———. *Mandate of Heaven: A New Generation of Entrepreneurs, Dissidents, Bohemians, and Technocrats Lays Claim to China's Future.* New York: Simon and Schuster, 1994.

———. "The Odyssey of Comrade Fang." *Los Angeles Times Magazine*, October 1, 2007.

———. *Watch Out for the Foreign Guests: China Encounters the West.* New York: Pantheon Books, 1980.

Schell, Orville and David Shambaugh, eds. *The China Reader: The Reform Era.* New York: Random House, 1994.

Schiffrin, Harold Z. *Sun Yat-sen, Reluctant Revolutionary.* Boston: Little, Brown, 1980.

Schoppa, R. Keith. *Revolution and Its Past: Identities and Change in Modern Chinese History.* Upper Saddle River, NJ: Prentice Hall, 2006.

———. *Twentieth Century China: A History in Documents.* Oxford: Oxford University Press, 2004.

Schram, Stuart R., ed. *Mao Tse-Tung Unrehearsed.* Trans. John Chinney. Harmondsworth: Penguin, 1974.

———. *The Political Thought of Mao Tse-tung.* Harmondsworth: Penguin, 1969.

Schumpeter, Joseph A. *Capitalism, Socialism, and Democracy.* New York: Harper, 1942.

Schurmann, Franz. *Ideology and Organization in Communist China.* Berkeley: University of California Press, 1966.

Schwarcz, Vera. *The Chinese Enlightenment: Intellectuals and the Legacy of the May Fourth Movement of 1919.* Berkeley: University of California Press, 1986.

Schwartz, Benjamin I. *Chinese Communism and the Rise of Mao.* Cambridge, MA: Harvard University Press, 1951.

———. *In Search of Wealth and Power: Yen Fu and the West.* Cambridge, MA: Harvard University Press, 1964.

———. *The World of Thought in Ancient China.* Cambridge, MA: Harvard University Press, 1985.

Seagrave, Sterling. *Dragon Lady: The Life and Legend of the Last Empress of China.* New York: Random House, 1993.

———. *The Soong Dynasty.* New York: Harper and Row, 1985.

Selden, Mark, ed. *The People's Republic of China: A Documentary History of Revolutionary Change.* New York: Monthly Review Press, 1979.

———. ed. *The Yenan Way in Revolutionary China.* Cambridge, MA: Harvard University Press, 1971.

Service, John S. *Lost Chance in China: The World War II Despatches of John S. Service.* Ed. Joseph Esherick. New York: Random House, 1974.

Shambaugh, David L. *China Goes Global: The Partial Power.* New York: Oxford University Press, 2013.

———. ed. *Deng Xiaoping: Portrait of a Chinese Statesman.* Oxford: Clarendon Press, 1995.

Sharman, Lyon. *Sun Yat-sen: His Life and Its Meaning.* Stanford, CA: Stanford University Press, 1968.

Shen Hu. "China's Gini Index at 0.61." *Caixin* (Beijing), December 10, 2012.

Sheng, Yueh. *Sun Yat-sen University in Moscow and the Chinese Revolution: A Personal Account.* Lawrence: Center for East Asian Studies, University of Kansas, 1971.

Shih, Victor C. *Factions and Finance in China: Elite Conflict and Inflation*. Cambridge: Cambridge University Press, 2009.

Shirk, Susan L. *China: Fragile Superpower*. Oxford: Oxford University Press, 2008.

———. *The Political Logic of Economic Reform in China*. Berkeley: University of California Press, 1993.

Short, Philip. *Mao: A Life*. New York: Henry Holt, 1999.

Sima, Qian. *Selections from Records of the Historian*. Trans. Xianyi Yang and Gladys Yang. Beijing: Foreign Languages Press, 1979.

Snow, Edgar. *Journey to the Beginning: A Personal View of Contemporary History*. New York: Random House, 1958.

———. *People on Our Side*. New York: Random House, 1944.

———. *Red Star over China*. New York: Grove Press, 1968.

Solomon, Richard H. *Mao's Revolution and the Chinese Political Culture*. Berkeley: University of California Press, 1971.

Soong, May-ling, and Kai-shek Chiang. *This Is Our China: Selections from the Writings of Madame Chiang Kai-shek*. New York: Harper and Brothers, 1940.

Spector, Stanley. *Li Hung-chang and the Huai Army: A Study in Nineteenth-Century Chinese Regionalism*. Seattle: University of Washington Press, 1964.

Spence, Jonathan D. "The Enigma of Chiang Kai-shek." *New York Review of Books*, October 22, 2009.

———. *The Gate of Heavenly Peace: The Chinese and Their Revolution, 1895–1980*. New York: Penguin, 1982.

———. *God's Chinese Son: The Taiping Heavenly Kingdom of Hong Xiuquan*. New York: W. W. Norton, 1996.

———. *Mao Zedong*. New York: Viking, 1999.

———. *The Search for Modern China*. New York: Norton, 1990.

———. *To Change China: Western Advisers in China, 1620–1960*. Boston: Little, Brown, 1969.

Stilwell, Joseph W. *The Stilwell Papers*. Ed. Theodore H. White. New York: William Sloane Associates, 1948.

Stranahan, Patricia. *Underground: The Shanghai Communist Party and the Politics of Survival, 1927–1937*. Lanham, MD: Rowman and Littlefield, 1998.

Strand, David. *An Unfinished Republic: Leading by Word and Deed in Modern China*. Berkeley: University of California Press, 2011.

Su Tairen. *Deng Xiaoping shengping quanji lu* [Complete Record of the Life of Deng Xiaoping]. Beijing: Zhongyang wenxian chubanshe, 2003.

Sun, E-Tu Zen. "The Chinese Constitutional Missions of 1905–1906." *Journal of Modern History* 24, no. 3 (1952): 251–69.

Sun Yat-sen. *The Three Principles of the People*. 4th ed. Trans. Frank W. Price. Taipei: China Publishing, 1982.

———. "A Program of National Reconstruction," in De Bary et al, *Sources of Chinese Tradition*. New York, Columbia University Press.

Sun Zhongshan. *Sanmin Zhuyi*, [The Three Principles of the People]. Guangzhou: Guangdong renmin chubanshe, 2006.

Tai Wan-chin. "Chen Duxiu's Conversion from a Liberal Democrat to a Marxist-Leninist: Motivations and Impact." *Tamkang Journal of International Affairs* 11, no. 1 (2007).

Tan, Chester C. *The Boxer Catastrophe*. New York: Norton, 1971.

Tang, Xiaobing. *Global Space and the Nationalist Discourse of Modernity: The Historical Thinking of Liang Qichao*. Stanford, CA: Stanford University Press, 1996.

Taylor, Jay. *The Generalissimo: Chiang Kai-shek and the Struggle for Modern China*. Cambridge, MA: Belknap Press of Harvard University Press, 2009.

———. *The Generalissimo's Son: Chiang Ching-kuo and the Revolutions in China and Taiwan*. Cambridge, MA: Harvard University Press, 2000.

Teng, Ssu-yu. *Chang Hsi and the Treaty of Nanking, 1842*. Chicago: University of Chicago Press, 1944.

Teng, Ssu-yu, and John King Fairbank, eds. *China's Response to the West: A Documentary Survey, 1839–1923*. Cambridge, MA: Harvard University Press, 1982.

ter Haar, B. J. *The White Lotus Teachings in Chinese Religious History*. Leiden: E. J. Brill, 1992.

Thompson, Roger R. "The Lessons of Defeat: Transforming the Qing State After the Boxer War." *Modern Asian Studies* 37, no. 4 (2003): 769–73.

Thurston, Anne F. *A Chinese Odyssey: The Life and Times of a Chinese Dissident*. New York: Charles Scribner's Sons, 1991.

Trevor-Roper, Hugh. *Hermit of Peking: The Hidden Life of Sir Edmund Backhouse*. New York: Knopf, 1978.

Tsu, Jing. *Failure, Nationalism, and Literature: The Making of Modern Chinese Identity, 1895–1937*. Stanford, CA: Stanford University Press, 2005.

Tuchman, Barbara Wertheim. *Notes from China*. New York: Collier Books, 1972.

Tyler, Patrick. "China Detains and Then Frees a Top Dissident." *New York Times*, March 5, 1994.

———. *A Great Wall: Six Presidents and China*. New York: PublicAffairs, 2000.

"U.S.-China Joint Statement." The White House. http://www.whitehouse.gov/the-press-office/us-china-joint-statement (accessed February 28, 2013).

Vernoff, Edward, and Peter J. Seybolt. *Through Chinese Eyes: Tradition, Revolution and Transformation*. 3rd ed. New York: APEX Press, 2007.

Vittinghoff, Natascha. "Unity vs. Uniformity: Liang Qichao and the Invention of a 'New Journalism' for China." *Late Imperial China* 23, no. 1 (2002): 91–143.

Vogel, Ezra F. *Deng Xiaoping and the Transformation of China*. Cambridge, MA: Belknap Press of Harvard University Press, 2011.

Wakeman, Frederic E. *History and Will: Philosophical Perspectives of Mao Tse-tung's Thought*. Berkeley: University of California Press, 1973.

———. "The Huang-chao ching-shih wen-pien." *Ch'ing-shih wen-t'i*, 1, no. 1 (1969): 8–22.

———. "A Revisionist View of the Nanjing Decade: Confucian Fascism." In *Reappraising Republican China*, ed. Richard L. Edmonds, 141–78. Oxford: Oxford University Press, 2000.

Waley, Arthur. *The Opium War Through Chinese Eyes*. London: Allen and Unwin, 1958.

Wang, David Der-wei. *Fin-de-siècle Splendor: Repressed Modernities of Late Qing Fiction, 1849–1911*. Stanford, CA: Stanford University Press, 1997.

Wang, Dong. *China's Unequal Treaties: Narrating National History*. Lanham, MD: Lexington Books, 2005.

Wang, Fanxi. "Chen Duxiu, Founder of Chinese Communism." In Chen Duxiu, *Chen Duxiu's Last Articles and Letters, 1937–1942*, ed. Gregor Benton, 133–41. Honolulu: University of Hawaii Press, 1998.

Wang, Nora. "Deng Xiaoping: The Years in France." *China Quarterly* 92 (1982): 698–705.

Wang Shaoguang and Hu Angang. *The Chinese Economy in Crisis: State Capacity and Tax Reform*. Armonk, NY: M. E. Sharpe, 2001.

Wang, Zheng. *Never Forget National Humiliation: Historical Memory in Chinese Politics and Foreign Relations*. New York: Columbia University Press, 2012.

Warner, Marina. *The Dragon Empress: The Life and Times of Tz'u-hsi, Empress Dowager of China, 1835–1908*. New York: Macmillan, 1972.

Wei, Jingsheng. *The Courage to Stand Alone: Letters from Prison and Other Writings*. Trans. and ed. Kristina M. Torgeson. New York: Penguin, 1998.

Wei, Yuan. *A Chinese Account of the Opium War*. Trans. Edward H. Parker. Shanghai: Kelly and Walsh, 1888.

———. *Haiguo tuzhi* [Illustrated Study of Sea Powers]. Zhengzhou: Zhongzhou guji, 1999.

Wei Chaoyong, *"Xin zhongguo weilaiji" de lishi quannien jiqi zhengzhi lunli*, [An Historical View and the Political Ethics of "The Future of New China"]. *Zhejiang Xuekan*, no. 4, 2006.

Westad, Odd Arne. *Decisive Encounters: The Chinese Civil War, 1946–1950*. Stanford, CA: Stanford University Press, 2003.

———. *Restless Empire: China and the World Since 1750*. New York: Basic Books, 2012.

Weston, Timothy B. *The Power of Position: Beijing University, Intellectuals, and Chinese Political Culture, 1898–1929*. Berkeley: University of California Press, 2004.

White, Theodore H. *In Search of History: A Personal Adventure*. New York: Harper and Row, 1978.

White, Theodore H., and Annalee Jacoby. *Thunder Out of China*. New York: William Sloane Associates, 1946.

Wilbur, C. Martin. *Sun Yat-sen, Frustrated Patriot*. New York: Columbia University Press, 1976.

Wills, John E. *Mountain of Fame: Portraits in Chinese History*. Princeton, NJ: Princeton University Press, 1994.

Wolseley, Garnet Wolseley. *Narrative of the War with China in 1860*. London: Longman, Green, Longman, and Roberts, 1862.

Wong, Edward. "China's Communist Chief Acts to Bolster Military." *New York Times*, December 15, 2012.

Wong, Edward, and Jonathan Ansfield. "Rising Power of Generals Worries Party in Beijing." *International Herald Tribune*, October 2, 2012.

Wong, K. Scott. "Liang Qichao and the Chinese of America: A Re-evaluation of His 'Selected Memoir of Travels in the New World.'" *Journal of American Ethnic History* 11, no. 4 (1992): 3–24.

Woo, T. C. *The Kuomintang and the Future of the Chinese Revolution*. London: George Allen and Unwin, 1928.

Woodman, Sophia, "Wei Jingsheng's Lifelong Battle for Democracy," in Wei Jingsheng, *The Courage to Stand Alone: Letters from Prison and Other Writings*. New York: Viking, 1997.

Wright, Mary Clabaugh. *The Last Stand of Chinese Conservatism: The T'ung-chih Restoration, 1862–1874*. Stanford, CA: Stanford University Press, 1962.

Wu, Hung. *Remaking Beijing: Tiananmen Square and the Creation of a Political Space*. Chicago: University of Chicago Press, 2005.

Wu, Jinglian. *Understanding and Interpreting Chinese Economic Reform*. Oakland, CA: Texere, 2005.

Wu, Yung. *The Flight of an Empress*. Trans. Ida Pruitt. 1936. Westport, CT: Hyperion, 1973.

"Xi Pledges 'Great Renewal of Chinese Nation,'" *Xinhua*, November 29, 2012.

Xi Jinping. "Full Text of Xi's Address to the Media." *China Daily*, November 16, 2012.

Xiong, Yuezhi. "Difficulties in Comprehension and Differences in Expression: Interpreting American Democracy in the Late Qing." *Late Imperial China* 23 (2002): 1–27.

———. *Feng Guifen pingzhuan*. Nanjing: Nanjing daxue chubanshe, 2004.

Xu Che. *Yige zhenshi de Cixi taihou*. Beijing: Tuanjie chubanshe, 2007.

Yahuda, Michael. "Deng Xiaoping: The Statesman." *China Quarterly* 135, special issue: "Deng Xiaoping: An Assessment" (1993): 551–72.

Yang, Benjamin. *Deng: A Political Biography*. Armonk, NY: M. E. Sharpe, 1998.

Yang, Dali. *Remaking the Chinese Leviathan: Market Transition and the Politics of Governance in China*. Stanford, CA: Stanford University Press, 2006.

Yang, Jianli, and John Downer, eds. *Wei Jingsheng: The Man and His Ideas*. Pleasant Hill, CA: Foundation for China in the 21st Century, 1995.

Yang Jisheng. *Tombstone: The Great Chinese Famine, 1958–1962*. Ed. Edward Friedman,

Guo Jian, and Stacy Mosher. Trans. Stacy Mosher and Guo Jian. New York: Farrar, Straus and Giroux, 2012.

Yang Tianshi. *Wan Qing shishi* [Historical Events of the Late Qing]. Beijing: Zhongguo renmin daxue chubanshe, 2007.

Yu Guangyuan. *Deng Xiaoping Shakes the World: An Eyewitness Account of China's Party Work Conference and the Third Plenum (November–December 1978)*. Ed. Steven I. Levine and Ezra F. Vogel. Norwalk, CT: EastBridge, 2004.

Zhao, Suisheng. *China and Democracy: The Prospect for a Democratic China*. New York: Routledge, 2000.

———. "A State-Led Nationalism: The Patriotic Education Campaigns in Post-Tiananmen China." *Communist and Post-Communist Studies* 31, no. 3 (1998): 287–302.

Zhao, Ziyang. *Prisoner of the State: The Secret Journal of Zhao Ziyang*. Trans. and ed. Pu Bao, Renee Chiang, and Adi Ignatius. New York: Simon and Schuster, 2009.

Zheng, Xiaowei. "Loyalty, Anxiety, and Opportunism: Local Elite Activism During the Taiping Rebellion in Eastern Zhejiang, 1851–1864." *Late Imperial China* 30, no. 2 (2009): 39–83.

Zheng, Yi. *Scarlet Memorial: Tales of Cannibalism in Modern China*. Trans. and ed. T. P. Sym. Boulder, CO: Westview Press, 1996.

Zhu, Rongji. *Zhu Rongji jianghua shilu* [A True Record of Zhu Rongji's Speeches]. Beijing: Renmin chubanshe, 2011.

———. *Zhu Rongji Meets the Press*. Hong Kong: Oxford University Press, 2011.

Zhu, Wenhua. *Chen Duxiu zhuan* [A Biography of Chen Duxiu]. Beijing: Hongqi chubanshe, 2009.

Zhu Hong, *Chen Duxiu: Zuihou suiyue* [Chen Duxiu's Last Years of Arduous Struggle]. Shanghai: Dongfang Chuban Zhongxing, 2011.

Zong, Hairen, ed. "Zhu Rongji in 1999." *Chinese Law and Government* 35, no. 2 (2002): 3–91.

Notes

Chapter 1: Introduction

1. Liang, *Liang Qichao quanji*, 5609; see also Wang, *Fin-de-siècle Splendor*, 307–12, Wei, "Xinzhongguo weilai de lishi guannian jiqi zhengzhi lunli."
2. Liang, Ibid.
3. Lin, *Between Tears and Laughter*, 5.
4. Ibid., 5.
5. Han, *Han Feizi jijie*, 428.
6. Cohen, *Speaking of History*, 491–7.
7. Wang, *Never Forget National Humiliation*, 5. See also Gries, *China's Nationalism*, 43–5.
8. Tsu, *Failure, Nationalism and Literature*, 21.
9. Yan, quoted in Schwartz, *In Search of Wealth and Power*, 47.
10. Cited in Bergère, *Sun Yat-sen*, 354.

Chapter 2: Humiliation

1. Lovell, *The Opium War*, 240.
2. A brief English-language sketch of Wei Yuan can be found in Hummel's *Eminent Chinese of the Ch'ing Period* and a useful Chinese-language biography in Chen and Liu, *Wei Yuan pingzhuan*.
3. Rowe, *China's Last Empire*, 62.
4. On Qing Dynasty population estimates, see ibid., 91. On Qing period economy in the global context, Pomeranz, *The Great Divergence*; Rosental and Wong, *Before and Beyond Divergence*; and Maddison, *Chinese Economic Performance in the Long Run*.
5. For more on the Qing's military expansion, see Perdue, *China Marches West* and Mosca, *From Frontier Policy to Foreign Policy*.
6. Qianlong quoted in Cheng, Lestz, and Spence, eds., *The Search for Modern China*, 105. Hevia's *Cherishing Men from Afar* describes the Macartney visit from the Chinese perspective. The best treatment of the Emperor himself is Elliott, *Emperor Qianlong*.
7. Macartney, *An Embassy to China*, 165.
8. Rowe, *China's Last Empire*, 149–58.
9. Macartney, *An Embassy to China*, 143. See ter Harr, *The White Lotus Teachings in Chinese Religious History*.
10. For more on Liu Fenglu and the so-called Gongyang School of Confucianism, see

Elman, *Classicism, Politics, and Kinship*. On Wei's ties to Liu, see Chen and Liu, *Wei Yuan*, 58–70.

11. Chen and Liu, *Wei Yuan*, 19.
12. For an annotated translation of excerpts from *Statecraft*, see Dunstan, *Conflicting Counsels to Confuse the Age*. Also see Wakeman, "The Huang-chao ching-shih wen-pien"; Janku, "Preparing the Ground for Revolutionary Discourse."
13. Hsiao, *A History of Chinese Political Thought*, 464. For a careful historical introduction to Confucius and his teachings, *The Analects*, see Chin, *Confucius*. Key texts in the Confucian tradition are translated with commentary in De Bary, *Sources of Chinese Tradition*, and placed in sweeping historical context in Bol, *Neo-Confucianism in History*.
14. Sima Qian, *Selections from Records of the Historian*, 69–70.
15. Han, *Han Feizi jijie*, 428.
16. Han, *Han Fan Tzu: Basic Writings*, 112. On the ancient argument between Confucians and Legalists, see Schwartz, *The World of Thought in Ancient China*, and Graham, *Disputers of the Tao*. See also, Goldin, "Persistent Misconceptions About Chinese 'Legalism.'"
17. Quoted in Kuhn, *Origins of the Modern Chinese State*, 49.
18. De Bary, *Sources of Chinese Tradition*, 190.
19. Chen and Liu, *Wei Yuan*, 29.
20. British diplomat-scholar Edward Harper Parker translated Wei's narrative as *A Chinese Account of the Opium War*. For a critical perspective on Wei's bias in his telling of the story, see Polachek, *The Inner Opium War*.
21. Rowe takes a fresh look at the fiscal crisis faced by the Qing in "Money, Economy and Polity in the Daoguang-Era Paper Currency Debates." Waley's *The Opium War Through Chinese Eyes* draws on Lin Zexu's own diary to tell his version of the story. The British side of the Opium War is finely told in Fay, *The Opium War*.
22. Wei, *Opium War*, 6–7.
23. Ibid., 6.
24. Fay, *The Opium War*, 194.
25. *Chinese Repository* 9, 10 (1841): 508.
26. Details on Anstruther's captivity are drawn from *Chinese Repository* 9, 6 (1840): 422–23; 10, 4 (1841): 191–204; 10, 9 (1841): 506–10. Wei's "Briefing on England" is included in *Haiguo tuzhi*, 348–49.
27. Wei, *Opium War*, 21.
28. MacPherson, *Two Years in China*, 4.
29. Wei, *Opium War*, 26.
30. Wei's poem cited in Chen and Liu, *Wei Yuan*, 30. Lei Bo of Peking University kindly assisted with the translation.
31. Quoted in Teng and Fairbank, eds., *China's Response to the West*, 28.
32. Wei, *Opium War*, 66.
33. Ibid.
34. Quoted in Fay, *Opium War*, 361.
35. A fascinating firsthand account from the perspective of the Chinese negotiating team is translated by Teng in *Chang Hsi and the Treaty of Nanking*. Cassel has recently shown how Chinese did their best to turn extraterritoriality in their own favor in *Grounds of Judgment*.
36. Wei, *Opium War*, 80.
37. Ibid., 81.
38. Bickers tells the story with verve in *The Scramble for China*.
39. Wei, quoted in De Bary et al., *Sources of Chinese Tradition*, 208.
40. Ibid., 208.
41. Barnett, "Wei Yuan and Westerners."

42. Wei's estimates are cited in Mitchell, "The Limits of Reformism," 201.
43. Wei, quoted in Leonard, *Wei Yuan*, 102.
44. Leonard, *Wei Yuan*, 2.
45. Wei, quoted in ibid., 164.
46. Leonard, *Wei Yuan*, 197.
47. Wei, quoted in *China's Response*, 34.
48. Ibid.
49. Wei, quoted in De Bary, *Sources of Chinese Tradition*, 211.
50. Quoted in Xiong, "Interpreting American Democracy in the Late Qing," 9.
51. Ibid.
52. Kuhn, *Origins of the Modern Chinese State*, 47.

Chapter 3: Self-Strengthening

1. Macartney, *An Embassy to China*, ix.
2. Ibid., 39.
3. Hurd, *The Arrow War*.
4. Hevia, *English Lessons*, 48, 107.
5. Ibid., 89–90.
6. Wolseley, *Narrative of the War with China*, 226–27.
7. Ibid., 278.
8. Ibid., 280.
9. Quoted in Spence, *To Change China*, 74–75.
10. Wolseley, *Narrative of the War with China*, 280.
11. Ibid., 281.
12. Ibid.
13. Boulger, *Life of Gordon*, 46.
14. Quoted in Teng and Fairbank, *China's Response to the West*, 76.
15. The fullest treatment of Feng Guifen in English is Montgomery, "The 'Remonstrance' of Feng Kuei-fen." For a detailed biography in Chinese, see Xiong, *Feng Guifen pingzhuan*.
16. Xiong, *Feng Guifen*, 286.
17. See Miyazaki, *China's Examination Hell*, and Elman, *A Cultural History of Civil Examinations*.
18. Quoted in Polachek, *Inner Opium War*, 193.
19. Feng, *Jiaobinlu kangyi*, 49.
20. See Chu and Liu, *Li Hung-chang*, 6.
21. Xiong, *Feng Guifen*, 71.
22. For an ancient use of the phrase, see Guan, *Guanzi*, 384.
23. For more on the Taipings, see Spence, *God's Chinese Son*, and Platt, *Autumn in the Heavenly Kingdom*.
24. Based on his son's manuscript diary, quoted in Xiong, *Feng Guifen*, 102–3. For more on Wang Tao, see Cohen, *Between Tradition and Modernity*. On Shanghai's early history as a treaty port, see Bergère, *Shanghai*.
25. Xiong, *Feng Guifen*, 99.
26. Feng, *Jiaobinlu kangyi*, 48–49.
27. Ibid., 49.
28. Ibid., 51.
29. Quoted in Fairbank, *Trade and Diplomacy on the China Coast*, 19.
30. Feng, *Jiaobinlu kangyi*, 48.
31. See Zheng, "Loyalty, Anxiety, and Opportunism," 63–64.
32. Feng, *Jiaobinlu kangyi*, 55.
33. Ibid., 49.

34. Ibid.
35. Feng, quoted in Montgomery, "'Remonstrance,'" 108.
36. Ibid., 86.
37. Feng, quoted in Min, *National Polity and Local Power*, 234–35. The original manuscript is apparently no longer held in the Shanghai Library, but a transcription is preserved in Chen, "*Guanyu Jiaobinlu kangyi.*"
38. Feng, quoted in Montgomery, "'Remonstrance,'" 99.
39. Ibid., 68.
40. Ibid., 70.
41. Feng, *Jiaobinlu kangyi*, 33.
42. Ibid., 75.
43. Ibid.
44. Ibid., 57.
45. For more on Zeng, see Porter, *Tseng Kuo-fan's Private Bureaucracy.*
46. Discussed in Spector, *Li Hung-chang and the Huai Army.*
47. Loti, *The Last Days of Pekin*, 164.
48. See Hummel, *Eminent Chinese of the Ch'ing Period*, 1:242.
49. Xiong, *Feng Guifen*, 186.
50. Zeng quoted in Teng and Fairbank, *China's Response*, 62.
51. On Zeng's offer to publish Feng, see *China's Response*, 50.
52. See Chu and Liu, *Li Hung-chang and Early Modernization*, 29–30, and Wright, *The Last Stand of Chinese Conservatism*, 76.
53. Liu, *Li Hung-chang and Early Modernization*, 23.
54. Li Hongzhang (Feb. 1863), in *China's Response*, 69.
55. Li Hongzhang (June 1863), in *China's Response*, 72.
56. Quoted in Liu, *Li Hung-chang and Early Modernization*, 7. On the General Bureau, see Hsu, *China's Entrance into the Family of Nations.*
57. Feng, *Jiaobinlu kangyi*, 57.
58. Ibid., 56.
59. Quoted in Teng and Fairbank, *China's Response*, 75.
60. Xiong, *Feng Guifen*, 143–44.
61. Wo-jen's Objection to Western Learning, in *China's Response*, 76.
62. Zongli Yamen's Rebuttal, in *China's Response*, 77.
63. See Montgomery, "'Remonstrance,'" 18.
64. Discussed in Kuhn, *Origins of the Modern Chinese State*, 58–73.

Chapter 4: Western Methods, Chinese Core

1. Headland, *Court Life in China*, 70.
2. Seagrave, *Dragon Lady*, 12. For more on Backhouse, see Trevor-Roper, *Hermit of Peking.*
3. Backhouse, *Décadence Mandchoue*, 61.
4. Ibid., 198.
5. Ibid., 71.
6. Cixi's life has long attracted writers of historical fiction, from Pearl Buck's *Imperial Woman* to Anchee Min's *Empress Orchid* and *The Last Empress*. Unfortunately, Cixi still awaits a scholarly biographical treatment in English. Xu, *Yige zhenshi de Cixi taihou* is a useful Chinese-language biography.
7. Yang, *Wan Qing shishi*, 53.
8. Backhouse, *Décadence Mandchoue*, 28.
9. Rhoads, *Manchus and Han*, 79. Also see Kwong, "Imperial Authority in Crisis."
10. Zeng, quoted in Kwong, *A Mosaic of the Hundred Days*, 36–37.
11. Wenxiang (1874), quoted in *China's Response*, 90.

12. Xue Fucheng (1878), quoted in *China's Response*, 117.
13. Li's efforts are described in Chu and Liu, *Li Hung-chang and China's Early Modernization*, and Feuerwerker, *China's Early Industrialization*.
14. Li Hongzhang (1872), quoted in *China's Response*, 109.
15. See Mokros, "Reconstructing the Imperial Retreat." On the Qing's fiscal problems, see Feuerwerker, *The Chinese Economy, 1870–1949*.
16. See Liu, "The Ch'ing Restoration."
17. Cixi (1878), quoted in Teng and Fairbank, *China's Response*, 105.
18. Li Hongzhang (1882), quoted in Chu and Liu, *Li Hung-chang and Early Modernization*, 10. On Li's reputation for corruption, see 273–75.
19. Wang Tao (1880), quoted in Cohen, *Between Tradition and Modernity*, 232.
20. On the rise of the Purists, see Rankin, " 'Public Opinion' and Political Power," and Eastman, "Ch'ing-i and Chinese Policy Formation."
21. Quoted in Eastman, *Throne and Mandarins*, 105.
22. See Elman, "Naval Warfare and the Refraction of China's Self-Strengthening Reforms," 298.
23. Li Hongzhang (1885), quoted in Teng and Fairbank, *China's Response*, 119–20.
24. Itō Hirobumi, quoted in Paine, *Sino-Japanese War*, 82.
25. Itō discusses the impact of his trips abroad, starting with his European tour in 1862, in Itō, *A Maker of New Japan*.
26. Sun Yat-sen (1893), quoted in Cheng, Lestz, and Spence, *The Search for Modern China*, 169–71.
27. See Bergère, *Sun Yat-sen*, 39–41.
28. On the remodeling of the stone boat, see Hayter-Menzies, *The Empress and Mrs. Conger*, 222.
29. Backhouse, *Décadence Mandchoue*, 59.
30. The classic book on the tributary system is Fairbank, *Chinese World Order*, although new Qing historians such as Pamela Crossley, James Millward, and Peter Perdue have shown that the Manchus created their own distinctive approach to foreign relations.
31. The best military history of the war is Paine, *Sino-Japanese War*. Also see Fung, "Testing the Self-Strengthening."
32. Li Hongzhang, quoted in Tan, *The Boxer Catastrophe*, 15.
33. Li Hongzhang, quoted in Teng and Fairbank, *China's Response*, 126.
34. See Paine, *Sino-Japanese War*, 262.
35. Ibid., 267.
36. See Makito, *The Sino-Japanese War*.
37. Jansen discusses the influence of Chinese statecraft writings in Japan in *The Making of Modern Japan*, 270–71, 318.
38. Ibid., 355.
39. See Rhoads, *Stepping Forth into the World*.
40. See Itō, *Commentaries on the Constitution of the Empire of Japan*.
41. Jansen, *Modern Japan*, 377.
42. Ibid., 426.
43. On Li's world tour, see Dong, *Li Hongzhang de waijiao shengya*.
44. Spence, *The Search for Modern China*, 225.
45. Nathan, *Chinese Democracy*, 138–39.
46. For an overview of late nineteenth-century intellectual trends, see Chang, "Intellectual Change and the Reform Movement." Also see Eastman, "Political Reformism in China."
47. On the founding of the Imperial University, see Weston, *The Power of Position*.
48. Missionary Samuel Woodbridge translated Zhang Zhidong's essay in Chang, *China's Only Hope*.

49. Quoted in Wakeman, *History and Will*, 143.
50. Itō's audience with Guangxu is excerpted in Teng and Fairbank, *China's Response*, 179–80.
51. Seagrave, *Dragon Lady*, 11.
52. For documentary evidence of Kang Youwei's plot to assassinate Cixi, see Yang, *Wan Qing shishi*, 59.
53. Quoted in Der Ling, *Two Years in the Forbidden City*, 291.
54. See Liang, *Wuxu zhengbian ji*, 87–88.
55. Quoted in Chung, "The Image of the Empress Dowager Tz'u-hsi," 104.
56. Martin, *The Siege in Peking*, 51.
57. *People's Daily*, Sept. 22, 1989, cited in Fewsmith, *China Since Tiananmen*, 37.
58. Der Ling, *Two Years*, 225.
59. Ibid., 260.
60. Ibid., 253, 282.
61. Wu, *Flight of an Empress*, 141.
62. Warner, *Dragon Empress*, 121.
63. Der Ling, *Two Years*, 68.
64. Quoted in Hart, *The I.G. in Peking*, 2:1230. For more on the Boxers, see Cohen, *History in Three Keys*, Esherick, *The Origins of the Boxer Uprising*, and Bickers and Tiedemann, *The Boxers, China, and the World*.
65. Der Ling, *Two Years*, 181.
66. Ibid., 184.
67. Reynolds, *China*, 201–2.
68. Ibid., 203. Also see Horowitz, "Breaking the Bonds of Precedent," and Thompson, "The Lessons of Defeat."
69. Yang, *Wan Qing shishi*, 61.
70. Der Ling, *Two Years*, 183–84.
71. Headland, *Court Life in China*, 193–94.
72. Conger, *Letters from China*, 41.
73. Ibid., 220. Also see Hayter-Menzies, *The Empress and Mrs. Conger*.
74. Headland, *Court Life in China*, 102.
75. Ibid., 102–3.
76. Carl, *With the Empress Dowager of China*.
77. Der Ling, *Two Years*, 356.
78. See Reynolds, *China*.
79. Quoted in Harrison, *The Man Awakened from Dreams*, 88.
80. Quoted in Horowitz, "Breaking the Bonds of Precedent," 791.
81. Sun, "Chinese Constitutional Missions," 266.
82. Quoted in Rhoads, *Manchus and Han*, 17.
83. Rhoads, *Manchus and Han*.
84. Bland and Backhouse, *China Under the Empress Dowager*, 471–75.
85. McAleavy, *A Dream of Tartary*, 186.
86. Yan Fu, quoted in Teng and Fairbank, *China's Response*, 150–51.

Chapter 5: New Citizen

1. Liang, *Liang Qichao wenxuan*, 41.
2. See Liang, "My Autobiographical Account at Thirty," 6. Liang's life and thought have received superb treatment in English in Levenson, *Liang Ch'i-ch'ao and the Mind of Modern China*; Huang, *Liang Ch'i-ch'ao and Modern Chinese Liberalism*; Chang, *Liang Ch'i-ch'ao and Intellectual Transition in China*; Tang, *Global Space and the Nationalist Discourse of Modernity*. Nathan explores Liang's ideas in depth

in *Chinese Democracy*, and Mishra puts him in a pan-Asian context in *From the Ruins of Empire*. A notable recent biography in Chinese is Jie, *Liang Qichao zhuan*.

3. See Miles, *The Sea of Learning*.
4. The best treatment of Liang's family life is Fairbank, *Liang and Lin*.
5. Xu Jiyu (1848), in Teng and Fairbank, *China's Response*, 42.
6. Liang, quoted in Levenson, *Liang Ch'i-ch'ao*, 17.
7. For more on Kang's ideas, see Hsiao, *A Modern China and a New World*. His story is also elegantly told in Spence, *The Gate of Heavenly Peace*.
8. On Liang's links to Richard, see Chang, *Liang Ch'i-ch'ao*, 71.
9. Liang, *Intellectual Trends in the Ch'ing Period*, 113.
10. Liang, *Wuxu zhengbian ji*, 3.
11. See Wang, *Never Forget National Humiliation*, 151.
12. Liang, *Intellectual Trends*, 98.
13. See Ding and Zhao, *Liang Qichao nianpu changbian*, 25.
14. Liang, *Intellectual Trends*, 102.
15. See Vittinghoff, "Unity vs. Uniformity," 110.
16. On the significance of these new societies and publications, and Liang's role, see Chang, "Intellectual Change and the Reform Movement," 292–95. Also see Judge, *Print and Politics*.
17. Chang, *Liang Ch'i-ch'ao*, 124.
18. Liang, "Autobiographical Account at Thirty," 12.
19. Liang (1897), *Liang Qichao quanji*, 1:122.
20. Liang, *Liang Qichao zishu*, 31.
21. Liang, *Liang Qichao quanji*, 1:122.
22. Liang, quoted in Tang, *Global Space*, 17.
23. Liang, *Intellectual Trends*, 101. On the atmosphere in Hunan, see Platt, *Provincial Patriots*, 78–86.
24. Schwartz, *In Search of Wealth and Power*, 33. Also see Huang, *The Meaning of Freedom*.
25. Yan, quoted in Schwartz, *In Search of Wealth and Power*, 31.
26. Ibid., 33.
27. Ibid., 44
28. Ibid., 49.
29. Yan, quoted in Lin, *The Crisis of Chinese Consciousness*, 58.
30. Yan, quoted in Schwartz, *In Search of Wealth and Power*, 45–46.
31. Kang, quoted in Wakeman, *History and Will*, 141.
32. Kang, quoted in Chang, "Intellectual Change," 325.
33. See Karl and Zarrow, *Rethinking the 1898 Reform Period*; Kwong, *A Mosaic of the Hundred Days*.
34. On Itō's role, see Levenson, *Liang Ch'i-ch'ao*, 55.
35. Timothy Richard claimed to have met with Liang on September 23 and advised him to seek the protection of the Japanese legation. Richard, *Forty-five Years in China*, 266.
36. Levenson, *Liang Ch'i-ch'ao*, 56.
37. See Huang, *Liang Ch'i-ch'ao*, 41, and Tang, *Global Space*, 141, 160; also see Fogel, *The Role of Japan in Liang Qichao's Introduction of Modern Western Civilization to China*.
38. Liang, quoted in Tang, *Global Space*, 14.
39. Liang (1899), quoted in Levenson, *Liang Ch'i-ch'ao*, 64.
40. Liang (1898), quoted in Huang, *Liang Ch'i-ch'ao*, 46.
41. Liang (1901), *Liang Qichao zishu*, 37.
42. Liang (1902), *Liang Qichao quanji*, 2:663.

43. Liang (1902), ibid., 2:674.
44. Liang, quoted in Levenson, *Liang Ch'i-ch'ao*, 117.
45. Liang, quoted in Huang, *Liang Ch'i-ch'ao*, 31.
46. See Nathan, *Chinese Democracy*, 55.
47. Yan, quoted in Tang, *Global Space*, 48.
48. See Chang, *Liang Ch'i-ch'ao*, 145.
49. Liang (1902), *Liang Qichao quanji*, 2:759.
50. Liang (1902), ibid., 2:688.
51. Liang, quoted in Wakeman, *History and Will*, 151.
52. Liang, *Intellectual Trends*, 105.
53. Liang's travels are chronicled in Ding, *Liang Qichao nianpu changbian*, 174–91. Excerpts from his travelogue are translated in Arkush and Lee, *Land Without Ghosts*, 81–96.
54. Liang, *Liang Qichao quanji*, 2:1187.
55. See the discussion in Fitzgerald, *Awakening China*, 118. San Francisco's Chinatown was a lightning rod for anti-Chinese sentiment—mobs looted in 1877, setting the stage for the Chinese Exclusion Act of 1882. On Liang's obliviousness to anti-Chinese racism in the United States, see Wong, "Liang Qichao and the Chinese of America." Liang was also apparently unaware of the civil rights litigiousness of Chinese Americans; see McClain, *In Search of Equality*.
56. Liang, quoted in Arkush and Lee, *Land Without Ghosts*, 92–93.
57. Liang (1904), quoted in De Bary, *Sources of Chinese Tradition*, 300.
58. Liang, quoted in Arkush and Lee, *Land Without Ghosts*, 93.
59. Liang, *Intellectual Trends*, 103.
60. Liang, quoted in Huang, *Liang Ch'i-ch'ao*, 100.
61. Liang, quoted in Judge, "Public Opinion and the New Politics of Contestation," 70.
62. Huang, *Liang Ch'i-ch'ao*, 121.
63. Liang (1913), *Liang Qichao zishu*, 69.
64. Liang (1914), ibid., 76.
65. See Lai, *Liang Qichao de jingji mianxiang*.
66. Levenson, *Liang Ch'i-ch'ao*, 178.
67. On Liang's role in opposing the Yuan Shikai autocracy, see Ch'en, *Yuan Shih-k'ai*, 208–9, 220–34.
68. Liang, *Intellectual Trends*, 106.
69. Liang, quoted in Tang, *Global Space*, 189.
70. On Liang's pro-war position and his support for accepting loans from Japan, see Huang, *Liang Ch'i-ch'ao*, 135–39.
71. The best account of the East Asian implications of Versailles is Manela, *The Wilsonian Moment*.
72. Liang, quoted in Levenson, *Liang Ch'i-ch'ao*, 189.
73. Tang, *Global Space*, 175. On Liang's telegrams, see Chow, *The May Fourth Movement*, 90–94.
74. Tang, *Global Space*, 178.
75. Liang, quoted in Tang, *Global Space*, 182.
76. Liang, quoted in Levenson, *Liang Ch'i-ch'ao*, 200.
77. Yan, quoted in Schwartz, *In Search of Wealth and Power*, 235.
78. Tang, *Global Space*, 186.
79. Liang, quoted in Fairbank, *Liang and Lin*, 32.
80. Liang, quoted in Tang, *Global Space*, 191.
81. Liang, quoted in ibid., 193.
82. Liang, quoted in Huang, *Liang Ch'i-ch'ao*, 149.
83. See the discussion in Tang, *Global Space*, 196–98.
84. Levenson, *Liang Ch'i-ch'ao*, 191.

85. Fairbank, *Liang and Lin*, 37–38.
86. Liang, *Intellectual Trends*, 106.
87. Ibid.
88. Huang, *Liang Ch'i-ch'ao*, 7.
89. Snow, *Red Star over China*, 137.

Chapter 6: A Sheet of Loose Sand

1. Bergère, *Sun Yat-sen*, 25.
2. Musgrove, "Monumentality in Nanjing's Sun Yat-sen Memorial Park," 5.
3. Musgrove, "Building a Dream," 139.
4. Sun Yat-sen quoted in Schiffrin, *Sun Yat-sen*, 57.
5. See Jansen, *The Japanese and Sun Yat-sen*.
6. Bergère, *Sun Yat-sen*, 76.
7. Wilbur, *Sun Yat-sen*, 287.
8. Strand, *An Unfinished Republic*, 281.
9. Sharman, *Sun Yat-sen*, 322.
10. Strand, *An Unfinished Republic*, 241.
11. Sun, quoted in Sharman, *Sun Yat-sen*, 4.
12. Sun, quoted in Strand, *An Unfinished Republic*, 238.
13. Ponce, quoted in Jansen, *The Japanese and Sun Yat-sen*, 70.
14. Cantlie and Jones, *Sun Yat Sen and the Awakening of China*, 31.
15. Sun, quoted in Gordon, *Sun Yatsen*, 2.
16. Bergère, *Sun Yat-sen*, 36–40.
17. Wilbur, *Sun Yat-sen*, 13.
18. Sun, quoted in Cantlie and Jones, *Sun Yat Sen and the Awakening of China*, 41.
19. Cantlie and Jones, *Sun Yat Sen and the Awakening of China*, 51.
20. Sun, quoted in Gasster, "Reform and Revolution in China's Political Modernization," 79.
21. Quoted in Sharman, *Sun Yat-sen*, 127–28.
22. Sharman, *Sun Yat-sen*, 128.
23. Calhoun, quoted in Horner, *Rising China and Its Postmodern Fate*, 82.
24. Quoted in Schiffrin, *Sun Yat-sen*, 216.
25. Spence, *The Search for Modern China*, 277.
26. Musgrove, "Monumentality," 7–8.
27. Quoted in Schiffrin, *Sun Yat-sen*, 42–43.
28. Sun, quoted in Bergère, *Sun Yat-sen*, 361.
29. Quoted in Strand, *An Unfinished Republic*, 265; see 262–65 for more on Sun's return to Confucianism.
30. Quoted in Strand, *An Unfinished Republic*, 268.
31. Sun Yat-sen, *The Three Principles of the People*, vii. Translations are adapted from Frank Price with modifications made in accordance with the Chinese original, Sun Zhongshan, *Sanmin Zhuyi*.
32. Sun, *Three Principles*, 7.
33. Ibid., 24.
34. Bergère, *Sun Yat-sen*, 357.
35. Sun, *Three Principles*, 14.
36. Ibid., 31.
37. Ibid., 6.
38. Ibid., 14.
39. Ibid., 29.
40. Westad, *Restless Empire*, 60.
41. Sun, *Three Principles*, 9–10.

42. Wang Dong, *China's Unequal Treaties*, 64.
43. Sun, *Three Principles*, 25.
44. Ibid., 9–10.
45. Wang, *China's Unequal Treaties*, 65.
46. Sun, *Three Principles*, 49.
47. Ibid., 53.
48. Ibid., 60.
49. Ibid., 59.
50. Strand, *An Unfinished Republic*, 256.
51. Sun, quoted in Bergère, *Sun Yat-sen*, 372.
52. Strand, *An Unfinished Republic*, 272.
53. Sun, *Three Principles*, 92.
54. Sun, quoted in Strand, *An Unfinished Republic*, 263.
55. Sun, *Three Principles*, 61.
56. Ibid., 62.
57. Ibid., 87.
58. Ibid., 113.
59. Bergère, *Sun Yat-sen*, 382.
60. Sun, *Three Principles*, 121.
61. Ibid., 119.
62. Ibid., 128–29.
63. See De Bary, *Sources of Chinese Tradition*, Sun's 1918 "A Program for National Reconstruction," 779–783.
64. Ibid., 328–30.
65. Musgrove, "Building a Dream," 142.
66. Sun, *Three Principles*, 96.
67. Ibid.
68. Ibid., 97.
69. Martin, *Strange Vigour*, 210.
70. Schiffrin, *Sun Yat-sen*, 250.
71. Sun, quoted in, Pantsov and Levine, *Mao*, 128.
72. See Brandt, *Stalin's Failure in China*.
73. Iriye, *After Imperialism*, 11.
74. Sun, quoted in Schiffrin, *Sun Yat-sen*, 244.
75. Bergère, *Sun Yat-sen*, 309–10.
76. Westad, *Restless Empire*, 158.
77. Quoted in Schwartz, *Chinese Communism and the Rise of Mao*, 40.
78. Spence, *The Search for Modern China*, 335.
79. Spence, *Mao Zedong*, 63.
80. Quoted in Westad, *Restless Empire*, 159.
81. Pantsov and Levine, *Mao*, 126.
82. See Brandt, *Stalin's Failure in China*.
83. Sun, quoted in Bergère, *Sun Yat-sen*, 325.
84. Wilbur, *Sun Yat-sen*, 281.
85. Schiffrin, *Sun Yat-sen*, 269.
86. Bergère, *Sun Yat-sen*, 41.

Chapter 7: New Youth

1. Feigon, *Chen Duxiu*, 226.
2. Zhu, *Chen Duxiu*, 286.
3. Cadot-Wood, "Striving Toward a Lovable Nation," 134.

4. Zhu, *Chen Duxiu*, 287.
5. Kagan, "Chen Tu-hsiu's Unfinished Autobiography," 302.
6. Zhu, *Chen Duxiu*, 1–3.
7. Kagan, "Chen Tu-hsiu's Unfinished Autobiography," 302; Zhu, *Chen Duxiu*, 4–5.
8. Ibid., 305.
9. Zhu, *Chen Duxiu*, 6.
10. Chen, quoted in Zhu, *Chen Duxiu*, 13.
11. Feigon, *Chen Duxiu*, 32.
12. Kagan, "Chen Tu-hsiu's Unfinished Autobiography," 313.
13. Chen, quoted in Wang, "Chen Duxiu," 134.
14. Chen, quoted in Kagan, "Chen Tu-hsiu's Unfinished Autobiography," 314.
15. Kagan, "Chen Tu-hsiu's Unfinished Autobiography," 297.
16. Chen, quoted in Wang, "Chen Duxiu," 134.
17. Ibid.
18. Chen, quoted in Cadot-Wood, "Striving Toward a Lovable Nation," 134.
19. Feigon, *Chen Duxiu*, 37–39.
20. Chen, quoted in Lin, *The Crisis of Chinese Consciousness*, 68.
21. Feigon, *Chen Duxiu*, 66.
22. Quoted in Feigon, *Chen Duxiu*, 41.
23. Chen, quoted in ibid., 42.
24. Ibid., 47.
25. Ibid., 44.
26. Ibid.
27. Chen, quoted in Cadot-Wood, "Striving Toward a Lovable Nation," 36.
28. Ibid., 37.
29. Ibid., 63–65.
30. Leys, *The Burning Forest*, 219. Also, Lu, *Selected Works*, 2:327.
31. Chen, quoted in Lin, *The Crisis of Chinese Consciousness*, 59.
32. Li Dazhao, quoted in Schwartz, *Chinese Communism and the Rise of Mao*, 12.
33. Chen, in Teng and Fairbank, *China's Response to the West*, 241.
34. Feigon, *Chen Duxiu*, 128.
35. Chen, quoted in Lin, *Crisis of Chinese Consciousness*, 59.
36. Lu, *The Real Story of Ah-Q and Other Tales of China: The Complete Fiction of Lu Xun*, translated by Lovell, preface to "Outcry," 17.
37. Hsia, *The Gate of Darkness*, 148.
38. Lu, *The Real Story of Ah-Q and Other Tales of China*, translated by Julia Lovell, preface to "Outcry," 19.
39. Ibid.
40. Ibid., 31.
41. Ibid.
42. Cadot-Wood, "Striving Toward a Lovable Nation," 95.
43. Feigon, *Chen Duxiu*, 105.
44. Ibid., 104.
45. Chen, quoted in Teng and Fairbank, *China's Response to the West*, 242.
46. Fu Sinian, quoted in Schwarcz, *The Chinese Enlightenment*, 288.
47. Chao, "Chen Duxiu's Early Years," 181.
48. Chen, quoted in De Bary, *Sources of Chinese Tradition*, 353.
49. Chen, quoted in Teng and Fairbank, *China's Response to the West*, 242.
50. Ibid., 240.
51. Ibid.
52. Ibid., 241–46.
53. Meisner, "Cultural Iconoclasm, Nationalism, and Internationalism," 15.

54. Chen, cited in Barmé and Jaivin, *New Ghosts, Old Dreams*, 199.
55. Wang, "Chen Duxiu," 136.
56. Chen, quoted in Schwarcz, *The Chinese Enlightenment*, 61.
57. Chow, *The May Fourth Movement*, 70.
58. Ibid., 69.
59. Chen, quoted in Wang, "Chen Duxiu," 14.
60. Vernoff and Seybolt, *Through Chinese Eyes*, 70–72.
61. Zhu, *Chen Duxiu*, 4.
62. Ba Jin, *Random Thoughts*, 95–96.
63. Schwartz, *Chinese Communism*, 9.
64. Gentzler, *Changing China*, 168.
65. Ibid.
66. Quoted in Grieder, *Hu Shih and the Chinese Renaissance*, 66.
67. Zhu, *Chen Duxiu*, 37–42; see also two websites: http://news.hinhuanet.com/theory/201-03/05/c_121151787.htm and http://www.360doc/content/12/0626/15/2207798_220544882.shtml.
68. Cadot-Wood, "Striving Toward a Lovable Nation," 118.
69. Chen, quoted in Westad, *Restless Empire*, 152.
70. Meisner, *Li Ta-chao and the Origins of Chinese Marxism*, 97.
71. Mao, "Poor Wilson," in Mao, *Mao's Road to Power*, 1:338.
72. Meisner, *Li Ta-chao*, 98.
73. Rice, *Mao's Way*, 20.
74. Nathan, *Chinese Democracy*, 8.
75. Chow, *May Fourth*, 106–7.
76. Rice, *Mao's Way*, 20.
77. Schwarcz, *The Chinese Enlightenment*, 19.
78. Chen, quoted in Cadot-Wood, "Striving Toward a Lovable Nation," 108.
79. Lin, *The Crisis of Chinese Consciousness*, 60.
80. Cadot-Wood, "Striving Toward a Lovable Nation," 110, 147.
81. Chow, *May Fourth*, 135.
82. Chao, "Chen Duxiu's Early Years," 315.
83. Ibid., 316.
84. Ibid.
85. Mao, "The Arrest and Rescue of Chen Duxiu," in Mao, *Mao's Road to Power*, 1:328.
86. Chen Duxiu, "Yanjiu yu jianyu" ("The Research Institute and the Prison"), *Meizhou Pinglun* #15 (June 8, 1919). Also see Lanza, *Behind the Gate*, 141.
87. Lanza, *Behind the Gate*, 137.
88. Cadot-Wood, "Striving Toward a Lovable Nation," 119.
89. Chen, quoted in Feigon, *Chen Duxiu*, 152–53.
90. Ibid.
91. Chen, quoted in Schwartz, *Chinese Communism*, 22.
92. Schwartz, *Chinese Communism*, 21.
93. Westad, *Restless Empire*, 158.
94. Schwartz, *Chinese Communism*, 34.
95. Chen, quoted in Feigon, *Chen Duxiu*, 152–53.
96. Ibid., 152.
97. Schwarcz, *The Chinese Enlightenment*, 179; Feigon, *Chen Duxiu*, 235.
98. Feigon, *Chen Duxiu*, 196.
99. On Chen's last years, see Zhu Hong, *Chen Duxiu: Zuihou suiyue*.
100. Chen, "Letter to Liangen," in Benton, *Last Days*, 59.
101. Chen, "A Sketch of the Post-war World," in ibid., 85–86.

Chapter 8: Unification

1. Taylor, *The Generalissimo*, 242.
2. Chiang and Jaffe, *China's Destiny*, 100.
3. Taylor, *The Generalissimo*, 12–14.
4. Fenby, *Chiang Kai-shek*, 23.
5. Taylor, *The Generalissimo*, 17.
6. Chiang, quoted in Fenby, *Chiang Kai-shek*, 26.
7. Taylor, *The Generalissimo*, 29.
8. Fenby, *Chiang Kai-shek*, 39–43.
9. Taylor, *The Generalissimo*, 41.
10. Ibid., 27.
11. Ibid., 61.
12. Ibid., 73.
13. Wang, *China's Unequal Treaties*, 70.
14. Fenby, *Chiang Kai-shek*, 175.
15. Peffer, *China*, 281–83.
16. Eastman et al., *The Nationalist Era in China*, Eastman, "Nationalist China During the Nanking Decade, 1927–37," 1.
17. Chiang, quoted in Westad, *Restless Empire*, 164.
18. Musgrove, "Building a Dream," 144.
19. Ibid.
20. Schoppa, *Twentieth Century China*, 85.
21. Ibid., 87.
22. McAleavy, *The Modern History of China*, 100.
23. Eastman, *Nationalist Era in China*, 47.
24. Spence, *The Search for Modern China*, 424. Also, Westad, *Restless Empire*, 255.
25. Snow, *Journey to the Beginning*, 135.
26. Ibid., 135–36.
27. Westad, *Restless Empire*, 167, and Taylor, *The Generalissimo*, 79–82, on estimates in thousands. See also Spence, *The Search for Modern China*, 363.
28. Chiang, *Jiang Jieshi riji jiemi*, 2:504.
29. Ibid., 2:480.
30. Ibid., 2:492.
31. Woo, *The Kuomintang and the Future of the Chinese Revolution*, 246.
32. Chiang, *Jiang Jieshi riji jiemi*, 2:504.
33. Rabe, *The Good Man of Nanking*, 77.
34. Taylor, *The Generalissimo*, 152.
35. Snow, *People on Our Side*, 282.
36. White, *In Search of History*, 156.
37. Taylor, *The Generalissimo*, 259.
38. Chiang, *China's Destiny*, 79.
39. White, *In Search of History*, 156–57.
40. Ibid., 157.
41. Ibid., 160.
42. Taylor, *The Generalissimo*, 33.
43. Chiang, quoted in Chow, *The May Fourth Movement*, 344.
44. Chiang, quoted in Wakeman, "A Revisionist View of the Nanjing Decade," 170.
45. Chiang, *China's Destiny*, 157.
46. Ibid., 149.
47. Taylor, *The Generalissimo*, 216.
48. Ibid., 49–50.

49. Chiang and Jaffe, *China's Destiny*, 44.
50. Wang, *Never Forget National Humiliation*, 80.
51. Fairbank, Reischauer, and Craig, *East Asia: The Modern Transformation*, 714.
52. Chiang, *China's Destiny*, 123. Also, Cohen, *Speaking to History*, 73.
53. Cohen, *Speaking to History*, 2–35.
54. Ibid., 73–74.
55. Wang, *Never Forget National Humiliation*, 80–81. See also Chiang, *Jiang Jieshi riji jiemi*, multiple entries.
56. Quoted in ibid., 80–81, from Grace Huang's translation of Chiang's original, Cohen, *Speaking to History*, 73.
57. Cohen, *Speaking to History*, 231–32.
58. Chiang, *China's Destiny*, 84.
59. Ibid., 78.
60. Ibid., 29.
61. Ibid., 34.
62. Ibid., 97.
63. Callahan, cited in Wang, *Never Forget National Humiliation*, 64.
64. Stilwell, *The Stilwell Papers*, 110–222.
65. Stilwell, cited in Taylor, *The Generalissimo*, 216.
66. Stilwell, *The Stilwell Papers*, 133.
67. Service, *Lost Chance in China*, 90.
68. Snow, *People on Our Side*, 280.
69. Chiang, *China's Destiny*, 208.
70. Ibid., 103.
71. Confucius, *Analects*, 3.
72. Schoppa, *Twentieth Century China*, 79–80.
73. Fenby, *Chiang Kai-shek*, 246.
74. See Ferlanti, "The New Life Movement in Jiangxi Province, 1934–1938."
75. Wills, *Mountain of Fame*, 323–24.
76. Taylor, *The Generalissimo*, 45.
77. Wakeman, "Revisionist View," 141.
78. Ibid., 142.
79. Ibid. Also Taylor, *The Generalissimo*, 102.
80. Wakeman, "Revisionist View," 142.
81. Chiang and Jaffe, *China's Destiny*, 210.
82. Snow, *Journey to the Beginning*, 137.
83. Barnett, *China on the Eve of Communist Takeover*, 97.

Chapter 9: Not a Dinner Party

1. Snow, *Red Star over China*, 133.
2. Ibid., 132.
3. See, Lifton, *Revolutionary Immortality*, 82.
4. *Poems of Mao Zedong*, 41.
5. Pye, *Mao Tse-tung*, 36.
6. Fairbank, introduction to Snow, *Red Star over China*, 11–13.
7. Snow, *Red Star over China*, 132–33.
8. Ibid., 133.
9. Ibid., 132–33.
10. Confucius, *Analects*, Book 2.5.
11. Ibid., Book 4.18.
12. Snow, *Red Star over China*, 131.
13. Ibid.

14. Ibid.
15. Ibid., 133.
16. Ibid., 136.
17. Spence, *Mao Zedong*, 7.
18. Snow, *Red Star over China*, 136–37.
19. Wakeman, *History and Will*, 143.
20. Spence, *Mao Zedong*, 11.
21. Spence, *Mao Zedong*, 20–21.
22. Mao, *Mao's Road to Power* (henceforth MRTP), 1:xxi.
23. Ibid., 1:6.
24. Spence, *Mao Zedong*, 18.
25. Mao, MRTP, 1:6.
26. Spence, *Mao Zedong*, 20–26.
27. Feigon, *Mao: A Reinterpretation*, 19.
28. Mao, MRTP, 1:113.
29. Ibid., 1:115.
30. Ibid., 1:116.
31. Ibid., 1:120.
32. Ibid., 1:115.
33. Ibid., 1:5.
34. Ibid., 1:60.
35. Ibid., 1:119, 120.
36. Ibid., 1:113.
37. Ibid., 1:124.
38. Ibid., 1:120.
39. Ibid., 1:132.
40. Ibid., 1:xxi.
41. Meisner, *Li Ta-chao and the Origins of Chinese Marxism*, 93.
42. Short, *Mao*, 83.
43. Mao, MRTP, 1:385.
44. Ibid., 1:381–82.
45. Ibid., 1:386.
46. Ibid., 1:389.
47. Platt, *Provincial Patriots*, 194.
48. Ibid.
49. Mao, MRTP, 1:263–64.
50. Ibid.
51. Ibid., 1:318.
52. Pantsov and Levine, *Mao*, 101–2.
53. Mao, "On People's Democratic Dictatorship," in Mao, *Selected Works*, 4:412-413.
54. Ibid.
55. See Lenin's essay "What Is to Be Done?" in Lenin, *The Lenin Anthology*.
56. Spence, *Mao Zedong*, 54–55.
57. Pantsov and Levine, *Mao*, 101.
58. Ch'en, *Mao and the Chinese Revolution*, 112.
59. Mao, "On New Democracy," in Mao, *Selected Works* 2:367.
60. Ibid., 2:366.
61. Mao, MRTP, 2:429.
62. Ibid., 2:430.
63. Ibid., 2:431.
64. Ibid., 2:430.
65. Ibid., 2:432–33.
66. Ibid., 2:434–35.

67. Ibid., 2:430–31.
68. Ibid., 2:434–35.
69. Wakeman, *History and Will*, 92.
70. Mao, MRTP, 1:124.
71. Solomon, *Mao's Revolution*, 166.
72. Ch'en, *Mao Papers*, 114.
73. Schumpeter, *Capitalism, Socialism, and Democracy*, 82–85.
74. Wakeman, *History and Will*, 152.
75. Ibid., 151.
76. Mao, *Selected Works*, 2:688.
77. Spence, *The Search for Modern China*, 403–9.
78. Ibid., 407.
79. Mao, *Selected Works*, 1:318.
80. Ibid.
81. Ibid., 1:333.
82. Ch'en, *Mao Papers*, 33.
83. Snow, *Red Star over China*, 90.
84. Snow, *Journey to the Beginning*, 162.
85. Ibid.
86. Snow, *Red Star over China*, 90.
87. Fairbank, introduction to Barrett, *The Dixie Mission*, 8.
88. Barrett, *Dixie Mission*, 82.
89. Service, *Lost Chance in China*, 193–94.
90. Ibid., 194–97.
91. Ibid., 198.
92. Ibid., 308.
93. Feigon, *Mao: A Reinterpretation*, 66.
94. Selden, *The Yenan Way in Revolutionary China*, 190.
95. Brandt et al., Mao; Yenan Forum . . . in *A Documentary History of Chinese Communism*, 384.
96. Rice, *Mao's Way*, 98.
97. Chi et al., *Chinese English Dictionary of Contemporary Usage*, 297.
98. Goldman, *Literary Dissent in Communist China*, 18–19.
99. Schurmann, *Ideology and Organization*, 29.
100. Huang, "An Unforgettable Night in Yanan," 91.
101. Brandt et al., *A Documentary History of Chinese Communism*, 375.
102. Ibid., 383.
103. Ibid., 382.
104. Schram, *The Political Thought of Mao Zedong*, 179.
105. Brandt et al., *A Documentary History of Chinese Communism*, 386.
106. Ibid., 392.
107. Ibid., 396.
108. Ibid., 392.
109. Ibid., 407.
110. Spence, *The Gate of Heavenly Peace*, 291–94.
111. Goldman, *Literary Dissent in Communist China*, 25–26.
112. Dai, *Wang Shiwei and "Wild Lilies,"* xvii–xxxi.
113. McDougall, *Mao Zedong's Talks at the Yan'an Conference on Literature and Art*, 12.
114. Huang, "An Unforgettable Night in Yan'an," 92.
115. Ibid., 91–98.
116. Ibid., 93.
117. Mao, *Quotations from Chairman Mao*, 299.

118. McDougall, *Talks at the Yan'an Conference*, 61.
119. Mao, *Quotations from Chairman Mao*, 300.
120. Brandt et al., *A Documentary History of Chinese Communism*, 408.
121. Ibid., 418.
122. Huang, "An Unforgettable Night in Yanan," 95–96.

Chapter 10: Creative Destruction

1. Mao, "The Chinese People Have Stood Up," *Selected Works*, vol. 5, 17.
2. Wu, *Remaking Beijing*, 93–4.
3. Ibid., 59.
4. Lu Xun, "More Roses Without Blooms," *Selected Works of Lu Xun*, 2:249.
5. Mao, *Selected Works*, 4:374.
6. Wu, *Remaking Beijing*, 63. See also Lanza, *Behind the Gate*, 169–173.
7. Ibid., 23.
8. Hung, *Mao's New World*, 9, 36–47.
9. Ibid., 8, 46.
10. Wu, *Remaking Beijing*, 23.
11. Hung, *Mao's New World*, 27–34.
12. Ibid., 27–29 and Wu, *Remaking Beijing*, 7–8.
13. Becker, *City of Heavenly Tranquility*, 170.
14. Wu, *Remaking Beijing*, 64–5.
15. Barmé, *The Forbidden City*, 11.
16. Hung, *Mao's New World*, 35–36.
17. Ibid., 47.
18. Mao, *Introducing a Cooperative*, (April 15, 1958), *Selected Works*, vol 8. http://www.marxists.org/reference/archive/mao/selected-works/volume-8/mswv8_09.htm.
19. See Lifton, *Thought Reform and the Psychology of Totalism*.
20. Goldman, *From Comrade to Citizen*, 159; see also, Mei, *Hu Feng's Prison Years*.
21. Garside, *Coming Alive*, 33.
22. Mao, *Selected Works*, 4:374.
23. Mao, quoted in Selden, *The People's Republic of China*, 324.
24. Mao, quoted in Ch'en, *The Mao Papers*, 62–64.
25. Dikötter, *Mao's Great Famine*, 48.
26. Mao, quoted in Ch'en, *The Mao Papers*, 61.
27. Ibid., 57.
28. MacFarquhar, *The Great Leap Forward*.
29. Schram, *The Political Thought of Mao Tse-tung*, 102.
30. Schurmann, *Ideology and Organization*, 74.
31. Ibid., 76.
32. Li, *The Private Life of Chairman Mao*, 274.
33. Schurmann, *Ideology and Organization*, 279.
34. Yang, *Tombstone*, 108.
35. Spence, *The Search for Modern China*, 579.
36. Yang, *Tombstone*, 200–201.
37. Dikötter, *Mao's Great Famine*, 49.
38. Spence, *The Search for Modern China*, 579.
39. Krushchev, *Khrushchev Remembers*, 467–68.
40. Schram, *Mao Tse-Tung Unrehearsed*, 139.
41. Ibid., 146.
42. Yang, *Tombstone*, 13.
43. Dikötter, *Mao's Great Famine*, 320.
44. Spence, *The Search for Modern China*, 592.

45. MacFarquhar and Schoenhals, *Mao's Last Revolution*, 10.
46. Mao, *Mao Tsetung Poems*, 49–50.
47. MacFarquhar and Schoenhals, *Mao's Last Revolution*, 13.
48. Spence, *The Search for Modern China*, 595.
49. MacFarquhar and Schoenhals, *Mao's Last Revolution*, 47.
50. Ibid., 104.
51. Ibid., 73–74.
52. Ch'en, *Mao Papers*, 24–25.
53. Ibid., 25.
54. Ibid., 25–26.
55. Milton and Milton, *The Wind Will Not Subside*, 147.
56. MacFarquhar and Schoenhals, *Mao's Last Revolution*, 102.
57. Deng, *Deng Xiaoping and the Cultural Revolution*, 12.
58. MacFarquhar and Schoenhals, *Mao's Last Revolution*, 102.
59. Ibid., 102.
60. Ibid., 85.
61. Ibid., 48.
62. Ibid., 85.
63. Han, *Han Fei Tzu*, 17–18.
64. Mao, *Mao Tsetung Poems*, 31–32.
65. MacFarquhar and Schoenhals, *Mao's Last Revolution*, 82.
66. Milton and Milton, "*The Wind Will Not Subside*," 139.
67. Vogel, *Deng*, 43.
68. Milton and Milton, "*The Wind Will Not Subside*," 146.
69. Karol, *The Second Chinese Revolution*, 189.
70. Schram, *Mao Unrehearsed*, 260.
71. MacFarquhar and Schoenhals, *Mao's Last Revolution*, 90.
72. Ibid., 72.
73. Ibid., 67, 92–94.
74. Ibid., 92.
75. Granqvist, *The Red Guard*, 100.
76. Ibid., 100.
77. MacFarquhar and Schoenhals, *Mao's Last Revolution*, 102.
78. Ibid., 108.
79. Gray and Cavendish, *Chinese Communism in Crisis*, 125.
80. Daubier, *A History of the Cultural Revolution*, 71; MacFarquhar and Schoenhals, *Mao's Last Revolution*, 107–8.
81. Snow, *Red Star over China*, 70.
82. Karol, *Second Chinese Revolution*, 188; and MacFarquhar and Schoenhals, *Mao's Last Revolution*, 109–10.
83. MacFarquhar and Schoenhals, *Mao's Last Revolution*, 109.
84. Ibid., 206.
85. Li, *The Private Life of Chairman Mao*, 482.
86. MacFarquhar and Schoenhals, *Mao's Last Revolution*, 159–161.
87. Mao, "On New Democracy," in *Selected Works*, 2:340.
88. Tuchman, *Notes from China*, 77–78.
89. Ibid., 79–87.
90. Kissinger, *Years of Renewal*, 142.
91. Ibid., 881.
92. Ibid., 144.
93. Ibid., 152.
94. Ibid., 154.
95. Ibid., 152.

96. Ibid., 154.

97. See Heilmann and Perry, *Mao's Invisible Hand*, "Embracing Uncertainty," 1–29.

Chapter 11: Black Cat, White Cat

1. Drawn from Schell, *Watch Out for the Foreign Guests*.

2. On TV viewership in China, see Vogel, *Deng Xiaoping and the Transformation of China*, 337.

3. Butterfield, "Apathy Replaces Marxist Idealism Among Chinese," *New York Times*, December 30, 1980.

4. Deng Xiaoping, August 21, 1985, in *Selected Works of Deng Xiaoping*, 3:139.

5. The authoritative biography of Deng in English is Vogel's masterly *Deng Xiaoping and the Transformation of China*. Also useful are Yang, *Deng: A Political Biography*, Evans, *Deng Xiaoping and the Making of Modern China*, and the essays compiled by Shambaugh in *Deng Xiaoping: Portrait of a Chinese Statesman*. Deng's daughter's memoirs add some personal color to the story of his life—Deng, *Deng Xiaoping and the Cultural Revolution* and *My Father Deng Xiaoping: The War Years*.

6. Yang, *Deng*, 29.

7. Deng, *Deng Xiaoping zishu*, 2.

8. Deng, *Deng Xiaoping and the Cultural Revolution*, 29.

9. Yang, *Deng*, 32.

10. For more, see Wang, "Deng Xiaoping: The Years in France," 698–705, and Levine, *The Found Generation*.

11. Deng, *My Father*, 101. Also see Vogel, *Deng*, 22.

12. Deng and Chiang were in the same class of twenty students and developed a close rapport. See Taylor, *The Generalissimo's Son*, 33.

13. Quoted in Deng, *My Father*, 126. On the teaching of Leninism, see Sheng, *Sun Yatsen University in Moscow and the Chinese Revolution*, 64.

14. As Vogel comments, "If anything was sacred for Deng, it was the Chinese Communist Party" (*Deng*, 262).

15. Pye, "Deng Xiaoping and China's Political Culture," in Shambaugh, *Deng Xiaoping*, 24.

16. See Stranahan, *Underground: The Shanghai Communist Party and the Politics of Survival, 1927–1937*.

17. Mao, "Problems of War and Strategy," *Mao's Road to Power*, 6:552.

18. See Deng, *Deng Xiaoping zishu*, 110.

19. On Deng's sacrilege against Chiang, see Deng, *My Father*, 507. On the Huai-Hai campaign, see Westad, *Decisive Encounters*.

20. Goldstein, *A History of Modern Tibet*, 181.

21. Khrushchev, *Memoirs of Nikita Khrushchev*, vol. 3: *Statesman, 1953–1964*, 439.

22. Deng, January 16, 1980, *Selected Works*, 2:228.

23. Vogel, *Deng*, 41–43.

24. Quoted in Yang, *Deng*, 151. Deng was speaking to the Seventh Plenum of the Third Communist Youth League (July 7, 1962). Ruan Ming, who was present in the audience, reports that Deng attributed the line, a Sichuanese proverb, to Liu Bocheng; see Ruan, *Deng Xiaoping: Chronicle of an Empire*, 4. Also see Su, *Deng Xiaoping shengping quanji lu*, 482–83; Deng, *Deng Xiaoping wenxuan*, 1:304–9.

25. Mencius, *Mencius*, 447 (6B.15).

26. Deng, March 25, 1984, in Deng, *Selected Works*, 3:64.

27. Deng, *Deng Xiaoping and the Cultural Revolution*, 46–47.

28. Ibid., 166.

29. Chin, *Teng Hsiao-ping: A Political Biography*, 59–60.

30. Deng, Deng Xiaoping tongzhi de "Wo de zishu." Thanks to Professor Ezra Vogel and librarian Nancy Hearst for locating this text in Harvard's collection.
31. Ibid.
32. Deng, Deng Xiaoping and the Cultural Revolution, 185.
33. Yang, Deng, 175.
34. Deng, Deng Xiaoping and the Cultural Revolution, 227.
35. Deng, Speech by Chairman of the Delegation.
36. Deng, September 16, 1978, Selected Works, 2:142.
37. Kissinger, On China, 324.
38. Vogel, Deng, 86.
39. CCP Central Documentary Research Office, Deng Xiaoping sixiang nianpu, 5:14–15.
40. See Cheng and Xia, Deng Xiaoping yu 1975 nian zhengdun.
41. Deng, August 18, 1975, Selected Works, 2:46.
42. See MacFarquhar and Schoenhals, Mao's Last Revolution, 387–88.
43. Deng, August 18, 1975, Selected Works, 2:44.
44. Vogel, Deng, 89.
45. According to official data compiled by the National Bureau of Statistics in China, GDP growth increased from 2.3 percent in 1974 to 8.7 percent in 1975, and then dropped steeply to -1.6 percent in 1976. Thanks to Barry Naughton for pointing out these figures.
46. Wu, Remaking Beijing, 37.
47. The most vivid account of April 1976 can be found in Garside, Coming Alive.
48. Quoted in Spence, The Search for Modern China, 646.
49. Garside, Coming Alive, 17–19.
50. Ibid., 110–14.
51. Ibid., 115.
52. Thurston, A Chinese Odyssey, 282.
53. Goldman, From Comrade to Citizen, 27.
54. Garside, Coming Alive, 124.
55. Ibid., 128–31.
56. Thurston, A Chinese Odyssey, 284.
57. Garside, Coming Alive, 132.
58. Fraser, The Chinese, 218.
59. Baum, Burying Mao, 38.
60. Yang, Deng, 178.
61. Quoted in Franz, Deng, 261.
62. Quoted in Franz, Deng, 261.
63. Strictly speaking, Deng's first use of the set phrase "reform and opening" does not appear until 1987. See Deng, March 8, 1987, Selected Works, 3:211.
64. Deng, December 13, 1978, Selected Works, 2:165.
65. Deng, May 25, 1988, Selected Works, 3:259.
66. Deng, Selected Works, 2:161.
67. Ibid., 2:154.
68. Ibid., 2:165.
69. Quoted in Vogel, Deng, 218.
70. Tyler, A Great Wall, 276.
71. Vogel, Deng, 221.
72. Wong and Ansfield, "Rising Power of Generals Worries Party in Beijing," International Herald Tribune, August 2, 2012.
73. Zhao, Prisoner of the State, 206.
74. Deng, August 21–23, 1980, Selected Works, 2:330.

75. Deng, May 24, 1977, *Selected Works*, 2:51; also see Salisbury, *The New Emperors*, 329.
76. Deng, August 18, 1980, *Selected Works*, 2:319.
77. Deng, January 16, 1980, *Selected Works*, 2:228.
78. Deng, August 19, 1977, *Selected Works*, 2:81.
79. Schell, *Watch Out for the Foreign Guests*, 143.
80. Deng, May 24, 1977, *Selected Works*, 2:53.
81. Yang and Downer, *Wei Jingsheng: The Man and His Ideas*, 42.
82. Nathan, *Chinese Democracy*, 11.
83. Yang and Downer, *Wei Jingsheng*, 40; Nathan, *Chinese Democracy*, 10.
84. Nathan, *Chinese Democracy*, 4.
85. Ibid., 9.
86. Garside, *Coming Alive*, 223.
87. Yang and Downer, *Wei Jingsheng*, 43.
88. Fraser, *The Chinese*, 245.
89. Deng, December 13, 1978, *Selected Works*, 2:155.
90. Goldman, *From Comrade to Citizen*, 32.
91. Ibid., 35.
92. Woodman, "Biography of Wei Jingsheng," 1.
93. Wei, *The Courage to Stand Alone*, 209–10.
94. Ibid., 206.
95. Ibid., 208–9.
96. Ibid., 212.
97. Garside, *Coming Alive*, 263.
98. Nathan, *Chinese Democracy*, 33.
99. Schell, *The China Reader*, 163.
100. Nathan, *Chinese Democracy*, 34.
101. Yang and Downer, *Wei Jingsheng*, 94.
102. Goldman, *From Comrade to Citizen*, 45–46.
103. Yang and Downer, *Wei Jingsheng*, 202.
104. Woodman, "Biography of Wei Jingsheng," 5.
105. Yang and Downer, *Wei Jingsheng*, 226.
106. Wei, *Courage*, 225.
107. Garside, *Coming Alive*, 281.
108. Ibid., 278; Nathan, *Chinese Democracy*, 34.
109. Nathan, *Chinese Democracy*, 37.
110. Deng, March 18, 1978, *Selected Works*, 2:106–7.
111. Deng, October 6, 1984, *Selected Works*, 3:85.
112. Naughton, "Deng Xiaoping: The Economist," in Shambaugh, *Deng Xiaoping.*
113. Deng, November 26, 1979, *Deng Xiaoping wenxuan*, 2:231. This passage is not included in the English version of Deng's *Selected Works*.
114. According to Zhao, Deng used this formulation repeatedly. Zhao, *Prisoner of the State*, 119.
115. Shirk, *The Political Logic of Economic Reform in China.*
116. Cited in Vogel, *Deng*, 156.
117. Cited in ibid., 437.
118. See Lau, Qian, and Roland, "Reform Without Losers." For more on rural capitalism, see Huang, *Capitalism with Chinese Characteristics.*
119. See Lau, Qian, and Roland, "Reform Without Losers," 18. Also see Naughton, *Growing Out of the Plan.*
120. Deng, June 30, 1984, in *Selected Works*, 3:73; April 26, 1987, 3:223.
121. Yu, *Deng Xiaoping Shakes the World*, 130–31.

122. Deng, January 12, 1983, *Selected Works*, 3:33.
123. Deng, February 24, 1984, *Selected Works*, 2:61–62.
124. Vogel, *Deng*, 398.
125. Zhao, *Prisoner of the State*, 102.
126. Deng, September 16, 1978, *Selected Works*, 2:142.
127. Zhao, *Prisoner of the State*, 107.
128. Deng, October 22, 1984, *Selected Works*, 3:97.
129. See Schell, *Mandate of Heaven*, 357.
130. Vogel, *Deng*, 418.
131. Deng, September 1, 1982, *Selected Works*, 3:14.
132. Burns, "Deng Asserts Ties to West Are Vital to Fight Poverty."
133. Yang, *Deng*, 227.

Chapter 12: Turmoil

1. Quotations by Fang, Lizhi in this chapter are uncited but drawn from Schell, *Discos and Democracy*, 121–139, and Schell, "China's Andrei Sakharov." Also see Fang, *Bringing Down the Great Wall*.
2. Yang, *Deng*, 285.
3. Deng, April 16, 1987, *Selected Works*, 3:219.
4. Zhao, *Prisoner of the State*, 248–49.
5. See Deng, August 18, 1980, *Selected Works* 2:302–25.
6. Salisbury, *The New Emperors*, 329.
7. Deng, December 30, 1986, *Selected Works*, 3:195.
8. Deng, June 12, 1987, *Selected Works*, 3:238.
9. Deng, June 26, 1983, *Selected Works*, 3:41–42.
10. Schell, *Discos*, 213–14.
11. Deng, quoted in Baum, "Road to Tiananmen," in MacFarquhar, *The Politics of China*, 398. On Deng being "shocked" by 1986 protests, see Zhao, *Prisoner*, 172.
12. Deng, January 13, 1987, *Selected Works*, 3:200.
13. Deng, March 30, 1979, *Selected Works*, 2:178–79.
14. Deng, December 30, 1986, *Selected Works*, 3:194.
15. Deng, January 13, 1987, *Selected Works*, 3:198.
16. Woodman, "Wei Jingsheng Biography," 10; also see Tyler, "China Detains and Then Frees a Top Dissident."
17. Zhao, *Prisoner*, 175.
18. See Schell, "China's Andrei Sakharov."
19. Schell, *Mandate of Heaven*, 46.
20. Ibid., 47.
21. Ibid., 48–49.
22. Cited in Ogden et al., *China's Search for Democracy*, 117.
23. Gorbachev, *Memoirs*, 489.
24. See Chinoy, *China Live*.
25. Kahn, "Better Fed than Red."
26. Cited in Vogel, *Deng*, 575.
27. See Brook, *Quelling the People*.
28. Deng, June 9, 1989, *Selected Works*, 3:294–95.
29. This section draws from Schell, *Mandate of Heaven*, 197–206.
30. Schell, "The Odyssey of Comrade Fang."
31. Deng, June 16, 1988, *Selected Works*, 3:302.
32. Deng, November 23, 1989, *Selected Works*, 3:334.
33. Deng, December 1, 1989, *Selected Works*, 3:336.

34. See Zhao, "A State-Led Nationalism."
35. Deng, January 18–February 21, 1992, *Selected Works*, 3:365.
36. Deng, December 24, 1990, *Selected Works*, 3:351.
37. Huang, *Ying daoli*, 131.
38. Schell, *Mandate of Heaven*, 324. Also see MacFarquhar, "Deng's Last Campaign," *New York Review of Books*, December 17, 1992.
39. Deng, *Deng Xiaoping wenxuan*, 3:370.
40. Schell, *Mandate of Heaven*, 345.
41. Deng, January 18–February 21, 1992, *Selected Works*, 3:360. On Mao's use of the phrase, see Vogel, *Deng*, 440.
42. Deng, *Selected Works*, 3:365.
43. Vogel, *Deng*, 674.
44. See Yahuda, "Deng Xiaoping: The Statesman," 160; also see Deng, September 24, 1982, in Shambaugh, ed., *Deng Xiaoping, Selected Works*, 3:23.
45. Yang, *Deng*, 226.
46. See Vogel, *Deng*, 714; Shambaugh, *China Goes Global*, 19.
47. Schell, *Mandate of Heaven*, 331–63.
48. See Evans, *Deng*, 306–8.
49. Yang, *Deng*, 261.
50. Ibid., 150.
51. Deng, August 21–23, 1980, *Selected Works*, 2:331.

Chapter 13: Entering the World

1. For full press conference transcript see www.presidency.wasb.edu/wg/pod?=56229.
2. Gilley, *Tiger on the Brink*, 103.
3. Gao and He, *Tie mian zaixiang*, 218.
4. Ibid., 222–23.
5. Quoted in Gilley, *Tiger*, 144.
6. Ibid., 144.
7. Ibid., 101.
8. Kristof, "Shanghai's Mayor Gains Credit as Pragmatist."
9. Quoted in Fewsmith, *China Since Tiananmen*, 49.
10. Ibid.
11. Zhu, June 21, 2000, *Zhu Rongji Meets the Press*, 103.
12. Zhu, June 5, 2001, *Zhu Rongji jianghua shilu*, 4:161.
13. Gao and He, *Tiemian zaixiang*, 72.
14. Schell, *Mandate of Heaven*, 344.
15. Zhu, March 25, 1992, *Zhu Rongji jianghua shilu*, 1:134.
16. Yan, quoted in Teng and Fairbank, *China's Response*, 150–51.
17. Zhu, March 25, 1992, *Zhu Rongji jianghua shilu*, 1:139.
18. Zhu, September 28, 1992, *Zhu Rongji jianghua shilu*, 1:223.
19. Baum, *Burying Mao*, 350.
20. Gilley, *Tiger*, 293.
21. Vogel, *Deng*, 451.
22. Baum, *Burying Mao*, 333.
23. Gilley, *Tiger*, 188; Mufson, "Economic Pragmatist to Be China Premier." *Washington Post*, March 5, 1998.
24. Eckholm and Faison, "China's New Premier: Fast Riser Who Tamed Economy in Chaos." *New York Times*, March 16, 1998.
25. Cooper and Madigan, "China: The Year of the Inflation Dragon." *Bloomberg*, October 10, 1994.

26. See Shirk, *The Political Logic of Economic Reform*, 149–96.
27. Kristof, "No Praise, Please! He Wants to Be the Premier." *New York Times*, August 25, 1992.
28. McGregor, *The Party*, 45–46.
29. Zhu, March 24, 1998, *Zhu Rongji jianghua shilu*, 3:4.
30. See Li, *China's Leaders*, 149–50.
31. Naughton, *The Chinese Economy*, 100.
32. Zhu, November 25, 1993, *Zhu Rongji jianghua shilu*, 1:408.
33. Zhu, January 15, 1994, *Zhu Rongji Meets Press*, 21.
34. Wang and Hu, *The Chinese Economy in Crisis*, 198–99.
35. Quoted in ibid., 225.
36. Zhu Rongji, January 15, 1994, *Zhu Rongji Meets the Press*, 22, 24.
37. Yang, *Remaking the Chinese Leviathan*, 73. Also see Naughton, "China's Economic Think Tanks," 633.
38. Shih, *Factions and Finance in China*, 154.
39. Brahm, *Zhu Rongji and the Transformation of Modern China*, 18–19.
40. Lardy, *China's Unfinished Economic Revolution*, 174.
41. Yang, *Leviathan*, 85.
42. Shih, *Factions and Finance*, 14.
43. Ibid., 175.
44. Chandler, "Wall Street's War for China," *Fortune*, May 17, 2006; Anderlini, "Ag-Bank IPO Officially the World's Biggest," *Financial Times*, August 13, 2010.
45. Landler, "Bankruptcy the Chinese Way," *New York Times*, January 22, 1999.
46. Wu, *Understanding and Interpreting Chinese Economic Reform*, 86.
47. Zhu, March 15, 2001, *Zhu Rongji Meets the Press*, 248.
48. Zhu, March 6, 1993, *Zhu Rongji Meets the Press*, 8.
49. Huang, *Capitalism with Chinese Characteristics*, 23; Shih, *Factions and Finance*, 189.
50. Quoted in Zong, ed., "Zhu Rongji in 1999," 88.
51. Zhu, *Zhu Rongji Meets the Press*, 371, 383, 385.
52. Ibid., 383, 389, 394.
53. Lampton, *The Making of Chinese Foreign and Security Policy in the Era of Reform*, 181.
54. "DCI Statement on the Belgrade Chinese Embassy Bombing," House Permanent Select Committee on Intelligence Open Hearing, July 22, 1999.
55. "Beijing Halts Rights, Arms Talks with U.S." *Chicago Sun-Times*, May 11, 1999.
56. Zong, "Zhu Rongji in 1999," 81.
57. Ibid., 83.
58. Chu, Farley, and Kuhn, "Chinese Attack U.S. Missions as Protests Intensify." *Los Angeles Times*, May 10, 1999.
59. Quoted in Gries, *China's New Nationalism*, 105.
60. Zong, "Zhu Rongji in 1999," 50.
61. Quoted in Gries, *New Nationalism*, 129.
62. Zhu, November 30, 1999, *Zhu Rongji Meets the Press*, 415.
63. Zhu, March 15, 2000, *Zhu Rongji Meets the Press*, 213.
64. Shirk, *China: Fragile Superpower*, 230–31.
65. Zhu Rongji, March 15, 2002, *Zhu Rongji Meets the Press*, 269.
66. Garnaut, "China's Elite Fail to Share Fruits of Growth." *The Age*, October 1, 2007.
67. Chen and Wu, *Will the Boat Sink the Water?*, 137–38.
68. Zhu, *Zhu Rongji Meets the Press*, 310–11.
69. Shih, *Factions and Finance*, 184.
70. Lam, *Chinese Politics in the Hu Jintao Era*, 233.
71. Zhu, May 13, 1993, *Zhu Rongji jianghua shilu*, 1:286.

72. Zhu, June 21, 2000, *Zhu Rongji Meets the Press*, 103.
73. Ibid., 105–6.
74. Zhu, April 13, 1999, *Zhu Rongji Meets the Press*, 386.
75. Zhu, March 15, 2001, *Zhu Rongji Meets the Press*, 243.
76. Zhu, October 22, 2001, *Zhu Rongji Meets the Press*, 163.
77. Zong, "Zhu Rongji in 1999," 57.
78. Nathan and Gilley, *China's New Rulers*, 195.
79. Zhu, August 30, 2001, *Zhu Rongji Meets the Press*, 145.

Chapter 14: No Enemies, No Hatred

1. Liu, quoted in Barmé, "Confession, Redemption, and Death," in Hicks, *The Broken Mirror*, 56.
2. Liu, *No Enemies, No Hatred*, 237.
3. Liu, *June Fourth Elegies*, xxv.
4. Liu, *No Enemies, No Hatred*, xv.
5. Liu, quoted in Barmé, "Confession, Redemption, and Death," 53.
6. Yang, translator's afterword, in Liu, *June Fourth Elegies*, 214.
7. Barmé and Jaivin, *New Ghosts, Old Dreams*, 385.
8. Yang, translator's afterword, in Liu, *June Fourth Elegies*, 215.
9. Barmé, "Confession, Redemption, and Death," 57.
10. Ibid., 59.
11. Ibid., 52.
12. Yang, translator's afterword, in Liu, *June Fourth Elegies*, 225.
13. Liu, quoted in Barmé, "Confession, Redemption, and Death," 81.
14. Ibid., 62.
15. Ibid., 61.
16. Barme and Jaivin, *New Ghosts, Old Dreams*, p. 67–9.
17. Fathers and Higgins, *Tiananmen: The Rape of Beijing*, 90.
18. Ogden et al., *China's Search for Democracy*, 357.
19. Ibid., 358.
20. Ibid., 360–61.
21. See Dardess, *Blood and History in China* for historical echoes of student martyrology.
22. Schell, *Mandate of Heaven*, 138–9.
23. Barme, "Confessions, Redemptions, Death," 79.
24. Schell, *Mandate of Heaven*, 152–53.
25. Fathers and Higgins, *Tiananmen: The Rape of Beijing*, 122.
26. Schell, *Mandate of Heaven*, 169 and Perry Link, Introduction, *No Enemies, No Hatred*, xvii.
27. Yang, translator's afterword, in Liu, *June Fourth Elegies*, 218.
28. Liu, *No Enemies, No Hatred*, 293.
29. Ibid., 237–8.
30. Lu Xun, *Random Thoughts Under the Lamp* quoted in Schell, *Mandate of Heaven*, faceplate. For different translation, also see *Selected Works of Lu Xun*, 2:135.
31. Liu, *No Enemies, No Hatred*, 10.
32. Goldman, *Comrade to Citizen*, 13–14.
33. Liu's letter to Liao Yiwu was written in 2000 and can be found in *No Enemies, No Hatred*, 288.
34. Link Introduction, ibid., xiii.
35. Liu, *No Enemies, No Hatred*, 118.
36. Ibid., 117.
37. Chen Duxiu, quoted in Lanza, *Behind the Gate, 141.*

38. Link Introduction, *No Enemies, No Hatred*, xviii.
39. Ibid., 241.
40. Ibid., 322–23.
41. Ibid., 321–22.
42. "Full Text of Hu Jintao's Speech at CPC Anniversary Gathering," *Xinhua*, July 1, 2011.
43. Liu, *No Enemies, No Hatred*, 223.
44. Ibid.
45. Ibid., 226.
46. Ibid.
47. Ibid., 227.
48. "Premier: China Confident in Maintaining Economic Growth," *Xinhua*, March 16, 2007.
49. Shen Hu, "China's Gini Index at 0.61," *Caixin*, December 10, 2012.
50. Devichand, "Millions 'Left Behind' in Rural China," *BBC News*, May 12, 2010; Flannery, "China's Billionaire Boom," *Forbes*, October 27, 2010.
51. Freeman, "The Accuracy of China's 'Mass Incidents,'" *Financial Times*, March 2, 2010.
52. Orlik, "Unrest Grows as Economy Booms," *Wall Street Journal*, September 26, 2011.
53. Hu Jintao, "Adhering to the Socialist Cultural Development Path with Chinese Characteristics and Striving to Build a Country with a Strong Socialist Culture," *Qiushi Journal*, April 2012.
54. Liu, *No Enemies, No Hatred*, 189.
55. Havel, *Václav Havel: Living in Truth*, 55.
56. Ai Weiwei Twitter feed, cited in *Wall Street Journal*, "A Dissident's Tips for Survival," December 29–30, 2012.
57. Liu, *No Enemies, No Hatred*, 295.
58. Ibid., 83–84.
59. Ibid., 62–63.
60. Ibid.
61. Ibid., 83.
62. Ibid., 246.
63. Ibid., 245.
64. Ibid., 249.
65. Ibid., 255.
66. Ai, "The Olympics Was a Strange, Surreal Nightmare," China Boom Project (http://chinaboom.asiasociety.org/period/overdrive/0/155).
67. Ai, "China Excluded Its People from the Olympics. London Is Different," *The Guardian*, July 25, 2012.
68. Dalai Lama, "Forty-Ninth Anniversary," *Central Tibetan Administration*, March 10, 2008 (http://tibet.net/2008/03/10/statement-of-his-holiness-the-dalai-lama-on-the-forty-ninth-anniversary-of-the-tibetan-national-uprising-day-10-march-2008).
69. Barnett, "Thunder from Tibet," *New York Review of Books*, May 1, 2008; Miles, "Siege of Lhasa," *The Economist*, March 17, 2008.
70. Hu Jintao, "China's Response," *PBS Newshour with Jim Lehrer*, May 9, 1999 (www.pbs.org/newshour/bb/europe/jan-june99/china_statement_5-9.html).
71. Fewsmith, "'Social Management' as a Way of Coping with Heightened Social Tensions," *China Leadership Monitor* 36, January 26, 2012, 6.
72. Jacobs and Ansfield, "Well-Oiled Security Apparatus in China Stifles Calls for Change," *New York Times*, February 28, 2011.
73. Fewsmith, *China Since Tiananmen*, 260–61.

74. China Internet Network Information Center, http://www.internetworldstats.com .asia/cn.htm.

75. Liu, *No Enemies, No Hatred*, xxi.

76. Ibid., 203.

77. Ibid., 211.

78. Ibid., 204.

79. Ibid., 209.

80. Ibid., 205.

81. Ibid., 301.

82. Ibid., 303, 305.

83. Ibid., 309–10.

84. Osnos, "Liu Xiaobo Wins the Nobel Peace Prize," *The New Yorker*, October 10, 2010 (http://www.newyorker.com/online/blogs/evanosnos/2010/10/liu-xiaobo.html #ixzz1yFIymNdK).

85. Liu, *No Enemies, No Hatred*, 315.

86. Ibid., xx.

87. Ibid., 315–16.

88. Ibid., 319.

89. Ibid., 318.

90. Ibid., 322.

91. Ibid., 323–26.

92. Mo et al., "Criminal Defense in Sensitive Cases," 73–74.

93. Liu, *No Enemies, No Hatred*, xvii.

94. Ibid., 322.

95. "International Reaction to Liu Xiaobo Nobel Peace Prize," *BBC News*, October 28, 2010 (http://bbc.co.uk/news/world-europe-11499931).

96. Fang, "Liu Xiaobo and Illusions About China," *New York Times*, October 11, 2010.

97. Barmé, *Confessions, Redemption, Death*, 80.

98. Liu, *No Enemies, No Hatred*, 304.

Chapter 15: Conclusion

1. On Sun's efforts see: Bergere, *Sun Yat-sen*, 50–55. On self-strengtheners' hopes for a mid-dynastic revival see: Wright, *Last Stand of Chinese Conservatism*. For a contemporary analysis see Wang, *Never Forget National Humiliation*, 237–42.

2. Quoted in Wang, *Never Forget National Humiliation*, 130.

3. Wang, *Never Forget National Humiliation*, 238.

4. Quoted in Wang, *Never Forget National Humiliation*, 132.

5. Xi Jinping, "Address to the Media," *China Daily*, November 16, 2012.

6. Xi Jinping, "Xi Pledges Great Renewal of Chinese Nation," *Xinhua News Service*, November 29, 2012.

7. Simon Rabinovitch, " 'Strong Army' Xi: The Other Side of China's Reformer," *The Financial Times*, December 13, 2012.

8. See: "China Top Legislature Concludes Annual Session," *Shanghai Daily*, March 17, 2013: http://mobile.shanghaidaily.com/article/?id=526199.

9. Schwartz, *In Search of Wealth and Power*, 120.

10. Schram, *MRTP*, 2:430.

11. Quoted in Leys, *Broken Images*, 25.

12. Ibid., 29; also see Hsia, *The Gate of Darkness*, 146–62.

13. Schoppa, *Twentieth Century China: A History in Documents*, 141.

14. Fairbank, Foreword, in Lo and Kinderman, *In the Eye of the Typhoon*, ix.

15. Liang, quoted in Arkush and Lee, *Land Without Ghosts*, 93.
16. MacFarquhar and Schoenhals, *Mao's Last Revolution*, 3.
17. Heilmann and Perry, eds., *Mao's Invisible Hand*, 5, 15.
18. Ibid., 3.
19. Ibid., 11–15.
20. Ibid., 7.
21. Ibid., 12.
22. Heilman, "Policy Making Through Experimentation," in Heilman and Perry, eds., *Mao Invisible Hand*, 87–89.
23. See Nathan, "Authoritarian Resistance."
24. Fairbank, Reischauer, and Craig, *East Asia: The Great Transformation*, 884.
25. See Cohen, *Discovering History*.
26. Fukuyama, "The End of History," 1.
27. Ibid., 7–8.
28. Quoted in Hicks, *The Broken Mirror*, 160.
29. Spence, *"The Search for Modern China,"* 1st ed., 747.
30. Schell, *Mandate of Heaven*, 441.
31. See Halper, *The Beijing Consensus*.
32. See: http://www.china-embassy.org/eng/xw/t662061.htm.
33. Nye, *Soft Power*, x.
34. White House, "U.S.-China Joint Statement," Beijing, November 17, 2009.
35. Deng, *Deng Xiaoping wenxuan*, 3:370.
36. Wong, "China Communist Chief Acts to Bolster Military," *New York Times*, December 15, 2012.
37. Lu Xun, "Nahan" ("Outcry"), trans. by authors, *Lu Xun Xiaoshuoji*, 91.
38. De Bary et al., *Sources of Chinese Tradition*, 781.
39. Buckley, "Vows of Change in China Belie Private Warning," *New York Times*, February 14, 2013.
40. Deng, (Jan. 28–Feb. 18, 1991) *Selected Works of Deng Xiaoping*, 3:355.
41. Editorial, *The Financial Times*, January 8, 2013; "Battling the Censors," *Economist*, January 13, 2013.
42. http://news.xinhuanet.com/english/china/2013–03_132240.
43. Hille, "Return of Warlike Rhetoric from China," *The Financial Times*, January 22, 2013.

Photo Credits

Index

Page numbers in *italics* refer to illustrations.

Grateful acknowledgment is made to the following for permission to reprint previously published material:

The Belknap Press of Harvard University Press: Excerpt from No Enemies, No Hatred: Selected Essays and Poems by Liu Xiaobo, edited by Perry Link, Tienchi Martin-Liao, and Liu Xia, pp. 62–63, Cambridge, MA: The Belknap Press of Harvard University Press, Copyright © 2012 by The President and Fellows of Harvard College. Reprinted by permission of The Belknap Press of Harvard University Press.

Harvard University Press: Excerpts from China's Response to the West: A Documentary Survey, 1839–1923 by Ssu-yü Tĕng and John King Fairbank, pp. 150–151, 240, Cambridge, MA: Harvard University Press, Copyright © 1954, 1979 by The President and Fellows of Harvard College. Copyright renewed 1982 by Ssu-yü Tĕng and John King Fairbank. Reprinted by permission of Harvard University Press.

Institute of East Asian Studies, University of California Berkeley: Excerpt from p. 82 of Dixie Mission: The United States Army Observer Group in Yenan, 1944 by David Dean Barrett (China Research Monograph #6, Center for Chinese Studies, UC Berkeley, 1970). Copyright © 1970 by The Regents of the University of California. Reprinted by permission.

Princeton University Press: Excerpt from Chen Duxiu: Founder of the Chinese Communist Party by Lee Feigon, copyright © 1983 by Princeton University Press. Reprinted by permission of Princeton University Press.

University of California Press c/o Copyright Clearance Center: Excerpts from Speaking to History: The Story of King Goujian in Twentieth-Century China by Paul A. Cohen, copyright © 2008 by The Regents of the University of California; excerpt from Land Without Ghosts: Chinese Impressions of America from the Mid-Nineteenth Century to the Present by R. David Arkush and Leo O. Lee, editors, copyright © 1953 by Regents of the University of California. Reprinted by permission of University of California Press c/o Copyright Clearance Center.

University of California Press c/o Copyright Clearance Center and Vera Schwarcz: Excerpt from The Chinese Enlightenment: Intellectuals and the Legacy of the May Fourth Movement of 1919 by Vera Schwarcz, copyright © 1986 by Vera Schwarcz. Digital rights are controlled by Vera Schwarcz. Reprinted by permission of University of California Press c/o Copyright Clearance Center and Vera Schwarcz.

ABOUT THE AUTHORS

ORVILLE SCHELL was educated at Harvard University and the University of California, Berkeley and is the author of numerous books and articles on China. The former dean of the Graduate School of Journalism at Berkeley, he is presently the Arthur Ross Director of the Center on U.S.-China Relations at the Asia Society in New York City.

JOHN DELURY received his Ph.D. in modern Chinese history at Yale University, where he wrote his dissertation on the seventeenth-century Confucian political thinker Gu Yanwu. He taught Chinese history and politics at Brown, Columbia, and Peking University, and was associate director of the Asia Society's Center on U.S.-China Relations. He is currently an assistant professor of East Asian studies at Yonsei University in Seoul, South Korea.

ABOUT THE TYPE

This book was set in Sabon, a typeface designed by the well-known German typographer Jan Tschichold (1902–74). Sabon's design is based upon the original letter forms of Claude Garamond and was created specifically to be used for three sources: foundry type for hand composition, Linotype, and Monotype. Tschichold named his typeface for the famous Frankfurt typefounder Jacques Sabon, who died in 1580.